NATO HANDBOOK

2001

NATO Office of Information and Press

1110 Brussels - Belgium

ISBN 92-845-0146-6

HB0801EN

NORTH ATLANTIC TREATY ORGANISATION (NATO)

MEMBER COUNTRIES

Belgium, Canada, Czech Republic, Denmark, France, Germany, Greece, Hungary, Iceland, Italy, Luxembourg, the Netherlands, Norway, Poland, Portugal, Spain, Turkey, United Kingdom and United States.

The North Atlantic Treaty, signed in Washington in April 1949, created an Alliance for collective defence as defined in Article 51 of the United Nations Charter. The Treaty is of indefinite duration. The fourth of April 1999 marked the 50th anniversary of the Treaty.

In accordance with Article 10 of the Treaty, the Alliance remains open to accessions by other European states in a position to further its principles and to contribute to the security of the North Atlantic area. In 1952, Greece and Turkey joined the original twelve member countries of the Alliance, followed in 1955 by the Federal Republic of Germany and in 1982 by Spain. In July 1997, at a Summit Meeting in Madrid, the Heads of State and Government of the Alliance invited three more countries to begin accession talks, and on 12 March 1999 the Czech Republic, Hungary and Poland formally became members of NATO. The Alliance now links 17 European countries with the United States and Canada.

In parallel with the internal and external transformation of the Alliance which has taken place since the end of the Cold War, NATO has established the Euro-Atlantic Partnership Council or "EAPC" as a forum for consultation and cooperation with Partner countries throughout the Euro-Atlantic area. It has developed an intensive programme of practical cooperation and regular consultation with 26 countries participating in the Partnership for Peace initiative launched in 1994. It has created new structures reflecting intensified cooperation with Russia and partnership with Ukraine as well as an enhanced dialogue with interested Mediterranean countries. It has undergone far-reaching internal and external reform and has made itself the instrument of peace and stability in the Euro-Atlantic area at the start of the new millennium.

During 1999, NATO celebrated its 50th anniversary year. A further Summit Meeting was held in Washington in April 1999, during the height of the conflict in Kosovo, when NATO countries conducted an air campaign to end the ethnic cleansing and repression of human rights perpetrated by the government of the Federal Republic of Yugoslavia. The conflict ended in late June 1999, following the withdrawal of the Serb forces and the deployment of the NATO-led

Kosovo Force (KFOR) tasked by the UN Security Council with the implementation of the Military Technical Agreement concluded on 9 June.

The Washington Summit focused on the ongoing crisis in Kosovo and addressed issues relating to future stability in South Eastern Europe. Other decisions taken in Washington included the approval and publication of a revised Alliance Strategic Concept; adoption of a Membership Action Plan; endorsement of measures to further enhance the Partnership for Peace programme; and the launching of new initiatives designed to adapt the defence capabilities of NATO member countries to changing requirements and to inject new momentum into efforts to limit the proliferation of weapons of mass destruction.

Subsequent developments within the Alliance have focused in particular on strengthening the European Security and Defence Identity within the Alliance and on developing structures for cooperation between NATO and the European Union, following decisions taken by the EU to develop its operational role in relation to crisis management and peacekeeping.

****

The NATO Emblem was adopted as the symbol of the Atlantic Alliance by the North Atlantic Council in October 1953. The circle is the symbol of unity and cooperation and the compass rose suggests the common road to peace taken by the member countries of the Atlantic Alliance.

TABLE OF CONTENTS

PART I

CHAPTER 1:   WHAT IS NATO?

CHAPTER 2:   THE TRANSFORMATION OF THE ALLIANCE

CHAPTER 3:   THE OPENING UP OF THE ALLIANCE

CHAPTER 4:   THE EUROPEAN SECURITY AND DEFENCE IDENTITY (ESDI)

CHAPTER 5: THE ALLIANCE'S OPERATIONAL ROLE IN PEACEKEEPING

CHAPTER 6: THE ALLIANCE'S ROLE IN ARMS CONTROL

PART II

CHAPTER 7: POLICY AND DECISION-MAKING

CHAPTER 8: PROGRAMMES AND ACTIVITIES

CHAPTER 9:   COMMON-FUNDED RESOURCES: NATO BUDGETS AND
              FINANCIAL MANAGEMENT

CHAPTER 10:   CIVILIAN ORGANISATION AND STRUCTURES

CHAPTER 11:   MILITARY ORGANISATION AND STRUCTURES

EDITORIAL NOTE

Since the publication of the 50th Anniversary edition of the NATO Handbook, three more countries have joined the Alliance and a number of other major developments have taken place. These include the initiation in March 1999 of NATO's air campaign against the military structures of the Serb Government responsible for carrying out the policy of ethnic cleansing in Kosovo; the deployment of the NATO-led Kosovo Force (KFOR) in June 1999, and new initiatives taken at the Washington Summit in April 1999, including the publication of the Alliance's new Strategic Concept.

These events are reflected in this edition, as well as other important developments including changes relating to NATO's military command structure; the development of the European Security and Defence Identity (ESDI); implementation of the Defence Capabilities Initiatives (DCI); developments concerning the Partnership for Peace (PfP) and the Euro-Atlantic Partnership Council (EAPC); implementation of the Membership Action Plan (MAP); evolution of NATO-Russia and NATO-Ukraine relations; the widening of the Alliance's Mediterranean Dialogue; progress in relation to the South East Europe Initiative; and developments in other spheres of Alliance activity such as implementation of arms control measures and non-proliferation of weapons of mass destruction.

"How to use this Handbook" provides a guide to the contents of the principal chapters detailing the recent evolution of policy in the main spheres of Alliance activity (Part I); and an outline of the contents of subsequent chapters describing NATO's organisation and structures (Part II). The Preface to this edition offers an overview of the principal developments shaping Alliance policy over the course of the last decade.

The information contained in this edition covers developments up to the end of March 2001. Information concerning the most recent developments affecting the Alliance as well as official statements and communiqués are accessible on the NATO web site (www.nato.int).

FOREWORD BY THE SECRETARY GENERAL

This new edition of the NATO Handbook provides a comprehensive overview of the North Atlantic Alliance at the beginning of the new millennium. It portrays an Alliance profoundly influenced and transformed by the tumultuous changes of the previous decade, ready to take on the fourfold challenge which it faces today.

Firstly, it must fulfil its fundamental and continuing responsibility to its members by guaranteeing their security and independence. Secondly, it must extend security further afield to Partner countries throughout Europe, through bilateral partnerships and multilateral cooperation. Thirdly, and simultaneously, it must stand ready to back the efforts of the international community to prevent crises and conflict or, when they occur, to prevent their spread and assist those involved in them to resolve them by political means rather than the use of military force.

And fourthly, to achieve these goals, it must create a fairer balance in the transatlantic partnership which is at the core of the North Atlantic Alliance, by strengthening the European role in crisis management and peacekeeping. This process is about reinforcing the Alliance and providing crisis management capabilities which NATO can support without necessarily assuming the leading role itself in every crisis which occurs in Europe. It is about introducing greater flexibility and better options for preventing or ending conflict, not about changing the basis of the collective defence for which the Alliance remains the essential guarantor.

The Alliance described in this Handbook is certainly not one which has found itself short of a role after the end of the Cold War, despite predictions by some analysts that it would lose its *raison d'être*. Rather it is an Alliance which has had to manage its own essential process of modernisation and change without any lapse in its operational ability to fulfil its task, nor delays in developing the means to perform the new functions required of it by its member countries. Its dilemma has not been how to identify a new role for itself but rather how best to seize the opportunity of fulfilling the security agenda established for it by the member countries at its creation, namely to safeguard the freedom, common heritage and civilisation of their peoples. Far from creating a role for itself, the challenge facing NATO has been to ensure that its existing roles are not compromised by too many or too vast demands on its resources.

NATO is not a world policeman, but it has a proven, successful track record as a catalyst for generating effective multinational forces, such as SFOR in Bosnia and Herzegovina and KFOR in Kosovo, able to ensure the implementation of peace agreements and to lay the basis for future stability in areas of conflict in the Euro-Atlantic area. It is not a club in which membership is available on demand but it is an intergovernmental security alliance, which brings burdens and responsibilities as well as benefits to its member countries. It is not a monolithic, self-determining entity but it is a covenant among member countries which they can use for the purposes which they agree in common, but which is also constrained by the limitations on its scope, resources and ability to act which they themselves impose. And finally, it is not a vehicle for power projection by individual member countries but rather a framework which permits each member country to determine its national interest in the broader context of consensus among the members of the Alliance as a whole.

The nations have demonstrated their attachment to these values in successive decisions designed to adapt the Alliance to changed circumstances and modern needs. Their efforts have been underpinned by the success of the different forms of partnership established with non-member countries, bilaterally through practical cooperation in the Partnership for Peace and politically, through consultations in the multilateral forum of the Euro-Atlantic Partnership Council. The value attached to these cooperative efforts is manifest in the clear aspiration to join the Alliance demonstrated by many of the countries participating in them but is also evident from the constructive participation by countries which have no current aspirations to join the Alliance. In addition, the degree of cooperation achieved in the bilateral relationship between NATO and Russia has served to underline the huge gains for all concerned which are to be had from this process, despite inevitable difficulties encountered along the way. Between NATO and Ukraine too, a level of understanding and cooperation has been achieved which has positive consequences for all.

Alliance decisions emanating from the series of Summit meetings which have charted its course since the end of the Cold War have laid the basis for extending further afield the culture of dialogue and cooperation on security issues established among NATO member countries for many years. Increasingly, through the work of the NATO-led forces supporting the peace process in Bosnia and Herzegovina and in Kosovo, this culture is influencing the process of reconciliation between communities and is helping to lay the groundwork for future cooperation in the much troubled Balkan region. In other fields too, such as the Alliance's Mediterranean Dialogue, the foundation of openness and understanding essential for future cooperation is being laid.

The main developments in each of these crucial areas of Alliance activity are described within these pages. Also depicted is the process of adaptation enabling major steps to be taken in rebalancing the transatlantic relationship which is at the core of cooperation in the Alliance. This is a multi-faceted task which has embraced, on the one hand, consultations and cooperation with the institutions involved in developing the European role in defence and security, namely the Western European Union and now, increasingly, the European Union; and, on the other, practical measures to put in place the operational capabilities needed if these arrangements are to deliver the improvements in European security and the overall strengthening of cooperation in the Alliance which they are intended to bring about. The evolution of the European Security and Defence Identity (ESDI) and the implementation of the Alliance's Defence Capabilities Initiative (DCI), which has ramifications for the whole Alliance but will also underpin ESDI, are integral to the agenda which the Alliance is pursuing. Their successful completion is central to the challenges I face during my stewardship of the Alliance as its Secretary General.

There is only one yardstick for measuring the success of all of these initiatives and activities and that is the extent to which they serve the interests of the citizens of the Euro-Atlantic area as a whole. Only if they bring about greater security, increased stability and better mechanisms for handling crises will they be perceived to have served their purpose. There is therefore an ever greater need for the choices and decisions involved to be well known and understood by a broad sector of public opinion in NATO and in its Partner countries alike. Without that, governments can achieve very little in the longer term. They therefore have a responsibility to ensure that policies pursued in their joint national interests are submitted to public scrutiny, supported by the relevant facts and figures and rationale.

I am therefore pleased to be able to commend this book to the attention of all those who may have the chance to refer to it and to invite them to participate professionally and privately in the discussion which these issues merit. There are no absolutes in the process of securing the best and most stable environment for the future political, economic and social development of our countries, only hard choices. Making the right ones is the job of governments, but taking an active part in the discussion process and if necessary challenging conventional thinking, is the task of public opinion. Organisations like NATO must therefore also be prepared to make available as much information as possible. Without it, discussion of these serious and complex issues risks being unbalanced and misleading. So I am glad to be able to introduce this Handbook and I am confident that better understanding of the information it contains will contribute positively to the public debate and deliberation to which security issues must be constantly subjected.

George Robertson

HOW TO USE THIS HANDBOOK

Part I of the Handbook begins with a summary of the origins of the Alliance and of its fundamental security tasks (Chapter 1), followed by an appraisal of factors which have combined to create the new security environment since the end of the Cold War and to render possible the transformation of NATO which has taken place as a consequence (Chapter 2).

Subsequent chapters of Part I describe, firstly, the opening up of the Alliance, both through its enlargement process and through the multilateral and bilateral forms of cooperation established under the Euro-Atlantic Partnership Council, the Partnership for Peace, the Mediterranean Dialogue, the NATO-Russia Founding Act and the NATO-Ukraine Distinctive Partnership (Chapter 3); secondly, the emergence of the European Security and Defence Identity within the Alliance and the intensification of relevant forms of cooperation initially with the Western European Union and more recently with the European Union (Chapter 4); and thirdly the practical operational work undertaken by NATO in the peacekeeping field and in the sphere of arms control and measures to limit the proliferation of weapons of mass destruction (Chapters 5 to 6).

Part II of the Handbook describes the manner in which policy is formulated and decisions are taken within the Alliance and summarises the different roles of the principal NATO policy and decision-making bodies (Chapter 7). Subsequent chapters address the programmes and activities which are the mainstay of the Alliance's effectiveness in the many different fields of planning and cooperation which together constitute the security agenda of today. Information is provided on the logistics, standardisation, communications, armaments, air traffic management and air defence activities which render it possible for the forces of member countries and NATO Partner countries to operate together. Information is also given on activities in the field of civil emergency planning and disaster relief; on scientific cooperation; and on cooperation in the environmental and societal spheres (Chapter 8).

Underpinning these programmes and activities are the organisational arrangements and structures needed to facilitate the exchange of information, consultation and decision-making processes as well as administrative and budgetary aspects in these different fields. Chapters 7 to 14 of the Handbook therefore provide information on the procedures which enable decisions to be made; the mechanisms which govern the management of resources and the administration of common-funded budgets; and the civilian and military organisation, structures and agencies which have been established by NATO to ensure that its tasks can be carried out in accordance with the decisions taken collectively by the member countries.

The importance of the work undertaken by other international organisations in the security field, independently or in cooperation with the Alliance, as well as the mutually reinforcing nature of their roles, is reflected in Chapter 15, which addresses the wider institutional framework for security.

Finally, in Chapter 16, three further influences on the evolution of security policy are described, namely the NATO Parliamentary Assembly, which provides the interface at the international level between the legislative and executive aspects of the formulation of security policy in individual member and partner countries; the Atlantic Treaty Association which brings together a number of non-governmental associations involved in informing their publics about NATO's role and policies; and the Interallied Confederation of Reserve Officers, which provides the international focus for related activities among civilians in the different member countries serving as reserve officers.

Abbreviations in common use and sources of further information are listed in Appendices 1 and 2.

The NATO Handbook is published by the NATO Office of Information and Press under the authority of the Secretary General as a reference book on the Alliance and on Alliance policies. The formulations used reflect as closely as possible the consensus among the member nations which is the basis for all Alliance decisions. However the Handbook is not a formally agreed NATO document and therefore may not represent the official opinions or positions of individual governments on every issue discussed.

Additional information on NATO, as well as the official texts of communiqués and statements issued by the North Atlantic Council, can be found on NATO's web site (www.nato.int).

PREFACE

NATO TODAY - FROM ROME TO WASHINGTON

From time to time, at determining moments in NATO's history, the Alliance meets at summit level with the participation of Heads of State and Government. The presence of Prime Ministers and Presidents, and their direct participation in the process of taking decisions by consensus, raises the public profile of such meetings and bestows on them increased historical significance.

By 1991, the major transformation of the international security environment marking the end of the 1980's was dictating the shape of the new NATO which was to emerge over the next few years. The first of a series of four Summit Meetings which were to plot the course of the Alliance's adaptation during the coming decade, took place in Rome in November 1991. It was to be followed by a further Summit Meeting in Brussels in January 1994 and two further decisive meetings in Madrid in July 1997 and in Washington in April 1999.

The momentum of change instigated by these meetings was maintained by frequent meetings of Foreign Ministers and Defence Ministers in the intervening periods. The Foreign Ministers' meeting in Sintra, Portugal, in May 1997, in particular, heralded moves to extend security cooperation further afield and to provide appropriate structures for managing the process.

THE ROME SUMMIT - NOVEMBER 1991

The Strategic Concept adopted by NATO Heads of State and Government in Rome in November 1991 outlined a broad approach to security based on dialogue, cooperation and the maintenance of a collective defence capability. It brought together political and military elements of NATO's security policy into a coherent whole, establishing cooperation with new partners in Central and Eastern Europe as an integral part of the Alliance's strategy. The Concept provided for reduced dependence on nuclear weapons and major changes in NATO's integrated military forces, including substantial reductions in their size and readiness, improvements in their mobility, flexibility and adaptability to different contingencies and greater use of multinational formations. Measures were also taken to streamline NATO's military command structure and to adapt the Alliance's defence planning arrangements and procedures, particularly in the light of future requirements for crisis management and peacekeeping.

At the Rome Summit Meeting, Allied leaders also issued a Declaration on Peace and Cooperation, which defined the future tasks and policies of NATO in relation to the overall institutional framework for Europe's future security and in relation to the evolving partnership and cooperation with the countries of Central and Eastern Europe. It underlined the Alliance's support for the steps being taken in the countries of Central and Eastern Europe towards reform; offered practical assistance to help them to succeed in this difficult transition; invited them to participate in appropriate Alliance forums; and extended to them the Alliance's experience and expertise in political, military, economic and scientific spheres. To this end, a North Atlantic Cooperation Council (NACC) was established to oversee the future development of this partnership.

Following the publication of the Rome Declaration, additional measures were taken at Ministerial Meetings of Foreign and Defence Ministers and by the North Atlantic Council in Permanent Session to further the process of adaptation and transformation of the Alliance. Three areas of activity merit particular mention, namely the institutional, political framework created to develop the relationship between NATO and its Cooperation Partners in Central and Eastern Europe; the development of cooperation in the defence and military spheres; and NATO's role in the field of crisis management and peacekeeping.

Firstly, in the institutional context, the first significant event was the inaugural meeting of the North Atlantic Cooperation Council which took place on 20 December 1991, with the participation of the Foreign Ministers or representatives of NATO countries and of six Central and Eastern European countries as well as the three Baltic states. The role of the NACC was to facilitate cooperation on security and related issues between the participating countries at all levels and to oversee the process of developing closer institutional ties as well as informal links between them. The 11 states on the territory of the former Soviet Union forming the Commonwealth of Independent States (CIS) became participants in this process in March 1992. Georgia and Albania joined the process in April and June 1992 respectively and, by 1997, when the NACC was replaced by the Euro-Atlantic Partnership Council (EAPC), there were 22 NACC Cooperation Partners. NACC cooperation was implemented on the basis of Work Plans, initially established annually but, from 1995 onwards, encompassing two-year periods. The Euro-Atlantic Partnership Council took this process a practical step further and developed an EAPC Action Plan (1998-2000) as the basis for its future work.

Secondly, in the defence and military spheres, NATO Defence Ministers met with Cooperation Partners for the first time on 1 April 1992 to consider ways of deepening dialogue and promoting cooperation on issues falling within their competence. The Military Committee held its first meeting in cooperation session on 10 April 1992. Regular meetings took place with Cooperation

Partners both at the level of Defence Ministers and in the Military Committee forum. In parallel, with these multilateral meetings, bilateral contacts and co-operation developed between Ministries of Defence and at the military level.

Thirdly, against the background of the crises in the former Yugoslavia and elsewhere, attention increasingly turned towards NATO's role in the field of crisis management and peacekeeping and particularly its support for UN peacekeeping activities relating to the former Yugoslavia. The main initiatives undertaken by NATO in this respect are described in Chapter 5.

Consultations and cooperation in the NACC were wide-ranging but focused in particular on political and security-related matters: peacekeeping; conceptual approaches to arms control and disarmament; defence planning issues and military matters; democratic concepts of civilian-military relations; the conversion of defence production to civilian purposes; defence expenditure and budgets; scientific cooperation and defence-related environmental issues; dissemination of information about NATO in the countries of Cooperation Partners; policy planning consultations; and civil/military air traffic management.

THE BRUSSELS SUMMIT - JANUARY 1994

In January 1994, at the Summit Meeting of the North Atlantic Council in Brussels, NATO launched a major new initiative to enhance stability and security throughout Europe. An invitation was issued to NACC and other states to join in a new and far-reaching programme of cooperation with NATO known as the Partnership for Peace (PfP). The Partnership has since developed into a fundamental component of security in the Euro-Atlantic area and occupies a central role in the NATO of today. The Partnership for Peace Invitation was addressed to all states participating in the North Atlantic Cooperation Council (NACC), and other states participating in the Conference of Security and Cooperation in Europe (CSCE), able and willing to contribute to the programme. The activities which each Partner undertakes are based on jointly elaborated Individual Partnership Programmes. The scope and objectives of the Partnership and its evolution and subsequent enhancement are described in Chapter 3.

At Sintra, in May 1997, the NACC was succeeded by the Euro-Atlantic Partnership Council (EAPC), whose purpose was to launch a new stage of cooperation. The principles of the EAPC were developed in close cooperation between the Alliance and its Partner countries and were expressed in the EAPC Basic Document.

The adoption of the EAPC Basic Document signalled the determination of the then 44 participating countries to raise political and military cooperation between them to a qualitatively new level. The document reaffirmed the joint commitment of the member countries to strengthening and extending peace and stability in the Euro-Atlantic area. The shared values and the principles underlying this commitment are set out in the Framework Document of the Partnership for Peace (PfP) (see NATO Handbook - Documentation, published separately). The EAPC in fact provides the overall framework for political and security-related consultations and for enhanced cooperation under the Partnership for Peace.

In December 1997 the EAPC endorsed an Action Plan which reflected the desire of EAPC members to develop a stronger, more operational partnership between them. One of the underlying aims of the Action Plan was to give political and security-related consultations and cooperation in the EAPC framework even greater focus and depth and to increase transparency among the 44 participating states. EAPC Foreign Ministers also endorsed the principle of establishing a Euro-Atlantic Disaster Response Coordination Centre and Euro-Atlantic Disaster Response Unit.

The EAPC provides opportunities for result-oriented multilateral consultations, enhanced practical cooperation, increased consultation and cooperation on regional matters, and increased transparency and confidence in security matters among all EAPC member states.

Two important principles underpin the success of cooperation between Allies and Partners in both the Partnership for Peace and the EAPC framework. Firstly inclusiveness: opportunities for political consultation and practical cooperation are open to all Allies and Partners equally; and secondly, mechanisms for self-differentiation: Partners are able to decide individually the level and areas of their cooperation with the Alliance. In line with these principles, the EAPC can meet in plenary session or in a limited format involving the member countries of the Alliance and open-ended groups of Partner countries to focus on functional matters or, on an ad hoc basis, on appropriate regional matters. The number of cooperative activities undertaken under EAPC auspices also increased. Based on the principles of inclusiveness and self-differentiation, further activities took place on defence economic issues, science, defence-related environmental issues, cooperation in peacekeeping, and civil emergency preparedness.

PfP in its enhanced form remains a clearly identifiable element of practical cooperation in defence-related and military fields within the flexible framework of the EAPC. Most Partner countries have also established Diplomatic Missions at NATO, which contribute significantly to communications and contacts in all these spheres.

THE MADRID SUMMIT - JULY 1997

The Summit Meeting held in Madrid in July 1997 was a landmark event which saw the accomplishment of major initiatives undertaken by the Alliance during the preceding five or six years. At the same time, it heralded the transition to a new and challenging phase in NATO's development, in which innovative structures and policies introduced to respond to new circumstances would be tried and tested in practice. The task of Alliance leaders at Madrid was therefore to pull together the central strands of future Alliance policy as a whole and to ensure their overall integrity and coherence.

At the Madrid Summit Meeting, the extent of the Alliance's commitment to internal and external transformation was fully demonstrated through further concrete and far-reaching measures in all the key areas of concern: the beginning of accession talks with the Czech Republic, Hungary and Poland and the endorsement of an "open door" policy on future accessions; enhancement of the Partnership for Peace and the establishment of a new forum in the shape of the EAPC to take cooperation forward; the opening of a brand new chapter in NATO-Russia relations; the formalisation of a growing partnership with Ukraine; the intensification of the dialogue with Mediterranean countries; progress with respect to the European Security and Defence Identity within NATO; and the definition of the Alliance's radically reformed military command structure. This full agenda bore witness to a NATO able to take on new challenges without prejudice to its traditional tasks and to base its future role on its proven ability to adapt to evolving security requirements.

THE WASHINGTON SUMMIT - APRIL 1999

From 23-25 April 1999, NATO held the 15th Summit in its 50 year history in Washington, DC. The Summit took place during an exceptional period in the Alliance's history in the midst of a commemoration of its 50th Anniversary, tempered by an unprecedented NATO air campaign aimed at bringing peace to Kosovo. Although much of the focus at the Summit was necessarily on the crisis in Kosovo, NATO leaders nonetheless put their imprimatur on a host of other programmes and accomplishments with long-term implications for the Alliance.

The achievements of Washington fulfilled the promise of the Madrid Summit held two years earlier. At Madrid, the Alliance had invited the Czech Republic, Hungary and Poland to begin accession talks and promised that the door would remain open to others. In Washington, the leaders of these three countries took their place for the first time at the Summit table, and the Alliance unveiled an initiative designed to help other interested countries prepare for possible membership in the future. *"The three new members will not be the last"* Alliance leaders stated in the Washington Summit Communiqué.

At Madrid, NATO leaders had pledged to enhance the Partnership for Peace programme and the full range of Alliance partnership activities; in Washington, leaders noted the progress achieved in this regard and unveiled new initiatives designed to continue the work. At Madrid, Alliance leaders had requested a review of the Strategic Concept (in essence the roadmap of Alliance tasks and the means to achieve them); in Washington a new Strategic Concept was approved, reflecting the transformed Euro-Atlantic security landscape at the end of the 20th century. At Madrid, NATO and Ukraine had signed a Charter on a Distinctive Partnership; in Washington NATO leaders and the Ukrainian President held their first Summit meeting and acknowledged the importance of Ukraine to Euro-Atlantic security and stability.

The work of the Washington Summit is reflected comprehensively in the Washington Summit Communiqué and the Strategic Concept. The Communiqué describes the major themes of the Summit and of the Alliance at this key period in its history. The Strategic Concept equips the Alliance for the security challenges and opportunities of the 21st century and guides its future political and military development.

The concrete accomplishments of the Summit - in the form of decisions and programmes - set the stage for the Alliance to enter the 21st century. While recognising that the Euro-Atlantic security climate had changed dramatically over the last ten years, the Strategic Concept also acknowledged *"the appearance of complex new risks to Euro-Atlantic peace and stability, including oppression, ethnic conflict, economic distress, the collapse of political order, and the proliferation of weapons of mass destruction."* It set out the Alliance's purposes and tasks for the future and reflected the resolve of Alliance member countries to maintain the necessary military capabilities to accomplish the full range of Alliance missions.

An important feature of the transforming posture of NATO is the development of the European Security and Defence Identity (ESDI) within the Alliance. At the Washington Summit, Alliance leaders welcomed the progress achieved so far and called for continuing work to make ESDI a reality. NATO also launched a Defence Capabilities Initiative, designed to help Alliance military forces become more mobile, interoperable, sustainable and effective. Similarly, the Alliance introduced changes in the integrated military command structure reflecting the transformed security environment. These changes are designed to enable NATO to carry out its operations more efficiently.

The Washington Summit Communiqué outlined another new Alliance initiative, on Weapons of Mass Destruction (WMD). NATO's principal aim with regard to these destructive weapons is to *"prevent proliferation from occurring, or, should it occur, to reverse it through diplomatic means."* In order to respond more effectively to the challenges of proliferation, NATO has established a WMD Centre within the International Staff at NATO Headquarters. The Centre seeks to coordinate an integrated political-military approach by encouraging debate and understanding of WMD issues in NATO; enhancing existing programmes to increase military readiness to operate in a WMD environment; and increasing the exchange of information on WMD destruction assistance programmes among allied countries.

Even as they welcomed three new members to their first Summit, NATO leaders emphasised that the door would remain open to others. A Membership Action Plan (MAP), the *"practical manifestation of the Open Door,"* was unveiled at the Summit. The MAP is a programme of activities from which interested countries may choose, on the basis of national decisions and self-selection. The programme covers five areas: political and economic issues, defence/military issues, resources, security and legal issues. NATO stressed that the programme should not be considered a list of criteria for membership, and that active participation in PfP and EAPC remains essential for countries interested in possible future membership. However, any decision on membership would be made on a case-by-case basis in accordance with the Madrid Summit Declaration and the Washington Summit Declaration.

After the Summit-level meeting of the North Atlantic Council, leaders or representatives from the member countries of the Euro-Atlantic Partnership Council also met in Washington. EAPC leaders discussed the situation in Kosovo and expressed their support for the demands of the international community, and their abhorrence of the policies of violence, repression and ethnic cleansing being carried out in Kosovo by the authorities of the Federal Republic of Yugoslavia. Leaders expressed their support for broad-based security and for economic and democracy-building efforts for the south-eastern Europe region. They also endorsed a report entitled *"Towards a Partnership for the 21st Century - The Enhanced and more Operational Partnership"*, aimed at improving the ability of the Alliance and Partner forces to operate together in the future.

Although Russia declined to participate in the Washington Summit because of events in Yugoslavia, NATO leaders reiterated their commitment to partnership with Russia under the NATO-Russia Founding Act. They also underscored the fact that close relations between NATO and Russia are of mutual interest and of great importance to stability and security in the Euro-Atlantic area.

NATO leaders also held their first-ever summit with the President of Ukraine. Both sides welcomed the progress in their Distinctive Partnership and discussed a variety of Euro-Atlantic security issues.

The Washington Summit Communiqué reiterated the importance of NATO's Mediterranean Dialogue as an integral part of the Alliance's cooperative approach to security. NATO leaders directed the Alliance to pursue early implementation of enhancements to the political and practical cooperation initiated under the Dialogue.

The achievements of the Washington Summit were both practical and conceptual, the fruit of several years of work. They also reflected the immediate priorities of NATO member countries, in particular the urgency of bringing to an end the conflict in Kosovo and restoring the rights of the people of Kosovo.

ENDING THE CONFLICT IN KOSOVO

On the evening of 9 June 1999, a Military Technical Agreement was concluded between NATO and the Federal Republic of Yugoslavia. Consistent with the agreement between the Yugoslav government and the special envoys of the European Union and of Russia reached on 3 June, the Military Technical Agreement provided in particular for the immediate withdrawal of Yugoslav security forces from Kosovo.

On 10 June 1999, the NATO Secretary General, Javier Solana, was able to announce that the air operations against Yugoslavia had been suspended. On the same day, the United Nations Security Council passed Resolution 1244, welcoming Yugoslav acceptance of the principles for a political solution, including an immediate end to violence and the rapid withdrawal of Yugoslav military, police and paramilitary forces. The Resolution also announced the establishment of " international civil and security presences in Kosovo" to operate under UN auspices. The NATO-led Kosovo Force (KFOR), created to fulfil the security part of this mandate, entered Kosovo on 12 June and completed its initial deployment by 20 June. Further details of these events are given in Chapter 5.

In the aftermath of the Kosovo conflict, by far the most urgent items on the Alliance's agenda were the implementation of the agreement ending the conflict, the restoration of peace, the return of the refugees and the protection of the people of Kosovo, regardless of their ethnic origins. The coming together of forces from NATO countries, Russia, Ukraine and many other non-NATO countries to achieve these goals owed much to the experience gained from the continuing deployment of the Stabilisation Force (SFOR) in Bosnia and

Herzegovina. Many of the countries involved were also active participants in NATO's Partnership for Peace, a factor which has contributed significantly to the role these multinational forces have been able to play in laying the basis for future stability in the region.

In the ensuing months, the influence of the Kosovo conflict was also to be seen in the implementation of a number of the initiatives introduced at the Washington Summit in April 1999 and subsequent decisions taken by the Alliance. In particular, it gave added impetus to the move to establish a stronger European Security and Defence Identity and to build up European capabilities commensurate with the task of intervening in crisis management and peacekeeping roles in the event of future conflict in which the Alliance as a whole might not be involved. This process is described in Chapter 4.

NEW SECRETARY GENERAL

In March 2000, a year after the Alliance's intervention in Kosovo, NATO's new Secretary General, Lord Robertson, issued a report summarising the achievements resulting from the military operation and the deployment of KFOR and outlining the challenges which remained.

Lord Robertson, former Minister of Defence of the United Kingdom, took up his appointment as NATO Secretary General on 14 October 1999. On his first day in office, outlining the priorities he saw for the Alliance in the coming months, he gave particular emphasis to three areas of immediate concern and long-term significance for the Alliance.

First, NATO must play its full role in the stabilisation of the Balkans in the wake of the Kosovo crisis and ensure that the NATO peacekeeping missions both in Bosnia and Herzegovina and in Kosovo create as rapidly as possible the conditions for a self-sustaining peace.

Second, he underscored the need to reinforce the European role in NATO, characterising this as an urgent necessity if NATO is to be as strong in the future as it has been in the past. The Alliance must develop good, effective and efficient links with the European Union, as the latter develops its role in this area. Stating that *"more Europe in NATO does not mean less North America"*, Lord Robertson emphasised the fact that the transatlantic relationship remains the key to NATO's effectiveness and that without a strong transatlantic connection, there could be no real stability in Europe or protection for its democratic values.

Third, he focused on the immediate priority of establishing closer relations between NATO and Russia, pointing to the resumption of meetings of the

NATO-Russia Permanent Joint Council as a highly positive development in this process.

This edition of the NATO Handbook describes the evolution of NATO policies in these and other areas of Alliance activity. For ease of reference the book has been divided into two parts, the first detailing the cooperative work being undertaken in specific fields to further Alliance objectives and outlining the context in which policy is evolving; and the second, describing the relevant procedural and structural arrangements which have been put in place to facilitate the exchange of information, consultation, decision-making and operational tasks which are fundamental to the process.

PART I

CHAPTER 1

WHAT IS NATO?

The Origins of the Alliance

Fundamental Security Tasks

What is NATO?

The Origins of the Alliance

From 1945 to 1949, faced with the pressing need for economic reconstruction, Western European countries and their North American allies viewed with concern the expansionist policies and methods of the USSR. Having fulfilled their own wartime undertakings to reduce their defence establishments and to demobilise forces, Western governments became increasingly alarmed as it became clear that the Soviet leadership intended to maintain its own military forces at full strength. Moreover, in view of the declared ideological aims of the Soviet Communist Party, it was evident that appeals for respect for the United Nations Charter, and for respect for the international settlements reached at the end of the war, would not guarantee the national sovereignty or independence of democratic states faced with the threat of outside aggression or internal subversion. The imposition of undemocratic forms of government and the repression of effective opposition and of basic human and civic rights and freedoms in many Central and Eastern European countries as well as elsewhere in the world, added to these fears.

Between 1947 and 1949 a series of dramatic political events brought matters to a head. These included direct threats to the sovereignty of Norway, Greece, Turkey and other Western European countries, the June 1948 coup in Czechoslovakia, and the illegal blockade of Berlin which began in April of the same year. The signature of the Brussels Treaty of March 1948[1] marked the determination of five Western European countries - Belgium, France, Luxembourg, the Netherlands and the United Kingdom - to develop a common defence system and to strengthen the ties between them in a manner which would enable them to resist ideological, political and military threats to their security.

Negotiations with the United States and Canada then followed on the creation of a single North Atlantic Alliance based on security guarantees and mutual commitments between Europe and North America. Denmark, Iceland, Italy, Norway and Portugal were invited by the Brussels Treaty powers to become participants in this process. These negotiations culminated in the signature of the Treaty of Washington in April 1949, bringing into being a common

---

1   The Brussels Treaty of 1948, revised in 1984, represented the first step in the post-war reconstruction of Western European security and brought into being the Western Union and the Brussels Treaty Organisation. It was also the first step in the process leading to the signature of the North Atlantic Treaty in 1949 and the creation of the North Atlantic Alliance. The Brussels Treaty is the founding document of the present day Western European Union (WEU).

security system based on a partnership among these 12 countries. In 1952, Greece and Turkey acceded to the Treaty. The Federal Republic of Germany[2] joined the Alliance in 1955 and, in 1982, Spain also became a member of NATO. The Czech Republic, Hungary and Poland joined NATO in 1999.

The North Atlantic Alliance was founded on the basis of a Treaty between member states entered into freely by each of them after public debate and due parliamentary process. The Treaty upholds their individual rights as well as their international obligations in accordance with the Charter of the United Nations. It commits each member country to sharing the risks and responsibilities as well as the benefits of collective security and requires of each of them the undertaking not to enter into any other international commitment which might conflict with the Treaty.

Between the creation of the Alliance and the present day, half a century of history has taken place. For much of this time the central focus of NATO was providing for the immediate defence and security of its member countries. Today this remains its core task, but its immediate focus has undergone fundamental change. The key features of this transformation are summarised in the relevant chapters of the Handbook.

FUNDAMENTAL SECURITY TASKS

NATO's essential purpose is to safeguard the freedom and security of all its members by political and military means in accordance with the North Atlantic Treaty and the principles of the United Nations Charter. The Alliance has worked since its inception for the establishment of a just and lasting peaceful order in Europe based on common values of democracy, human rights and the rule of law. This central Alliance objective has taken on renewed significance since the end of the Cold War because, for the first time in the post-war history of Europe, the prospect of its achievement has become a reality.

NATO embodies the transatlantic link by which the security of North America is permanently tied to the security of Europe. It is the practical expression of effective collective effort among its members in support of their common security interests.

The fundamental principle underpinning the Alliance is a common commitment to mutual cooperation among the member states, based on the indivisibility of their security. Solidarity and cohesion within the Alliance ensure that

---

2   In 1990, with the unification of Germany, the former German Democratic Republic came under the security protection of the Alliance as an integral part of the united country.

no member country is forced to rely upon its own national efforts alone in dealing with basic security challenges. Without depriving member states of their right and duty to assume their sovereign responsibilities in the field of defence, the Alliance enables them to realise their essential national security objectives through collective effort. In short, the Alliance is an association of free states united in their determination to preserve their security through mutual guarantees and stable relations with other countries.

The North Atlantic Treaty of April 1949 - which is the legal and contractual basis for the Alliance - was established within the framework of Article 51 of the United Nations Charter, which reaffirms the inherent right of independent states to individual or collective defence. As the preamble to the Treaty states, the aim of the Allies is to *"promote peaceful and friendly relations in the North Atlantic Area."* However, at the time of the Treaty's signature, the immediate purpose of NATO was to defend its members against a potential threat resulting from the policies and growing military capacity of the former Soviet Union.

The North Atlantic Treaty Organisation (NATO) provides the structure which enables the goals of the Alliance to be implemented. It is an intergovernmental organisation in which member countries retain their full sovereignty and independence. The Organisation provides the forum in which they consult together on any issues they may choose to raise and take decisions on political and military matters affecting their security. It provides the structures needed to facilitate consultation and cooperation between them, in political, military and economic as well as scientific and other non-military fields.

The resulting sense of equal security among the members of the Alliance, regardless of differences in their circumstances or in their national military capabilities, contributes to stability in the Euro-Atlantic area. It creates conditions which favour increased cooperation among Alliance members as well as between members of the Alliance and other countries.

The means by which the Alliance carries out its security policies include the maintenance of a sufficient military capability to prevent war and to provide for effective defence; an overall capability to manage crises affecting the security of its members; and active promotion of dialogue with other nations and of a cooperative approach to European security, including measures to bring about further progress in the field of arms control and disarmament.

To achieve its essential purpose, as an Alliance of nations committed to the Washington Treaty and the United Nations Charter, the Alliance performs the following fundamental security tasks:

"Security: To provide one of the indispensable foundations for a stable Euro-Atlantic security environment, based on the growth of democratic institutions and commitment to the peaceful resolution of disputes, in which no coun-

try would be able to intimidate or coerce any other through the threat or use of force.

Consultation: To serve, as provided for in Article 4 of the Washington Treaty, as an essential transatlantic forum for Allied consultations on any issues that affect their vital interests, including possible developments posing risks for members' security, and for appropriate coordination of their efforts in fields of common concern.

Deterrence and Defence: To deter and defend against any threat of aggression against any NATO member state as provided for in Articles 5 and 6 of the Washington Treaty.

And in order to enhance the security and stability of the Euro-Atlantic area:

- *Crisis Management: To stand ready, case-by-case and by consensus, in conformity with Article 7 of the Washington Treaty, to contribute to effective conflict prevention and to engage actively in crisis management, including crisis response operations.*

- *Partnership: To promote wide-ranging partnership, cooperation, and dialogue with other countries in the Euro-Atlantic area, with the aim of increasing transparency, mutual confidence and the capacity for joint action with the Alliance."* [3]

The structures created within NATO enable member countries to coordinate their policies in order to fulfil these fundamental tasks. They provide for continuous consultation and cooperation in political, economic and other non-military fields as well as the formulation of joint plans for the common defence; the establishment of the infrastructure and basic installations and facilities needed to enable military forces to operate; and arrangements for joint training programmes and exercises. Underpinning these activities is a complex civilian and military structure involving administrative, budgetary and planning staffs, as well as agencies which have been established by the member countries of the Alliance in order to coordinate work in specialised fields - for example, the communications needed to facilitate political consultation and command and control of military forces and the logistics support needed to sustain military forces. This structure is described in Part II.

---

[3]   From the Alliance's Strategic Concept issued at the Washington Summit Meeting in April 1999.

CHAPTER 2

THE TRANSFORMATION OF THE ALLIANCE

Europe's New Security Environment

New Institutions

The Strategic Concept of the Alliance

The Role of Allied Military Forces and the Transformation of
the Alliance's Defence Posture

NATO's Defence Capabilities Initiative

NATO's Nuclear Forces in the New Security Environment

THE TRANSFORMATION OF THE ALLIANCE

EUROPE'S NEW SECURITY ENVIRONMENT

On the fourth of April 1989, the Alliance celebrated the fortieth anniversary of the signing of the North Atlantic Treaty. The event coincided with the beginning of a period of profound change in the course of East-West and international relations and a far-reaching transformation of the security environment. The role of the North Atlantic Alliance has been fundamental in bringing about the conditions for change described in these pages. By providing the basis for the collective defence and common security of its member countries and preserving a strategic balance in Europe throughout the Cold War period, the Alliance has safeguarded their freedom and independence. In accordance with the North Atlantic Treaty it continues to fulfil these core functions and has assumed new tasks in addition. It is building on the foundations it has created in order to promote stability based on common democratic values and respect for human rights and the rule of law throughout Europe.

The following sections describe the origins and course of these developments; the progress achieved towards the realisation of many of the long-standing goals of the Alliance; and the principal issues of concern facing member countries and NATO's Partner countries as they continue to adapt their policies and shape their common institutions to meet new challenges.

The Origins of the Changed Security Environment

The roots of the changes which have transformed the political map of Europe can be traced to a number of developments during the 1960s and 1970s which were to have far-reaching implications. While there were many aspects to these developments, three events stand out in particular, namely: the adoption by the Alliance, in December 1967, of the Harmel doctrine based on the parallel policies of maintaining adequate defence while seeking a relaxation of tensions in East-West relations; the introduction by the Government of the Federal Republic of Germany in 1969 of Chancellor Willy Brandt's "Ostpolitik", designed to bring about a more positive relationship with Eastern European countries and the Soviet Union within the constraints imposed by their governments' domestic policies and actions abroad; and the adoption of the CSCE[1] Helsinki Final Act in August 1975, which established new standards

---

1   The Conference on Security and Cooperation in Europe (CSCE) was renamed the Organisation on Security and Cooperation in Europe (OSCE) in January 1995.

for the discussion of human rights issues and introduced measures to increase mutual confidence between East and West.

A series of similarly important events marked the course of East-West relations during the 1980s. These included NATO's deployment of Intermediate-Range Nuclear Forces in Europe following the December 1979 double-track decision on nuclear modernisation and arms control; the subsequent Washington Treaty signed in December 1987, which brought about the elimination of US and Soviet land-based INF missiles on a global basis; early signs of change in Eastern Europe associated with the emergence and recognition, despite later setbacks, of the independent trade union movement "Solidarity" in Poland in August 1980; the consequences of the December 1979 Soviet invasion of Afghanistan and the ultimate withdrawal of Soviet forces from Afghanistan in February 1989; and the March 1985 nomination of Mikhail Gorbachev as General Secretary of the Soviet Communist Party.

In March 1989, in the framework of the CSCE, promising new arms control negotiations opened in Vienna, between the 23 countries of NATO and the Warsaw Treaty Organisation, on reductions in conventional forces in Europe (CFE). The NATO Summit Meeting held in Brussels at the end of May 1989 against this background was of particular significance. Two major statements of Alliance policy were published, namely a declaration marking the fortieth anniversary of the Alliance, setting out goals and policies to guide the NATO Allies during the fifth decade of their cooperation; and a Comprehensive Concept of Arms Control and Disarmament.

The 1989 Summit Declaration contained many extremely important elements. It recognised the changes that were underway in the Soviet Union as well as in other Eastern European countries and outlined the Alliance's approach to overcoming the division of Europe and achieving its long-standing objective of shaping a just and peaceful European order. It reiterated the continuing need for credible and effective deterrent forces and an adequate defence, and endorsed US President Bush's three part arms control initiative calling for a) an acceleration of the CFE negotiations in Vienna; b) significant reductions in additional categories of conventional forces, and c) major reductions in United States and Soviet military personnel stationed outside their national territory. The Summit Declaration set forth a broad agenda for expanded East-West cooperation in other areas, for action on significant global challenges and for measures designed to meet the Alliance's longer-term objectives.

Developments at the End of the Eighties

Developments of major significance for the entire European continent and for international relations as a whole continued as the year progressed. By the end of 1989 and the early weeks of 1990, significant progress had been made towards the reform of the political and economic systems of Poland and Hungary; and in the German Democratic Republic, Bulgaria, Czechoslovakia and Romania, steps had been taken towards freedom and democracy which went far beyond expectations.

The promise held out for over 40 years to bring an end to the division of Europe, and with it an end to the division of Germany, took on real meaning with the opening of the Berlin Wall in November 1989. Beyond its fundamental symbolism, the member countries of the Alliance saw this event as part of a wider process leading to a genuinely whole and free Europe. The process was as yet far from complete and faced numerous obstacles and uncertainties, but rapid and dramatic progress had nevertheless been achieved. Free elections had taken place or were planned in most Central and Eastern European countries; former divisions were being overcome; repressive border installations were being dismantled; and, within less than a year, on 3 October 1990, the unification of the two German states took place with the backing of the international community and the assent of the Soviet Government, on the basis of an international treaty and the democratic choice of the German people as a whole.

Both the fact and the prospect of reform brought about major positive changes in the relationships of Central and Eastern European countries with the international community, opening up a new and enriched dialogue involving East and West, which offered real hope in place of the fear of confrontation, and practical proposals for cooperation in place of polemics and stagnation.

Such changes were not accomplished without difficulty and, as events within the former Soviet Union and other parts of Central and Eastern Europe confirmed, could give rise to new concerns about stability and security. The bold course of reforms within the Soviet Union itself led to new challenges as well as severe internal problems. Moreover the dire economic outlook and the major difficulties experienced in many of the countries of Central and Eastern Europe in managing the transition from authoritarian government and a centrally planned economy to pluralist democracy and a free market combined to make political forecasting uncertain and subject to constant revision.

Throughout this period NATO continued to play a key role, providing the framework for consultation and coordination of policies among its member countries in order to diminish the risk of crises which could impinge on common security interests. The Alliance pursued its efforts to remove military imbalances; to bring about greater openness in military matters; and to build confidence through radical, but balanced and verifiable arms control agreements, verification arrangements and increased contacts at all levels.

The Hand of Friendship and Cooperation

At the Summit Meeting in London in July 1990, in the most far-reaching Declaration issued since NATO was founded, the Heads of State and Government announced major steps to transform the Alliance in a manner commensurate with the new security environment and to bring confrontation between East and West to an end. They extended offers to the governments of the Soviet Union and Central and Eastern European countries to establish regular diplomatic liaison with NATO and to work towards a new relationship based on cooperation. The Declaration had been foreshadowed a month earlier when NATO Foreign Ministers met in Scotland and took the exceptional step of issuing a "Message from Turnberry", extending an offer of friendship and cooperation to the Soviet Union and all other European countries. The announcement made by President Gorbachev in July 1990, accepting the participation of the united Germany in the North Atlantic Alliance, was explicitly linked to the positive nature of this Message and to the substantive proposals and commitments made by Alliance governments in London.

The London Declaration included proposals to develop cooperation in numerous different ways. Leaders and representatives of Central and Eastern European countries were invited to NATO Headquarters in Brussels. Many such visits took place and arrangements for regular contacts at the diplomatic level were made. The Secretary General of NATO also visited Moscow immediately after the London Summit Meeting to convey to the Soviet leadership the proposals contained in the Declaration and the Alliance's determination to make constructive use of the new political opportunities opening up.

A joint declaration and commitment to non-aggression was signed in Paris in November 1990, at the same time as the Treaty on Conventional Forces in Europe and the publication, by all CSCE member states, of the "Charter of Paris for a New Europe". The Joint Declaration formally brought adversarial relations to an end and reaffirmed the intention of the signatories to refrain from the threat or use of force against the territorial integrity or political independence of any state, in accordance with the purposes and principles of the UN Charter and the Helsinki Final Act (see Chapter 15). All other states participating in the CSCE were invited to join this commitment.

Within a short space of time, new military contacts were established, including intensified discussions of military forces and doctrines. Progress was made towards an "Open Skies" agreement, permitting overflights of national territory on a reciprocal basis in order to increase confidence and transparency with respect to military activities. Further talks were initiated to build on the CFE Treaty on reductions of conventional forces from the Atlantic to the Ural Mountains, including additional measures to limit manpower in Europe. Agreement was reached to intensify the CSCE process and to set new standards for the establishment and preservation of free societies. Measures were taken to enable the CSCE process, which had been successful in enhancing mutual confidence, to be further institutionalised in order to provide a forum for wider political dialogue in a more united Europe. Internally, NATO began a far-reaching review of its strategy in order to adapt it to the new circumstances.

The Gulf Crisis

Despite the positive course of many of these developments, new threats to stability can arise very quickly and in unpredictable circumstances, as the 2 August 1990 Iraqi invasion of Kuwait and subsequent developments in the Gulf area demonstrated. The Coalition Force formed under United States leadership to repel the invasion did not involve NATO directly, but the solidarity achieved within NATO in relation to the conflict played a significant role. The NATO countries used the Alliance forum intensively for political consultations from the outbreak of the crisis and took a prominent part in supporting United Nations efforts to achieve a diplomatic solution. When these failed, the direct contributions to the Coalition Force of NATO member countries, and their experience of sharing assets and working together within NATO, again played a part. Moreover, in an act incumbent upon the Alliance itself, elements of NATO's ACE Mobile Force were sent to Turkey in order to demonstrate the Alliance's collective defence commitment, under Article 5 of the North Atlantic Treaty, in the event of an external threat to Turkey's security developing from the situation in the Gulf.

Significantly, the unity of purpose and determined opposition by the international community to the actions taken by Iraq, offered positive evidence of the transformation which had taken place in relations between the Soviet Union and the West. The benefits resulting from the establishment of better contacts and increased cooperation between them were clearly apparent. This early recognition of mutual interests with respect to the security and stability of the entire Euro-Atlantic area contributed to the subsequent positive evolution of NATO-Russian relations culminating in 1997 with the signing of the NATO-Russia Founding Act.

The dangers inherent in the Gulf crisis reinforced the Alliance's determination to develop and enhance the level of its cooperation with the countries of Central and Eastern Europe, as well as with other countries, in accordance with the goals set by Alliance Heads of State and Government in the London Declaration. This determination was further reinforced by the events of 1991, including the repressive steps taken by the Soviet Government with regard to the Baltic states, prior to conceding their right to establish their own independence; the deteriorating situation and outbreak of hostilities in Yugoslavia, leading to the break-up of the Yugoslav Federation; and the attempted *coup d'état* in the Soviet Union itself which took place in August 1991.

NEW INSTITUTIONS

The North Atlantic Cooperation Council

Against the background of these events, 1991 was marked by an intensification of visits and diplomatic contacts between NATO and the countries of Central and Eastern Europe in accordance with the decisions taken by NATO Heads of State and Government in London. With the publication of the Rome Declaration in November 1991, the basis was laid for placing this evolving relationship on a more institutionalised footing. The establishment of the North Atlantic Cooperation Council (NACC) in December 1991 brought together the member countries of NATO and, initially, nine Central and Eastern European countries, in a new consultative forum. In March 1992, participation in the NACC was expanded to include all members of the Commonwealth of Independent States and by June 1992, Georgia and Albania had also become members.

The inaugural meeting of the NACC took place on 20 December 1991, just as the Soviet Union was ceasing to exist. Simultaneously, 11 former Soviet republics became members of the new Commonwealth of Independent States, entering a period of intense political and economic transformation, both internally and with respect to their international relations. Against this background, regional problems became increasingly dominant. In Nagorno-Karabakh, Moldova, Georgia and elsewhere, outbreaks of violence occurred and serious intra- and inter-state tensions developed.

However it was the deteriorating situation, continuing use of force and mounting loss of life in the territory of the former Yugoslavia which were the major causes of concern, marring the prospects for peaceful progress towards a new security environment in Europe. From the start of the crisis, the North Atlantic Council and the North Atlantic Cooperation Council consulted and supported efforts undertaken in other fora to restore peace.

During the same period, discussion of measures designed to strengthen the role of the CSCE in promoting stability and democracy in Europe, including proposals outlined in the Rome Declaration issued by the Alliance, culminated in the signature of the 1992 Helsinki Document ("The Challenges of Change") at the CSCE Summit Meeting held in July 1992. The document described, inter alia, new initiatives for the creation of a CSCE forum for security cooperation and for CSCE peacekeeping activities, for which both the North Atlantic Council and the North Atlantic Cooperation Council expressed full support.

The development of the North Atlantic Cooperation Council and the role of the Euro-Atlantic Partnership Council (EAPC) which replaced it in 1997 are described in more detail in subsequent chapters.

The Euro-Atlantic Partnership Council (EAPC)

The Euro-Atlantic Partnership Council (EAPC), was set up in 1997 to succeed the North Atlantic Cooperation Council. It brings together the 19 Allies and 27 Partners[2] in a forum providing for regular consultation and cooperation. It meets periodically at the level of Ambassadors and Foreign and Defence Ministers.

Heads of State and Government of the 46 members can also meet, when appropriate, as they did in Washington in April 1999. The EAPC Summit in Washington was an opportunity for open discussions on security-related cooperation within the EAPC in the 21st century. The leaders concentrated on key-security challenges in the EAPC area, in particular the situation in Kosovo.

Heads of State and Government endorsed two documents relating to further development of the Partnership for Peace. The first of these, the "Political-Military Framework for NATO-led PfP Operations", addressed the involvement of Partner countries in political consultations and decision-making, in operational planning and in command arrangements for future NATO-led operations in which they participate. The second document entitled "Towards a Partnership for the 21st Century - the Enhanced and More Operational Partnership" outlines the main elements designed to make the Partnership for Peace (PfP) more operational.

The EAPC played a valuable role as a forum for consultation on the crisis in Kosovo. A series of extraordinary meetings was held to keep Partners

---

2   Albania, Armenia, Austria, Azerbaijan, Belarus, Belgium, Bulgaria, Canada, Croatia, Czech Republic, Denmark, Estonia, Finland, France, Georgia, Germany, Greece, Hungary, Iceland, Ireland, Italy, Kazakhstan, Kyrgyz Republic, Latvia, Lithuania, Luxembourg, Moldova, Netherlands, Norway, Poland, Portugal, Romania, Russia, Slovakia, Slovenia, Spain, Sweden, Switzerland, Tajikistan, the former Yugoslav Republic of Macedonia(a), Turkey, Turkmenistan, Ukraine, United Kingdom, United States, Uzbekistan.

(a)   Turkey recognises the Republic of Macedonia with its constitutional name.

informed of the status of NATO planning and preparations for possible military options in Kosovo and to exchange views with Partners on developments.

EAPC activities complement Partnership for Peace (PfP) Programmes. They are based on a two-year action plan which focuses on consultation and cooperation on a range of political and security-related matters, including regional issues, arms control, international terrorism, peacekeeping, defence economic issues, civil emergency planning, and scientific and environmental issues.

Almost all of non-NATO EAPC members have established diplomatic missions accredited to NATO, expanding contacts between NATO and Partners and increasing the efficiency and effectiveness of cooperation.

An important achievement of the EAPC has been the establishment of the Euro-Atlantic Disaster Response Coordination Centre (EADRCC) at NATO headquarters, following a proposal by the Russian Federation. The Centre was inaugurated in June 1998 and was called upon immediately to support the UN High Commissioner for Refugees in relief efforts in Albania for refugees fleeing from Kosovo. Coordinated humanitarian assistance from NATO and Partner countries was stepped up in response to the escalating refugee crisis in the region since the end of March 1999. The EADRCC also played a significant role in coordinating humanitarian relief for flood-hit parts of western Ukraine.

The EAPC also helps to foster practical regional security cooperation through topical seminars which form part of the EAPC action plan. The first such regional cooperation seminar was hosted by Georgia in October 1998. Since then similar events have been held in Lithuania and Slovakia, Bulgaria and Uzbekistan.

Ideas for further practical initiatives are being explored, including ways in which the EAPC might support global humanitarian action against mines and ways of controlling transfers of small arms.

THE STRATEGIC CONCEPT OF THE ALLIANCE

At the Washington Summit meeting in April 1999, the NATO Allies approved a strategy to equip the Alliance for the security challenges and opportunities of the 21st century and to guide its future political and military development.

The updated Strategic Concept provides overall guidance for the development of detailed policies and military plans. It describes the *Purpose and Tasks of the Alliance* and examines its *Strategic Perspectives* in the light of the evolving strategic environment and security challenges and risks. The Concept sets out the *Alliance's Approach to Security in the 21st Century*, reaffirming the importance of the transatlantic link and of maintaining the Alliance's military capabilities. It examines the role of other key elements in the Alliance's broad approach to stability and security, namely the European Security and Defence Identity; conflict prevention and crisis management; partnership, cooperation and dialogue; enlargement; and arms control, disarmament and non-proliferation. The Concept also gives *Guidelines for the Alliance's Forces* based on the principles of Alliance strategy and the characteristics of the Alliance's force posture. This includes sections addressing the missions of Alliance military forces and guidelines for the Alliance's force posture, as well as the characteristics of conventional and nuclear forces.

The Strategic Concept was first published in 1991. The 1999 version, like its predecessor, is the authoritative statement of the Alliance's objectives and provides the highest level guidance on the political and military means to be used in achieving them.

The initial formulation of NATO strategy was known as "The Strategic Concept for the Defence of the North Atlantic Area". Developed between October 1949 and April 1950, it set out a strategy of large-scale operations for territorial defence. In the mid-1950s the strategy of "massive retaliation" was developed. It emphasised deterrence based on the threat that NATO would respond to any aggression against its member countries by every means at its disposal, specifically including nuclear weapons.

Discussions of possible changes in this strategic approach began later in the 1950s and continued until 1967 when, following intensive debate within the Alliance, "massive retaliation" was replaced by the strategy of "flexible response". This concentrated on giving NATO the advantages of flexibility and of creating uncertainty in the minds of any potential aggressor about NATO's response in the case of a threat to the sovereignty or independence of any single member country. The concept was designed to ensure that aggression of any kind would be perceived as involving unacceptable risks.

The above strategies were enshrined in classified documents, which provided guidance to national governments and points of reference for military planning activities. They were not addressed to the general public. Although the underlying concepts were well known, little public discussion about their details was possible because their effectiveness depended greatly on secrecy. They reflected the realities of the Cold War, the political division of Europe and the confrontational ideological and military situation that characterised East-West relations for many years.

As the Cold War continued, however, the Alliance also sought to reduce its dangers and to lay the grounds for progress towards a more positive relationship with the Soviet Union and other member countries of the Warsaw Pact. The Harmel Report, published in 1967, thus established defence and dialogue, including arms control, as the dual pillars of the Alliance's approach to security.

With the end of the Cold War era, the political situation in Europe and the overall military situation were transformed. A new Strategic Concept evolved during the two years following the fall of the Berlin Wall. This was debated and discussed within the Alliance and was completed in November 1991. Bearing little relation to previous concepts, it emphasised cooperation with former adversaries as opposed to confrontation. It maintained the security of its member nations as NATO's fundamental purpose but combined this with the specific obligation to work towards improved and expanded security for Europe as a whole. In other respects, too, the 1991 Strategic Concept differed dramatically from its predecessors. It was issued as a public document, open for discussion and comment by parliaments, security specialists, journalists and the wider public.

In 1997, NATO leaders agreed that the Concept should be reexamined and updated to reflect the changes that had taken place in Europe since its adoption, while confirming the Allies' commitment to collective defence and the transatlantic link and ensuring that NATO strategy is fully adapted to the challenges of the 21st century. Intensive work was undertaken throughout the Alliance, to conclude the revision by the time of the Washington Summit.

In common with all other Alliance business, the approval of the Concept required consensus on both the substance and the language of the document by all the member countries of the Alliance. Against the background of the accession of three new member countries, representatives of the Czech Republic, Hungary and Poland were present from the outset of the discussions.

The Strategic Concept is the authoritative statement of NATO's purposes and tasks and the highest level guidance on the political and military means to be used in achieving its objectives.

The 1999 Concept confirms that the Alliance's essential and enduring purpose is to safeguard the freedom and security of its members by political and military means. It affirms the values of democracy, human rights, and the rule of law and expresses the commitment of the Allies not only to common defence but to the peace and stability of the wider Euro-Atlantic area.

The strategy also defines the Alliance's fundamental security tasks, both in terms of collective defence, which has been at the centre of the Alliance since its establishment, and in terms of the new activities in the fields of crisis management and partnership that the Alliance is undertaking in order to enhance the security and stability of the Euro-Atlantic area.

The Concept describes the strategic environment and assesses the foreseeable security challenges and risks. It notes that in recent years the environment has been marked by continuing and generally positive change and that the Alliance has played an essential part in strengthening Euro-Atlantic security since the end of the Cold War.

With respect to risks, the document reaffirms the conclusion in the 1991 Strategic Concept that the threat of general war in Europe has virtually disappeared but that there are other risks and uncertainties facing the members of the Alliance and other states in the Euro-Atlantic region, such as ethnic conflict, the abuse of human rights, political instability, economic fragility, and the spread of nuclear, biological, and chemical weapons and their means of delivery.

One of the distinguishing features of the Alliance's 1991 strategy was its delineation of a broad approach to security, encompassing complementary political and military means and emphasising cooperation with other states that share the Alliance's objectives. This comprehensive approach remains a central feature of the new Strategic Concept and comprises the following essential elements:

The preservation of the transatlantic link. The Strategic Concept underlines the indivisibility of European and North American security and therefore the importance of a strong and dynamic partnership between Europe and North America.

The maintenance of effective military capabilities. The strategy calls for military capabilities that will be effective under the full range of foreseeable circumstances, from deterrence and collective defence to crisis response operations. The Strategic Concept also provides specific guidance on the necessary capabilities.

The development of the European Security and Defence Identity within the Alliance. The Strategic Concept confirms that the European Security and Defence Identity will continue to be developed within the Alliance on the basis of decisions taken by Alliance Foreign Ministers in Berlin in 1996 and thereafter. It states that this process will require close cooperation between NATO, the Western European Union and, if and when appropriate, the European Union[3].

The Concept affirms that this process will enable all European Allies to make a more coherent and effective contribution to the missions and activities

---

3   The evolution of policy relating to the European Security and Defence Identity and the respective roles of NATO, the Western European Union and the European Union are described in Chapter 4 and Chapter 15.

of the Alliance; it will reinforce the transatlantic partnership; and it will assist the European Allies to act by themselves as required through the readiness of the Alliance, on a case-by-case basis and by consensus, to make its assets and capabilities available for European-led operations in which NATO is not engaged militarily, taking into account the full participation of all European Allies if they were so to choose.

Conflict prevention and crisis management. The Concept defines an important role for the Alliance with respect to conflict prevention and crisis management, since crisis response operations like those in Bosnia and in Kosovo are likely to remain a key aspect of NATO's contribution to Euro-Atlantic peace and security.

Partnership, cooperation, and dialogue. The Concept emphasises the Alliance's determination to pursue its long-standing policy of partnership, cooperation and dialogue with all democratic Euro-Atlantic countries, in order to preserve peace, promote democracy and contribute to prosperity and progress. It points out that this approach is aimed at enhancing the security of all, excludes nobody, and helps to overcome divisions that could lead to conflict. It also describes the principal instruments of this policy - the Euro-Atlantic Partnership Council, the Partnership for Peace, the special relationships with Russia and Ukraine, and the Mediterranean Dialogue.

Enlargement. The Concept confirms the openness of the Alliance to new members under Article 10 of the Washington Treaty and restates NATO's expectation that it will extend further invitations in coming years.

Arms Control, Disarmament, and Non-Proliferation. Finally, the Strategic Concept sets out the Alliance's policy of support for Arms Control, Disarmament, and Non-Proliferation. It underlines the Alliance's intention to keep this aspect of its approach to security in harmony with its approach to defence; and also affirms that it will seek to enhance security and stability at the lowest possible level of forces consistent with its ability to fulfil the full range of its missions.

The final part of the Strategic Concept establishes guidelines for the Alliance's forces, translating the purposes and tasks of the preceding sections into practical - albeit necessarily general - instructions for NATO force and operational planners. The strategy calls for the continued development of the military capabilities needed for the full range of the Alliance's missions, from collective defence to peace support and other crisis response operations.

Among the capabilities highlighted as particularly important are the ability to engage opposing forces effectively; deployability and mobility; survivability of forces and infrastructure; sustainability, and interoperability - including interoperability with the forces of Partner countries. In addition, the strategy underlines the indispensable part that Alliance forces play in addressing the risks associated with the proliferation of nuclear, biological and chemical weapons and their means of delivery.

The Strategic Concept also stipulates that the Alliance will maintain for the foreseeable future an appropriate mix of nuclear and conventional forces based in Europe, kept up to date where necessary, at the minimum sufficient level.

THE ROLE OF ALLIED MILITARY FORCES AND THE TRANSFORMATION OF THE ALLIANCE'S DEFENCE POSTURE

Since the establishment of NATO, Allied forces have constituted the basis for effective deterrence and defence against the threat of war, which remained the principal security concern of the Allies for forty years. Their primary role remains that of guaranteeing the security and territorial integrity of member states.

The task of providing security through deterrence and collective defence remains unchanged. However, the quite different security situation of the 1990s has allowed Alliance forces to take on new roles in addition to fulfilling this primary function. For example, through the enhanced Partnership for Peace programme, and within the framework of the EAPC, the NATO-Russia Permanent Joint Council, the NATO-Ukraine Commission, and other forums created to intensify cooperation, Alliance military forces are playing an increasingly important part in facilitating transparency and creating greater confidence between NATO and its Partners. They also play a key role in the verification of arms control agreements. Above all, as operational peacekeeping forces, they have assumed the vital task of underpinning effective crisis management and conflict prevention arrangements, most notably in their role in implementing the Bosnian Peace Agreement and in providing the international security presence in Kosovo mandated by the United Nations.

The peacekeeping and crisis management roles of NATO forces have taken on increasing importance in parallel with the development of the Alliance's overall role in this field. Indeed, of all the challenges the Alliance has faced, none has called for more determination and unity of purpose than that of putting its military forces at the centre of multinational efforts to end the conflict and create the basis for a stable and peaceful future in the Balkans.

The first major combat mission in which military force was used by NATO as a tool of crisis management to support United Nations efforts to end the

Yugoslavian conflict took place in 1995. This action, known as "Operation Deliberate Force", was a significant factor in the process which culminated in the conclusion of a peace settlement in Bosnia. NATO was subsequently tasked at the end of 1995 with the implementation of the military aspects of the agreement by leading a multinational Implementation Force (IFOR), and the following year a Stabilisation Force (SFOR), both of which were established in accordance with United Nations mandates. In so doing NATO moved from a relatively limited role in supporting UN peacekeeping efforts to assuming full control of complex peace support operations involving the participation of forces from numerous Partner and other non-NATO countries. This practical, operational experience of cooperation in the military field has had wide repercussions, for example in generating enhanced political cooperation, not only between NATO and its Partners, but also with other countries. The process is benefiting security and stability in Europe as a whole.

The Alliance operation in Kosovo and its role in alleviating the humanitarian crisis in the neighbouring countries further reinforced NATO's role in crisis management. NATO contributed decisively, in particular through the conduct of its air campaign and the subsequent deployment of KFOR, to the international community's objective of creating the basis for long-term peace and stability in Kosovo.

The Kosovo air campaign, which demonstrated the cohesion and unity of the Alliance and its determination to act in the face of sustained violence and repression of human rights in Kosovo, reinforced the diplomatic efforts of the international community and achieved the key objectives of the NATO Allies and their Partners. The humanitarian catastrophe has ended; over 840 000 refugees have returned; a NATO-led international peace force (KFOR) has been successfully deployed; and the international community has assumed responsibility for the civil administration through the United Nations Mission in Kosovo (UNMIK).

The changing role of Allied military forces also reflects the Alliance's commitment to developing the European Security and Defence Identity within NATO. This process is now being carried forward in the context of the European Security and Defence Policy being developed by the European Union and is described in Chapter 4.

A further related illustration of the way in which Allied military forces are being adapted to new circumstances is the implementation of the military concept known as "Combined Joint Task Forces" (CJTFs). At the NATO Summit held in January 1994, Heads of State and Government endorsed the concept as an important part of the adaptation of Alliance structures to changes in the European security environment. The concept is designed to provide NATO with a flexible means to respond to new security challenges, including operations involving the participation of nations outside the Alliance. It is aimed at improving NATO's ability to deploy, at short notice, appropriate multinational and multiservice forces matched to the specific requirements of a particular military operation. It will also facilitate the integration of non-NATO participants in NATO-led peace support operations. Many of the features of the CJTF concept, which is still being developed, have been put into practice in the context of the NATO-led peacekeeping operations in the Balkans.

Arrangements for the assignment of forces to CJTFs by member nations follow normal NATO force planning procedures. Nevertheless, the flexibility which is built into the CJTF concept places considerable demands on arrangements for commanding and controlling the task forces, that is to say on CJTF headquarters. Core elements ("nuclei") of a small number of CJTF headquarters are therefore being established within selected "Parent" headquarters of NATO's Command Structure (see Chapters 11 and 12). CJTF headquarters rely primarily on pre-designated personnel - i.e. personnel undertaking other responsibilities when not operating in a CJTF context - in "Parent" headquarters, and on pre-trained augmentation personnel provided by other NATO headquarters and nations.

In summary, the continuing transformation of the Alliance's conventional force defence posture is a complex and far-reaching process which has to take into account all the above factors. Ultimately, in the event of crises which might lead to a military threat to the security of the Alliance members, NATO forces must be able to complement and reinforce political actions and contribute to the management of such crises and to their peaceful resolution. The maintenance of an adequate military capability and clear preparedness to act collectively therefore remain central. The structures and arrangements which have been built over many years enable member countries to benefit from the political, military and resource advantages of collective action and collective defence. These arrangements are based on an integrated structure, key features of which include collective force planning; common funding; common operational planning; multinational formations; headquarters and command arrangements; an integrated air defence system; a balance of roles of responsibilities among the Allies; the stationing and deployment of forces outside home territory when required; arrangements, including planning for crisis management and reinforcement; common standards and procedures for equipment, training and logistics; joint and combined doctrines and exercises when appropriate; and infrastructure, armaments and logistics cooperation. The inclusion of NATO's Partner countries in such arrangements or the development of similar arrangements for Partner countries, in appropriate areas, is also instrumental in enhancing cooperation and common efforts in Euro-Atlantic security matters.

The principal characteristics of the changes affecting NATO's military forces are reductions in size and readiness and increases in flexibility, mobility and multinationality. Underlying the changes themselves, in addition to the requirements dictated by the Alliance's new roles, two indispensable principles have remained sacrosanct: the commitment to collective defence as a core function which is fundamental to the Alliance; and the preservation of the transatlantic link as the guarantor of the Alliance's credibility and effectiveness.

The threat of war which confronted Europe for over four decades, as a result of ideological conflict, political hostility and military opposition, has very significantly diminished. Today, attention is focused much less on deterrence against the use of force, as foreseen under Article 5 of the North Atlantic Treaty, than on the much more likely peacekeeping, conflict prevention and crisis management tasks which NATO may face.

There are nevertheless risks from instability inherent in conflict situations which have arisen since the end of the Cold War, such as the situation in the former Yugoslavia, which illustrate the necessity for continued Alliance solidarity and the maintenance of an effective military capability able to meet a wide range of contingencies.

The net effect of changes affecting NATO forces themselves has been to transform NATO forces into a substantially reduced, but more mobile structure. Ground forces committed to the Alliance by member nations through NATO's integrated defence and force planning processes have been cut by 35 percent. Major naval vessels have been reduced by over 30 percent and air force combat squadrons by some 40 percent since the beginning of the 1990s. There have also been major reductions in the number of forces held at high states of readiness. In general, NATO forces have been reorganised in a manner which will facilitate their flexible regeneration and build-up whenever this becomes necessary for either collective defence or crisis management, including peace support operations.

NATO's Defence Capabilities Initiative

Launched at the Washington Summit meeting in April 1999, NATO's Defence Capabilities Initiative or DCI is designed to ensure that the Alliance can meet the security challenges of the 21st century and is prepared to deal effectively with crises like that in Kosovo, as well as maintaining the ability to fulfil its fundamental responsibilities for the defence of its member countries. In the words of Secretary General Lord Robertson: *"The Defence Capabilities Initiative is designed to ensure that all Allies not only remain interoperable, but that they also improve and update their capabilities to face the new security challenges."*

The Initiative covers almost all areas of military capability. This includes the mobility of forces; their logistical support; their ability to protect themselves and engage an enemy; and the command and control and information systems they use in order to ensure that, when necessary, they can deploy rapidly and efficiently to the locations where they may be needed to manage crises, if necessary, for extended periods.

During the Cold War, NATO's defence planning was primarily concerned with maintaining the capabilities needed to defend against possible aggression by the Soviet Union and Warsaw Pact. Today, the European security environment has become more complex. The most likely threats to security come from conflict on Europe's fringes, such as in the former Yugoslavia, or from proliferation of weapons of mass destruction. As a result, NATO must now be ready to deploy forces beyond Alliance borders to respond to crises, in addition to being able to defend against deliberate aggression.

Moreover, as in Bosnia and Herzegovina and Kosovo, where NATO forces are currently deployed, future Alliance military operations are likely to be markedly different from the kind of operation for which planning was undertaken during the Cold War. They will probably take place outside Alliance territory; they may last for many years; and they will involve troops of many nations working closely together - principally from member states but also, in some instances, from Partner countries. Moreover, crisis management tasks demand different skills from those required for fighting wars.

To meet these new security challenges, NATO has to ensure that its forces have the equipment, personnel and training needed to successfully carry out all their tasks. Lessons learned in Bosnia and Herzegovina and Kosovo, as well as the experience of earlier multinational operations involving NATO countries such as those in the Gulf, Somalia and Haiti, have demonstrated where changes are needed.

The Defence Capabilities Initiative was launched to ensure that NATO is ready for every eventuality. A High Level Steering Group was formed to oversee the programme. The Group, which is made up of senior officials from national capitals and chaired by the Deputy Secretary General of NATO, meets every few weeks to review progress and guide the process.

DCI will also contribute to the development of the European Security and Defence Identity, or ESDI, by strengthening European defence capabilities and the European pillar of NATO. This will enable the European allies to make a stronger and more coherent contribution to NATO (see Chapter 4).

DCI aims in particular to improve Alliance capabilities in the following five, overlapping areas:

- "mobility and deployability": i.e. the ability to deploy forces quickly to where they are needed, including areas outside Alliance territory;

- "sustainability"; i.e. the ability to maintain and supply forces far from their home bases and to ensure that sufficient fresh forces are available for long-duration operations;

- "effective engagement"; i.e. the ability to successfully engage an adversary in all types of operations, from high to low intensity;

- "survivability": i.e. the ability to protect forces and infrastructure against current and future threats; and

- "interoperable communications": i.e. command, control and information systems which are compatible with each other, to enable forces from different countries to work effectively together.

To enhance NATO's ability to deploy forces in distant crisis areas, member states are investigating improved arrangements for transporting troops and equipment. This includes the sharing of resources and arrangements enabling commercial planes and ships to be called upon if necessary. The use of commercial resources would require arrangements for their use as well as unambiguous legal arrangements to be put in place well in advance.

Logistics is a crucial element in any military operation. The DCI aims to enhance the numbers and capabilities of Allies' logistic units. The scope for pooling of logistic capabilities is also being examined in order to increase efficiency. This will lead to the creation of Multinational Joint Logistic Centres as part of the Combined Joint Task Force Concept (see Chapter 12).

Modern technologies can permit military force to be applied in a discriminating way which reduces collateral damage and can shorten a conflict by demonstrating that continued aggression can not succeed. Such technologies include day/night and all-weather weapons systems and precision-guided munitions. DCI is also addressing these areas.

To improve the protection and survivability of forces engaged in military operations, NATO is looking at ways of enhancing military capabilities in these fields. Improvements are being examined in reconnaissance and surveillance systems; air defence systems; and systems to counteract the threat posed by weapons of mass destruction.

At the same time, as the forces of different countries work more and more closely together, for example in undertaking crisis management operations, the need increases to ensure that they can communicate effectively at every level.

The DCI aims to ensure that technological advances do not degrade communications interoperability. It also seeks to ensure that advances in technology are put to the best use in developing communications methods for military use.

NATO's Nuclear Forces in the New Security Environment

Since the end of the Cold War, the Alliance has taken far-reaching steps to adapt its overall policy and defence posture to the new security environment. In realising their new broad approach to security, which recognises the importance of political, economic, social and environmental factors in addition to the indispensable defence dimension, NATO member countries have taken full advantage of the opportunities provided by the momentous improvements in the security environment. NATO's nuclear strategy and force posture were among the first areas to be reviewed. They are also the areas that have been subjected to some of the most radical changes. The most significant changes are described below.

During the Cold War, NATO's nuclear forces played a central role in the Alliance's strategy of flexible response. To deter major war in Europe, nuclear weapons were integrated into the whole of NATO's force structure, and the Alliance maintained a variety of targeting plans which could be executed at short notice. This role entailed high readiness levels and quick-reaction alert postures for significant parts of NATO's nuclear forces.

In the new security environment, NATO has radically reduced its reliance on nuclear forces. Its strategy remains one of war prevention but it is no longer dominated by the possibility of nuclear escalation. Its nuclear forces are no longer targeted against any country, and the circumstances in which their use might have to be contemplated are considered to be extremely remote. NATO's nuclear forces continue to contribute, in an essential way, to war prevention. Their role is now more fundamentally political and they are no longer directed towards a specific threat. They are maintained at the minimum level sufficient to preserve peace and stability.

In keeping with the reduced salience of nuclear weapons in Alliance strategy, NATO's nuclear posture was radically reduced. As the Cold War ended, NATO's nuclear powers took unilateral steps to cancel planned modernisation programmes for their nuclear forces. France announced the early cessation of Hadès missile manufacturing. The United States and the United Kingdom cancelled plans for a nuclear tactical air-to-surface missile. As a precursor of later decisions to eliminate ground-launched nuclear systems, the United States also cancelled plans for a nuclear-capable follow-on system to the LANCE surface-to-surface missile and for the production of a new 155 mm nuclear artillery shell. France has, since 1991, reduced the types of nuclear delivery systems from six to two; today, the independent French nuclear forces consist only of four submarines carrying submarine-launched ballistic missiles (SLBM) and of Mirage 2000N aircraft with medium-range air-to-surface missiles.

Since 1992, the United Kingdom has given up its nuclear LANCE and tube artillery roles, its maritime tactical nuclear capability previously based on surface ships, and all air-launched nuclear weapons, thus eliminating the nuclear role for its dual-capable aircraft. Trident submarines are now Britain's only nuclear system.

In October 1991, following an initiative by US President Bush, NATO decided to reduce the number of weapons available for its sub-strategic[4] forces in Europe by over 85 percent. This reduction was completed in July 1992. As part of these reductions, all nuclear warheads for NATO's ground-launched sub-strategic forces (including nuclear artillery and surface-to-surface missiles) were eliminated and air-delivered gravity bombs were reduced by well over 50 percent. In addition, all nuclear weapons for surface maritime forces were removed. The elimination process included some 1 300 nuclear artillery weapons and 850 LANCE missile warheads. All of the nuclear warheads that had been assigned to these forces have been removed from the NATO inventory. Most of them have already been eliminated and the remaining weapons are to be eliminated in the near future.

The United States has also completely eliminated all naval non-strategic/sub-strategic systems except submarine-launched nuclear cruise missiles, which are no longer deployed at sea in peacetime. In addition, it completely terminated the nuclear role for its carrier-based dual-capable aircraft. Today, the only land-based nuclear weapons available to NATO are United States nuclear bombs capable of being delivered by dual-capable aircraft of several Allies.

NATO nuclear storage sites have also undergone a massive reduction (about 80 percent) as weapon systems have been eliminated and the number of weapons reduced. At the same time, a new, more secure and survivable weapon storage system has been installed.

---

4   The terms "strategic" and "sub-strategic" have slightly different meanings in different countries. Strategic nuclear weapons are normally defined as weapons of "intercontinental" range (over 5 500 kilometres), but in some contexts these may also include intermediate-range ballistic missiles of lower ranges. The term "sub-strategic" nuclear weapons has been used in NATO documents since 1989 with reference to intermediate and short-range nuclear weapons and now refers primarily to air-delivered weapons for NATO's dual-capable aircraft and to a small number of United Kingdom Trident warheads in a sub-strategic role (other sub-strategic nuclear weapons having been withdrawn from Europe).

With the end of the Cold War, in a further significant change, NATO ceased to maintain standing peacetime nuclear contingency plans and associated targets for its sub-strategic nuclear forces. As a result, NATO's nuclear forces no longer target any country. Taking further advantage of the improved security environment, NATO has taken a number of steps to decrease the number and readiness levels of its dual-capable aircraft.

In another unilateral initiative, in December 1996, NATO Foreign and Defence Ministers announced that enlarging the Alliance would not require a change in its greatly reduced nuclear posture and that NATO has *"no intention, no plan, and no reason to deploy nuclear weapons on the territory of new member countries, nor any need to change any aspect of NATO's nuclear posture or nuclear policy, and that it does not foresee any future need to do so"*. NATO's remaining much smaller sub-strategic forces will, for the foreseeable future, continue to meet the Alliance's deterrence requirements.

Nuclear Arms Control

NATO Allies have maintained a long-standing commitment to nuclear arms control, disarmament, and non-proliferation as an integral part of their security policy, firmly embedded in the broader political context in which Allies seek to enhance stability and security by lowering arms levels and increasing military transparency and mutual confidence. In its 1983 "Montebello Decision" the Alliance announced, and subsequently carried out, the withdrawal of 1 400 nuclear warheads from Europe. The 1987 US-Soviet Intermediate Range Nuclear Forces (INF) Treaty eliminated land-based intermediate range nuclear missiles on a global basis, thus bringing to fruition the arms control aspect of NATO's 1979 "dual-track decision".

The United States and the Russian Federation are deeply engaged in a process aimed at drastically reducing their strategic nuclear weapons. The Strategic Arms Reductions Treaty (START I), signed in July 1991 and in force since 1994, will reduce the deployed strategic weapons of both sides from well over 10 000 to 6 000. START II (signed in January 1993 and ratified by the US in January 1996 and by Russia in April 2000) will further reduce each side's strategic weapons to between 3 000 and 3 500 and will eliminate multiple independently-targetable re-entry vehicles (MIRV) from Inter-Continental Ballistic Missiles (ICBM), as well as provide for procedures for intrusive verification of compliance. Following the ratification of START II by Russia, the United States and Russia have indicated that they are prepared to engage in START III negotiations to further reduce strategic weapons to between 2 000 and 2 500 and to introduce measures relating to the transparency of strategic warhead inventories and destruction of strategic nuclear warheads.

In other related fields, NATO member countries are all parties to and fully support the nuclear Non-Proliferation Treaty (NPT) to which there are 187 signatory countries. They have urged all countries which have not yet done so to accede to and fully implement the Treaty. At the NPT five-yearly Review Conference in New York in May 2000, the five nuclear powers which are the permanent members of the UN Security Council - China, France, Russia, United Kingdom and United States - among other practical steps for implementing the treaty, committed to *"an unequivocal undertaking... to accomplish the total elimination of their nuclear arsenals leading to total disarmament".* This commitment represents a significant advance in the field of nuclear arms control and one which can be expected to exert a positive influence on the future arms control agenda.

NATO strongly supports efforts to reduce nuclear weapons in a prudent and graduated manner. The Alliance has consistently welcomed progress with the Strategic Arms Reduction Treaty (START) and has stressed the need for the entry into force of the START II Treaty, which could lead to further substantial reductions of strategic arsenals envisaged through a START III Treaty.

All these commitments and developments are in line with the Alliance's objective of ensuring security and stability at the lowest possible level of forces consistent with the requirements of defence.

Role of NATO's Remaining Nuclear Forces

The fundamental purpose of the nuclear forces that remain is political: to preserve peace and prevent coercion. They make the risks of aggression against NATO incalculable and unacceptable in a way that conventional forces alone cannot. Together with an appropriate mix of conventional capabilities, they also create real uncertainty for any country that might contemplate seeking political or military advantage through the threat or use of weapons of mass destruction against the Alliance. By deterring the use of nuclear, biological and chemical weapons, the Alliance's forces also contribute to Alliance efforts aimed at preventing the proliferation of these weapons and their delivery means.

The collective security provided by NATO's nuclear posture is shared among all members of the Alliance. Moreover, the presence of US nuclear forces based in Europe, committed to NATO, reinforces the political and military link between the European and North American members of the Alliance. At the same time, the participation of non-nuclear countries in the implementation of the Alliance's nuclear policies demonstrates Alliance solidarity as well as the common commitment of its member countries to maintaining their security and the widespread sharing among them of responsibilities and risks.

Political oversight of NATO's nuclear posture is also shared among member nations. NATO's Nuclear Planning Group provides a forum in which the Defence Ministers of nuclear and non-nuclear Allies alike (with the exception of France) participate in decisions on NATO's nuclear posture and in the development of the Alliance's nuclear policy. This is based on agreement among the member countries that NATO must retain - and must be seen to retain - a core of military capabilities with an appropriate mix of forces affording it the basic military strength necessary for collective self-defence. NATO's nuclear forces remain an essential element of that core capability, notwithstanding the dramatic changes in the security environment which have allowed NATO to undertake major reductions both in its nuclear posture and in its reliance on nuclear weapons.

CHAPTER 3

THE OPENING UP OF THE ALLIANCE

The Process of NATO Enlargement

Partnership for Peace

Cooperation between NATO and Russia

NATO's Partnership with Ukraine

The Alliance's Mediterranean Dialogue

NATO's South East Europe Initiative

THE OPENING UP OF THE ALLIANCE

THE PROCESS OF NATO ENLARGEMENT

"The Parties may, by unanimous agreement, invite any other European state in a position to further the principles of this Treaty and to contribute to the security of the North Atlantic area to accede to this Treaty. (...)"

Article 10, The North Atlantic Treaty Washington DC, 4 April 1949

Since the signature of the North Atlantic Treaty, seven countries have joined the initial 12 signatories, raising the total number of NATO Allies to 19. The Czech Republic, Hungary and Poland joined the Alliance in March 1999, following an invitation issued at the 1997 Madrid Summit Meeting. The three latest member countries participated in their first Summit meeting as members in Washington in April 1999. At that time, NATO leaders underlined the continuing openness of the Alliance to further new members and pledged that NATO would continue to welcome new members in a position to further the principles of the Treaty and contribute to peace and security in the Euro-Atlantic area.

The Alliance expects to extend further invitations in coming years to nations willing and able to assume the responsibilities and obligations of membership, when it considers that the inclusion of these nations would serve the overall political and strategic interests of the Alliance and would enhance overall European security and stability.

NATO leaders also launched a Membership Action Plan, specifically designed to provide advice and feedback to countries aspiring to joint the Alliance.

The 1995 Study on NATO's Enlargement

In January 1994 at the Brussels Summit, Allied leaders reaffirmed that the Alliance was open to membership of other European states in a position to further the principles of the Washington Treaty and to contribute to security in the North Atlantic area.

Following a decision by Allied Foreign Ministers in December 1994, the "why and how" of future admissions into the Alliance were examined by the Allies during 1995. The resulting "Study on NATO Enlargement" was shared with interested Partner countries in September 1995 and made public. The principles outlined in the Study remain the basis for NATO's open approach to inviting new members to join. With regard to the "why" of NATO enlargement, the Study concluded that, with the end of the Cold War and the disappearance of the Warsaw Treaty Organisation, there was both a need for and a unique opportunity to build improved security in the whole of the Euro-Atlantic area, without recreating dividing lines.

NATO enlargement is a further step towards the Alliance's basic goal of enhancing security and extending stability throughout the Euro-Atlantic area, complementing broader trends towards integration, notably the enlargement of the European Union (EU) and the strengthening of the Organisation for Security and Cooperation in Europe (OSCE) (See Chapter 15). It threatens no one. NATO will remain a defensive Alliance whose fundamental purpose is to pre-serve peace in the Euro-Atlantic area and to provide security to its members.

The Study further concluded that the enlargement of the Alliance will con-tribute to enhanced stability and security for all countries in the Euro-Atlantic area in numerous ways. It will encourage and support democratic reforms, including the establishment of civilian and democratic control over military forces. It will foster the patterns and habits of cooperation, consultation and consensus-building which characterise relations among the current Allies and will promote good-neighbourly relations in the whole Euro-Atlantic area. It will increase transparency in defence planning and military budgets, thereby rein-forcing confidence among states, and will reinforce the tendency toward inte-gration and cooperation in Europe. Furthermore, it will strengthen the Alliance's ability to contribute to European and international security and support peace-keeping under the United Nations or OSCE; and it will strengthen and broaden the transatlantic partnership.

With regard to the "how" of enlargement, the Study confirmed that, as in the past, any future extension of the Alliance's membership would be through accession of new member states to the North Atlantic Treaty in accordance with its Article 10. Once admitted, new members would enjoy all the rights and assume all obligations of membership under the Treaty. They would need to accept and conform with the principles, policies and procedures adopted by all members of the Alliance at the time that they join. The Study made clear that willingness and ability to meet such commitments, not only on paper but in practice, would be a critical factor in any decision taken by the Alliance to invite a country to join.

States which are involved in ethnic disputes or external territorial disputes, including irredentist claims, or internal jurisdictional disputes, must settle those disputes by peaceful means in accordance with OSCE principles, before they can become members.

The Study also noted that the ability of interested countries to contribute militarily to collective defence and to peacekeeping and other new missions of the Alliance would be a factor in deciding whether to invite them to join the

Alliance. Ultimately, the Study concluded, Allies would decide by consensus whether to invite each new member to join, basing their decision on their judgement - at the time such a decision has to be made - of whether the membership of a specific country would contribute to security and stability in the North Atlantic area or not. No country outside the Alliance has a veto or 'droit de regard' over the process of enlargement or decisions relating to it.

At the Madrid Summit in July 1997, at the end of a careful and comprehensive process of deliberation and of intensified, individual dialogue with interested partner countries, Allied Heads of State and Government invited the Czech Republic, Hungary and Poland to begin accession talks with NATO. Following this decision, negotiations took place with each of the invited countries in Autumn 1997 and Accession Protocols for each of the three were signed in December 1997. These Accession Protocols were ratified by all 16 Allies according to their respective national procedures and by the new members. The three countries formally acceded to the Treaty in March 1999.

NATO enlargement is an open, continuing process, not a single event.

The Process of Accession

The main stages leading up to the accession of the three new member countries were as follows:

- **10 January 1994**. At the NATO Summit in Brussels, the 16 Allied leaders said they expected and would welcome NATO enlargement that would reach to democratic states to the East. They reaffirmed that the Alliance, as provided for in Article 10 of the Washington Treaty, was open to membership of other European states in a position to further the principles of the Washington Treaty and to contribute to security in the North Atlantic area.

- **September 1995**. The Alliance adopted the Study on NATO Enlargement which described factors to be taken into account in the enlargement process. It also stipulated that the process should take into account political- and security-related developments throughout Europe. The Study remains the basis for NATO's approach to inviting new members to join.

- **During 1996**, an intensified individual dialogue was undertaken with 12 interested Partner countries. These sessions improved their understanding of how the Alliance works and gave the Alliance a better understanding of where these countries stood in terms of their internal development as well as the resolution of any disputes with neighbouring countries. The Study identified this as an important precondition for membership.

- **10 December 1996**. The NATO Allies began drawing up recommendations on which country or countries should be invited to start accession talks, in preparation for a decision to be made at the Madrid Summit of July 1997.

- **Early 1997**. Intensified individual dialogue meetings took place with 11 Partner countries, at their request. In parallel, NATO military authorities undertook an analysis of relevant military factors concerning countries interested in NATO membership.

- **8 July 1997**. Allied leaders, meeting in Madrid, invited the Czech Republic, Hungary and Poland to start accession talks with the Alliance. They also reaffirmed that NATO would remain open to new members.

- **September and November 1997**. Accession talks were held with each of the three invited countries. At the end of the process, the three countries sent letters of intent confirming commitments undertaken during the talks.

- **16 December 1997**. NATO Foreign Ministers signed Protocols to the North Atlantic Treaty on the accession of the three countries.

- **During 1998**, Allied countries ratified the Protocols of Accession according to their national procedures.

- **12 March 1999**. After completion of their own national legislative procedures, the Foreign Ministers of the Czech Republic, Hungary and Poland deposited instruments of accession to the North Atlantic Treaty in a ceremony in Independence, Missouri, in the United States. This marked their formal entry into the Alliance.

- **16 March 1999**. The national flags of the three new member states were raised at a ceremony at NATO headquarters, Brussels.

During this period, a number of measures were successfully completed by each of the perspective member countries in order to ensure the effectiveness of their future participation in the Alliance. These included measures in the security sphere (e.g. arrangements for receiving, storing and using classified information), as well as in areas such as air defence, infrastructure, force planning and communication and information systems.

The Membership Action Plan (MAP)

The Membership Action Plan (MAP) is designed to assist those countries which wish to join the Alliance in their preparations by providing advice, assistance and practical support on all aspects of NATO membership. Its main features are:

- the submission by aspiring members of individual annual national programmes on their preparations for possible future membership, covering political, economic, defence, resource, security and legal aspects;

- a focused and candid feedback mechanism on aspirant countries' progress on their programmes that includes both political and technical advice, as well as annual 19+1 meetings at Council level to assess progress;

- a clearing-house to help coordinate assistance by NATO and by member states to aspirant countries in the defence/military field;

- a defence planning approach for aspirants which includes elaboration and review of agreed planning targets.

NATO Foreign Ministers will keep the enlargement process, including the implementation of the Membership Action Plan, under continual review. NATO leaders will review the process at their next Summit meeting which will be held no later than 2002.

The launching of the Membership Action Plan (MAP) in April 1999 has helped the countries aspiring to NATO membership to increasingly focus their preparations on meeting the goals and priorities set out in the Plan. Moreover, its implementation has ceased to be a matter concerning only ministries of foreign affairs and defence. With the establishment of inter-ministerial meetings at the national level, fulfilling the objectives of the Plan is increasingly engaging other government departments in a coordinated and systematic effort.

The nine countries that have declared an interest in joining NATO and are participating in the MAP are Albania, Bulgaria, Estonia, Latvia, Lithuania, Romania, Slovakia, Slovenia, and the former Yugoslav Republic of Macedonia[1].

The MAP gives substance to NATO's commitment to keep its door open. However, participation in the MAP does not guarantee future membership, nor does the Plan consist simply of a checklist for aspiring countries to fulfil. Decisions to invite aspirants to start accession talks will be taken within NATO by consensus and on a case-by-case basis.

---

1   Turkey recognises the Republic of Macedonia with its constitutional name.

The MAP provides for concrete feedback and advice from NATO to aspiring countries on their own preparations directed at achieving future membership. It provides for a range of activities designed to strengthen each aspirant country's candidacy. The MAP does not replace the Partnership for Peace (PfP) programme. The aspirants' participation in PfP and its Planning and Review Process (PARP) has been tailored to their needs. Full participation in PfP/PARP is essential because it allows aspirant countries to develop interoperability with NATO forces and to prepare their force structures and capabilities for possible future membership.

Like PfP, the MAP is guided by the principle of self-differentiation: aspirant countries are free to choose the elements of the MAP best suited to their own national priorities and circumstances. All aspirants have submitted an Annual National Programme on preparations for possible membership, covering political and economic, defence/military, resource, security and legal issues. They set their own objectives, targets and work schedules. These programmes are expected to be updated each year by aspirant countries but can be amended at any time.

NATO is following the progress made by each aspirant and providing political and technical advice. Meetings of the North Atlantic Council with each of the aspirants are taking place to discuss progress. Throughout the year, meetings and workshops with NATO civilian and military experts in various fields allow for discussion of the entire spectrum of issues relevant to membership. An annual consolidated progress report on activities under the MAP will be presented to NATO foreign and defence ministers at their regular spring meetings each year.

Aspirant countries are expected to achieve certain goals in the political and economic fields. These include settling any international, ethnic or external territorial disputes by peaceful means; demonstrating a commitment to the rule of law and human rights; establishing democratic control of their armed forces; and promoting stability and well-being through economic liberty, social justice and environmental responsibility.

Defence and military issues focus on the ability of the country to contribute to collective defence and to the Alliance's new missions. Full participation in PfP is an essential component. Through their individual PfP programmes, aspirants can focus on essential membership related issues. Partnership Goals for aspirants include planning targets which are covering those areas which are most directly relevant for nations aspiring NATO membership.

Resource issues focus on the need for any aspirant country to commit sufficient resources to defence to allow them to meet the commitments that future membership would bring in terms of collective NATO undertakings.

Security issues centre on the need for aspirant countries to make sure that procedures are in place to ensure the security of sensitive information.

Legal aspects address the need for aspirants to ensure that legal arrangements and agreements which govern cooperation within NATO are compatible with domestic legislation.

PARTNERSHIP FOR PEACE

Aim and scope

Partnership for Peace (PfP) is a major initiative introduced by NATO at the January 1994 Brussels Summit Meeting of the North Atlantic Council. The aim of the Partnership is to enhance stability and security throughout Europe. The Partnership for Peace Invitation was addressed to all states participating in the North Atlantic Cooperation Council (NACC)[2] and other states participating in the Conference for Security and Cooperation in Europe (CSCE)[3] able and willing to contribute to the programme. The invitation has since been accepted by a total of 30 countries. The accession to the Alliance of the three former PfP countries Czech Republic, Hungary and Poland brings the current number of PfP participants to 27. The activities which each Partner undertakes are based on jointly elaborated Individual Partnership Programmes.

The PfP programme focuses on defence-related cooperation but goes beyond dialogue and cooperation to forge a real partnership between each Partner country and NATO. It has become an important and permanent feature of the European security architecture and is helping to expand and intensify political and military cooperation throughout Europe. The programme is helping to increase stability, to diminish threats to peace and to build strengthened security relationships based on the practical cooperation and commitment to democratic principles which underpin the Alliance. In accordance with the PfP Framework Document which was issued by Heads of State and Government at the same time as the PfP Invitation Document, NATO undertakes to consult with any active Partner if that Partner perceives a direct threat to its territorial integrity, political independence, or security.

---

2   The NACC was replaced by the Euro-Atlantic Partnership Council (EAPC) in May 1997. The EAPC has 46 member Countries.

3   The Conference on Security and Cooperation in Europe (CSCE) became an Organisation (OSCE) at the beginning of 1995. It has 55 member states, comprising all European states together with the United States and Canada.

All members of PfP are also members of the Euro-Atlantic Partnership Council (EAPC) which provides the overall framework for cooperation between NATO and its Partner countries. However, the Partnership for Peace retains its own separate identity within the framework provided by the EAPC and maintains its own basic elements and procedures. It is founded on the basis of a bilateral relationship between NATO and each one of the PfP countries.

Objectives

The Framework Document includes specific undertakings to be made by each participant to cooperate with NATO in fulfilling the objectives of the programme as a whole. They are as follows:

- to facilitate transparency in national defence planning and budgeting processes;

- to ensure democratic control of defence forces;

- to maintain the capability and readiness to contribute to operations under the authority of the United Nations and/or the responsibility of the OSCE;

- to develop cooperative military relations with NATO, for the purpose of joint planning, training and exercises, in order to strengthen the ability of PfP participants to undertake missions in the field of peacekeeping, search and rescue, humanitarian operations, and others as may subsequently be agreed;

- to develop, over the longer term, forces that are better able to operate with those of the members of the North Atlantic Alliance.

The Framework Document also states that active participation in the Partnership for Peace will play an important role in the evolutionary process of including new members in NATO.

Procedures and Structures

Any country wishing to join the Partnership for Peace is first invited to sign the Framework Document. In addition to describing the objectives of the Partnership, this describes the basic principles on which PfP is founded. By virtue of their signature, countries reiterate their political commitment to the preservation of democratic societies and to the maintenance of the principles of international law. They reaffirm their commitment to fulfil in good faith the obligations of the Charter of the United Nations and the principles of the Universal Declaration on Human Rights; to refrain from the threat or use of force against the territorial integrity or political independence of any state; to respect existing borders; and to settle disputes by peaceful means. They also reaffirm their commitment to the Helsinki Final Act and all subsequent CSCE/OSCE documents and to the fulfillment of the commitments and obligations they have undertaken in the field of disarmament and arms control.

After signing the Framework Document, the next step in the procedure is for each Partner to submit a Presentation Document to NATO. This document indicates the steps which will be taken to achieve the political goals of the Partnership, the military and other assets the Partner intends to make available for Partnership purposes, and the specific areas of cooperation which the Partner wishes to pursue jointly with NATO.

Based on the statements made in the Presentation Document, and on additional proposals made by NATO and each Partner country, an Individual Partnership Programme (IPP) is jointly developed and agreed. This covers a two-year period. The IPP contains statements of the political aims of the Partner in PfP, the military and other assets to be made available for PfP purposes, the broad objectives of cooperation between the Partner and the Alliance in various areas of cooperation, and specific activities to be implemented in each one of the cooperation areas in the IPP.

The selection of activities is made by each Partner separately, on the basis of its individual requirements and priorities, from a list of activities contained in a Partnership Work Programme (PWP). This principle of self-differentiation is an important aspect of PfP which recognises that the needs and situations of each Partner country vary and that it is for each one of them to identify the forms of activity and cooperation most suited to their needs. The Work Programme contains a broad description of the various possible areas of cooperation and a list of available activities for each area. The PWP, like each IPP, also covers a two year period and is reviewed every year. It is prepared with the full involvement of Partners.

Areas of Cooperation

Enhanced PfP cooperation covers a wide spectrum of possibilities, both in the military field and in the broader defence-related but not strictly military area. The areas of cooperation listed in the current Partnership Work Programme 2001-2002 are as follows:

1. air defence related matters;

2. airspace management/control;

3. consultation, command and control, including communications and information systems, navigation and identification systems, interoperability aspects, procedures and terminology;

4. civil emergency planning;

5. crisis management;

6. democratic control of forces and defence structures;

7. defence planning, budgeting and resource management;

8. planning, organisation and management of national defence procurement programmes and international cooperation in the armaments field;

9. defence policy and strategy;

10. planning, organisation and management of national defence research and technology;

11. military geography;

12. global humanitarian mine action;

13. language training;

14. consumer logistics;

15. medical services;

16. meteorological support for NATO/Partner forces;

17. military infrastructure;

18. NBC defence and protection;

19. conceptual, planning and operational aspects of peacekeeping;

20. small arms and light weapons;

21. operational, material and administrative aspects of standardisation;

22. military exercises and related training activities;

23. military education, training and doctrine.

Political-Military Steering Committee on Partnership for Peace (PMSC/PfP)

The Political-Military Steering Committee on Partnership for Peace is the basic working body with responsibility for PfP matters. It meets in various configurations, either with Allies only or with Allies and Partners.

The main responsibilities of the PMSC include advising the North Atlantic Council with respect to PfP questions; being responsible for the overall coordination of the Partnership Work Programme; developing political-military guidelines for use by the NATO Military Authorities for the preparation of their input to the Partnership Work Programme with respect to military exercises and activities; providing guidance for the preparation of the Individual Partnership Programmes, and for submitting them to the Council for approval; and developing and coordinating work in relation to the Partnership Planning and Review Process (PARP) (see below).

The military aspects of cooperation in PfP are developed by the NATO Military Authorities on the basis of guidance proposed by the PMSC and agreed by the Council. The PfP working forum on the military side is the Military Committee Working Group on Cooperation (MCWG(COOP)), which acts as a consultative body for the Military Committee. The MCWG(COOP) meets either with Allies only or with Allies and Partner countries. The Military Committee also meets with Partners to discuss military aspects of cooperation in PfP.

Partnership Coordination Cell (PCC)

The Partnership Coordination Cell is a unique PfP structure, based at Mons (Belgium) where the Supreme Headquarters Allied Powers Europe (SHAPE) is also located. It was established under the authority of the North Atlantic Council and executes its tasks under the direct authority of both NATO Strategic Commanders.

The task of the PCC is to coordinate joint military activities within PfP and to carry out the military planning necessary to implement the military aspects of the Partnership Work Programme, notably with respect to exercises and related activities in such fields such as peacekeeping, humanitarian operations and search and rescue. The PCC also participates in the evaluation of such military activities. Detailed operational planning for military exercises is the responsibility of the military commands conducting the exercise.

The Cell is headed by a Director. Its staff, which has international status, consists of NATO personnel and, since the beginning of 1998, also includes personnel from Partner countries. Staff officers from Partner Missions are also attached to the PCC for liaison purposes.

At NATO Headquarters, Partner countries have established full Diplomatic Missions formally accredited to NATO, as well as senior military representation to the Military Committee.

Examples of enhancements of PfP

Building on the decisions taken in 1997 to enhance PfP, one of the important steps implemented early on was the establishment of PfP Staff Elements (PSEs) in various NATO military headquarters at the strategic and regional levels. A second phase of this process, involving the creation of PSEs at the sub-regional level, is under consideration. Each PSE consists of a nucleus of Allied and Partner officers with international status working together on planning for exercises and conducting other cooperative functions. Some 56 Partner personnel and a similar number of NATO personnel are involved in the eight PSEs that have been established. This includes seven Partner officers serving at the Partnership Coordination Cell (PCC) at Mons, alongside their colleagues from NATO countries.

Partner countries are represented at meetings of the NATO Military Committee in EAPC/PfP format by senior officers serving within the missions of Partner countries established at NATO and designated as their country's military representative.

The Partnership for Peace Planning and Review Process (PARP)

The PfP Framework Document commits NATO to developing with the Partner countries a planning and review process, designed to provide a basis for identifying and evaluating forces and capabilities which might be made available for multinational training, exercises and operations in conjunction with Alliance forces. Initially PfP operations were limited to peacekeeping, search and rescue and humanitarian operations. However, as part of the enhancements of PfP introduced since 1997, PfP operations and corresponding planning and evaluation requirements have been expanded to encompass the full range of the Alliance's new missions, including peace support operations.

The Planning and Review Process is offered to Partners on an optional basis and draws on NATO's extensive experience in defence planning. It is in essence a biennial process involving both bilateral and multilateral elements. For each two-year planning cycle, Partners wishing to participate in the process undertake to provide information on a wide range of subjects including their defence policies, developments with regard to the democratic control of the armed forces, national policy relating to PfP cooperation, and relevant financial and economic plans. The information is provided in response to a "Survey of Overall PfP Interoperability" issued by NATO in the Autumn every second year. Participating countries also provide an extensive overview of their armed forces and detailed information of the forces which they are prepared to make available for PfP cooperation.

On the basis of each Partner's response, a Planning and Review Assessment is developed. A set of Partnership Goals is also prepared, in order to set out the measures each Partner needs to introduce in order to make its armed forces better able to operate in conjunction with the armed forces of Alliance countries. After bilateral and multilateral consultations, the Planning and Review Assessment and the Interoperability Objectives are jointly approved by the Alliance and the Partner country concerned. A Consolidated Report, which summarises each of the agreed assessments and the forces being made available by each Partner, is agreed by the representatives of the Allies and of all Partners participating in the process. The report is brought to the attention of EAPC Ministers.

The first PARP cycle was launched in December 1994 with 15 Partners participating. A Consolidated Report on its achievements was presented to Alliance and Partner Ministers in spring 1995. Building on the success of this first cycle, a number of measures were adopted to broaden and deepen the process for the next cycle which was launched in October 1996. The second cycle, for which 18 Partners signed up, provided a further demonstration of the inherent strength of the process. There was a significant increase in the breadth and quality of information exchanged, resulting in a much clearer picture of the forces being made available by Partners. The number and substance of Interoperability Objectives were also substantially increased, further adding to the measures available for enhancing the Partner countries' capabilities and their ability to operate with Alliance forces.

The process of developing and preparing the individual assessments and the Consolidated Report in spring 1997 led the way for the development of recommendations for further enhancement of the process. This coincided with measures being taken to enhance the PfP programme as a whole and contributed to the work of the Senior Level Group on PfP Enhancement. The effect of the recommendations, which were approved by Ministers at their meetings in spring 1997, is to increase the parallels between the PARP process and the defence planning process which takes place within NATO itself. For example, political guidance is to be developed for each cycle, agreed by the Defence Ministers of the countries participating in PARP in conjunction with the

Consolidated Report. This political guidance will play a very similar role to the Ministerial Guidance which has long formed a key part of Alliance defence planning procedure. In addition, the Interoperability Objectives have been renamed Partnership Goals, reflecting the fact that their future scope will extend beyond the development of interoperability, into other defence planning fields.

PARP has contributed significantly to the close cooperation of Partner countries in the NATO-led peace operations in former Yugoslavia. In addition, PARP is helping to strengthen the political consultation element in PfP and to provide for greater Partner involvement in PfP decision-making and planning. PARP is also a crucial element in preparing prospective members of NATO for accession.

An enhanced and more operational Partnership

Partnership emerged as a central underlying theme at the 1999 Washington Summit. Plans were approved by Heads of State and Government for an enhanced and more operational Partnership which will provide additional tools to support the Alliance's role in Euro-Atlantic security. The Summit decisions brought to fruition a number of important enhancements to Partnership for Peace launched at the Madrid Summit in 1997. These aimed to make PfP more operational and to give Partners a greater role in PfP planning and decision-making. In addition, the updated Strategic Concept adopted in Washington established crisis management and Partnership as part of the fundamental security tasks of the Alliance. The strengthened Partnership will also contribute to the effectiveness of two other Summit initiatives, the Defence Capabilities Initiative and the Membership Action Plan. In addition, PfP can be expected to play a key role in fostering security and stability in the Balkan region in the wake of the Kosovo crisis.

Taken together, the Washington decisions further cement the Partnership's role as a permanent fixture of Euro-Atlantic security for the next century.

Cornerstones of the Partnership

The Political Military Framework (PMF) for NATO-led PfP operations provides for Partner involvement in political consultation and decision-making, in operational planning, and in command arrangements for NATO-led PfP operations. The document addresses four phases: (1) a non-crisis phase, (2) a consultation phase prior to initiation of military planning, (3) a planning and consultation phase between initiation of military planning and execution of the operation, and (4) an execution phase.

In terms of Partner involvement, a distinction is made between "potential contributing nations", "recognised potential contributing nations", and "contributing nations". Since summer 1999, the principles and guidelines of the PMF are being implemented, for example in the context of Partner country participation in the Kosovo Force (KFOR) established in June 1999.

The PMF will complement and support the Alliance's Combined Joint Task Force (CJTF) concept (see Chapter 12).

The expanded and adapted PfP Planning and Review Process (PARP) (see above) will closely resemble the Alliance's force planning process. PARP will introduce Partnership Goals to define forces and capabilities declared by Partners for PfP activities. Ministerial Guidance procedures will help shape these forces and capabilities.

PfP will continue to develop on the basis of enhanced defence-related and military cooperation, which allows for significantly expanding the involvement of Partner countries in the PfP work of NATO committees, increasing the presence of officers from Partner countries in NATO military structures, and increasing the scope and complexity of NATO/PfP exercises.

Reinforcing operational capabilities

The experience in Bosnia and Herzegovina had shown the importance of the contribution made by cooperation in PfP to effective multinational peace support operations. The increased operational dimension of PfP emphasised at the Washington Summit could therefore take into account the lessons learned and practical experience gained in the IFOR/SFOR operations in Bosnia and address the specific challenges to military effectiveness and interoperability that such multinational operations present.

A new Operational Capabilities Concept (OCC) has been developed within PfP to improve the ability of Alliance and Partner forces to operate together in future NATO-led PfP operations. It will also provide increased flexibility in putting together tailored force packages to mount and sustain future NATO-led PfP operations. The OCC will focus on the forces and capabilities potentially available for such operations. The enhanced peacetime working relationships developing progressively between Partner and Alliance headquarters and staffs, and between Allied and Partner formations, will facilitate the integration of these forces into NATO-led forces. Other central features will be a database and assessment and feedback mechanisms on the operational capabilities of forces declared by Partners.

The OCC represents a new and more integrated approach to military cooperation and links together the different elements of Partnership for Peace.

Closer and more focused forms of military cooperation generated by the OCC will improve cooperation in peacetime and result in Partner country forces which are more effective militarily and better prepared to operate with those of the Alliance. This will help Partner countries to prepare follow-on forces for the Stabilisation Force in Bosnia and Herzegovina (SFOR) and for the Kosovo Force (KFOR) and for other NATO-led operations which may be undertaken in the future.

The OCC also establishes a link between normal cooperation in the context of the Partnership for Peace and the NATO force generation process which is activated in a crisis. Over time, it will help to generate forces and capabilities adapted to the requirements for Alliance-led crisis management operations and to improve the effectiveness of cooperation in the field. The improvement of capabilities will have significant impact on the cost/benefit ratio of participation in Partnership for Peace and will give added value to the Partnership as a whole.

The Operational Capabilities Concept will also have benefits for other Alliance initiatives, for example improving the contribution made by the Partnership for Peace to the CJTF concept (see Chapter 12) and to the implementation of the Membership Action Plan. Together with Planning and Review Process (PARP) described earlier, it also establishes a mechanism which will enable decisions taken in the context of the Defence Capabilities Initiative (DCI) (see Chapter 2) to be reflected in the future development of PfP.

The Operational Capabilities Concept and the steps for its implementation were endorsed at the autumn 1999 Ministerial meetings. Its main elements are being implemented step by step, focusing on the establishment of a database on the pool of forces and capabilities declared by Partner countries as being available for PfP exercises and operations and on related assessment and feedback mechanisms.

Better coordination of efforts for training and education

The more operational Partnership also includes measures to improve training and education efforts, through a PfP Training and Education Enhancement Programme (TEEP), designed to meet the current and future demands of the Partnership. Even though training and education typically remains a national responsibility, the programme is helping to improve interoperability and promote greater cooperation and dialogue among the wider defence and security communities in NATO and Partner nations, thus ensuring the best use of human and other resources.

TEEP encompasses six main elements, namely:

- linkages and collaboration amongst NATO and PfP training and education institutions;
- feedback and assessment related to PfP activities;
- interoperability tools for Partners;
- exercise planning tools and methods offered to Partners;
- advice by NATO in the field of national training and education strategies;
- advanced distributed learning and simulation.

Most elements of the Programme have been put in place and are in their first year of implementation. Two areas are still being developed, namely:

Linkages and Collaboration. To date, NATO has recognised and accorded the status of PfP Training Centre to seven institutions, in Austria, Greece, Slovenia, Sweden, Switzerland, Turkey and Ukraine. A periodic Conference of PfP Training Centres and other PfP training and education institutions provides a forum where all participants can explore ways to exchange information, experience and expertise, investigate where coordination is possible to avoid duplication, and examine how to make the best use of resources.

Advanced Distributed Learning and Simulation. The aim in this sphere is to use distant learning technologies (similar, for example, to internet courses) and to develop a NATO framework for distant learning and simulation management for use in the education and training of military personnel for NATO-led PfP operations and PfP related tasks. The objective is to build a combined resource of multipurpose training and education tools, with a clear focus on operational requirements. In the first phase of the project, work has begun on the development of a prototype as well as an interim overall policy for the future organisation and management of the resource.

The Partnership's potential for crisis management

The decisions taken at Washington mark a further stage in the development of the Partnership and of the EAPC in view of the latter's potential for crisis management. It has already proved its worth as a forum for political consultations on topics ranging from Bosnia and Herzegovina and Kosovo to humanitarian demining and continues to develop. Combined with the improvements in PfP, it is helping to provide NATO and its Partner countries with the tools needed to improve security and stability in the Euro-Atlantic area as a whole.

Since its introduction, the Partnership has played a valuable role in supporting NATO's overall effort towards conflict prevention and crisis management. Practical PfP cooperation has been instrumental in preparing NATO and Partner forces for joint operations. The interoperability achieved through PfP contributed to the successful integration of Partner forces in IFOR/SFOR and subsequently in KFOR.

However, PfP's role is not restricted to its contributions to military operations. Quite apart from its focus on transparency, reform, collaboration and interoperability, the Partnership has made concrete contributions to NATO's conflict prevention and crisis management efforts in general. Well before the air campaign in Kosovo and the subsequent deployment of KFOR, PfP mechanisms were being used in Albania and the former Yugoslav Republic of Macedonia[4] to signal NATO's commitment to the region and to deal with spill-over effects of the crisis.

Programmes specifically tailored to the situation in these countries have been integral elements of the Alliance's overall approach to the crisis in Kosovo. NATO assisted the efforts of the government of the former Yugoslav Republic of Macedonia[4] to improve its crisis management, civil emergency planning, logistic and other capabilities to deal with the effects of the Kosovo crisis. Assistance programmes for Albania, put in place first after the internal crisis of 1997, helped rebuild the Albanian armed forces and deal with other consequences of that crisis, notably problems caused by the destruction and looting of explosive ordnance storage sites. The NATO/PfP Cell in Tirana is a visible demonstration of the Alliance's interest and commitment in the region.

Both the EAPC and PfP will continue to evolve to meet the challenges of the changing security environment in the Euro-Atlantic area. Neither of them has reached its full potential in preventing, managing and defusing crises. Indeed, achieving that potential is one of the Partnership's major future challenges.

PfP experience in promoting stability through conflict prevention and crisis management has been put to use in the development of NATO's South East Europe Initiative (SEEI). PfP is making a substantial contribution to SEEI by applying its practical approach to the stimulation and development of regional cooperation in South East Europe. Regional actors take the lead in a great variety of activities which are modelled on PfP but further enhanced by a region-wide, rather than country-specific, focus. NATO complements these efforts by activities that it conducts itself. The customised application of PfP tools to South East Europe is helping to create a model for regional security coopera-

---

4   Turkey recognises the Republic of Macedonia with its constitutional name.

tion which has relevance and utility beyond this region. In this context, a South East Europe Common Assessment Paper on Regional Security Challenges and Opportunities (SEECAP) has been negotiated among countries of the region to set out their common perceptions of security risks, with a view to promoting an agenda for cooperative actions to deal with regional challenges. A South East Europe Security Cooperation Steering Group (SEEGROUP) has also been established to strengthen practical cooperation. This forms another component of the Partnership's increasing role in conflict prevention and crisis management in the Euro-Atlantic area that is destined to develop further in the future.

Cooperation in Peacekeeping

The Political-Military Steering Committee/Ad Hoc Group on Cooperation in Peacekeeping (PMSC/AHG), which operates in the framework of the EAPC, serves as the main forum for consultations on political and conceptual issues related to peacekeeping, and for the exchange of experience and the discussion of practical measures for cooperation. The PMSC/AHG reports periodically to meetings of Foreign and Defence Ministers on these matters. All meetings of the PMSC/AHG include Partners. A representative of the OSCE Chairman-in-Office regularly attends the meetings of the Group and, occasionally, a representative of the United Nations also participates.

In the course of its work, the Group has produced two detailed reports on cooperation in peacekeeping. The first report from 1993 - known as the "Athens Report" - dealt with conceptual approaches to peacekeeping. A second report, the "Follow-On to the Athens Report" of 1995, revisited these issues in the light of experiences gained since 1993.

In 1995, drawing on the extensive peacekeeping experience available, including the experience of the conflict in the former Yugoslavia, the members of the Ad Hoc Group completed a compendium of "Lessons Learned in Peacekeeping Operations". The paper reflects national experiences gained by Allied and Partner countries in areas such as the preparation, implementation and operational aspects of such operations. By exchanging national experiences, Euro-Atlantic Partnership Council members aim to develop further practical approaches to peacekeeping.

In 1999, the PMSC/AHG produced a "Compendium of Views and Experiences on the Humanitarian Aspects of Peacekeeping", reflecting the high level of common understanding developed among the participating nations and other international organisations and non-governmental organisations active in the field of humanitarian assistance.

The Group has continued to exchange views on "Principles, Methods and Experiences on Early Warning and Conflict Prevention" and is further expanding contacts and discussions with the UN, OSCE and other relevant organisations on this topic.

COOPERATION BETWEEN NATO AND RUSSIA

Overview of NATO-Russia Relations

Since the end of the Cold War, NATO has attached particular importance to the development of constructive and cooperative relations with Russia. Over the past ten years, NATO and Russia have succeeded in achieving substantial progress in developing a genuine partnership and overcoming the vestiges of earlier confrontation and competition in order to strengthen mutual trust and cooperation.

Since 1991, the Alliance and Russia have been working together on a variety of defence and security-related issues. In 1994, Russia joined the Partnership for Peace Programme, further enhancing the emerging broad NATO-Russia dialogue. Russia's participation in the implementation of the Peace Agreement for Bosnia and Herzegovina was a particularly significant step towards a new cooperative relationship. For the first time, Allied and Russian contingents worked side by side in a multinational military operation.

By signing the NATO-Russia Founding Act on Mutual Relations, Cooperation and Security in May 1997, NATO and Russia institutionalised and substantially enhanced their partnership. They committed themselves to further developing their relations on the basis of common interests and created a new forum to achieve this goal: the NATO-Russia Permanent Joint Council (PJC). Since July 1997 the PJC has been the principal venue for consultation between NATO and Russia. Its central objective is to build increasing levels of trust by providing a mechanism for regular and frank consultations. Since the conclusion of the Founding Act, considerable and encouraging progress has been made in intensifying consultation and cooperation. The PJC has developed into an important venue in which to consult, to promote transparency and confidence-building and to foster cooperation.

Initial constructive work in the PJC was, however, increasingly overshadowed by the emerging crisis in Kosovo. This development culminated in Russia's suspension of cooperation within the PJC on 24 March 1999, as a result of NATO's air campaign to end the Kosovo conflict. After the end of the Kosovo campaign, Russia returned to the PJC, but for some months limited its agenda to topics related to Kosovo. Russia also agreed to contribute a significant number of troops to the NATO-led Kosovo Force (KFOR), as provided for in UN Security Council Resolution 1244.

Following the setbacks encountered in 1999, a visit to Moscow by NATO Secretary General Lord Robertson in February 2000 helped to restore a broader relationship, going beyond the Kosovo agenda. As a result of that visit, NATO and Russia once again are actively engaged in implementing the objectives of the Founding Act. Building on the positive momentum achieved during the Secretary General's visit, monthly PJC meetings and regular Ministerial meetings of the PJC have provided a further positive impetus to NATO-Russia cooperation across the board. This has included the opening of a NATO Information Office in Moscow by the NATO Secretary General in February 2001 and the beginning of consultations on the establishment of a NATO Military Liaison Mission in Moscow.

The Evolution of NATO-Russia Relations

Building upon early cooperation in the framework of the North Atlantic Cooperation Council (NACC) from 1991 onwards, Russia joined the Partnership for Peace (PfP) in 1994 and agreed to pursue "Broad, Enhanced Dialogue and Cooperation" with NATO beyond PfP.

Meetings between NATO member countries and Russia at Ministerial, Ambassadors' and experts' levels led to the exchange of information and consultations on wide-ranging issues of common interest, such as peacekeeping, ecological security and science. In the public information field, new initiatives included arrangements for improving access to information about NATO in Russia. As an initial step, a NATO information officer was posted to the NATO Contact Point Embassy in Moscow in the summer of 1995, later to be joined by a second officer.

Close cooperation between Russia and NATO on the implementation of the military aspects of the 1995 Peace Agreement on Bosnia and Herzegovina added a major new dimension to the evolving security partnership. The unprecedented participation of Russian troops, along with contingents from Allied and other Partner countries, in the NATO-led Implementation Force (IFOR) and subsequently in the Stabilisation Force (SFOR) which succeeded it, reflected shared goals and joint political responsibility for the implementation of the Peace Agreement. Today, Russia contributes about 1 200 troops to SFOR, which numbers approximately 20 000 in all. Russia's participation also provides a concrete demonstration of the fact that NATO and Russia can collaborate effectively in the construction of cooperative security in Europe. Joint efforts in SFOR and cooperation within the framework of the Partnership for

Peace have assisted both sides in overcoming misperceptions about each other.

Significant initiatives have also been taken in other fields. In March 1996, a Memorandum of Understanding on Civil Emergency Planning and Disaster Preparedness was signed between NATO and the Ministry of the Russian Federation for Civil Defence, Emergencies and the Elimination of Consequences of Natural Disasters (EMERCOM). This has subsequently borne fruit, in particular through the establishment of a Euro-Atlantic Disaster Response Coordination Centre and a Euro-Atlantic Disaster Response Unit in May 1998, proposals for which had been initiated by Russia.

The NATO-Russia Founding Act

At their meeting on 10 December 1996, Foreign Ministers of NATO requested the Secretary General to explore with Russia the scope for an agreement to deepen and widen NATO-Russia relations and to provide a framework for their future development. Four months of intensive negotiations between Secretary General Solana and Russian Foreign Minister Primakov led to agreement on a ground-breaking document. The "Founding Act on Mutual Relations, Cooperation and Security between NATO and the Russia Federation" was signed in Paris on 27 May 1997 by the Heads of States and Governments of the North Atlantic Alliance, the Secretary General of NATO and the President of the Russian Federation.

The Founding Act is the expression of an enduring commitment, under-taken at the highest political level, to work together to build a lasting and inclu-sive peace in the Euro-Atlantic area. It creates the framework for a new secu-rity partnership and for building a stable, peaceful and undivided Europe. It commits the Alliance and Russia to forging a closer relationship, not only in their own interest, but also in the wider interest of all other states in the Euro-Atlantic region.

The preamble of the document sets out the historical and political context of NATO-Russia relations, recalling the fundamental transformation both NATO and Russia have undergone since the days of the Cold War. The four sections of the document outline the principles and mechanisms governing the partner-ship between NATO and Russia.

Section I spells out the guiding principles on which the NATO-Russia part-nership is based. Section II creates a new forum for implementing consultation and cooperation under the Founding Act: the NATO-Russia Permanent Joint Council (PJC). Section III outlines areas for consultation and cooperation. Section IV covers political-military issues, including the reiteration of the political commitment by NATO member states that they have "no intention, no plan and no reason" to deploy nuclear weapons on the territory of new members of the Alliance.

In sum, the Founding Act represents a reciprocal commitment to help build together a stable, peaceful and undivided continent on the basis of partnership and mutual interest.

The NATO-Russia Permanent Joint Council

The NATO-Russia Permanent Joint Council (PJC) met for the first time on 18 July 1997 and quickly became the hub of efforts to build confidence, overcome misperceptions, and develop a pattern of regular consultations and cooperation.

The PJC meets on a monthly basis at the level of Ambassadors and military representatives and twice a year at the level of Ministers of Foreign Affairs and Defence, as well as at the level of Chiefs of Staff or Chiefs of Defence. It may also meet at the level of Heads of State and Government.

On 18 March 1998, the Russian Federation formally established its Mission to NATO and appointed a Senior Military Representative as an integral part of its Mission, to facilitate military and defence-related cooperation.

In the first three years of its existence, the PJC addressed a wide range of topics of direct interest to both sides. Among them were:

- the situation in the former Yugoslavia;

- meetings of Military Representatives under the auspices of the PJC;

- measures to promote cooperation, transparency and confidence between NATO and Russia;

- the contribution by NATO and Russia and the role of the PJC to the security architecture of the Euro-Atlantic region;

- political and defence efforts against the proliferation of weapons of mass destruction;

- nuclear weapons issues;

- strategies and doctrines of NATO and Russia;

- peacekeeping;

- disarmament and arms control;

- search and rescue at sea;

- retraining of military officers;

- combating international terrorism;

- defence-related scientific cooperation;

- defence-related environmental issues;

- civil emergency planning and disaster relief.

Under the political umbrella of the PJC, a close network of working groups, experts' meetings, joint projects and staff level contacts emerged, to follow-up and implement consultations of the PJC itself.

The Kosovo Conflict

As the situation in Kosovo deteriorated in 1998, NATO and Russia made full use of the PJC mechanism to consult on the crisis. In June 1998, the PJC met at the level of Defence Ministers and condemned Belgrade's massive and disproportionate use of force as well as violent attacks by Kosovar extremists. Ministers reaffirmed their determination to contribute to international efforts to resolve the crisis.

In the autumn of 1998, NATO and Russia both expressed support for diplomatic efforts to secure a political solution and to avert a humanitarian catastrophe, and stressed the need for immediate, full and irreversible compliance with relevant UN Security Council Resolutions. As the situation worsened in early 1999, NATO informed Russia about its decision to issue an Activation Order for a limited air response and phased air operation to help put an end to the intolerable humanitarian situation in Kosovo and to support efforts aimed at a political solution. On 30 January 1999, the North Atlantic Council issued a warning to the Belgrade government that failure to meet the demands of the international community would lead NATO to take whatever measures were necessary to avert a humanitarian catastrophe.

Russia did not share the Allies' view on the possible use of military force to end the conflict and to enforce the international community's demands reflected in relevant UN Security Council Resolutions. Nevertheless, in February 1999, both NATO and Russia emphasised their full support for the peace talks taking place in Rambouillet. On 23 March, when the talks failed and all diplomatic avenues to end the conflict had been exhausted, NATO decided that there was no alternative to the use of force.

When NATO airstrikes over Kosovo began, Russia temporarily suspended consultation and cooperation in the framework of the PJC. Without formally withdrawing from the Founding Act, Russia also ceased to participate in meetings in the framework of the Euro-Atlantic Partnership Council and expelled the two NATO information officers from Moscow. However, military cooperation in Bosnia and Herzegovina continued.

In the wake of the Military Technical Agreement signed by NATO and Yugoslav military commanders on 9 June 1999 and UN Security Council Resolution 1244 of 12 June, the basis for an international security presence in Kosovo (KFOR) was established. Russia's participation in KFOR was made possible by the signing of a separate agreement in Helsinki. The integrated force became operational as Serb forces withdrew from the province and the work of restoring peace and stability began. Today, Russia contributes about 3 250 troops to the 43 000-strong Kosovo force.

Resumption and Broadening of NATO-Russia Cooperation

Monthly meetings of the PJC resumed in July 1999, but Russia limited the agenda to topics relating to Kosovo. Committed, on its part, to the full range of cooperation foreseen in the NATO-Russia Founding Act, NATO urged Russia to resume cooperation across the board, as agreed in the 1999 PJC Work Programme.

This was to be a gradual process. When NATO Secretary General Lord Robertson visited Moscow on 16 February 2000, following a Russian invitation, a joint statement was issued in which NATO and Russia agreed to a gradual return to broad cooperation on the basis of the Founding Act. The PJC meetings that followed this visit again had a broader agenda. In particular, frank and open exchanges on respective military strategies and doctrines have demonstrated the role the PJC can play in dispelling misperceptions and enhancing transparency and confidence.

In Florence in May 2000, Foreign Ministers of NATO and Russia agreed to further intensify their dialogue in the PJC and to seek improved cooperation on a broad range of issues. They approved a PJC Work Programme for the remainder of 2000 and confirmed agreement on the establishment of a NATO Information Office in Moscow as foreseen in the Founding Act. In Florence, Russia also resumed its participation in the Euro-Atlantic Partnership Council. At a meeting at the level of Defence Ministers in June 2000, Russian Defence Minister Sergeyev, echoing the view of NATO countries, stated that there was no alternative to NATO-Russia cooperation. The statement issued at the end of the meeting also recognised the important role of the partnership for stability and security in the Euro-Atlantic area. It recorded agreement to intensify dialogue and cooperation in the defence and military field on the basis of common interest, reciprocity and transparency, as laid down in the Founding Act.

The situation in Kosovo, and the shared determination of NATO and Russia to ensure the full implementation of UN Security Council Resolution 1244, remained high on the agenda of the Permanent Joint Council. It issued firm warnings against acts of provocation or other attempts to undermine the peace process in the region and took note of ever more converging views on the situation in the Balkans.

At the PJC Ministerial meeting in December 2000, NATO and Russia reaffirmed their commitment to build, within the framework of the PJC, a strong, stable and equal partnership in the interest of security and stability in the Euro-Atlantic area. Ministers exchanged letters on the establishment of a NATO Information Office in Moscow. They also approved an ambitious Work Programme for 2001, which included promising new items, such as cooperation in the field of search and rescue at sea and defence reform. Defence Ministers also agreed to begin consultations on the opening of a NATO Military Liaison Mission in Moscow.

Against the background of enhanced dialogue and improved cooperation, NATO Secretary General Lord Robertson again visited Moscow on 19-21 February 2001. The Secretary General of NATO and the Russian leadership took positive stock of what had been achieved over the previous year and discussed how the potential of the Founding Act could be tapped more effectively. During this visit, the NATO Secretary General officially inaugurated the NATO Information Office in Moscow, which is expected to contribute significantly to public understanding of NATO and of the evolving relations between NATO and Russia.

Future prospects

Cooperation in SFOR and KFOR are striking examples of how NATO and Russia can indeed interact successfully to achieve common goals. They have indicated that they will continue to work together closely on the ground, both in Bosnia and Herzegovina and in Kosovo.

They also face numerous common security challenges in other areas. Working together to address these challenges is in the interest of both sides and contributes to the further strengthening of the basis of mutual trust which is essential for peace and stability in the Euro-Atlantic area[5].

---

5   In December 2000, PJC Foreign Ministers adopted an ambitious Work Programme for 2001, inclu-
      ding cooperation in the field of search and rescue at sea, considered by both sides as one of the
      most promising area of future practical interaction between NATO and Russia.

NATO's Partnership with Ukraine

A visit to Ukraine by the North Atlantic Council in March 2000 injected new momentum into the Distinctive Partnership between NATO and Ukraine established in Madrid in July 1997.

The meeting in Kyiv of the NATO-Ukraine Commission - the first time this body, which directs the Partnership, had met in Ukraine - was an occasion for the 19 NATO allies and Ukraine to review the full range of their cooperation. It was hailed as a significant step for bringing Ukraine closer to the Euro-Atlantic community of nations.

The signing of the Charter on a Distinctive Partnership in Madrid in 1997 shifted cooperation between NATO and Ukraine on to a new plane and gave formal recognition to the importance of an independent, stable and democratic Ukraine to Europe as a whole.

The Charter is in line with Ukraine's declared strategy of increasing its integration in European and transatlantic structures. It is the basis on which NATO and Ukraine agree to consult in the context of Euro-Atlantic security and stability and in areas such as conflict prevention, crisis management, peace support and humanitarian operations.

Seminars, joint working group meetings and other cooperative programmes have focused on areas such as defence reform and the reshaping of the defence establishment, civil-military relations, budgeting and resource planning. Seminars on retraining retiring Ukrainian military personnel and on military downsizing and conversion have also been held.

Joint work in civil emergency planning and disaster preparedness is also a major area of cooperation with direct practical benefits for Ukraine. A Memorandum of Understanding on civil emergency planning was concluded in December 1997, providing for cooperation in this field. A disaster relief exercise was subsequently scheduled for September 2000, in the Transcarpathia region of Ukraine, to test humanitarian assistance procedures in the event of further flooding.[6]

---

6   Transcarpathia 2000 took place in the framework of the Partnership for Peace programme from 20-28 September 2000. It involved disaster response teams from Belarus, Croatia, Hungary, Moldova, Poland, Romania, Slovakia, Slovenia, Sweden, Switzerland and Ukraine as well as the participation of the UN Office for the Coordination of Humanitarian Affairs. Disaster response scenarios exercised included search and rescue, life support and medical care, water purification and cleaning of contamination in rivers, and railway accident situations involving toxic spills. In the early spring of 2001, this mechanism was put to the test when renewed flooding in Transcarpathia created the need for a coordinated response.

Other strong areas of cooperation are the scientific field, in which NATO has supported the Ukrainian scientific community through grants; economic aspects of security; and training. In this latter context NATO has launched a programme of foreign language teaching for up to 100 Ukrainian military officers.

The NATO Information and Documentation Centre opened by the NATO Secretary General in May 1997 has become a focal point for information activities to explain the benefits of the Distinctive Partnership with NATO to the Ukrainian public. The Centre is the first such centre to be opened in any NATO Partner country. It has since played an important role in explaining Alliance policies and overcoming misperceptions.

In December 1998 a Memorandum of Understanding was signed, enabling two NATO Liaison Officers to be stationed in Kyiv to facilitate Ukraine's full participation in the Partnership for Peace. The NATO Liaison Office was established in 1999, facilitating contacts between NATO and civil and military agencies involved in Ukrainian participation in the Partnership for Peace and in the implementation of the NUC Work Plan.

Other positive developments include the ratification on 1 March 2000 by the Ukrainian Parliament of the Partnership for Peace Status of Forces Agreement (SOFA) and its additional protocol. This development should facilitate increased Ukrainian participation in the Partnership for Peace. The Parliament also gave its approval to Ukraine's adherence to the Open Skies Treaty, making an important contribution to transparency in arms control.

The Evolution of NATO's Relationship with Ukraine

NATO's relations with Ukraine began to develop soon after the country achieved independence in 1991. Ukraine immediately joined the North Atlantic Cooperation Council (NACC), and became an active participant. It joined the Partnership for Peace programme in 1994, and was among the founding members of the Euro-Atlantic Partnership Council which replaced the NACC in May 1997.

When President Kuchma visited NATO on 1 June 1995, he signalled his country's wish to upgrade NATO-Ukraine relations to a new level. Three months later, on 14 September 1995, Foreign Minister Udovenko visited NATO to accept formally the Ukrainian PfP Individual Partnership Programme and to hold discussions with the North Atlantic Council on issues related to European security. A Joint Press Statement was issued, outlining the general principles of NATO-Ukraine relations in the context of the Partnership for Peace and in other areas.

Further meetings were held at different levels in 1996 and 1997. A Ukrainian Mission to NATO, including a military representative, was also established as well as Ukrainian representation in the Partnership Coordination Cell (PCC) adjacent to the headquarters of SHAPE at Mons, Belgium. In accordance with the decision taken by the NATO-Ukraine Commission at its meeting in Luxembourg in May 1998, a NATO Liaison Officer was subsequently assigned to Kyiv, to facilitate Ukraine's full participation in the Partnership for Peace and to enhance cooperation between NATO and the Ukrainian military authorities in general. Ukraine remains an active participant in PfP and has hosted a number of PfP exercises on its own territory. The ratification of a Partnership for Peace Status of Forces Agreement (SOFA) by the Ukrainian parliament has made it possible for this potential, including the use of the Yavoriv Training Centre in Western Ukraine, to be further exploited.

Ukraine has made significant contributions to international peacekeeping activities. It contributed an infantry battalion of 550 men to the NATO-led Implementation Force in Bosnia (IFOR), following the conclusion of the Dayton Peace Agreement. Similarly, it participated in the Stabilisation Force (SFOR) which replaced IFOR, contributing a mechanised infantry battalion and helicopter squadron involving some 400 men. Although no longer contributing to SFOR, Ukraine is a contributor to the NATO-led Kosovo Force (KFOR) and has also participated in the International Police Task Force and in the UN force in Eastern Slavonia.

The Charter for a Distinctive Partnership

At the time of the July 1997 Summit Meeting of NATO Heads of State and Government in Madrid, NATO leaders and Ukrainian President Kuchma signed a "Charter for a Distinctive Partnership between NATO and Ukraine", which had been initialled a few weeks earlier, in Sintra, Portugal. In signing the Charter, the member countries of NATO reaffirmed their support for Ukrainian sovereignty and independence, as well as its territorial integrity, democratic development, economic prosperity and status as a non-nuclear weapons state, and for the principle of inviolability of frontiers. These are regarded by the Alliance as key factors of stability and security in Central and Eastern Europe and on the continent as a whole.

Ukraine's decision to support the indefinite extension of the Treaty on Non-Proliferation of Nuclear Weapons (NPT) and its contribution to the withdrawal and dismantling of nuclear weapons based on its territory were warmly welcomed by NATO. The assurances given to Ukraine, as a non-nuclear weapon state party to the NPT, by all five nuclear-weapon states which are parties to the Treaty were also regarded as significant factors.

In addition to the Memorandum of Understanding on Civil Emergency Planning and Disaster Preparedness, signed between NATO and Ukraine on 16 December 1997, which established civil emergency planning as a major area of cooperation, other cooperative programmes cover a broad range of topics. Consultation and cooperation take place, through joint seminars and meetings of joint working groups, in many different fields, including civil-military relations; democratic control of the armed forces, and Ukrainian defence reform; defence planning, budgeting, policy, strategy and national security concepts; defence conversion; NATO-Ukraine military cooperation and interoperability; military training and exercises; economic aspects of security; science and technology issues; environmental security issues including nuclear safety; aerospace research and development; and civil-military coordination of air traffic management and control. A NATO-Ukraine Joint Working Group (JWG) on Defence Reform has been established to pursue further efforts in this area.

The NATO-Ukraine Commission

The North Atlantic Council meets periodically with Ukrainian representatives, as a rule not less than twice a year, in the forum established by the Charter called the NATO-Ukraine Commission. The role of the Commission is to assess implementation of the Charter and to discuss ways to improve or further develop cooperation.

A NATO-Ukraine Summit Meeting was held in Washington in April 1999 and, in March 2000, the NATO-Ukraine Commission met for the first time in Kyiv. The Political Committee of NATO visited Ukraine three times between 1997 and 2000 and held a variety of consultations and information exchanges in Kyiv and other Ukrainian cities.

Future Prospects

The positive developments described above have helped to establish a firm basis for future cooperation and are indicative of the fields in which progress has already been made. Robust participation in PfP, which involves programmes of practical defence-related activities in which many NATO countries and Partner countries participate, enables Ukraine to measure its defence establishment against those of its European neighbours and to establish more effectively its role in European security. Ukraine's participation in the Euro-Atlantic Partnership Council (EAPC) also contributes to this process.

THE ALLIANCE'S MEDITERRANEAN DIALOGUE

The Mediterranean Dialogue is an integral part of the Alliance's cooperative approach to security and is based on the recognition that security in the whole of Europe is closely linked to security and stability in the Mediterranean region.

The Dialogue was launched in 1994. Six countries joined the Dialogue initially, namely Egypt, Israel, Jordan, Mauritania, Morocco and Tunisia. Algeria became a participant in February 2000. The Dialogue is aimed at creating good relations and better mutual understanding throughout the Mediterranean, as well as promoting regional security and stability. It provides for political discussions with the participating countries. Its work is organised through an annual Work Programme focusing on practical cooperation in security and defence-related areas, information, civil emergency planning and science.

The Dialogue complements other related but distinct international initiatives under the auspices of the European Union (EU) and the Organisation for Security and Cooperation in Europe (OSCE).

Activities take various forms, including invitations to participants from Dialogue countries to take part in courses at the NATO School in Oberammergau, Germany and the NATO Defense College in Rome. Such courses cover peacekeeping issues; arms control; environmental protection; civil-military cooperation for civil emergency planning; and European security cooperation. A number of international fellowships have also been made available to researchers from Dialogue countries.

In principle, activities within the Dialogue take place on a self-funding basis. However, Allies may decide - on a case-by-case basis - to consider requests for financial assistance in support of Mediterranean partners' participation in the Dialogue. The level of participation varies from country to country.

At the Washington Summit in April 1999, Alliance leaders decided to enhance both the political and practical dimensions of the Dialogue. Among other things this would create further opportunities for discussion and for strengthening cooperation in areas where NATO can bring added value. This applies particularly in the military field, and in other areas where Dialogue countries have expressed interest.

Evolution of the Mediterranean Dialogue

The Mediterranean Dialogue has its origins in the Brussels Summit Declaration of January 1994. NATO Heads of State and Government referred to positive developments in the Middle East Peace Process as *"opening the way to consider measures to promote dialogue, understanding and confidence-building between the countries in the region"* and encouraged *"all efforts conducive to strengthening regional stability"*. At their meeting in December 1994 NATO Foreign Ministers declared their readiness *"to establish contacts, on a case-by-case basis, between the Alliance and Mediterranean non-member countries with a view to contributing to the strengthening of regional stability"*. To this end, they directed the Council in Permanent Session *"to continue to review the situation, to develop the details of the proposed dialogue and to initiate appropriate preliminary contacts"*. This resulted, in February 1995, in invitations to Egypt, Israel, Mauritania, Morocco and Tunisia to participate in a Dialogue with NATO. An invitation was extended to Jordan in November 1995, and to Algeria in February 2000.

The aim of the Dialogue is to contribute to security and stability in the Mediterranean, to achieve a better mutual understanding, and to correct misperceptions about NATO among Mediterranean Dialogue countries. It is based on the recognition that security in Europe is closely linked with security and stability in the Mediterranean and that the Mediterranean dimension is one of the security components of the European security architecture.

The Dialogue is progressive, and in principle is based on bilateral relations between each participating country and NATO. However it allows for multilateral meetings on a case-by-case basis. It offers all Mediterranean partners the same basis for discussion and for joint activities and aims to reinforce other international efforts involving Mediterranean Dialogue countries, such as those undertaken by the Barcelona process[7], the Middle East peace process and the OSCE, without either duplicating such efforts or intending to create a division of labour.

The Mediterranean Dialogue consists of a political dialogue combined with participation in specific activities.

The political dialogue consists of regular bilateral political discussions. These provide an opportunity for extensive briefings on NATO's activities, including its outreach and partnership programmes, its internal adaptation and its general approach to building cooperative security structures. In turn,

---

7   In November 1995, 15 EU member states and 12 non-member Mediterranean countries (Algeria, Cyprus, Egypt, Israel, Jordan, Lebanon, Malta, Morocco, Syria, Tunisia, Turkey and the Palestinian Authority) signed the Barcelona Declaration which spelt out the framework of the Euro-Mediterranean Partnership (also known as the Barcelona Process). The Declaration outlines three major goals: 1. a political and security partnership aimed at creating a common area of peace and stability; 2. an economic and financial partnership designed to establish a common area of prosperity; and 3. a social, cultural and human partnership to increase exchanges between the civil societies of the countries involved. The Barcelona Process envisages the establishment of a complete free trade area by the year 2010.

Mediterranean Dialogue countries are invited to share their views with NATO on stability and security in the Mediterranean region.

Mediterranean Dialogue countries have been invited to participate in specific activities such as science, information and civil emergency planning, and to take part in courses at NATO schools in fields such as peacekeeping; arms control and verification; the responsibilities of military forces with regard to environmental protection; civil emergency planning; and NATO European security cooperation. Participation in these courses is on a self-funding basis. In order to increase transparency, certain activities in the military field have been added.

NATO's Mediterranean Dialogue has evolved at a steady pace since it was launched in 1994. The 1997 Madrid Summit added a new and more dynamic direction to it by establishing a Mediterranean Cooperation Group. This created a forum involving Allied member states directly in the political discussions with Dialogue countries, in which views could be exchanged on a range of issues relevant to the security situation in the Mediterranean, as well as on the future development of the Dialogue.

NATO's SOUTH EAST EUROPE INITIATIVE

NATO's South East Europe Initiative (SEEI) was launched at the Washington Summit in order to promote regional cooperation and long term security and stability in the region.

The initiative was based on 4 pillars: a Consultative Forum on Security Issues on South East Europe; an open-ended Ad Hoc Working Group (AHWG) on Regional Cooperation in South East Europe under the auspices of the EAPC in Political Committee Session; Partnership for Peace working tools; and targeted security cooperation programmes for countries in the region.

The Consultative Forum includes NATO countries; six Partner countries in the South East Europe neighbourhood (Albania, Bulgaria, Croatia, Romania, the former Yugoslav Republic of Macedonia[8], Slovenia); and Bosnia and Herzegovina. It met initially at Summit level on the margins of the NATO Summit in Washington in April 1999 and has subsequently met at Ambassadorial level at NATO headquarters in Brussels.

---

8   Turkey recognises the Republic of Macedonia with its constitutional name.

The EAPC-AHWG identified ideas for further development to promote regional cooperation which have been incorporated into a set of activities modelled on activities carried out under NATO's Partnership for Peace programme.

The methodology of the Partnership for Peace initiative has been used to address a number of issues which are important to South East Europe, including transparency in defence planning, crisis management and defence management. Activities such as workshops on these topics have thus been designed to have a region-wide focus. Some of these are led by the participating countries in the region, facilitated by NATO, and others by NATO itself. Designed to complement each other, they are helping to promote stability through regional cooperation and integration. A South East Europe Security Coordination Group has been established to coordinate regional projects.

A complementary programme of targeted security cooperation with Croatia, building on PfP mechanisms, was introduced in spring 2000. Croatia joined the Partnership for Peace in May 2000. NATO also has a special security cooperation programme with Bosnia and Herzegovina outside PfP, which likewise complements other South East Europe Initiative activities.

NATO is also providing advice and expertise on the retraining of military officers made redundant by force structure reforms in Bulgaria and Romania. This is a NATO project being carried out in the framework of the Stability Pact for South Eastern Europe[9], in cooperation with the World Bank, with funding arranged between the World Bank and the countries involved. It is therefore a project which reflects the mutually reinforcing character of the international and institutional actions being taken in this field.

---

9   The Stability Pact was initiated by the European Union in May 1999. It was subsequently adopted at an international conference held in Cologne on 10 June 1999 and placed under the auspices of the OSCE. It is designed to contribute to lasting peace, prosperity and stability in South Eastern Europe through coherent and coordinated action, by bringing together the countries of the region, other interested countries and organisations with capabilities to contribute. It establishes specific mechanisms to coordinate their joint efforts.

CHAPTER 4

THE EUROPEAN SECURITY AND DEFENCE IDENTITY

Evolution of the ESDI

NATO-WEU Cooperation

NATO-EU Relations

THE EUROPEAN SECURITY AND DEFENCE IDENTITY (ESDI)

EVOLUTION OF THE ESDI

The Alliance is committed to reinforcing its European pillar through the development of an effective European Security and Defence Identity (ESDI) which could respond to European requirements and at the same time contribute to Alliance security. By assuming greater responsibility for their own security, the European member countries will help to create a stronger and more balanced transatlantic relationship which will strengthen the Alliance as a whole.

Accordingly, at their meeting in Washington in April 1999, Alliance Heads of State and Government set in train work on the further development of the European Security and Defence Identity. Discussions were initiated to address a number of specific aspects, namely:

- means of ensuring the development of effective mutual consultation, cooperation and transparency between the European Union (EU) and the Alliance, based on the mechanisms established between NATO and the Western European Union (WEU);

- the participation of non-EU European Allies;

- practical arrangements for EU access to NATO planning capabilities and NATO's assets and capabilities.

An essential part of the development of ESDI is the improvement of European military capabilities. The Alliance's Defence Capabilities Initiative (DCI), launched in Washington, is designed to ensure the effectiveness of future multinational operations across the full range of NATO missions and will play a crucial role in this process. Objectives arising from the DCI and the efforts of the EU to strengthen European capabilities are mutually reinforcing.

The principles which form the basis for future work on ESDI, set out at the Washington Summit and in subsequent meetings, are as follows:

- The Alliance acknowledges the resolve of the European Union to have the capacity for autonomous action so that it can take decisions and approve military action where the Alliance as a whole is not engaged.

- As this process goes forward, NATO and the EU should ensure the development of effective mutual consultation, cooperation and transparency, building on the mechanisms existing between NATO and the WEU.

- Alliance leaders applaud the determination of both EU members and other European Allies to take the necessary steps to strengthen their defence capabilities, especially for new missions, avoiding unnecessary duplication.

- They attach the utmost importance to ensuring the fullest possible involvement of non-EU European Allies in EU-led crisis response operations, building on existing consultation arrangements within the WEU, also noting Canada's interest in participating in such operations under appropriate modalities.

- They are determined that the decisions taken in Berlin in 1996, including the concept of using separable but not separate NATO assets and capabilities for WEU-led operations, should be further developed.

Work on these arrangements, which will respect the requirements of NATO operations and the coherence of its command structure, deals with questions such as:

- assured EU access to NATO planning capabilities able to contribute to military planning for EU-led operations;

- the presumption of availability to the EU of pre-identified NATO capabilities and common assets for use in EU-led operations;

- identification of a range of European command options for EU-led operations and further developing the role of the Deputy Supreme Allied Commander, Europe, in order for him to assume fully and effectively his European responsibilities;

- further adaptation of NATO's defence planning system to incorporate more comprehensively the availability of forces for EU-led operations.

By the early 1990s, it seemed to many in Europe and North America that the time had come for a rebalancing of the relationship between the two sides of the Atlantic and for concrete steps to be taken by the European member countries to assume greater responsibility for their common security and defence. European countries embarked upon a process designed to provide a genuine European military capability without unnecessary duplication of the command structures, planning staffs and military assets and capabilities already available within NATO, while simultaneously strengthening their contribution to the Alliance's missions and activities. Such an approach was seen as responding both to the European wish to develop a Common Foreign and Security Policy, and to the need for a balanced partnership between the North American and European member countries of the Alliance.

Developing the European Security and Defence Identity within NATO is an integral part of the adaptation of NATO's political and military structures. At the same time, it is an important element of the development of the European Union (EU). Both of these processes have been carried forward on the basis of the European Union's Treaties of Maastricht in 1991 and Amsterdam in 1997, corresponding declarations made by the Western European Union and the European Union, and decisions taken by the Alliance at successive Summit meetings held in Brussels in 1994, Madrid in 1997 and Washington in 1999, as well as in NATO Ministerial meetings.

With the Treaty on European Union, which was signed in Maastricht in December 1991 and entered into force on 1 November 1993, the leaders of the European Community agreed on the development of a Common Foreign and Security Policy (CFSP) *"including the eventual framing of a common defence policy which might in time lead to a common defence"*. This agreement included reference to the Western European Union as an integral part of the development of the European Union created by the Treaty; and a request to the WEU to elaborate and implement decisions and actions of the European Union which had defence implications. At the meeting of the WEU which took place in Maastricht in December 1991 concurrently with the meeting of the European Council, WEU Member states issued a declaration agreeing on the need for a genuine European security and defence identity and a greater European responsibility in defence matters.

In January 1994, NATO Heads of State and Government welcomed the entry into force of the Maastricht Treaty and the launching of the European Union as a means of strengthening the European pillar of the Alliance and allowing the European members of NATO to make a more coherent contribution to the security of all the Allies. They reaffirmed that the Alliance was the essential forum for consultation among its members and the venue for agreement on policies bearing on the security and defence commitments of Allies under the Washington Treaty. They also welcomed the close and growing cooperation between NATO and the Western European Union, achieved on the basis of agreed principles of complementarity and transparency. They further announced that they stood ready to make collective assets of the Alliance available, on the basis of consultations in the North Atlantic Council, for WEU operations undertaken by the European Allies in pursuit of their Common Foreign and Security Policy.

NATO Heads of State and Government directed the North Atlantic Council to examine how the Alliance's political and military structures might be developed and adapted in order to conduct the Alliance's missions, including peacekeeping, more efficiently and flexibly; and to reflect the emerging European Security and Defence Identity. As part of this process, the concept of Combined Joint Task Forces (CJTFs) was developed. The CJTF concept, described in Chapter 12, is aimed at providing improved operational flexibility and permitting the more flexible and mobile deployment of forces needed to respond to the new demands of all Alliance missions. It was designed inter alia to provide separable but not separate deployable headquarters that could be employed by the Western European Union.

At their meetings in Berlin and Brussels in June 1996, NATO Foreign and Defence Ministers decided that the European Security and Defence Identity should be built within NATO, as an essential part of the internal adaptation of the Alliance. This would enable all European Allies to make a more coherent and effective contribution to the missions and activities of the Alliance. It would allow them to act themselves as required and would simultaneously reinforce the transatlantic partnership. Taking full advantage of the Combined Joint Task Force concept, the strengthened European identity would be based on sound military principles supported by appropriate military planning, and would permit the creation of militarily coherent and effective forces capable of operating under the political control and strategic direction of the WEU.

At the Summit Meeting in Madrid in July 1997, NATO Heads of State and Government welcomed the major steps taken with regard to the creation of the ESDI within the Alliance. The North Atlantic Council in Permanent Session was requested to complete its work in this sphere expeditiously, in cooperation with the WEU.

NATO-WEU COOPERATION

As a result of the decisions to develop ESDI within NATO, arrangements were made to ensure that the further adaptation of the Alliance covered all aspects of NATO support for a WEU-led operation. These included:

- taking WEU requirements into account in NATO's new defence planning procedures for developing forces and capabilities. The WEU began contributing to the Alliance defence planning process in 1997 by providing an input to the 1997 Ministerial Guidance (see Chapter 7);

- introducing procedures for identifying NATO assets and capabilities on which the WEU might wish to draw with the agreement of the North Atlantic Council;

- establishing multinational European command arrangements within NATO, which could be used to prepare, support, command and conduct an operation under the political control and strategic direction of the WEU. (Under these arrangements the Deputy Supreme Allied Europe Commander (Deputy SACEUR) is given a distinct role, both in normal times and in the context of WEU-led operations, in relation to the forces to be made available to the WEU);

- introducing consultation and information-sharing arrangements to provide the coordination needed throughout a WEU-led operation undertaken with NATO support;

- developing military planning and exercises for illustrative WEU missions.

In practice these arrangements were designed to ensure that if a crisis arose in which the WEU decided to intervene (and the Alliance chose not to), it could request the use of Alliance assets and capabilities, possibly including a CJTF headquarters, for conducting an operation under its own political control and strategic direction.

The assets requested could then be made available for the WEU's use by the North Atlantic Council on a case-by-case basis. Conditions for their transfer to the WEU, as well as for monitoring their use and for their eventual return or recall, would be registered in a specific agreement between the two organisations. During the operation, NATO would monitor the use of its assets and regular political liaison with the WEU would be maintained. European commanders from the NATO command structure could be nominated to act under WEU political control. The assets would be returned to NATO at the end of the operation or when required. Throughout the operation, including its preparatory phase, NATO and the WEU would consult closely.

Decisions were taken at the EU's Cologne Summit meeting in June 1999 to give the EU the means and capabilities needed for the implementation of a common European security and defence policy (ESDP). In accordance with these decisions, the role undertaken by the WEU with respect to the development of the European Security and Defence Identity has been progressively assumed by the European Union.

In the intervening period, NATO continued to work with the WEU to complete and implement arrangements to facilitate cooperation between the two organisations in the event of a WEU-led crisis management operation making use of NATO assets and capabilities. Further work was undertaken to refine arrangements for the use of such assets and for information-sharing. Joint testing and evaluation of procedures and exercising of common elements and forces were undertaken. A joint NATO-WEU crisis management exercise was held in February 2000. At their meeting in Marseilles in November 2000, WEU Ministers decided to suspend routine NATO-WEU consultation mechanisms, apart from those that would be required during the transition period.

NATO-EU Relations

The Helsinki meeting of the Council of the European Union held in December 1999 established a "Headline Goal" for EU member states in terms of their military capabilities for crisis management operations. The aim is to enable the EU to deploy, by the year 2003, and sustain for at least one year, military forces of up to 60 000 troops to undertake the full range of the so-called Petersberg tasks set out in the Amsterdam Treaty of 1997. These consist of humanitarian and rescue tasks; peacekeeping tasks; and tasks of combat forces in crisis management, including peacemaking. Their role would be to undertake military operations led by the EU in response to international crisis, in circumstances where NATO as a whole is not engaged militarily. This process is part of the EU's resolve to develop a common European policy on security and defence which would underpin its Common Foreign and Security Policy militarily. It will avoid unnecessary duplication with NATO structures and does not imply the creation of a European army.

In addition, the EU decided to create permanent political and military structures, including a Political and Security Committee, a Military Committee and a Military Staff, to ensure the necessary political guidance and strategic direction to such operations. The EU also decided to develop arrangements for full consultation, cooperation and transparency with NATO and to ensure the necessary dialogue, consultation and cooperation with European NATO members which are not members of the EU on issues related to European security and defence policy and crisis management.

The dialogue between the Alliance and the European Union is steadily intensifying in accordance with the decisions taken at Washington and subsequently, and in the light of developments in the EU. Meetings of the European Council in Nice and of the North Atlantic Council in Brussels in December 2000 registered further progress. Alliance Foreign Ministers stated that they shared the goal endorsed by EU member states for a genuine partnership in crisis management between NATO and the EU. Both organisations agreed that consultations and cooperation will be developed between them on questions of common interest relating to security, defence and crisis management, so that crises can be met with the most appropriate military response and effective crisis management ensured.

On the basis of the December 2000 meetings an exchange of letters took place in January 2001, between the Secretary General and the Swedish Presidency of the EU, on holding joint meetings at Ambassadorial level and Ministerial level. The arrangement envisages at least three meetings at Ambassadorial level and one meeting at Ministerial level every six months (i.e. during each EU Presidency). However both organisations are committed to stepping up consultations in times of crisis. Thus regular meetings of the EU Political and Security Committee and the North Atlantic Council now take place and the two organisations are rapidly moving from the theory of ESDI/ESDP to consultation and cooperation on concrete and topical issues, such as the situation in the Western Balkans.

Since mid-2000, joint NATO-EU Ad Hoc Working Groups have been meeting to discuss security issues (for example, procedures for the exchange of classified information, including intelligence); modalities for EU access to Alliance assets and capabilities; capability goals (including issues relating to the Alliance's defence planning system); and permanent consultation arrangements, taking into account all relevant factors including those relating to participation. In spring 2001, the Secretary General of NATO was invited for the first time to brief the EU General Affairs Council on NATO policy.

In summer 2000, NATO and the EU Council Secretariat established an interim security agreement between the two organisations governing the exchange of classified information. Both organisations are working towards the conclusion of a permanent NATO-EU security agreement.

During the second half of 2000, Alliance experts contributed military and technical advice to the work of EU experts on the establishment of a catalogue of forces and capabilities for the EU Headline Goal, in preparation of the EU's Capabilities Commitment Conference held in November 2000. At their meeting in December 2000, Alliance Foreign Ministers expressed NATO's readiness to provide further expert advice upon request by the EU, subject to the necessary decisions.

Within NATO, work on the principal issues facing the further development of ESDI continues, in particular the identification of a range of European command options; the presumption of availability of pre-identified assets and capabilities; assured access to NATO operational planning capabilities; and the adaptation of Alliance defence planning.

CHAPTER 5

THE ALLIANCE'S OPERATIONAL ROLE IN PEACEKEEPING

The Process of Bringing Peace to the Former Yugoslavia

The Furtherance of the Peace Process in Bosnia and Herzegovina

NATO's Role in Relation to the Conflict in Kosovo

Human Rights Violations in the Kosovo Area and KFOR Assistance
for Humanitarian Causes

THE ALLIANCE'S OPERATIONAL ROLE IN PEACEKEEPING

THE PROCESS OF BRINGING PEACE TO THE FORMER YUGOSLAVIA

The political basis for the Alliance's role in the former Yugoslavia was established at the North Atlantic Council meeting in Ministerial session in Oslo, in June 1992. At that time NATO Foreign Ministers announced their readiness to support, on a case-by-case basis, in accordance with their own procedures, peacekeeping activities under the responsibility of the Conference on Security and Cooperation in Europe (CSCE) (subsequently renamed the Organisation for Security and Cooperation in Europe or OSCE). This included making available Alliance resources and expertise for peacekeeping operations.

In December 1992, NATO Foreign Ministers stated that the Alliance was also ready to support peacekeeping operations under the authority of the United Nations Security Council, which has the primary responsibility for international peace and security. Ministers reviewed peacekeeping and sanctions or embargo enforcement measures already being undertaken by NATO countries, individually and as an Alliance, to support the implementation of UN Security Council resolutions relating to the conflict in the former Yugoslavia. They indicated that the Alliance was ready to respond positively to further initiatives that the UN Secretary General might take in seeking Alliance assistance in this field.

Monitoring and Enforcement Operations

Between 1992 and 1995 the Alliance took several key decisions which led to operations by NATO naval forces, in conjunction with the Western European Union, to monitor and subsequently enforce the UN embargo and sanctions in the Adriatic; and by NATO air forces, first to monitor and then to enforce the UN no-fly zone over Bosnia and Herzegovina. The Alliance also provided close air support to the UN Protection Force (UNPROFOR) in Bosnia and Herzegovina and authorised air strikes to relieve the strangulation of Sarajevo and other threatened areas denominated by the UN as Safe Areas. Decisive action by the Alliance in support of the UN, together with a determined diplomatic effort, broke the siege of Sarajevo, led to a genuine cease-fire and made a negotiated solution to the conflict possible in autumn 1995.

Evolution of the Conflict

The evolution of the conflict and the process which culminated in the signing of the Bosnian Peace Agreement were long and drawn out. The successive actions taken by the Alliance in support of the United Nations between 1992 and 1995 are chronicled below.

Throughout this period, NATO conducted contingency planning for a range of options to support UN activities relating to the conflict. Contingency plans were provided to the UN for enforcement of the no-fly zone over Bosnia and Herzegovina; the establishment of relief zones and safe havens for civilians in Bosnia; and ways to prevent the spread of the conflict to Kosovo and the former Yugoslav Republic of Macedonia[1]. Contingency plans were also made available for the protection of humanitarian assistance, the monitoring of heavy weapons, and the protection of UN forces on the ground.

July 1992

NATO ships belonging to the Alliance's Standing Naval Force Mediterranean, assisted by NATO Maritime Patrol Aircraft (MPA), began monitoring operations in the Adriatic. These operations were undertaken in support of the UN arms embargo against all republics of the former Yugoslavia (UN Security Council Resolution (UNSCR) 713) and sanctions against the Federal Republic of Yugoslavia (Serbia and Montenegro) (UNSCR 757).

October 1992

Aircraft belonging to NATO's Airborne Early Warning and Control System (AWACS) began monitoring operations in support of UNSCR 781, which established a no-fly zone over Bosnia and Herzegovina. Data on possible violations of the no-fly zone was passed to UN authorities on a regular basis.

November 1992

As an extension of maritime monitoring operations, NATO and WEU forces in the Adriatic began enforcement operations in support of the sanctions and embargo imposed by the UN (UNSCR 787). Operations were no longer restricted to registering possible violations but included stopping, inspecting and diverting ships when required.

March 1993

On 31 March the UN Security Council passed Resolution 816, which authorised enforcement of the no-fly zone over Bosnia and Herzegovina and extended the ban to cover flights by all fixed-wing and rotary-wing aircraft except those authorised by UNPROFOR.

---

1   Turkey recognises the Republic of Macedonia with its constitutional name.

April 1993

A NATO enforcement operation (Deny Flight) began on 12 April. Initially it involved some 50 fighter and reconnaissance aircraft (later increased to more than 200) from various Alliance nations, flying from airbases in Italy and from aircraft carriers in the Adriatic. By December 1995, almost 100 000 sorties had been flown by fighter planes and supporting aircraft.

June 1993

At a joint session of the North Atlantic Council and the Council of the Western European Union on 8 June, a combined NATO/WEU concept of operations was approved for the enforcement of the UN arms embargo in the Adriatic. The resulting operation (Sharp Guard) included a single command and control arrangement under the authority of the Councils of both organisations. Operational control of the combined NATO/WEU Task Force was delegated, through NATO's Supreme Allied Commander Europe (SACEUR), to the Commander Allied Naval Forces Southern Europe (COMNAVSOUTH) in Naples.

During the enforcement operation approximately 74 000 ships were challenged by NATO and WEU forces, nearly 6 000 were inspected at sea and just over 1 400 were diverted and inspected in port. No ships were reported to have broken the embargo, though six attempted to do so and were stopped.

With the termination of the UN arms embargo on 18 June 1996, Operation Sharp Guard was suspended. The NATO and WEU Councils stated that both organisations were prepared to resume it, in accordance with UNSCR 1022, if UN sanctions were reimposed.

August 1993

A number of decisions were taken by the North Atlantic Council, following the adoption of a resolution by the UN Security Council in relation to the overall protection of Safe Areas (UNSCR 836). On 2 August, in the face of continued attacks, it agreed to make immediate preparations for undertaking stronger measures against those responsible, including air strikes, if the strangulation of Sarajevo and other areas continued and if interference with humanitarian assistance to the region did not cease. NATO Military Authorities were tasked to draw up operational options for air strikes, in close coordination with UNPROFOR.

On 9 August, the North Atlantic Council approved a series of "Operational Options for Air Strikes in Bosnia and Herzegovina" recommended by the NATO Military Committee. These options addressed the targeting identification process as well as NATO/UN command and control arrangements for air strikes.

January 1994

At the Brussels Summit, Alliance leaders reaffirmed their readiness to carry out air strikes in order to prevent the strangulation of Sarajevo and of other Safe Areas and threatened areas in Bosnia and Herzegovina.

February 1994

On 9 February, the North Atlantic Council, responding to a request by the UN Secretary General, authorised the Commander of Allied Forces Southern Europe (CINCSOUTH) to launch air strikes - at the request of the UN - against artillery and mortar positions in or around Sarajevo determined by UNPROFOR to be responsible for attacks against civilian targets in that city. The Council also decided that all heavy weapons had to be withdrawn from a 20-kilometre exclusion zone around Sarajevo or placed under UNPROFOR control within 10 days. After the expiry of the 10-day period, heavy weapons of any of the Parties found within the exclusion zone, unless under UNPROFOR control, would be subject to air strikes.

On 28 February, four warplanes violating the no-fly zone over Bosnia and Herzegovina were shot down by NATO aircraft in the first military engagement ever to be undertaken by the Alliance.

April 1994

Following a request from the UN, NATO aircraft provided Close Air Support on 10-11 April to protect UN personnel in Gorazde, designated by the UN as a Safe Area.

On 22 April, in response to a request by the UN Secretary General to support the UN in its efforts to end the siege of Gorazde and to protect other Safe Areas, the North Atlantic Council announced that air strikes would be launched unless Bosnian Serb attacks ceased immediately.

By 24 April, Bosnian Serb forces had pulled back three kilometres from the centre of Gorazde and humanitarian relief convoys and medical teams were allowed to enter the city. The Council declared that air strikes would be launched against remaining Bosnian Serb heavy weapons within a 20-kilometre Exclusion Zone around the centre of Gorazde from 27 April.

Air strikes were also authorised if other UN-designated Safe Areas (Bihac, Srebrenica, Tuzla and Zepa) were attacked by heavy weapons from any range. These areas could also become Exclusion Zones if, in the judgement of NATO and UN Military Commanders, there was a concentration or movement of heavy weapons within a radius of 20 kilometres around them.

July 1994

NATO military authorities were tasked to undertake contingency planning to assist the UN forces in withdrawing from Bosnia and Herzegovina and/or Croatia if that became unavoidable.

August 1994

On 5 August, at the request of UNPROFOR, NATO aircraft attacked a target within the Sarajevo Exclusion Zone. Agreement was reached by NATO and UNPROFOR to order this action after weapons were seized by Bosnian Serbs from a weapons collection site near Sarajevo.

September 1994

On 22 September, following a Bosnian Serb attack on an UNPROFOR vehicle near Sarajevo, NATO aircraft carried out an air strike against a Bosnian Serb tank at the request of UNPROFOR.

November 1994

On 19 November, in implementation of UNSCR 958, the North Atlantic Council approved the extension of Close Air Support to Croatia for the protection of UN forces in that country.

NATO aircraft attacked the Udbina airfield in Serb-held Croatia on 21 November, in response to attacks launched from that airfield against targets in the Bihac area of Bosnia and Herzegovina.

On 23 November, after attacks launched from a surface-to-air missile site south of Otoka (north-west Bosnia and Herzegovina) on two NATO aircraft, air strikes were conducted against air defence radars in that area.

May 1995

After violations of the Exclusion Zones and the shelling of Safe Areas, NATO forces carried out air strikes on 25 and 26 May against Bosnian Serb ammunition depots in Pale. Some 370 UN peacekeepers in Bosnia were taken hostage and subsequently used as human shields at potential targets in a bid to prevent further air strikes.

On 30 May, NATO Foreign Ministers meeting in Noordwijk, the Netherlands, condemned the escalation of violence in Bosnia and the hostile acts against UN personnel by the Bosnian Serbs.

June 1995

Plans for a NATO-led operation to support the withdrawal of UN forces were provisionally approved by the North Atlantic Council. The Alliance expressed its hope that its planning and preparations would serve to underpin a continued UN presence in the area.

By 18 June, the remaining UN hostages had been released. UN peace-keeping forces which had been isolated at weapons collection sites around Sarajevo were withdrawn.

July 1995

On 11 July, the UN called for NATO Close Air Support to protect UN peacekeepers threatened by Bosnian Serb forces advancing on the UN-declared Safe Area of Srebrenica. Under the control of the UN, targets identified by the UN were attacked by NATO aircraft. Despite NATO's air support, the Safe Area of Srebrenica fell to Bosnian Serb forces. The nearby Safe Area of Zepa was overrun by Bosnian Serb forces shortly after.

On 25 July, the North Atlantic Council authorised military planning aimed at deterring an attack on the Safe Area of Gorazde, and the use of NATO air power if this Safe Area was threatened or attacked.

August 1995

On 1 August, the Council took similar decisions aimed at deterring attacks on the Safe Areas of Sarajevo, Bihac and Tuzla. On 4 August NATO aircraft conducted air strikes against Croatian Serb air defence radars near Udbina air-field and Knin in Croatia.

On 30 August, following continued attacks by Bosnian Serb artillery on Sarajevo, NATO aircraft commenced a series of air strikes against Bosnian Serb military targets in Bosnia, supported by the UN Rapid Reaction Force on Mt. Igman. The air operations were initiated after UN military commanders concluded that a mortar attack in Sarajevo two days earlier had come from Bosnian Serb positions.

The operations were decided upon jointly by the Commander in Chief, Allied Forces Southern Europe (CINCSOUTH) and the Force Commander, UN Peace Forces, in accordance with the authority given to them under UN Security Council Resolution 836, in line with the North Atlantic Council's decisions of 25 July and 1 August 1995 endorsed by the UN Secretary General.

The common objectives of NATO and the UN were to reduce the threat to the Sarajevo Safe Area and to deter further attacks there or on any other Safe Area; to bring about the withdrawal of Bosnian Serb heavy weapons from the total Exclusion Zone around Sarajevo; and to secure complete freedom of movement for UN forces and personnel and non-governmental organisations, as well as unrestricted use of Sarajevo Airport.

September 1995

On 20 September, the NATO and UN Force Commanders concluded that the Bosnian Serbs had complied with the conditions set down by the UN and air strikes were discontinued. They stressed that any attack on Sarajevo or any other Safe Area, or other non-compliance with the provisions of the Sarajevo Exclusion Zone, or interference with freedom of movement or with the functioning of Sarajevo airport, would be subject to investigation and possible resumption of air strikes.

October 1995

On 4 October, three missiles were fired by NATO aircraft at Bosnian Serb radar sites at two different locations after anti-aircraft radar had locked on to Alliance aircraft.

On 9 October, in response to a request for air support from UN peace forces which had come under artillery shelling from Bosnian Serb guns for a second consecutive day, NATO aircraft attacked a Bosnian Serb Army Command and Control bunker, near Tuzla.

November 1995

As prospects for peace in Bosnia improved, the Alliance reaffirmed its readiness to help to implement a peace plan. Preparations were stepped up for a NATO-led force to implement the military aspects of the peace agreement. On 21 November, the Bosnian Peace Agreement between the Republic of Bosnia and Herzegovina, the Republic of Croatia and the Federal Republic of Yugoslavia (Serbia and Montenegro) was initialled in Dayton, Ohio (USA).

The conclusion of the Peace Agreement enabled the UN Security Council to suspend sanctions (UNSCR 1022) and to phase out its arms embargo, subject to certain conditions (UNSCR 1021).

Enforcement of sanctions by NATO and the WEU ceased on 22 November 1995 but could be reinstated if UN conditions were not met.

December 1995

The Bosnian Peace Agreement was signed in Paris on 14 December.

The NATO enforcement operation (Deny Flight), begun in April 1993, was terminated. On 15 December, the UN Security Council adopted UNSCR 1031, transferring authority for such operations from the UN to NATO from 20 December and giving NATO a mandate to implement the military aspects of the Peace Agreement.

The airspace over Bosnia and Herzegovina was subsequently controlled by the Implementation Force (IFOR) (see below) as part of its task.

The North Atlantic Council also decided that, in accordance with Security Council Resolution 1037, Operation Joint Endeavour should provide Close Air Support for the UN Task Force in the region of Eastern Slavonia (UNTAES).

Control of the airspace over Bosnia and Herzegovina and the provision of Close Air Support to UNTAES continued under the Stabilisation Force (SFOR) which succeeded IFOR on 20 December 1996. Provision of Close Air Support to UNTAES terminated in January 1998 on completion of the UNTAES mandate.

The NATO-led Implementation Force (IFOR)

IFOR's Command Structure

As stipulated in Annex 1A of the Peace Agreement, Operation Joint Endeavour was a NATO-led operation under the political direction and control of the Alliance's North Atlantic Council. The Implementation Force (IFOR) had a unified command structure. Overall military authority rested in the hands of NATO's Supreme Allied Commander Europe (SACEUR), at that time General George Joulwan. General Joulwan designated Admiral Leighton-Smith (NATO's Commander in Chief Southern Command (CINCSOUTH)) as the first Commander in Theatre of IFOR (COMIFOR). In November 1996, when IFOR Headquarters was transferred from Allied Forces Southern Europe (AFSOUTH) to Allied Land Forces Central Europe (LANDCENT), General Crouch became Commander in Theatre. He was replaced by General Shinseki in July 1997. Details of the subsequent command structure of IFOR and of its successor force, SFOR, are given in the SFOR website (www.nato.int.sfor).

Major IFOR Milestones

An Advance Enabling Force of 2 600 troops began deploying to Bosnia and Croatia on 2 December 1995. Their task was to establish the headquarters, communications and logistics necessary to receive the main body of some 60 000 IFOR troops being deployed to the area. The deployment of the main force was activated on 16 December, after final approval by the North Atlantic Council of the Operational Plan (OPLAN) and the UN Security Council's Resolution 1031 of 15 December authorising IFOR's mission.

The transfer of authority from the Commander of UN Peace Forces to the Commander of IFOR took place on 20 December, 96 hours after the NATO Council's approval of the main deployment. On that day, all NATO and non-NATO forces participating in the operation came under the command and/or control of the IFOR Commander.

By 19 January 1996, 30 days after IFOR's deployment (D+30), the Parties to the Agreement had withdrawn their forces from the zone of separation on either side of the agreed cease-fire line. As of 3 February (D+45), all forces had been withdrawn from the areas to be transferred. The transfer of territory between Bosnian entities was completed by 19 March (D+90), and a new zone of separation was established along the inter-entity boundary line.

Under the terms of the Peace Agreement, all heavy weapons and forces were to be in cantonments or to be demobilised by 18 April (D+120). This represented the last milestone in the military annex to the Peace Agreement. Technical problems prevented the Parties to the Peace Agreement from completing the withdrawal and demobilisation or cantonment of heavy weapons and forces by the deadline. However by 27 June 1996, the revised deadline set by the Supreme Allied Commander Europe (SACEUR), the cantonment of heavy weapons was completed.

Civilian Implementation

To achieve lasting peace in Bosnia and Herzegovina, full implementation of the civilian aspects of the Peace Agreement is also crucial. By implementing the military aspects of the Agreement, IFOR contributed to the creation of a secure environment conducive to civil and political reconstruction. It also provided substantial support for civilian tasks within the limits of its mandate and available resources. The Implementation Force worked closely with the Office of the High Representative (OHR), the International Police Task Force (IPTF), the International Committee of the Red Cross (ICRC), the UN High Commissioner for Refugees (UNHCR), the Organisation for Security and Cooperation in Europe (OSCE), the International Criminal Tribunal for the former Yugoslavia (ICTY) and many others, including more than 400 non-governmental organisations active in the area. It offered a range of support facilities to these organisations, such as emergency accommodation, medical treatment and evacuation, vehicle repair and recovery, as well as transport assistance, security information and advice, and other logistical support.

IFOR also provided a broad range of support to the OSCE, assisting in that organisation's task of preparing, supervising and monitoring the elections that took place on 14 September 1996. Following these elections, IFOR provided support to the Office of the High Representative in assisting the Parties in building new common institutions.

IFOR military engineers were able to repair and open more than 50 percent of the roads in Bosnia and Herzegovina, and to rebuild or repair over 60 bridges, including those linking the country with Croatia. They were also involved in the de-mining and repair of railroads and the opening up of airports to civilian traffic, in restoring gas, water and electricity supplies, in rebuilding schools and hospitals, and in restoring key telecommunication assets.

The NATO-led Stabilisation Force (SFOR)

From IFOR to SFOR

After the peaceful conduct of the September 1996 elections in Bosnia, IFOR had successfully completed its mission. However, it was clear that much remained to be accomplished on the civil side and that the environment would continue to be potentially unstable and insecure. One week after the elections, at an informal meeting in Bergen, Norway, NATO Defence Ministers concluded that the Alliance needed to reassess how it might continue to provide support for the establishment of a secure environment after the end of IFOR's mandate in December 1996.

One month later, the North Atlantic Council approved detailed political guidance for a study to be undertaken by the NATO Military Authorities of post-IFOR security options. In November and December 1996, a two-year consolidation plan was established in Paris and elaborated in London under the auspices of the Peace Implementation Council established under the Peace Agreement. On the basis of this plan and of the Alliance's own study of security options, NATO Foreign and Defence Ministers concluded that a reduced military presence was needed to provide the stability necessary for consolidating the peace. They agreed that NATO should organise a Stabilisation Force (SFOR), which was subsequently activated on 20 December 1996, the day on which IFOR's mandate expired.

SFOR's Role and Mandate

Under UN Security Council Resolution 1088 of 12 December 1996, the Stabilisation Force was authorised to implement the military aspects of the Peace Agreement as the legal successor to IFOR, operating under Chapter VII of the UN Charter (peace enforcement). Rules of engagement adopted for SFOR were the same as for IFOR, authorising the robust use of force if it should be necessary for SFOR to accomplish its mission and to protect itself.

The primary task given to SFOR was to contribute to the secure environment necessary for the consolidation of peace. Its specific tasks included:

- deterring or preventing a resumption of hostilities or new threats to peace;
- consolidating IFOR's achievements and promoting a climate in which the peace process could continue to move forward;
- providing selective support to civilian organisations, within its capabilities.

It also stood ready to provide emergency support to UN forces in Eastern Slavonia.

SFOR's size, with around 31 000 troops in Bosnia, was about half that of IFOR. Building on general compliance with the terms of the Dayton Agreement achieved during the IFOR mission, the smaller-sized force was able to concentrate on the implementation of all the provisions of Annex 1A of the Peace Agreement. This involves:

- stabilisation of the current secure environment in which local and national authorities and other international organisations can work; and

- providing support to other agencies (on a selective and targeted basis because of the reduced size of the forces available).

NATO envisaged an 18-month mission for SFOR, reviewing force levels after six and 12 months to enable the focus to be moved from stabilisation to deterrence, with a view to completing the mission by June 1998. The six month review in June 1997 concluded that, with the exception of a force adjustment during the municipal elections in September, no other significant changes to the size and capabilities of SFOR would take place until the North Atlantic Council, in consultation with the non-NATO SFOR contributors, had undertaken a thorough assessment of the security situation in Bosnia and Herzegovina after the elections.

SFOR's Command Structure

The Stabilisation Force has a unified command and is a NATO-led operation under the political direction and control of the Alliance's North Atlantic Council, as stipulated by Annex 1 A of the Peace Agreement. Overall military authority is in the hands of NATO's Supreme Allied Commander Europe (SACEUR).

Participation of non-NATO Nations

Every NATO nation with armed forces committed troops to SFOR, as was also the case with IFOR. Iceland, the only NATO country without armed forces, provided medical support. All 18 non-NATO nations which participated in IFOR also participated in SFOR, namely Albania, Austria, Bulgaria, Czech Republic, Estonia, Finland, Hungary, Latvia, Lithuania, Poland, Romania, Russia, Sweden and Ukraine - all of which are Partnership for Peace countries - plus Egypt[2], Jordan[2], Malaysia and Morocco[2]. Four more countries (Argentina,

---

2   Participant in NATO's Mediterranean Dialogue.

Ireland, Slovakia and Slovenia) have also joined SFOR, bringing the total of non-NATO participating nations to 22.

Non-NATO nations have been incorporated into the operation on the same basis as forces from NATO member countries. Special arrangements apply to Russian forces participating in SFOR but, in general, all participating forces receive their orders from the SFOR Commander through the multinational divisional headquarters. The SFOR headquarters in Sarajevo has personnel from 25 NATO and non-NATO nations.

Contributing non-NATO countries have liaison officers at SHAPE and have been involved in planning operations and in generating the necessary forces through the International Coordination Centre. At NATO headquarters, contributing non-NATO countries are consulted at key junctures and have the opportunity to express their views or to associate themselves with the decisions of the North Atlantic Council. The main mechanism for political consultation among the contributing countries was the so-called "NAC+N" format (now referred to as "EAPC(SFOR)"), consisting of the North Atlantic Council meeting with non-NATO contributing countries. Consultation with non-NATO contributors has also taken place in the context of the meetings of the EAPC and of the Policy Coordination Group (PCG) in SFOR format.

Participation by non-NATO countries not only contributes to the accomplishment of the SFOR mission but has a wider significance. It provides all the participating forces from Partnership Countries with practical experience of operating with NATO forces and demonstrates that NATO and non-NATO countries can work closely together in a NATO-led operation in the cause of peace. This has a broad impact on the region and contributes to enhanced security in the whole of Europe and beyond.

Civilian Aspects

Full implementation of the civilian aspects of the Peace Agreement continues to be a crucial factor in building the basis for a lasting peace. Like the Implementation Force, the Stabilisation Force provides support for civilian tasks, but with fewer forces at its disposal has to prioritise its efforts and to apply them selectively.

As directed by the North Atlantic Council, SFOR provided the secure environment for the municipal elections that took place in September 1997. It also provided other forms of support to the OSCE in the preparation and conduct of these elections. It continues to support the OSCE in its role of assisting the Parties in the implementation of agreements reached on Confidence and Security Building Measures and on Sub-Regional Arms Control. The latter limits the holdings of heavy weapons by the Parties in order to eliminate the danger of a sub-regional arms race and to bring about an overall reduction of heavy weaponry in the area.

Direct support to the Office of the High Representative (OHR) is provided by making available technical expertise and assistance in telecommunications and engineering, air transportation, and assets used for information purposes. Support of this kind is provided on a routine basis.

SFOR also continues to support UNHCR in its tasks in arranging for the return of refugees and displaced persons. It does this by helping to implement procedures designed to facilitate returns to the Zone of Separation, negotiated among the various organisations concerned and the Parties to the Peace Agreement, for example by ensuring that no weapons other than those of SFOR itself are brought back into the Zone. SFOR also supports UNHCR by assessing infrastructure, housing, economic and social factors in over 80 cities. Information is then shared with the Repatriation Information Centre to assist in maintaining its data-base on projects related to the agreements on returns.

Like its IFOR predecessor, SFOR continues to work closely with the UN International Police Task Force (IPTF) through surveillance, communications and transportation, and by providing security for its activities. SFOR's law enforcement support team continues to provide technical assistance to the IPTF and supports the implementation of the IPTF checkpoint policy. The implementation of the Brcko Arbitration Agreement of 15 February 1997 is also supported by SFOR by providing a secure environment in and around Brcko and by supporting the Brcko Supervisor, the International Police Task Force, UNHCR and other agencies involved in its implementation.

The support already provided by IFOR to the International Criminal Tribunal for the former Yugoslavia (ICTY) has been maintained by SFOR. This includes the provision of security and logistic support of ICTY investigative teams, and surveillance and ground patrolling of alleged mass grave sites. The North Atlantic Council has authorised SFOR to detain and transfer to the ICTY persons indicted for war crimes when SFOR personnel come into contact with them while carrying out their duties. A number of such persons have been detained and immediately transferred to the jurisdiction of the ICTY in The Hague. Several indicted persons have surrendered themselves voluntarily.

Support for civil implementation is provided by local forces and by SFOR's Civil-Military Task Force (CMTF). The CMTF, located in Sarajevo, consists of approximately 350 military personnel. Initially drawn mainly from US Army reserves, the Task Force has subsequently become multinational. CMTF personnel have mid-level and senior civilian skills in 20 functional areas, including law, economics and finance, agriculture, industry, commerce and business, structural engineering, transportation, utilities, housing, social services (education, public health, etc.), cultural affairs, government, management and political science.

THE FURTHERANCE OF THE PEACE PROCESS IN BOSNIA AND HERZEGOVINA

Continuation of a NATO-led Multinational Military Presence

In December 1997, NATO Foreign and Defence Ministers took a number of additional decisions in relation to the implementation of the Peace Agreement in Bosnia and Herzegovina. Recognising the fragility of the peace, despite positive achievements in several fields, they reiterated NATO's commitment to the establishment of a single, democratic and multiethnic state. They applauded the measures being taken by the Office of the High Representative in Bosnia to facilitate the implementation of the Peace Agreement by using its full authority to promote the resolution of difficulties through binding decisions on issues identified by the Peace Implementation Council. The NAC also acted upon the consensus emerging in the Peace Implementation Council and elsewhere on the need for a military presence to continue beyond the expiry of SFOR's mandate, and requested the NATO's Military Authorities to present options.

On 20 February 1998, the Council issued a statement announcing that, subject to the necessary UN mandate, NATO would be prepared to organise and lead a multinational force in Bosnia and Herzegovina following the end of SFOR's current mandate in June 1998, and directed the Military Authorities to initiate the necessary planning.

The new force would retain the name "SFOR" and would operate on a similar basis, in order to deter renewed hostilities and to help to create the conditions needed for the implementation of the civil aspects of the Peace Agreement. At the same time the Council projected a transitional strategy, involving regular reviews of force levels and progressive reductions as the transfer of responsibilities to the competent common institutions, civil authorities and international bodies became possible.

In view of the generally stable situation in Bosnia and Herzegovina, the North Atlantic Council directed NATO's Military Authorities in the autumn of 1999 to restructure and reduce the size of the Stabilisation Force. As a result, force levels have since been reduced to approximately 23 000 troops. These forces are provided by 17 NATO member countries and 17 non-NATO nations, among them 12 Partner countries, including a 1 200-strong Russian contingent. For the foreseeable future, an SFOR presence will be needed to ensure the maintenance of a secure environment and to underpin the work being undertaken to further the civilian reconstruction process.

There have nevertheless been encouraging signs of progress in this context. Refugee returns, and in particular the rate of spontaneous returns, accelerated in 1999 and 2000 reflecting growing confidence among the population that they can return to their former homes and villages in relative safety. Moreover, the results of municipal elections in April 2000 indicated decreased support for nationalist parties and some increase in political diversity. A further event which served to promote stability was the peaceful demilitarisation of Brcko.

Despite these positive developments, dissatisfaction was expressed at the meeting of the Peace Implementation Council in Brussels in May 2000 with the pace of progress in the implementation of the civilian aspects of the Peace Agreement and with the fact that, after five years, more progress had not been made in key areas. The Peace Implementation Council established three priority areas: deepening economic reform; accelerating the return of displaced persons and refugees; and fostering democratically accountable common institutions.

As part of this process, the North Atlantic Council has tasked SFOR with providing guidance and advice to the Standing Committee on Military Matters (SCMM). Further reference to the role of the SCMM is made in the following section.

On 11 November 2000 elections took place in Bosnia and Herzegovina. A state-level government was finally constituted on 22 February 2001 by a number of moderate parties that came together to form an Alliance for Change. This was the first government which did not include the major nationalist parties of the three ethnic groups in the country.

Security Cooperation Activities

In December 1997, in addition to decisions relating to SFOR, the Council initiated a series of further actions labelled Security Cooperation Activities. These are quite distinct from SFOR operations designed to ensure compliance by all sides with the military aspects of the Dayton Peace Agreement. Their purpose is to promote confidence and cooperation among the armed forces of Bosnia and Herzegovina and to encourage the development of democratic practices and central defence mechanisms, such as the Standing Committee on Military Matters (SCMM).

An initial set of Security Cooperation Activities endorsed by the Council included setting up courses for military and civilian defence officials of Bosnia and Herzegovina at the NATO School in Oberammergau, Germany. These courses are designed to promote reconciliation, dialogue and mutual understanding among the former warring factions within the three entities that which make up the country and their constituent parties. The programme also involves visits and seminars designed to help defence officials in Bosnia and Herzegovina to familiarise themselves with NATO and to increase their understanding of the role of the international community in laying the foundations for future peace and stability in their country. In addition, an assessment was undertaken to establish how NATO could best assist the government of Bosnia and Herzegovina in making its central defence institution, the SCMM, fully effective.

The SCMM is one of the common institutions set up by the Dayton Peace Agreement and is responsible for coordinating the armed forces of Bosnia and Herzegovina. It is composed of the Presidents of the ethnic groups within the country, namely the Bosnian Croats, the Bosnian Muslims, and the Bosnian Serbs; the Defence Ministers and Chiefs of Defence of the Bosniac-Croat Federation and of the Republika Srpska; and national and international observers, as well as a Secretariat. It is strongly supported by NATO and is developing its role in dealing with defence issues at the state level.

The Security Cooperation Activities sponsored by NATO are coordinated through the SCMM and involve representation from both the Bosniac-Croat Federation and the Republika Srpska, as well as from the three ethnic groups. Courses are conducted on security cooperation issues. Results are judged by participants and organisers alike to be positive. Without losing sight of its original goals, the Security Cooperation Programme (SCP) is focusing increasingly on more specific objectives. In cooperation with other international bodies, for example, and as part of the Programme, NATO is helping Bosnia and Herzegovina to respond to tasks identified in the May 2000 Work Plan drawn up by the Peace Implementation Council. These include the restructuring of the Entity Armed Forces, the strengthening of a common defence institution at state level, and the development of a common security policy for the country.

Reduction of the Entity Armed Forces (EAF)

Following a 15 percent reduction in 1999, the Entity Armed Forces (EAF) were to achieve a second round of 15 percent reductions in active manpower by the end of 2000. SFOR is monitoring the situation and is also working with

EAF Commanders on the development of common security and defence policies designed to ensure that the future structure of EAF is affordable and meets security requirements.

Weapon Collection (Operation HARVEST)

In 1998 SFOR began to collect and destroy unregistered weapons and ordnance held in private hands, to improve the overall safety of the citizens and to build confidence in the peace process. About 11 000 arms, 10 000 mines and 35 000 hand grenades as well as 3 700 000 rounds of ammunition (2 800 000 in 1999 and 900 000 in 2000) have been collected since the beginning of the operation, significantly reducing the threat to the local population. The aim of Project Harvest 2000 was to build upon the success of the work undertaken in 1999 by shifting the responsibility for the collection of weapons and ordnance to the national authorities and their armed forces. The operation is continuing in 2001.

War Crimes/ War Criminals

The apprehension of war criminals is the responsibility of the national authorities. Nevertheless, SFOR has been providing security and logistic support to investigative teams of the International Criminal Tribunal for the former Yugoslavia (ICTY), as well as surveillance and ground patrolling of alleged mass gravesites. Since 1996, NATO forces have been involved in the detention and transfer to The Hague of 37 people indicted for war crimes.

Upper Airspace Control

Under the Dayton Peace Accords, SFOR is responsible for normalising the airspace over Bosnia and Herzegovina by fostering a stable, safe and secure airspace environment that can eventually be returned to civilian control. A step in this direction was made in January 2000, when the upper airspace over Bosnia and Herzegovina was returned to civilian control. Plans are being made for a reduction of NATO military flight operations to make way for normalisation of the medium level airspace, with a view to full normalisation of the airspace by the end of 2001.

UNHCR/Refugees and Displaced Persons

Since November 1995, the security provided by SFOR has resulted in more than 723 000 returns (368 000 refugees and 355 000 displaced persons). The effective implementation of property laws is a crucial part of the process. The overall figure for repossession of houses and flats reached 51 500 cases by December 2000. However the pace of progress remains slow and only 21 percent of all claims lodged with the Commission for Real Property Claims (CRPC) have been decided.

NATO's Role in Relation to the Conflict in Kosovo

Background to the Conflict

Kosovo lies in southern Serbia and has a mixed population of which the majority are ethnic Albanians. Until 1989, the region enjoyed a high degree of autonomy within the former Yugoslavia, when Serbian leader Slobodan Milosevic altered the status of the region, removing its autonomy and bringing it under the direct control of Belgrade, the Serbian capital. The Kosovar Albanians strenuously opposed the move.

During 1998, open conflict between Serbian military and police forces and Kosovar Albanian forces resulted in the deaths of over 1 500 Kosovar Albanians and forced 400 000 people from their homes. The international community became gravely concerned about the escalating conflict, its humanitarian consequences, and the risk of it spreading to other countries. President Milosevic's disregard for diplomatic efforts aimed at peacefully resolving the crisis and the destabilising role of militant Kosovar Albanian forces were also of concern.

On 28 May 1998, the North Atlantic Council, meeting at Foreign Minister level, set out NATO's two major objectives with respect to the crisis in Kosovo, namely:

- to help to achieve a peaceful resolution of the crisis by contributing to the response of the international community; and

- to promote stability and security in neighbouring countries with particular emphasis on Albania and the former Yugoslav Republic of Macedonia[3].

On 12 June 1998 the North Atlantic Council, meeting at Defence Minister level, asked for an assessment of possible further measures that NATO might take with regard to the developing Kosovo crisis. This led to consideration of a large number of possible options.

---

3   Turkey recognises the Republic of Macedonia with its constitutional name.

On 13 October 1998, following a deterioration of the situation, the NATO Council authorised Activation Orders for air strikes. This move was designed to support diplomatic efforts to make the Milosevic regime withdraw forces from Kosovo, cooperate in bringing an end to the violence and facilitate the return of refugees to their homes. At the last moment, following further diplomatic initiatives by NATO and US officials, President Milosevic agreed to comply and the air strikes were called off.

UN Security Council Resolution (UNSCR) 1199 among other things expressed deep concern about the excessive use of force by Serbian security forces and the Yugoslav army, and called for a cease-fire by both parties to the conflict. In the spirit of the Resolution, limits were set on the number of Serbian forces in Kosovo, and on the scope of their operations, following a separate agreement concluded with the Serb government.

It was agreed, in addition, that the Organisation for Security and Cooperation in Europe (OSCE) would establish a Kosovo Verification Mission (KVM) to observe compliance on the ground and that NATO would establish an aerial surveillance mission. The establishment of the two missions was endorsed by UN Security Council Resolution 1203. Several non-NATO nations agreed to contribute to the surveillance mission.

In support of the OSCE, the Alliance established a special military task force to assist with the emergency evacuation of members of the KVM, if renewed conflict should put them at risk. This task force was deployed in the former Yugoslav Republic of Macedonia[4] under the overall direction of NATO's Supreme Allied Commander Europe.

Despite these steps, the situation in Kosovo flared up again at the beginning of 1999, following a number of acts of provocation on both sides and the use of excessive and disproportionate force by the Serbian Army and Special Police. Some of these incidents were defused through the mediation efforts of the OSCE verifiers but by mid-January the situation had deteriorated further after escalation of the Serbian offensive against Kosovar Albanians.

Renewed international efforts were made to give new political impetus to finding a peaceful solution to the conflict. The six-nation Contact Group[5] established by the 1992 London Conference on the former Yugoslavia met on 29 January. It was agreed to convene urgent negotiations between the parties to the conflict, under international mediation.

---

4   Turkey recognises the Republic of Macedonia with its constitutional name.

5   France, Germany, Italy, Russia, the United Kingdom and the United States.

NATO supported and reinforced the Contact Group's efforts by agreeing on 30 January to the use of air strikes if required, and by issuing a warning to both sides in the conflict. These concerted initiatives culminated in initial negotiations in Rambouillet near Paris from 6 to 23 February, followed by a second round in Paris from 15 to 18 March. At the end of the second round of talks, the Kosovar Albanian delegation signed the proposed peace agreement, but the talks broke up without a signature from the Serbian delegation.

Immediately afterwards, Serbian military and police forces stepped up the intensity of their operations against the ethnic Albanians in Kosovo, moving extra troops and tanks into the region, in a clear breach of compliance with the October agreement. Tens of thousands of people began to flee their homes in the face of this systematic offensive.

On 20 March, the OSCE Kosovo Verification Mission was withdrawn from the region, having faced obstruction from Serbian forces to the extent that they could no longer continue to fulfil their task. US Ambassador Holbrooke then flew to Belgrade in a final attempt to persuade President Milosevic to stop attacks on the Kosovar Albanians or face imminent NATO air strikes. Milosevic refused to comply, and on 23 March the order to carry out air strikes was given (Operation Allied Force).

NATO's Objectives

NATO's objectives in relation to the conflict in Kosovo were set out in the Statement issued at the Extraordinary Meeting of the North Atlantic Council held at NATO on 12 April 1999 and were reaffirmed by Heads of State and Government in Washington on 23 April 1999:

- a verifiable stop to all military action and the immediate ending of violence and repression;

- the withdrawal from Kosovo of the military, police and paramilitary forces;

- the stationing in Kosovo of an international military presence;

- the unconditional and safe return of all refugees and displaced persons and unhindered access to them by humanitarian aid organisations;

- the establishment of a political framework agreement for Kosovo on the basis of the Rambouillet accords, in conformity with international law and the Charter of the United Nations.

Throughout the conflict the achievement of these objectives, accompanied by measures to ensure their full implementation, was regarded by the Alliance as the prerequisite for bringing to an end the violence and human suffering in Kosovo.

On 10 June 1999, after an air campaign lasting 77 days, NATO Secretary General Javier Solana announced that he had instructed General Wesley Clark, Supreme Allied Commander Europe, to suspend NATO's air operations. This decision was taken after consultations with the North Atlantic Council and confirmation from General Clark that the full withdrawal of Yugoslav forces from Kosovo had begun.

The withdrawal was in accordance with the Military Technical Agreement concluded between NATO and the Federal Republic of Yugoslavia on the evening of 9 June. The agreement was signed by Lieutenant General Sir Michael Jackson on behalf of NATO, and by Colonel General Svetozar Marjanovic of the Yugoslav Army and Lieutenant General Obrad Stevanovic of the Ministry of Internal Affairs on behalf of the Governments of the Federal Republic of Yugoslavia and Republic of Serbia. The withdrawal was also consistent with the agreement between the Federal Republic of Yugoslavia and the European Union and Russian special envoys, President Ahtisaari of Finland and Mr. Victor Chernomyrdin, former Prime Minister of Russia, reached on 3 June.

On 10 June the UN Security Council passed Resolution 1244 welcoming the acceptance by the Federal Republic of Yugoslavia of the principles for a political solution to the Kosovo crisis, including an immediate end to violence and a rapid withdrawal of its military, police and paramilitary forces. The Resolution, adopted by a vote of 14 in favour and none against, with one abstention (China), announced the Security Council's decision to establish an international civil and security presence in Kosovo, under United Nations auspices.

Acting under Chapter VII of the UN Charter, the Security Council decided that the political solution to the crisis would be based on the general principles adopted on 6 May by the Foreign Ministers of the Group of Seven industrialised countries and the Russian Federation - the Group of 8 - and the principles contained in the paper presented in Belgrade by the President of Finland and the Special Representative of the Russian Federation which was accepted by the Government of the Federal Republic of Yugoslavia on 3 June. Both documents were included as annexes to the Resolution.

The principles included, among others, an immediate and verifiable end to violence and repression in Kosovo; the withdrawal of the military, police and paramilitary forces of the Federal Republic of Yugoslavia; deployment of an effective international civil and security presence, with substantial NATO participation in the security presence and unified command and control; establishment of an interim administration; the safe and free return of all refugees; a political process providing for substantial self-government; the demilitarisation of the Kosovo Liberation Army (KLA); and a comprehensive approach to the economic development of the crisis region.

The Security Council authorised Member States and relevant international organisations to establish the international security presence, and decided that its responsibilities would include deterring renewed hostilities, demilitarising the KLA and establishing a secure environment for the return of refugees and in which the international civil presence could operate. The Security Council also authorised the UN Secretary General to establish the international civil presence and requested him to appoint a Special Representative to control its implementation.

Following the adoption of UNSCR 1244, General Jackson, designated as the Commander of the force and acting on the instructions of the North Atlantic Council, made immediate preparations for the rapid deployment of the security force mandated by the United Nations Security Council.

The NATO-led Kosovo Force (KFOR)

The first elements of KFOR entered Kosovo on 12 June 1999. As agreed in the Military Technical Agreement, the deployment of the force was synchronised with the departure of Serb forces from Kosovo. By 20 June, the Serb withdrawal was complete and KFOR had accomplished its initial deployment task.

At its full strength KFOR comprised some 50 000 personnel. All 19 NATO members and 20 non-NATO countries participate in KFOR under unified command and control (among them 16 Partner countries, including a Russian contingent of 3 200 men).

Also on 20 June, following confirmation by the Supreme Allied Commander Europe (SACEUR) that Serb security forces had vacated Kosovo, the Secretary General of NATO announced that, in accordance with the Military Technical Agreement, he had formally terminated the air campaign.

Throughout the crisis, NATO forces were at the forefront of the humanitarian efforts to relieve the suffering of the many thousands of refugees forced to flee Kosovo by the Serbian ethnic cleansing campaign. In the former Yugoslav Republic of Macedonia[6] NATO troops built refugee camps, refugee reception centres and emergency feeding stations, and moved many hundreds of tons of humanitarian aid to those in need. In Albania, NATO deployed substantial forces to provide similar forms of assistance and assisted the UN High

---

6   Turkey recognises the Republic of Macedonia with its constitutional name.

Commission for Refugees - UNHCR - with the coordination of humanitarian aid flights, as well as supplementing these flights by using aircraft supplied by member countries. The Euro-Atlantic Disaster Response Coordination Centre (EADRCC) established at NATO in June 1998 also played an important role in the coordination of support to UNHCR relief operations.

Of particular concern to NATO countries and to the international community as a whole, from the outset of the crisis, was the situation of the Kosovar Albanians remaining in Kosovo, whose plight was described by refugees leaving the province. All indications pointed to organised persecution involving mass executions; exploitation of civilians as human shields; rape; mass expulsions; burning and looting of homes and villages; destruction of crops and livestock; suppression of identity, origins and property ownership by the confiscation of documents; hunger, starvation and exhaustion; and many other abuses of human rights and international norms of civilised behaviour.

Support for neighbouring countries

The Alliance fully recognised the immense humanitarian, political, and economic problems facing the countries in the region as a result of the conflict in Kosovo. In particular, Alliance efforts focused on providing immediate practical assistance in dealing with the refugee crisis by reassigning NATO forces in the region to humanitarian tasks.

At the beginning of April 1999, the NATO Commander in the former Yugoslav Republic of Macedonia[7] was given full authority to coordinate NATO's assistance to that country and to establish a forward headquarters in Albania, in coordination with the Albanian authorities and the UNHCR, in order to assess the humanitarian situation and provide support. The North Atlantic Council also tasked the NATO Military Authorities to undertake further planning to this end. Subsequent assistance included the provision of emergency accommodation and building of refugee camps, and assisting humanitarian aid organisations by providing transport and other forms of help including the distribution of food and aid. NATO countries provided financial and other support to Albania and the former Yugoslav Republic of Macedonia[7] and gave reassurances that they would respond to any challenges to their security by Yugoslavia stemming from the presence of NATO forces and their activities on their territories.

NATO Heads of State and Government in Washington set out their vision for achieving lasting peace, stability and future prosperity, based on increasing

---

7   Turkey recognises the Republic of Macedonia with its constitutional name.

integration of the countries in the region into the European mainstream, working hand in hand with other international institutions towards these goals. They established a process of individual consultations and discussions between the 19 NATO countries and the countries of the region and undertook to promote regional cooperation within the Euro-Atlantic Partnership Council (EAPC). They also agreed to use the resources of the Partnership for Peace (PfP) to provide more direct and focused assistance in addressing their security concerns. The Alliance welcomed related measures being taken in other forums, including the European Union proposal to convene a conference on a stability pact for South Eastern Europe at the end of May 1999. The Alliance also recognised that the G7 group of countries and financial institutions like the World Bank and the International Monetary Fund would play a vital role in the process of reconstruction following the end of the Kosovo crisis.

The situation in Kosovo is closely monitored by the North Atlantic Council. At Ministerial meetings held in May 2000, NATO countries reaffirmed their determination to play a full part in meeting the aims of the international community, as set out in UNSCR 1244, to work towards a peaceful, multiethnic, multicultural and democratic Kosovo in which all its people can enjoy universal rights and freedoms. NATO Foreign Ministers expressed strong support for the work being undertaken by the United Nations Mission in Kosovo (UNMIK) and the UN Secretary General's Special Representative and for the continuing high level of cooperation between UNMIK and KFOR. They also reaffirmed their determination to ensure that KFOR force levels and capabilities will be maintained at the levels required by the challenges it will face. These include maintaining a secure environment in a still unsettled Kosovo, discouraging and preventing ethnic violence, providing security and protection for all minorities, assisting the return of refugees, whether of Albanian, Serb, or other communities, and supporting the OSCE in the conduct of free, fair and safe elections.

In spring 2001, following violent clashes on the border with Kosovo, involving forces of the former Yugoslav Republic of Macedonia[8] and ethnic Albanian extremist groups reportedly based on Kosovo, KFOR initiated additional actions including increased ground and aerial patrols, anti-smuggling operations, and search and seizure operations. Reconnaissance and surveillance flights were also increased, as were intelligence gathering efforts.

---

8   Turkey recognises the Republic of Macedonia with its constitutional name.

HUMAN RIGHTS VIOLATIONS IN THE KOSOVO AREA AND KFOR ASSISTANCE FOR HUMANITARIAN CAUSES

The creation of conditions in which the underlying political problems of Kosovo can be resolved is a challenging and long-term task. Given the scale of the growing humanitarian crisis that faced Kosovo in the spring of 1999 and the destruction and violence directed by the Milosevic government in Belgrade, the situation has improved greatly. There is still a long way to go but the facts and figures below represent a solid list of achievements which are paving the way for the future stability of the province and the security of the region as a whole.

The findings of the OSCE Kosovo Verification Mission, which was sent to Kosovo from January to March 1998, pointed to organised and systematic atrocities carried out by Serb and Yugoslav forces against Albanian communities. Expulsions, arbitrary arrests and killings and other human rights violations and methods of intimidation were already in evidence. The Mission's report found that violations were committed on both sides of the ethnic divide during the conflict but that the suffering was overwhelmingly on the Kosovo Albanian side at the hands of the Yugoslav and Serbian military and security apparatus. The chief prosecutor of the International Criminal Tribunal for the former Yugoslavia (ICTY) has reported that some 526 mass graves have been identified in Kosovo and more than 4 000 bodies exhumed. A further 300 sites are being investigated.

Refugees

The scale of the problem involved in the relocation of displaced persons and refugees in Kosovo has been a major concern. By the beginning of April 1999, the United Nations High Commission for Refugees estimated that the campaign of ethnic cleansing had resulted in 226 000 refugees in Albania, 125 000 in the former Yugoslav Republic of Macedonia[9], and 33 000 in Montenegro. By the end of May 1999, over 230 000 refugees had arrived in the former Yugoslav Republic of Macedonia[9], over 430 000 in Albania and some 64 000 in Montenegro. Approximately 21 500 refugees had reached Bosnia and over 61 000 had been evacuated to other countries. An estimated 1.5 million people, i.e. 90 percent of the population of Kosovo, had been expelled from their homes and within Kosovo itself, some 580 000 people had been rendered homeless. Approximately 225 000 Kosovar men were believed to be missing and as many as 5 000 Kosovars executed.

---

9   Turkey recognises the Republic of Macedonia with its constitutional name.

Assistance given by NATO forces to alleviate the refugee situation included providing equipment and building camps to house 50 000 refugees in Albania; assistance in expanding camps in the former Yugoslav Republic of Macedonia[10]; providing medical support and undertaking emergency surgery; transporting refugees to safety; and providing transport for humanitarian aid and supplies.

NATO forces flew in many thousands of tons of food and equipment into the area. By the end of May 1999, over 4 666 tons of food and water, 4 325 tons of other goods, 2 624 tons of tents and nearly 1 600 tons of medical supplies had been transported to the area.

Positive progress has been made with regard to returns. Approximately 1 300 000 refugees and displaced persons, from inside Kosovo and abroad, have been able to return to their homes and villages. However some 200 000 Kosovar Serbs and up to 40 000 people from other minorities are still displaced within the Federal Republic of Yugoslavia.

In May 2000, a Joint Committee on Returns (JCR) was established to explore ways and means for the safe and sustainable return especially of Kosovar Serb residents. KFOR, the United Nations Mission to Kosovo (UNMIK), and other international organisations have helped to coordinate and support resettlement activities, within their means and capabilities, and to limit the potential for ethnic violence. KFOR forces have increased their presence in minority enclaves to provide more security in the wake of localised violence against Kosovo Serbs and other minorities.

Reconstruction

In June 1999 there were more than 128 000 damaged and destroyed houses in Kosovo. By 31 January 2001, about 18 000 houses had been reconstructed, with more than 8 000 still under construction. Activity has also focused on repair and renovation of the electrical power system, restoration of roads and railroads and the reparation of bridges.

Medical assistance

Medical assistance has been another major sphere of activity for KFOR, with over 50 000 civilian patients receiving treatment annually.

---

10   Turkey recognises the Republic of Macedonia with its constitutional name.

Security

Kosovo today is a vastly different place from the Kosovo that KFOR found when it arrived in the province in June 1999. Its capital, Pristina, is now a bustling centre of cars, traffic, commerce and open shops, as are other major towns. Most citizens of Kosovo enjoy a measure of security and normal life that has been denied to them for years. Continuous efforts are made to make Kosovo safe for all. KFOR conducts up to 800 patrols every day, guards over 550 key sites and mans over 250 vehicle checkpoints. On any single day, two out of three KFOR soldiers are deployed in security operations.

One of the highest priorities for KFOR is improving security for the ethnic minorities. Over 50 percent of its manpower is engaged in the protection of minority (mainly Serb) populations in Kosovo. This includes guarding individual homes and villages, transporting people to schools and shops, patrolling, monitoring checkpoints, protecting sites and assisting the local people. KFOR forces have also been deployed in Mitrovica to ensure security on either side of the river Ibar.

There has been a significant reduction in incidents of accidents involving unexploded ordinance, including mines and cluster bombs, due to the work being undertaken by civilian demining companies working under contract to United Nations Mine Action and Coordination Centres as well as KFOR.

Border controls

KFOR continues to control the border area, using a combination of foot, vehicle and helicopter patrols to man eight crossing points and to support the UN Mission in Kosovo (UNMIK) at four others, as well as providing aerial surveillance.

KFOR is constantly engaged in border security tasks. Vehicles are thoroughly searched or subjected to document checks and random searches at border crossings. Close coordination is maintained with border guards on both sides and with UNMIK border police and customs officials at most official border and boundary crossings.

Following the escalation of border violence in spring 2001, NATO authorities successfully brokered a cease fire on 12 March 2001. The North Atlantic Council subsequently decided to implement a phased and conditioned reduction of the Ground Safety Zone (GSZ) around Kosovo as provided for by the Military Technical Agreement, based on the plan submitted by the new Yugoslav government under President Kostunica (Covic Plan).

Civil Implementation

In June 1999, there were no civil structures and no administrative services in Kosovo. By contrast, all executive, legislative and judicial structures have now been integrated into Joint Integrated Administrative Structures (JIAS). Of the 19 administrative departments to be established under the JIAS, the first four were set up in February 2000 and others have been gradually set up since.

On 2 February 2000, the Kosovar Albanian leader, Dr. Ibrahim Rugova, formally announced the dissolution of the so-called shadow government and associated structures. The President of the Parliament, Mr. Idriz Ajeti, confirmed the dissolution.

The expanded Kosovo Transitional Council held its second session on 16 February 2000 with 28 members in attendance, including the Catholic bishop. Administrators have since been appointed in all 29 municipalities. Budgets have been allocated for all core local government activities. In October 2000, the Organisation for Security and Cooperation in Europe (OSCE) played an important role in the planning of municipal elections, including voter registration, under security arrangements provided by KFOR, in coordination with UNMIK, to protect freedom of movement in the area.

The elections were conducted without major incident, resulting in victory for the moderate Democratic League of Kosovo party (LDK), led by Dr. Rugova. Together with the outcome of the December 2000 Serbian elections, in which the Democratic Opposition of Serbia party (DOS), led by Vojislav Kostunica, succeeded in overthrowing the regime of former President Milosevic, this is expected to have far reaching political implications throughout the region.

Law and Order

In June 1999, when KFOR arrived in Kosovo the weekly murder rate was 50. By spring 2000 the figure had dropped to 7 per week, comparable with many large European cities. Much of the violence can now be attributed to criminal activities, as opposed to acts motivated by ethnic hatred. Such acts nevertheless continue to take place. However an important part of KFOR resources continues to be engaged in patrolling and manning checkpoints and protecting patrimonial sites, as part of the process of restoring law and order.

The Kosovo Police Service (KPS) established by the OSCE and committed to fair and impartial law enforcement for the population as a whole, now has some 3 100 active police and is beginning to contribute significantly to the establishment of law and order. The goal for 2001 is to achieve a force level of

4 000 active Kosovo police. This is a significant step towards self-sufficiency and one that should lead to reduced dependence on the UNMIK Police.

International assistance is also helping to rebuild the judicial and penal system, including the appointment of a substantial number of international judges.

Rotation of Headquarters Staff

The Kosovo Force comes under the overall command of the Supreme Allied Commander Europe (SACEUR).

Operational command of KFOR was initially assumed by the Allied Command Europe (ACE) Rapid Reaction Corps (ARRC), which is the land component of the ACE Rapid Reaction Forces. It subsequently passed to Headquarters Allied Land Forces Central Europe (LANDCENT), a Principal Subordinate Command under the former Subordinate Command known as Allied Forces Central Europe (AFCENT).

In April 2000, operational command of KFOR passed from Allied Forces Central Europe (LANDCENT) to the 5-nation Eurocorps[11]. This was in line with the agreement reached between the nations contributing to the Eurocorps and NATO as a whole, that the corps could be made available to support operations under NATO command. Operational command passed to AFSOUTH in early 2001. In April 2001, NATO's Northern region HQ (Regional Command North) takes over operational command of the force.

---

11   Belgium, France, Germany, Luxembourg and Spain.

CHAPTER 6

THE ALLIANCE'S ROLE IN ARMS CONTROL

**Developments relating to Nuclear, Biological
and Chemical Weapons**

**Developments relating to Conventional Arms Control
and Disarmament**

Alliance Policy on WMD Proliferation

THE ALLIANCE'S ROLE IN ARMS CONTROL

NATO's policy of support for arms control, disarmament and non-proliferation plays a major role in the achievement of the Alliance's security objectives. NATO has a longstanding commitment in this area and continues to ensure that its overall objectives of defence, arms control, disarmament and non-proliferation remain in harmony.

At their Summit Meeting in Washington in April 1999, NATO leaders decided to increase Alliance efforts to counter the proliferation of Weapons of Mass Destruction (WMD) and their means of delivery. The WMD Initiative has initiated a more vigorous and structured debate on WMD issues. The principal goal of the Alliance and its members remains to prevent proliferation from occurring or, should it occur, to reverse it through diplomatic means.

As stated in the Strategic Concept of 1999, the Alliance is committed to contribute actively to the development of arms control, disarmament, and non-proliferation agreements as well as to Confidence and Security Building Measures (CSBMs). Member countries consider confidence building, arms control, disarmament and non-proliferation as important components of conflict prevention and recognise that the Alliance can play a vital role in this field by promoting a broader, more comprehensive and more verifiable international arms control and disarmament process. NATO's partnership, cooperation and dialogue programmes offer a unique opportunity to promote these objectives and contribute to the overall goal of increasing confidence and security and developing a cooperative approach to international security.

At the Washington Summit NATO Allies agreed, in the light of overall strategic developments and the reduced salience of nuclear weapons, to consider options for confidence and security building measures, verification, non-proliferation and arms control and disarmament. Since the Summit, the responsible NATO bodies have undertaken an extensive and comprehensive evaluation of overall developments and have examined a number of options for the future.

A summary of the principal developments in this field is given below.

DEVELOPMENTS RELATING TO NUCLEAR, BIOLOGICAL AND CHEMICAL WEAPONS

The proliferation of Nuclear, Biological and Chemical (NBC) weapons and their means of delivery are a matter of serious concern for the Alliance. In spite of welcome progress in strengthening international non-proliferation regimes, major challenges with respect to proliferation remain. The Alliance recognises that proliferation can occur despite efforts to prevent it and can pose a direct military threat to the Allies' populations, territory, and forces.

Some states, including some on NATO's periphery and in other regions, sell or acquire or try to acquire NBC weapons and delivery means. Other, non-state actors have also shown the potential to create and use some of these weapons.

NATO has greatly reduced its reliance on nuclear forces in the last decade and major reductions have been made in the forces themselves by the three member countries of the Alliance which maintain nuclear forces, namely the United States, France and the United Kingdom. However, the existence of powerful nuclear forces outside the Alliance constitutes a significant factor which the Alliance has to take into account if security and stability in the Euro-Atlantic area are to be maintained. Russia still retains a large number of nuclear weapons of all types. China has continued to modernise its nuclear forces over the last decade. In addition, in 1998, India and Pakistan both carried out nuclear tests, posing a serious challenge to nuclear non-proliferation agreements and increasing dangers associated with regional conflict.

In June 1999, the United States and Russia affirmed their existing obligations under the Anti-Ballistic Missile (ABM) Treaty to consider possible changes in the strategic situation that have a bearing on the Treaty and possible proposals for further increasing its viability. The United States has subsequently proposed changes to the Treaty in order to permit deployment of a limited missile defence system. Bilateral discussions and multilateral consultations, both on the ABM Treaty and on a third round of Strategic Arms Reductions Talks (START III), are taking place.

In September 2000, the United States and Russia also agreed on a Strategic Stability Cooperation Initiative as a constructive basis for strengthening trust between them and for developing measures to enhance strategic stability and to counter the proliferation of weapons of mass destruction, missiles and missile technologies world-wide.

The Nuclear Non-Proliferation Treaty (NPT)

For many years, the Nuclear Non-Proliferation Treaty has been the cornerstone of international agreements on global non-proliferation and of the process of bringing about nuclear disarmament. The Treaty was extended indefinitely at the 1995 NPT Review and Extension Conference. It was also decided to strengthen the review process and to adopt a set of "Principles and

Objectives for Nuclear Non-Proliferation and Disarmament" in order to promote effective implementation of the Treaty.

At the 2000 NPT Review Conference held in New York between 24 April and 19 May 2000, a comprehensive, substantive final document was adopted. Its conclusions reflect continued support for universal NPT adherence, strict compliance with the NPT's provisions, strengthened International Atomic Energy Agency (IAEA) safeguards, and future steps toward nuclear disarmament.

One of the most significant practical achievements of the Review Conference was agreement on the entry into force of the Comprehensive Nuclear Test-Ban Treaty (CTBT), as soon as the required ratifications have been completed. NATO member countries are committed to working to secure the necessary signatures and ratification in order to achieve an early entry into force of the Treaty. The Review Conference also emphasised the importance of making progress towards a treaty to ban the production of fissile material for nuclear weapons or other nuclear explosive devices and called for negotiations on this subject in the framework of the Conference on Disarmament to be resumed.

Biological and Chemical Weapons

The proliferation of biological and chemical weapons is widely recognised as a growing international security problem, both for interstate conflict and as a potential dimension of terrorism.

The 1925 Geneva Protocol bans the use of chemical and biological weapons. States Parties to the Biological and Toxin Weapons Convention (BTWC), which entered into force in 1975, agree not to develop, produce, stockpile or acquire biological agents and related equipment used for hostile purposes. In 1994 a Special Conference established an Ad Hoc Group of States Parties to the Convention to examine possible verification measures and proposals to strengthen the Convention. The fourth Review Conference in 1996 agreed that a Protocol should be completed as soon as possible before the commencement of the fifth Review Conference in 2001. During their meeting held in Florence on 24 May 2000, NATO Ministers reiterated their commitment to this objective.

A Chemical Weapons Convention banning chemical weapons, negotiated at the Conference on Disarmament between 1980 and 1992, entered into force in 1997. Each party to the Convention agrees not to develop, produce, acquire, stockpile or retain chemical weapons, not to use or prepare to use chemical weapons and not to assist others in acting against the provisions of the Convention. The Convention also requires States Parties to destroy any chemical weapons in their possession, and to destroy their chemical weapon production facilities.

Missiles and other means of delivery

The proliferation of missile technology is another issue of significant concern. Established in 1987, the Missile Technology Control Regime (MTCR) brings together 32 states (including all 19 NATO members) that seek to limit the proliferation of missiles and missile technology. The MTCR partners control exports of a common list of controlled items in accordance with a common export control policy.

DEVELOPMENTS RELATING TO CONVENTIONAL ARMS CONTROL AND DISARMAMENT

Over the course of the last several years, there have been a number of promising developments in the area of conventional arms control and related confidence and security building measures. These include:

The Adaptation of the CFE Treaty

The Conventional Forces in Europe (CFE) Treaty of 19 November 1990 imposed legally-binding limits on five categories of treaty limited equipment and included provisions for exceptionally comprehensive information exchange and notifications, as well as intrusive on-site inspection and verification arrangements. More than 3 000 inspections have taken place. This transparency in arms holdings is a unique feature in an arms control treaty. The Treaty brought about dramatic reductions in treaty limited equipment within Europe. More than 50 000 pieces of equipment have been destroyed or removed. During the Treaty Review Conference in 1996, the States Parties recognised the need to adapt the CFE Treaty in order to allow it to continue to sustain its key role in European security arrangements.

Adaptation negotiations began in May 1996, reflecting the fact that fundamental changes had occurred since 1990 such as the reunification of Germany, the dissolution of the Warsaw Pact and the USSR, the emergence of new successor states which raised the Treaty's membership from 22 to 30 states, the process of democratisation in Central and Eastern Europe, and the end of the Cold War.

The adaptation process was completed with the signing of a legally-binding "Agreement on Adaptation" of the CFE Treaty at the Istanbul OSCE Summit in November 1999. In Istanbul, a "Final Act" was also adopted. This politically-binding text contains all of the undertakings relating to restraint and progressive reductions towards equipment entitlements which States Parties have offered additionally, in the context of the Treaty adaptation. The Agreement will enter into force following ratification by States Parties. Pending the completion of the ratification process, the full and continued implementation of the Treaty and its associated documents remains crucial.

The Vienna Document

At the Istanbul Summit in November 1999, the member states of the Organisation for Security and Cooperation in Europe (OSCE) also adopted the 1999 Vienna Document, which enhances the Confidence and Security Building Measures (CSBMs) introduced by the Vienna Documents of 1990, 1992 and 1994. The 1999 Vienna Document improves the current CSBMs and emphasises the importance of regional cooperation.

Open Skies

Another important element in creating greater openness in the military field is the March 1992 "Open Skies" Treaty, permitting overflights of national territory on a reciprocal basis.

The Treaty on Open Skies is intended to enhance confidence building, facilitate the monitoring of compliance with existing or future arms control agreements, and strengthen the capacity for the early recognition and subsequent management of crises by permitting reciprocal overflights of national territory.

A number of trial flights have subsequently taken place, but the complete regime of observation flights as set forth in the Treaty has not yet entered into force. Allies continue to support ratification of this Treaty, and have urged the remaining signatories, Russia and Belarus, to ratify it so that the Treaty can enter into force as soon as possible.

Small Arms and Light Weapons

There has been an increasing international awareness over the last decade of the need to prevent and reduce destabilising accumulations and flows of small arms and light weapons, particularly through illicit and irresponsible transfers. A number of initiatives have been undertaken at the global, regional and local levels. Since January 1999, practical work on this issue has been undertaken by the member states of the Euro-Atlantic Partnership Council (EAPC). The UN General Assembly has agreed to convene an international conference on the illicit arms trade in all its aspects in the year 2001.

Anti-Personnel Mines

Over the last decade, the international community has become increasingly active in efforts to counter the humanitarian problems and suffering caused by anti-personnel mines. NATO nations have demonstrated their commitment to tackling this issue.

In 1998, a new protocol to the 1980 Convention on Prohibitions or Restrictions on the Use of Certain Conventional Weapons was signed. Entitled "Protocol on Prohibitions or Restrictions on the Use of Mines, Booby Traps and Other Devices", it entered into force in December 1998. A Convention on the Prohibition of the Use, Stockpiling, Production, and Transfer of Anti-Personnel Mines and on their Destruction was signed in Ottawa on 3 December 1997. It came into force on 1 March 1999 and has been ratified by over 100 states.

ALLIANCE POLICY ON WMD PROLIFERATION

Recognising that proliferation of weapons of mass destruction constitutes a threat to international security, NATO Heads of State and Government directed the Alliance in 1994 to intensify and expand its efforts against proliferation. In June 1994 NATO Foreign Ministers issued the 'Alliance Policy Framework on Proliferation of Weapons of Mass Destruction', a public document stating that the principal goal of the Alliance and its member states is to prevent proliferation from occurring or, should it occur, to reverse it through diplomatic means. The document also noted that proliferation might nevertheless occur despite international non-proliferation norms and agreements, and that weapons of mass destruction and their delivery means can pose a direct military threat to NATO territory, populations and forces. Since 1994, the Alliance has increasingly focused on the range of defence capabilities needed to devalue WMD proliferation and use. Efforts are continuing to improve NATO's defence posture against WMD risks, in order to reduce the operational vulnerabilities of NATO military forces, while maintaining their flexibility and effectiveness in situations involving the presence, threat or use of NBC weapons.

The Alliance's WMD Initiative

In order to respond to the risks to Alliance security posed by the spread of weapons of mass destruction and their delivery means, the Alliance launched an Initiative in 1999, building upon previous work, to improve overall Alliance political and military efforts in this area. This WMD Initiative is helping to promote a more vigorous, structured debate, leading to better understanding among NATO countries of WMD issues and how to respond to them: for example by improving the quality and quantity of intelligence and information-sharing. In May 2000, a WMD Centre was established at NATO to support these efforts.

In addition, there are three senior NATO groups dealing with the Alliance's political and defence efforts against WMD proliferation, namely the Senior Politico-Military Group on Proliferation (SGP) and the Senior Defence Group on Proliferation (DGP), which deal respectively with the political and defence dimensions of NATO's response; and the Joint Committee on Proliferation (JCP), which coordinates and brings together the work on both aspects. The SGP considers a range of factors in the political, security and economic fields that may cause or influence proliferation and discusses political and economic means to prevent or respond to proliferation. The DGP addresses the military capabilities needed to discourage WMD proliferation, to deter threats and use of such weapons, and to protect NATO populations, territory and forces.

PART II

CHAPTER 7

POLICY AND DECISION-MAKING

The Principal Policy and Decision-Making Institutions of the Alliance

Consensus Politics and Joint Decision-Making

Crisis Management

The Defence Dimension

Nuclear Policy

The Economic Sphere

Public Information

POLICY AND DECISION-MAKING

THE PRINCIPAL POLICY AND DECISION-MAKING INSTITUTIONS OF THE ALLIANCE

The North Atlantic Council

The North Atlantic Council (NAC) has effective political authority and powers of decision, and consists of Permanent Representatives of all member countries meeting together at least once a week. The Council also meets at higher levels involving Foreign Ministers, Defence Ministers or Heads of Government but it has the same authority and powers of decision-making, and its decisions have the same status and validity, at whatever level it meets. The Council has an important public profile and issues declarations and communiqués explaining the Alliance's policies and decisions to the general public and to governments of countries which are not members of NATO.

The Council is the only body within the Alliance which derives its authority explicitly from the North Atlantic Treaty. The Council itself was given responsibility under the Treaty for setting up subsidiary bodies. Many committees and planning groups have since been created to support the work of the Council or to assume responsibility in specific fields such as defence planning, nuclear planning and military matters.

The Council thus provides a unique forum for wide-ranging consultation between member governments on all issues affecting their security and is the most important decision-making body in NATO. All member countries of NATO have an equal right to express their views round the Council table. Decisions are the expression of the collective will of member governments arrived at by common consent. All member governments are party to the policies formulated in the Council or under its authority and share in the consensus on which decisions are based.

Each government is represented on the Council by a Permanent Representative with ambassadorial rank. Each Permanent Representative is supported by a political and military staff or delegation to NATO, varying in size.

When the Council meets in this format, it is often referred to as the "Permanent Council". Twice each year, and sometimes more frequently, the Council meets at Ministerial level, when each nation is represented by its Minister of Foreign Affairs. Meetings of the Council also take place in Defence Ministers Sessions. Summit Meetings, attended by Heads of State or

Government, are held whenever particularly important issues have to be addressed or at seminal moments in the evolution of Allied security policy.

While the Council normally meets at least once a week, it can be convened at short notice whenever necessary. Its meetings are chaired by the Secretary General of NATO or, in his absence, by his Deputy. The longest serving Ambassador or Permanent Representative on the Council assumes the title of Dean of the Council. Primarily a ceremonial function, the Dean may be called upon to play a more specific presiding role, for example in convening meetings and chairing discussions at the time of the selection of a new Secretary General. At Ministerial Meetings of Foreign Ministers, one country's Foreign Minister assumes the role of Honorary President. The position rotates annually among the nations in the order of the English alphabet. An Order of Precedence in the Permanent Council is established on the basis of length of service, but at meetings of the Council at any level, Permanent Representatives sit round the table in order of nationality, following the English alphabetical order. The same procedure is followed throughout the NATO committee structure.

Items discussed and decisions taken at meetings of the Council cover all aspects of the Organisation's activities and are frequently based on reports and recommendations prepared by subordinate committees at the Council's request. Equally, subjects may be raised by any one of the national represen-tatives or by the Secretary General. Permanent Representatives act on instruc-tions from their capitals, informing and explaining the views and policy deci-sions of their governments to their colleagues round the table. Conversely they report back to their national authorities on the views expressed and positions taken by other governments, informing them of new developments and keep-ing them abreast of movement towards consensus on important issues or areas where national positions diverge.

When decisions have to be made, action is agreed upon on the basis of unanimity and common accord. There is no voting or decision by majority. Each nation represented at the Council table or on any of its subordinate committees retains complete sovereignty and responsibility for its own decisions.

The work of the Council is prepared by subordinate Committees with responsibility for specific areas of policy. Much of this work involves the Senior Political Committee (SPC), consisting of Deputy Permanent Representatives, sometimes reinforced by appropriate national experts, depending on the sub-ject. In such cases it is known as the SPC(R).The Senior Political Committee has particular responsibility for preparing most statements or communiqués to be issued by the Council and meets in advance of ministerial meetings to draft such texts for Council approval. Other aspects of political work may be handled by the regular Political Committee, which consists of Political Counsellors or Advisers from national delegations.

When the Council meets at the level of Defence Ministers, or is dealing with defence matters and questions relating to defence strategy, other senior committees, such as the Executive Working Group, may be involved as the principal advisory bodies. If financial matters are on the Council's agenda, the Senior Resource Board, or the Civil or Military Budget Committees, or the Infrastructure Committee, depending on which body is appropriate, will be responsible to the Council for preparing its work. Depending on the topic under discussion, the respective senior committee with responsibility for the subject area assumes the leading role in preparing Council meetings and following up on Council decisions.

The Secretariat of the Council is provided by the relevant Divisions and Offices of the International Staff, and in particular by the Executive Secretariat, which has a coordinating role in ensuring that Council mandates are executed and its decisions recorded and disseminated. The Executive Secretary is also the Secretary of the Council.

The Defence Planning Committee

The Defence Planning Committee (DPC) is normally composed of Permanent Representatives but meets at the level of Defence Ministers at least twice a year, and deals with most defence matters and subjects related to collective defence planning. With the exception of France, all member countries are represented in this forum. The Defence Planning Committee provides guidance to NATO's military authorities and, within the area of its responsibilities, has the same functions and attributes and the same authority as the Council on matters within its competence.

The work of the Defence Planning Committee is prepared by a number of subordinate committees with specific responsibilities and in particular by the Defence Review Committee, which oversees the Force Planning Process within NATO and examines other issues relating to the Integrated Military Structure. Like the Council, the Defence Planning Committee looks to the senior committee with the relevant specific responsibility for the preparatory and follow-up work arising from its decisions.

The Nuclear Planning Group

The Defence Ministers of member countries which take part in NATO's Defence Planning Committee meet at regular intervals in the Nuclear Planning Group (NPG), where they discuss specific policy issues associated with nuclear forces. These discussions cover a broad range of nuclear policy matters, including the safety, security and survivability of nuclear weapons, communications and information systems, deployment issues and wider questions of common concern such as nuclear arms control and nuclear proliferation. The Alliance's nuclear policy is kept under review and decisions are taken jointly to modify or adapt it in the light of new developments and to update and adjust planning and consultation procedures.

The work of the Nuclear Planning Group is prepared by an NPG Staff Group composed of members of the national delegations of countries participating in the NPG. The Staff Group carries out detailed work on behalf of the NPG Permanent Representatives. It meets regularly once a week and at other times as necessary.

The NPG High Level Group (HLG) was established as a senior advisory body to the NPG on nuclear policy and planning issues. In 1998/1999, in addition to its original portfolio, the HLG took over the functions and responsibilities of the then Senior Level Weapons Protection Group (SLWPG) which was charged with overseeing nuclear weapons safety, security, and survivability matters. The HLG is chaired by the United States and is composed of national policy makers and experts from capitals. It meets several times a year to discuss aspects of NATO's nuclear policy, planning and force posture, and matters concerning the safety, security, and survivability of nuclear weapons.

CONSENSUS POLITICS AND JOINT DECISION-MAKING

Policy formulation and implementation, in an Alliance of independent sovereign countries, depends on all member governments being fully informed of each other's overall policies and intentions and the underlying considerations which give rise to them. This calls for regular political consultation, whenever possible during the policy-making stage of deliberations before national decisions have been taken.

Political consultation in NATO began as a systematic exercise when the Council first met in September 1949, shortly after the North Atlantic Treaty came into force. Since that time it has been strengthened and adapted to suit new developments. The principal forum for political consultation remains the Council. Its meetings take place with a minimum of formality and discussion is frank and direct. The Secretary General, by virtue of his Chairmanship, plays an essential part in its deliberations and acts as its principal representative and spokesman both in contacts with individual governments and in public affairs.

Consultation also takes place on a regular basis in other forums, all of which derive their authority from the Council: the Political Committee at senior and other levels, the Policy Coordination Group, Regional Expert Groups, Ad Hoc Political Working Groups, an Atlantic Policy Advisory Group and other special committees all have a direct role to play in facilitating political consultation between member governments. Like the Council, they are assisted by an International Staff responsible to the Secretary General of NATO and an International Military Staff responsible to its Director, and through him, responsible for supporting the activities of the Military Committee.

Political consultation among the members of the Alliance is not limited to events taking place within the NATO Treaty area. Increasingly, events outside the geographical area covered by the Treaty have implications for the Alliance and therefore feature on the agenda of the Council and subordinate committees. The consultative machinery of NATO is readily available and extensively used by the member nations in such circumstances, even if NATO as an Alliance may not be directly involved. By consulting together they are able to identify at an early stage areas where, in the interests of security and stability, coordinated action may be taken.

Neither is the need for consultation limited to political subjects. Wide-ranging consultation takes place in many other fields. The process is continuous and takes place on an informal as well as a formal basis with a minimum of delay or inconvenience, as a result of the collocation of national delegations to NATO within the same headquarters. Where necessary, it enables intensive work to be carried out at short notice on matters of particular importance or urgency with the full participation of representatives from all governments concerned.

Consultation within the Alliance takes many forms. At its most basic level it involves simply the exchange of information and opinions. At another level it covers the communication of actions or decisions which governments have already taken or may be about to take and which have a direct or indirect bearing on the interests of their allies. It may also involve providing advance warning of actions or decisions to be taken by governments in the future, in order to provide an opportunity for them to be endorsed or commented upon by others. It can encompass discussion with the aim of reaching a consensus on policies to be adopted or actions to be taken in parallel. And ultimately it is designed to enable member countries to arrive at mutually acceptable agreements on collective decisions or on action by the Alliance as a whole.

Regular consultations on relevant political issues also take place with Partner countries in the context of the Euro-Atlantic Partnership Council as well as with Russia, principally through the NATO-Russia Permanent Joint Council (PJC); with Ukraine through the NATO-Ukraine Commission; and with participants in NATO's Mediterranean Dialogue, through the Mediterranean Cooperation Group. The principles which guide consultations in these forums are modelled on those which have long formed the basis for consultations within the Alliance itself and are conducted with the same openness and spirit of cooperation. The role of each of these institutions is described in more detail in the linked sections. Finally, there are provisions for NATO consultations with any active participant in the Partnership for Peace, if that Partner perceives a direct threat to its territorial integrity, political independence, or security.

In making their joint decision-making process dependent on consensus and common consent, the members of the Alliance safeguard the role of each country's individual experience and outlook while at the same time availing themselves of the machinery and procedures which allow them jointly to act rapidly and decisively if circumstances require them to do so. The practice of exchanging information and consulting together on a daily basis ensures that governments can come together at short notice whenever necessary, often with prior knowledge of their respective preoccupations, in order to agree on common policies. If need be, efforts to reconcile differences between them will be made in order that joint actions may be backed by the full force of decisions to which all the member governments subscribe. Once taken, such decisions represent the common determination of all the countries involved to implement them in full. Decisions which may be politically difficult, or which face competing demands on resources, thus acquire added force and credibility.

All NATO Member countries participate fully in the political level of cooperation within the Alliance and are equally committed to the terms of the North Atlantic Treaty, not least to the reciprocal undertaking made in Article 5 which symbolises the indivisibility of their security - namely to consider an attack against one or more of them as an attack upon them all.

The manner in which the Alliance has evolved nevertheless ensures that variations in the requirements and policies of member countries can be taken into account in their positions within the Alliance. This flexibility manifests itself in a number of different ways. In some cases differences may be largely procedural and are accommodated without difficulty. Iceland, for example, has no military forces and is therefore represented in NATO military forums by a civilian if it so wishes. In other cases the distinctions may be of a more substantive nature. France, a founding member of the Alliance in 1949, withdrew from the Alliance's integrated military structure in 1966 while remaining a full member of its political structures. Spain joined the Alliance in 1982, but in accordance with a national referendum held in 1986 initially remained outside NATO's integrated military structure.

At the 1997 Madrid Summit, Spain announced its readiness to participate fully in the Alliance's emerging new command structure, once this had been agreed. In December 1997, an agreement was reached on a new command structure as a whole, and in particular on the type, number and location of military headquarters. In their end of year communiqués, NATO Foreign and Defence Ministers welcomed Spain's announcement that it would join the new military structure and take part in the new command structure which had just been agreed.

Distinctions between NATO member countries may also exist as a result of their geographical, political, military or constitutional situations. The participation of Norway and Denmark in NATO's military dispositions, for example, must comply with national legislation which does not allow nuclear weapons or foreign forces to be stationed on their national territory in peacetime. In another context, military arrangements organised on a regional basis may involve only the forces of those countries directly concerned or equipped to participate in the specific area in which the activity takes place. This applies, for example, to the forces contributed by nations to the ACE Mobile Force and to NATO's Standing Naval Forces.

CRISIS MANAGEMENT

The importance attached by NATO member countries to crisis management issues is reflected in the Strategic Concept published in 1999 which identifies crisis management as one of the Alliance's fundamental security tasks. It states that in order to enhance the security and stability of the Euro-Atlantic area, NATO stands ready, case-by-case and by consensus, in conformity with Article 7 of the Washington Treaty, to contribute to effective conflict prevention and to engage actively in crisis management, including crisis response operations. Maintaining an overall capability to manage crises successfully is an integral part of the Alliance's approach to preserving peace and reinforcing Euro-Atlantic security and stability.

The Alliance's crisis management policy has been adapted since the end of the Cold War to take account of the radically different nature of the risks which it now faces. It is based on three mutually reinforcing elements: dialogue; cooperation with other countries; and the maintenance of NATO's collective defence capability. Each of these is designed to ensure that crises affecting Euro-Atlantic security can be prevented or resolved peacefully.

Consultation among NATO member countries plays an essential role in crisis management and takes on particular significance in times of tension and crisis. In such circumstances rapid decision-making, based on consensus on the measures which need to be taken in the political, military and civil emergency fields, depends on immediate and continuous consultation between member governments. The principal NATO forums for the intensive consultation required in this context are the Council and the Defence Planning Committee, supported by the Policy Coordination Group, the Political

Committee, the Military Committee and the Senior Civil Emergency Planning Committee. Other NATO committees may also play a role when required.

The practices and procedures which are then involved form the Alliance's crisis management arrangements. Facilities, including communications, in support of the process are provided by the NATO Situation Centre, which operates on a permanent 24-hour basis. Exercises to test and develop crisis management procedures are held at regular intervals in conjunction with national capitals and NATO Strategic Commanders. Crisis management arrangements, procedures and facilities, as well as the preparation and conduct of crisis management exercises, are coordinated by the Council Operations and Exercise Committee (COEC), which also coordinates crisis management activities with Partner countries.

In view of the important contribution that Partner countries can make in this field, crisis management is also one of the agreed fields of activity in the Partnership for Peace Work Plan and is included in Individual Partnership Programmes. Activities include briefings and consultations, expert visits, crisis management courses, Partner participation in the annual NATO-wide crisis management exercise, and the provision of generic crisis management documents to Partners. Crisis management is also identified as an area for consultation and cooperation in the Founding Act on Mutual Relations, Cooperation and Security Between NATO and the Russian Federation, and in the Charter on a Distinctive Partnership between NATO and Ukraine (see Chapter 3). It is also an area of discussions in the context of the Mediterranean Dialogue.

THE DEFENCE DIMENSION

In the present political and strategic environment in Europe, the success of the Alliance's role in preserving peace and preventing war depends, even more than in the past, on the effectiveness of preventive diplomacy and on the successful management of crises affecting security. The political, economic, social and environmental elements of security and stability are thus taking on increasing importance.

Nonetheless, the defence dimension of the Alliance remains indispensable and contributes to the maintenance of stability in Europe as well as to crisis management. Reorganisation of Alliance forces since the end of the Cold War now enables NATO to react to a much wider range of contingencies. However, the maintenance of an adequate military capability and clear preparedness to act collectively in the common defence remain central to the Alliance's security objectives. Ultimately this capability, combined with political solidarity, is designed to prevent any attempt at coercion or intimidation, and to ensure that military aggression directed against the Alliance can never be perceived as an option with any prospect of success, thus guaranteeing the security and territorial integrity of member states and protecting Europe as a whole from the consequences which would ensue from any threat to the Alliance.

The framework for NATO's defence planning process is provided by the underlying principles which are the basis for collective security as a whole: political solidarity among member countries; the promotion of collaboration and strong ties between them in all fields where this serves their common and individual interests; the sharing of roles and responsibilities and recognition of mutual commitments; and a joint undertaking to maintain adequate military forces to support Alliance strategy and policy.

In determining the size and nature of their contribution to collective defence, member countries of NATO retain full sovereignty and independence of action. Nevertheless, the nature of NATO's defence structure requires that in reaching their individual decisions, member countries take into account the overall needs of the Alliance. They therefore follow agreed defence planning procedures which provide the methodology and machinery for determining the forces needed for the implementation of Alliance policies, for coordinating national defence plans and for establishing force planning goals which are in the interests of the Alliance as a whole[1]. The planning process takes many factors into account, including changing political circumstances, assessments provided by NATO's Military Commanders of the forces required to fulfil their tasks, technological developments, the importance of an equitable division of roles, risks and responsibilities within the Alliance, and the individual economic and financial capabilities of member countries. The process thus ensures that all relevant considerations are jointly examined to enable the best use to be made of collective national resources which are available for defence.

Close coordination between international civil and military staffs, NATO's military authorities, and governments is maintained through an annual exchange of information on national plans. This exchange of information enables each country's intentions to be compared with NATO's overall requirements and, if necessary, to be reconsidered in the light of new Ministerial political directives, modernisation requirements and changes in the roles and responsibilities of the forces themselves. All these aspects are kept under continual review and are scrutinised at each stage of the defence planning cycle.

As part of the adaptation of the Alliance, a review of the Alliance's defence planning process was carried out. Its conclusions were endorsed by Ministers in June 1997. A single, coherent and streamlined process is now in place which

---

1   France does not take part in the Force Planning.

will ensure that NATO continues to develop the forces and capabilities needed to conduct the full range of Alliance missions. This includes providing support for operations which might be led by the European Union in the context of the European Security and Defence Identity. Also in that context, the process enables support to be made available, within the Alliance, for all European Allies with respect to their planning relating to the conduct of EU-led operations.

Since 1991, the starting point for defence planning has been the Alliance's Strategic Concept setting out in broad terms Alliance objectives and the means for achieving them. The original Strategic Concept has been superseded by the Alliance's new Strategic Concept approved by NATO Heads of State at their Washington Summit meeting in April 1999. More detailed guidance is given by Defence Ministers every two years, in a document known as "Ministerial Guidance". This gives guidance on defence planning in general and force planning in particular. It addresses the political, economic, technological and military factors which could affect the development of forces and capabilities of Allies; and sets out the priorities and areas of concern to be addressed by the NATO Military Authorities in drawing up their force goals in the first instance, and secondly by nations in their own planning. It deals with planning for forces and capabilities required both for collective defence and for contingencies falling outside the scope of Article 5 of the Washington Treaty[2]. It also provides guidance, where appropriate, on cooperation with other organisations, and following the 1997 review of the defence planning process included political guidance developed by the Western European Union (WEU) defining the likely scope of European-led operations.

Specific planning targets for the armed forces of each member country are developed on the basis of Ministerial guidance. These targets, known as "Force Goals", generally cover a six-year period, but in certain cases look further into the future. Like the guidance provided by Defence Ministers, they are updated every two years.

Allied defence planning is reviewed annually and given direction by Ministers of Defence in an "Annual Defence Review". In response to a Defence Planning Questionnaire (DPQ) issued every year, governments of member countries prepare and submit to the Alliance their force plans and their defence spending plans for the five-year period covered by the review. The Annual Defence Review is designed to assess the contribution of member countries to

---

2   Article 5 of the North Atlantic Treaty deals primarily with deterrence against the use of force against members of the Alliance and embodies the principle that an attack against any one of them is considered as an attack against all. Alliance activities falling outside the scope of Article 5 are referred to collectively as "Non-Article 5 Operations".

the common defence in relation to their respective capabilities and constraints and in the context of the Force Goals addressed to them. The Review culminates in the compilation of a common NATO Force Plan that provides the basis for NATO defence planning over a five-year time frame.

National replies to the Defence Planning Questionnaire are examined simultaneously by the International Staff (IS) and the NATO Military Authorities. The International Staff prepares draft "Country chapters" for each country. These set out in detail any unresolved differences between the NATO Force Goals and the country plans, including the extent to which national plans are consistent with the requirements of EU-led operations. They describe whether countries have fulfilled, or expect to fulfil, existing force commitments undertaken for the current year. Explanations of any shortcomings are set out, and national efforts are assessed against the background of their capabilities and constraints. The draft Country chapters are supplemented by Major NATO Commanders' assessments, which focus on force capabilities in relation to their operational requirements and missions.

The draft Country chapters are considered in "multilateral examinations". These include a review of the extent to which countries have fulfilled force commitments undertaken for the current year. They are directed particularly towards reconciling possible differences between country force plans and NATO Force Goals or plans. They are also intended to assess the degree to which the plans of appropriate individual Allies could support the requirements of EU-led operations and contribute to the coordination of the defence planning of individual Allies.

In the light of the Country chapters and of an assessment by the Military Committee, a General Report is submitted to the Defence Planning Committee. It recommends a NATO five-year force plan for adoption by Defence Ministers, and examines the overall balance, feasibility and acceptability of the force plan. It also contains sections on national compliance with their force commitments for the current year, and an assessment on how far the overall objectives and specific guidance, laid down in Ministerial Guidance, including that relating to requirements for EU-led operations, have been met. As part of Alliance consultations, additional "out-of-cycle" consultation with Allies is necessary when a country is contemplating important changes to commitments and plans approved by Ministers in the Defence Review and Force Goal process. This also occurs when the timetable for national decisions prevents consideration of these changes in the next Defence Review.

NUCLEAR POLICY

Changes in NATO's nuclear strategy and force posture are concrete illustrations of the many positive steps which have been taken in order to adapt to the new security environment. Under the momentous security improvements which have been achieved since the end of the Cold War, the Alliance has been able to reduce radically its reliance on nuclear forces. Moreover, its strategy while remaining one of war prevention, is no longer dominated by the possibility of escalation involving nuclear weapons.

NATO's nuclear forces contribute to European peace and stability by underscoring the irrationality of a major war in the Euro-Atlantic region. They make the risks of aggression against NATO incalculable and unacceptable in a way that conventional forces alone cannot. They also create uncertainty for any country that might contemplate seeking political or military advantage through the threat or use of Nuclear, Biological or Chemical (NBC)[3] weapons against the Alliance. By promoting European stability, helping to discourage threats relating to the use of weapons of mass destruction, and contributing to deterrence against such use, NATO's nuclear posture serves the interests not only of the Allies, but also of its Partner countries and of Europe as a whole.

NATO's reduced reliance on nuclear forces has been manifested in major reductions in the forces themselves. In 1991 NATO decided to reduce the number of weapons which had been maintained for its sub-strategic[4] forces in Europe by over 85 percent compared to Cold War levels. In addition to the reductions of sub-strategic forces, the strategic forces available to the NATO Allies are also being reduced.

The only land-based nuclear weapons which NATO retains in Europe are bombs for dual-capable aircraft. These weapons have also been substantially reduced in number and are stored in a smaller number of locations in highly secure conditions. The readiness levels of dual-capable aircraft associated with them have been progressively reduced, and increased emphasis has been given to their conventional roles. None of NATO's nuclear weapons are targeted against any country.

---

3   The terms NBC (Nuclear, Biological and Chemical weapons) and WMD (Weapons of Mass Destruction) can be used interchangeably.

4   The terms "strategic" and "sub-strategic" have slightly different meanings in different countries. Strategic nuclear weapons are normally defined as weapons of "intercontinental" range (over 5 500 kilometres), but in some contexts these may also include intermediate-range ballistic missiles of lower ranges. The term "sub-strategic" nuclear weapons has been used in NATO documents since 1989 with reference to intermediate and short-range nuclear weapons and now refers primarily to air-delivered weapons for NATO's dual-capable aircraft and to a small number of United Kingdom Trident warheads in a new sub-strategic role (other sub-strategic nuclear weapons having been withdrawn from Europe).

The Allies have judged that the Alliance's requirements can be met, for the foreseeable future, by this "sub-strategic" force posture. NATO has also declared that enlarging the Alliance will not require a change in its current nuclear posture. NATO countries have no intention, no plan, and no reason to deploy nuclear weapons on the territory of new members, nor any need to change any aspect of NATO's nuclear posture or nuclear policy, and they do not foresee any future need to do so.

The collective security provided by NATO's nuclear posture is shared among all members of the Alliance, providing reassurance to any member that might otherwise feel vulnerable. The presence of US nuclear forces based in Europe and committed to NATO provides an essential political and military link between the European and North American members of the Alliance. At the same time, the participation of non-nuclear countries in the Alliance nuclear posture demonstrates Alliance solidarity, the common commitment of its member countries to maintaining their security, and the widespread sharing among them of burdens and risks.

Political oversight of NATO's nuclear posture is also shared between member nations. NATO's Nuclear Planning Group provides a forum in which the Defence Ministers of nuclear and non-nuclear Allies alike participate in the development of the Alliance's nuclear policy and in decisions on NATO's nuclear posture.

Further information on the role of NATO's Nuclear Forces in the new security environment and on reductions in this field are given in Chapter 2.

THE ECONOMIC SPHERE

The basis for economic cooperation within the Alliance is Article 2 of the North Atlantic Treaty, which states that member countries "will seek to eliminate conflict in their international economic policies and will encourage economic collaboration between any or all of them". NATO's Economic Committee, which was established to promote cooperation in this field, is the only Alliance forum concerned exclusively with consultations on economic developments with a direct bearing on security policy. Analyses and joint assessments of security-related economic developments are key ingredients in the coordination of defence planning within the Alliance. They cover matters such as comparisons of military spending, developments within the defence industry, the availability of resources for the implementation of defence plans, and securing "value for money" in the defence sector of national economies.

The premise on which economic cooperation within the Alliance is founded is that political cooperation and economic conflict are irreconcilable.

There must therefore be a genuine commitment among the members to work together in the economic as well as in the political field, and a readiness to consult on questions of common concern based on the recognition of common interests.

The member countries recognise that in many respects the purposes and principles of Article 2 of the Treaty are pursued and implemented by other organisations and international fora specifically concerned with economic cooperation. NATO therefore avoids duplication of work carried out elsewhere but reinforces collaboration between its members whenever economic issues of special interest to the Alliance are involved. This applies particularly to those which have security and defence implications. The Alliance therefore acts as a forum in which different and interrelated aspects of political, military and economic questions can be examined. It also provides the means whereby specific action in the economic field can be initiated to safeguard common Alliance interests.

In the context of the Alliance's overall security interests and in line with its evolving priorities, a wide range of economic issues have to be addressed. These include the study of defence expenditure and budgetary trends; the restructuring of defence industries; trends in defence industrial employment; and defence spending projections, their affordability and their implications for the size and structure of the armed forces.

In accordance with agreed Work Plans, activities conducted in the economic sphere of NATO cooperation with Partner Countries have concentrated on security aspects of economic developments, including defence budgets and defence expenditures and their relationship with the economy and the restructuring of defence industries. Defence economic issues also feature prominently in the Action Plan of the Euro-Atlantic Partnership Council for 2000-2002. The Action Plan specifically addresses the following topics:

- resource management in defence spending;
- transparency in defence planning and budgeting;
- transition from conscript to professional armies;
- management of former military sites;
- the restructuring of defence industries, including privatisation;
- regional matters.

A fruitful dialogue between Allied and Partner Countries has already taken place in the spheres of defence budgeting, important topics such as defence budget formulation, cost-benefit analysis of defence down-sizing, planning and management of national defence programmes, legislative oversight of defence budgets, economic aspects of conscript versus professional armies, and the role of the private sector in defence.

Economic aspects of defence budgeting and defence expenditures will remain core subjects in the context of NATO's cooperation with Partner countries. In particular, efforts made in NATO countries to apply economic yardsticks to the management of defence budgets are likely to be particularly relevant. Examples of areas in which the experience of NATO countries is being made available include:

- new management principles, drawing on experiences in the commercial sector, directed towards the establishment of defence agencies responsible for ensuring reliable delivery of goods and services within the constraints of a given budget;

- the extension of competition to defence services, in the form of contracting out, market-testing, and external financing;

- the improvement of cost-limitation methods, and the reconsideration of priorities in the context of a reduction of available resources.

Economic cooperation is also important in the context of the restructuring of defence industries. The conversion of defence industries, as well as other issues such as the retraining of former military personnel, represent some of the areas of mutual interest for consultation and cooperation between NATO and Russia. They also represent areas for consultation and cooperation between NATO and Ukraine.

Unlike specialised financial institutions, NATO does not have the mandate or resources to fund the development of specific economic cooperation programmes. However, the Alliance has endeavoured to promote dialogue and exchange of experience with experts from Partner countries involved in managing the restructuring process.

In pursuing this type of cooperation, it has become increasingly clear that there is no single model for restructuring of defence industries. Although there are common problems and challenges, it is in the interest of each country to pursue its own specific policies, taking into account its political, social and economic environment. In order to better understand this dualism and to draw appropriate joint lessons, special emphasis is placed on the analysis of practical experiences of defence restructuring. This part of the work includes individual case studies and draws on the experiences of a broad range of relevant agencies, national administrations, the management side of private and public companies, and local and regional authorities. It also allows the sectorial and regional dimensions of defence restructuring to be taken into account.

Cooperation in this area will continue to be centred on practical aspects of the restructuring and adaptation of the defence industry sector, taking into account regional differences. In general terms, developments in the demand side of the defence market, as well as the response of the supply side through industrial restructuring, and the economic consequences of the latter, need to be carefully monitored. Moreover, defence industries are losing their singularity and are being increasingly obliged to bow to market forces. It is therefore also crucial to analyse effects on the economy of the privatisation of defence companies.

Security aspects of economic developments are discussed at an annual NATO Economics Colloquium and other seminars and workshops. The Economics Colloquium is attended by experts from business, universities and national and international administrations, and provides a framework for an intensive exchange of ideas and experiences in the economic sphere. Themes addressed at recent Economic Colloquia have included the social and human dimensions of economic developments and reforms in Cooperation Partner countries; the status of such reforms, their implications for security and the opportunities and constraints associated with them; and privatisation in Cooperation Partner countries[5].

PUBLIC INFORMATION

Responsibility for explaining national defence and security policy and each member country's role within the Alliance rests with the individual member governments. The choice of methods to be adopted and resources to be devoted to the task of informing their publics about the policies and objectives of NATO varies from country to country and is also a matter for each member nation to decide. All NATO governments recognise both the democratic right of their peoples to be informed about the international structures which provide the basis for their security, and the importance of maintaining public understanding and support for their countries' security policies.

The role of NATO's Office of Information and Press is to complement the public information activities undertaken within each country, providing whatever assistance may be required; to manage the Organisation's day-to-day relations with the press and media; and to provide information to respond to the interest in the Alliance from non-member nations. A large part of that interest stems from the Alliance's cooperation and partnership with the member countries of

---

5   The May 2001 Economics Colloquium held in Bucharest addressed the interrelationship between Regional Economic Cooperation, Security and Stability. The proceedings of the annual Colloquia are published annually in book form and may be obtained from the NATO Information and Press (Distribution Unit). The proceedings are also published on Internet (http://www.nato.int).

the Euro-Atlantic Partnership Council (EAPC), from its special bilateral relationship with Russia and its partnership with Ukraine, and from its developing Mediterranean Dialogue.

In addition, the focus of world public attention on Bosnia and Herzegovina and on Kosovo has called for a corresponding increase in information programmes to explain NATO's role in bringing the conflicts in the former Yugoslavia to an end and creating the conditions for future stability in the region. Other developments in the Alliance, including the implementation of the Partnership for Peace initiative, the restructuring of NATO military forces and the internal transformation of the Alliance, the strengthening of the European identity within the Alliance as well as the external transformation of NATO, have all contributed to the growth of public interest and the need for adequate information to be provided to respond to it.

With the opening up of the Alliance to new members, and specifically the accession of three new member countries, a further significant dimension has been added to the information challenge. In the Czech Republic, Hungary and Poland, the individual governments face a continuing need to explain the implications of membership of NATO to their publics. In each of their countries, knowledge of NATO, of civil-military relations within the Alliance, and of Alliance decision-making procedures, has been limited and sometimes adversely influenced by earlier negative public perceptions, entrenched attitudes, and lack of reliable information. The NATO Office of Information and Press therefore has a particular obligation to assist each of the three governments and to respond to public interest from their respective countries within the means at its disposal. In addition, there has been an increased focus on security issues and on NATO in each of the nine countries participating in the Membership Action Plan (MAP) approved at the Washington Summit Meeting in April 1999 (see Chapter 3). NATO's information activities are therefore being adapted to enable an adequate response to be made to the requirement for information on the Alliance to be made more widely available in each of these countries.

The overall objectives of the Alliance's press and information policies are to contribute to public knowledge of the facts relating to security and to promote public involvement in a well informed and constructive debate on the security issues of the day as well as the objectives of future policy. Each of the action plans and work programmes drawn up to implement the goals of the principal initiatives taken by NATO countries in recent years contain specific sections addressing information requirements for meeting these objectives. This applies to the EAPC Action Plan adopted by EAPC Foreign Ministers, to the work programmes of the NATO-Russia Permanent Joint Council and of the NATO-Ukraine Commission, and to the work envisaged in the context of NATO's Mediterranean Dialogue.

The programmes administered under the Information budget of the NATO Headquarters consist of activities which take place within the Headquarters itself; external events administered by the Office of Information and Press at NATO; activities which take place under the auspices of governmental or non-governmental organisations outside the confines of the NATO Headquarters which may be supported by conceptual, practical or financial contributions from the Office of Information and Press; and events which are organised by other external agencies with direct or indirect assistance from NATO. The principal activities under each of these headings are described below.

In addition to NATO itself, a number of other organisations and agencies play an important role in providing access to information about Alliance related topics, disseminating written materials, exploiting the advantages of electronic communications through the Internet, and responding to public inquiries. The list of these additional bodies is extensive and includes national and multinational organisations. The following should be mentioned in particular:

• Public information offices and press offices of NATO member country governments and of governments in EAPC and Partner countries.

• Embassies of NATO member countries serving on a rotational basis as Contact Point Embassies in the capitals of Partner countries.

• National parliaments and the NATO Parliamentary Assembly (NPA), an international parliamentary forum created to promote Alliance goals and policies at the parliamentary level. The NPA has its headquarters in Brussels.

• National Atlantic Councils, Atlantic Committees or Atlantic Associations in Member and Partner countries, established as educational foundations dedicated to improving knowledge and understanding of Alliance goals and policies.

• Institutes and foundations established on a national or international basis in different countries throughout the Euro-Atlantic area, for the purposes of promoting policy research and academic input into the debate on security issues.

• Public Information Offices of the Alliance's military headquarters located in different member countries.

• Educational and training establishments of the Alliance such as the NATO Defense College in Rome, the NATO (SHAPE) School in Oberammergau, independent institutions such as the Marshall Centre in Oberammergau, and national defence establishments and colleges.

- International structures grouping together national chapters of their organisations, such as the Atlantic Treaty Association (ATA), bringing together the Atlantic Committees, Councils and Associations of Member and Partner countries; and the Interallied Confederation of Reserve Officers (CIOR), which incorporates Reserve Officer associations throughout the Alliance. The ATA has a small secretariat in Paris and a contact address in Brussels. The CIOR similarly has a Liaison Office at the NATO Headquarters in Brussels.

Further information on these organisations is given in Chapter 16.

The Office of Information and Press liaises directly with the Public Information Adviser's office in the International Military Staff with regard to information concerning the activities of the Military Committee.

The Office of Information and Press maintains a small regional information office in Reykjavik, Iceland. With this exception, there are no regional information offices in NATO member countries. Military headquarters belonging to the Alliance's integrated military structure, which are located in different parts of the Alliance, as well as a number of NATO agencies and organisations located outside the Brussels Headquarters, constitute an important part of the Alliance's identity and represent additional points of contact and sources of information.

As part of its extensive programme of cooperation with Partner countries, and specifically NATO's cooperative relationships with Russia and Ukraine, the North Atlantic Council has undertaken steps to improve access to information relating to the Alliance in these countries. In 1995, it approved the appointment of an Information Officer to be located in Moscow, working within the French Embassy, which was then the Contact Point Embassy for NATO in Russia.

This small information office was transferred to the German Embassy in 1996 when Germany took over the Contact Point role. Germany subsequently seconded a German Colonel of this office to assist NATO in developing information contacts and activities with the Russian armed forces.

In January 1998 an independent NATO Documentation Centre, housed within the premises of the Russian Institute for Scientific Information for the Social Sciences (INION), was opened in Moscow. Supported by NATO, the Centre has provided access to publications and documents relating to security issues and periodically has also published a bulletin addressed to academic and other interested audiences.

The activities of the Information Office and Documentation Centre were curtailed when Russia suspended cooperation with NATO, following the military action taken by the Alliance to end the crisis in Kosovo. During a visit to

Moscow by NATO Secretary General, Lord Robertson, in February 2000, agreement was reached which the NATO Allies hope will lead to a resumption of the full range of cooperation agreed in the NATO-Russia Founding Act. In February 2001, the NATO Secretary General again visited Moscow and formally inaugurated a NATO Information Office located in independent premises in the city centre.

A NATO Information and Documentation Centre opened in Kyiv in 1996. Staffed and financed by the Office of Information and Press, the Centre is accommodated within the Ukrainian Institute of International Affairs and provides access to documentation as well as providing a link to other information activities, including visits to NATO and NATO-sponsored seminars.

The addresses of the various offices and information centres referred to in this section are listed at the end of the Handbook, together with details of the NATO Integrated Data Service, which provides worldwide electronic access to NATO-related information.

The communications tools used by the NATO Office of Information and Press both directly and in support of the above outlets and intermediaries draw on conventional oral and written forms of providing information and promoting dialogue. The Office administers a major programme of visits, bringing up to 20 000 opinion formers annually to the political headquarters of the Alliance, for briefings and discussions with experts from NATO's International Staff, International Military Staff and National Delegations on all aspects of the Alliance's work and policies.

The Office of Information and Press issues a number of publications ranging from compilations of official texts and declarations to periodical and non-periodical publications which seek to contribute to an informed public debate on relevant aspects of security policy.

Official texts issued by the Alliance, normally in the form of communiqués and press statements, are formally negotiated documents articulating the agreed policy orientation of member countries on specific subjects or on the collectivity of policy issues reviewed periodically throughout the year. They constitute the Alliance's public archive and allow the process of policy-making and the evolution of decisions to be traced to the political events or circumstances to which they relate. All such texts are published in the two official languages of the Alliance and often in other languages.

In addition to these documents, the Office of Information and Press assists in the dissemination of statements issued by the Secretary General of NATO, who is the Organisation's principal spokesman, and of the texts of speeches by the Secretary General and other senior officials. These documents also assist in explaining policy and giving insights into the objectives and rationale which lie behind it.

Under the authority of the Secretary General, the Information Office publishes a periodical called the NATO Review and a range of handbooks, brochures, newsletters and other reference materials which can contribute to public knowledge and understanding. These items are printed, according to resources and requirements, in all the languages used in NATO countries in addition to the official languages, as well as in many Partner country languages.

Dissemination of written materials also relies increasingly on electronic media. Most of NATO public documentation and information materials are issued through the NATO Integrated Data Service. Details are given in "Sources of Further Information" (Appendix 2).

NATO has a separate Science Programme (described in Chapter 8), which publishes a newsletter and has its own series of scientific publications which are issued separately by specialised publishers in accordance with agreed commercial arrangements.

The personnel resources of the Office of Information and Press include a NATO Country Relations Section consisting of national Liaison Officers responsible for administering information programmes directed towards their own member countries. Such programmes consist of arranging visits to NATO, organising conferences and seminars at different locations throughout the Alliance, and assisting parliamentarians, academics, journalists and other relevant professional groupings in their countries in obtaining access to the publicly available information they require. An Outreach and Partner Relations Section fulfils a similar role in disseminating information in many of NATO's Partner countries. National Liaison Officers for NATO countries also contribute to this work, acting as programme officers for the Partner countries for which their national governments have the current "Contact Point" role through their national embassies in the different Partner countries.

Information programmes for individual nations may include the provision of conceptual, practical and limited financial support for relevant publishing activities of non-governmental organisations in Member and Partner countries. Similar assistance may also be given to the governments of Partner countries in preparing and issuing publications designed to inform public opinion about NATO-related issues.

In the academic field, NATO's information activities include the award of an annual Manfred Wörner Fellowship, named after the late former Secretary General of NATO, and the administration of a series of NATO-EAPC Fellowships open to scholars in NATO and Partner countries alike. The Fellowships, which consist of grants to assist recipients with travel and research costs, are awarded annually, on a competitive basis, on the recommendations of an independent jury, for the purpose of carrying out studies in subject areas generally relating to NATO policy areas and to the current political agenda of the Alliance.

Under the academic affairs programme, support is also given periodically to multinational conferences addressing major topics and themes in the security field.

The interest of the public in NATO policies and access to information in this sphere is manifested both directly and through the press and media coverage given to NATO-related developments and events. A central part of the work of the Office of Information and Press is therefore related to press activities and to the support provided by the NATO Press Service for accredited and other media representatives.

Press briefings and interviews with senior officials, background briefings, access to photographs, sound and video facilities and electronic transmission services all form part of the arrangements called for to meet the needs of the world's media. Major events or developments in the Alliance, such as Summit Meetings, may attract upwards of a thousand journalists to the Headquarters, for whom adequate provision must be made. Similar resources are called for at major events taking place away from the Headquarters, for example during Ministerial or Summit meetings held abroad. Support for journalists is provided by both the Press and Information Services within the Office of Information and Press, the focus of the Press Service being directed towards the immediate or short-term requirements, while the Information Office provides access to a wide range of background information on which media representatives can draw over a longer time frame.

The Press Spokesman and Press Service work in close daily contact with the Office of the Secretary General and support the Secretary General in his media and press contacts. The Press Service is also responsible for arranging contacts between other senior officials and the media and for the official accreditation of journalists attending NATO press events. Summaries and reviews of the international press and press agency reports are prepared by the Press Service on a daily basis for the benefit of the International Staffs, National Delegations, Diplomatic Missions and Liaison Officials working within the headquarters building. Information Liaison Officers and Press Office staff also prepare reviews of the national press in NATO and Partner countries for the use of the Secretary General and assist in the preparation of his official visits to these countries.

The Office of Information and Press also manages the NATO Headquarters Library serving the national and international staffs working within the Headquarters.

CHAPTER 8

PROGRAMMES AND ACTIVITIES

Consumer Logistics

Key Logistic Functions

Consumer Logistics and Peace Support Operations

Production and Logistics Organisations

Armaments Cooperation, Planning and Standardisation

Communications and Information Systems

Civil/Military Coordination of Air Traffic Management

Air Defence

Civil Emergency Planning

Scientific Cooperation

Environment and Society

PROGRAMMES AND ACTIVITIES

CONSUMER LOGISTICS[1]

The term "logistics" is used to mean different things in different contexts. There are also differences in the use of the term by NATO nations and in the categories of support for military operations which are regarded as being components of logistics. The NATO definition of logistics refers to *"the science of planning and carrying out the movement and maintenance of forces"*. In its most comprehensive sense, the term refers to aspects of military operations, which deal with the following spheres:

- Design and development, acquisition, storage, transport, distribution, maintenance, evacuation and disposition of materiel.

- Transport of personnel.

- Acquisition, construction, maintenance, operation and disposition of facilities.

- Acquisition or provision of services.

- Medical and Health Service Support.

The above categories inevitably involve a very wide range of services and responsibilities. In NATO, these are subdivided, from a decision-making as well as from an organisational point of view, into the following sectors:

- Production or acquisition aspects of logistics, which include planning, design development and procurement of equipment. These are primarily a national responsibility and are handled nationally. Cooperation and coordination within NATO nevertheless takes place in numerous spheres, largely under the auspices of the Conference of National Armament Directors (CNAD) and its subordinate bodies. Organisationally, production or acquisition aspects of logistics within NATO are principally the responsibility of the Defence Support Division of the International Staff on the civilian side and of the Armaments Branch, Logistics, Armaments and Resources Division of the International Military Staff on the military side.

- Consumer or operational aspects of logistics, which are generally understood as supply and support functions of forces. These are the

---

1   Many of the programmes and activities referred to in this section are implemented by organisations and agencies established by the North Atlantic Council or the NATO Military Committee to undertake specific tasks. Details are given in Chapter 14.

subject of the first part of this section, and fall mainly under the responsibility of the Senior NATO Logisticians' Conference (SNLC) and the NATO Pipeline Committee. The Committee of the Chiefs of Military Medical Services in NATO (COMEDS), NATO's senior military medical advisory body, has responsibility for advising the Military Committee on medical matters. From an organisational point of view, responsibility for consumer or operational aspects of logistics on the civilian side lies with the Security Investment, Logistics and Civil Emergency Planning Division of the International Staff. On the military side, they are the responsibility of the Logistics Branch, Logistics, Armaments and Resources Division of the International Military Staff.

Logistic Support for the Alliance's Strategic Concept

The Alliance's Strategic Concept, approved by NATO Heads of State and Government in April 1999, emphasises the mobile and multinational character of NATO forces and the need for flexible Alliance logistics to support them. The Senior NATO Logisticians' Conference recognised that the provision of logistic support, though fundamentally a national responsibility, also needs collective responsibility, improved coordination, cooperation and enhanced multinationality if this flexibility is to be achieved. It responded to the introduction of the new strategic concept by undertaking an analysis of its implications for logistic principles and policies. The importance of this topic is also emphasised in the Defence Capabilities Initiative launched at the Washington Summit in April 1999 (see Chapter 2). A Policy for Cooperation in Logistics is in the final stages of development and will shortly be considered by the North Atlantic Council. A NATO Concept for Cooperation in Logistics is also currently being developed.

Logistics Principles and Policies

New logistics principles and policies were endorsed by the Defence Planning Committee in 1992 in a document known as MC 319. These principles and policies have been thoroughly reviewed in the light of the practical experiences gained from NATO-led peacekeeping operations. A revised version was endorsed by the Council in 1997 (MC 319/1). Its principles and policies apply to peace, crisis and conflict situations, and include operations under Article 5 of the North Atlantic Treaty as well as "non-Article 5" operations[2]. They also apply to operations within the framework of the Combined Joint Task

---

2   Article 5 of the North Atlantic Treaty deals primarily with deterrence against the use of force against members of the Alliance and embodies the principle that an attack against any one of them is considered as an attack against all. Alliance activities falling outside the scope of Article 5 are referred to collectively as "Non-Article 5 Operations".

Force concept and for operations involving non-NATO nations in NATO-led operations.

These general principles have served as the springboard for the subsequent development of more specific principles and policies relating to functional areas of logistics, such as medical support (MC 326/1), host nation support (MC 334/1), and movement and transportation (MC 336/1).

Key Principles

Responsibility

Member nations and NATO authorities have a collective responsibility for logistic support of NATO's multinational operations. Each NATO military commander establishes logistic requirements and coordinates logistic planning and support within his area of responsibility.

Provision

Nations must ensure, individually or through cooperative arrangements, the provision of logistic resources to support the forces allocated to NATO during peace, crisis or conflict.

Authority

The NATO military commanders at the appropriate levels need to have sufficient authority over the logistic assets needed to enable them to employ and sustain their forces in the most effective manner. The same applies to non-NATO commanders of multinational forces participating in a NATO-led operation.

Cooperation and Coordination

Cooperation and coordination among the nations and NATO authorities is essential. Moreover, logistic cooperation between the civilian and military sectors within and between nations must make the best use of limited resources. Cooperative arrangements and mutual assistance among nations in the provision and the use of logistic resources can therefore ease the individual burden on each nation.

In considering the scope for developing different forms of cooperation in the field of consumer logistics in order to maximise such benefits, integrated multinational logistics support, role specialisation, common-funding of resources, and the application of the "lead-nation" principle are all investigated. The potential role of NATO Agencies such as the NATO Maintenance and Supply Agency (NAMSA) is also considered if it is likely to offer cost-effective solutions.

The need for coordination in the field of logistic support occurs at numerous levels and may not be confined to NATO itself. For "non-Article 5" operations, cooperation may need to be extended to non-NATO nations and where appropriate to the United Nations, the Western European Union, the Organisation for Security and Cooperation in Europe, the International Committee of the Red Cross and other relevant organisations.

Cooperative Logistics

The aim of cooperation in logistics is to enhance the overall logistics posture of the Alliance by maximising the effectiveness of logistics support to NATO and NATO-led or supported multinational operations; and by improving efficiency and achieving cost savings through economies of scale and elimination of duplication of efforts in peacetime, crisis and conflict.

The major principles governing cooperation in logistics in NATO are: primacy of operational requirements; collective responsibility; efficiency; and visibility and transparency.

The development of cooperative logistics arrangements in NATO is facilitated by a number of production and logistics agencies which have been created for this purpose. Foremost among these agencies is NAMSA - the NATO Maintenance and Supply Agency. The scope for effective cooperative logistics is enhanced by the use of modern techniques for the management and procurement of materiel. One example is a concept developed by NAMSA known as SHARE (Stock Holding and Asset Requirements Exchange). As its name implies, this is an arrangement which facilitates the sharing or exchange of stock holdings among users by providing an effective link between their specific needs on the one hand, and the availability of the corresponding assets on the other.

Multinational Logistics

The challenges facing the Alliance in the future, including limitations on resources, underscore the necessity of increased cooperation and multinationality in logistic support. Both the need to carry out operations (such as peace support) in locations where the logistics support provided by the normal national infrastructure is not available, and the need to integrate non-NATO military forces and their logistic support, underline the importance of a multinational joint logistics structure. This has to cover logistic requirements in the field of transportation, engineering and supply, as well as medical capabilities.

Multinational logistics is also an important force multiplier that optimises individual national logistic support efforts. It involves bilateral or multilateral arrangements which enhance the cost-effectiveness of individual national logistic support activities as well as their efficiency. Such arrangements can contribute significantly to the success of both the planning and the implementation aspects of logistic operations. A number of concepts and initiatives are being used to bring about increased multinationality in this field, including role specialisation and the lead nation concept, Multinational Integrated Logistics Units and Multinational Integrated Medical Units, Host Nation and Third Party Support, and the development of a Multinational Joint Logistic Centre.

KEY LOGISTIC FUNCTIONS

Mobility

Efficient and timely movement of forces is a pre-requisite for all military operations. Ensuring the strategic mobility of troops and materiel by providing adequate lift, transport facilities, equipment, and infrastructure is normally a major operational requirement. It includes the possible use of civilian resources and may involve the deployment, staging, and onward movement of large amounts of materiel and equipment. Planning and evaluation of capacity and capabilities can therefore be decisive in ensuring that varying political and military requirements can be met. The focal point for questions relating to strategic mobility in NATO is the Movement and Transportation Advisory Group (MAG), a sub-group of the Senior NATO Logisticians' Conference (SNLC). This body was created to foster cooperative approaches to the management side of movement, transportation and mobility matters between military and civilian agencies and between NATO and member nations.

Host Nation Support

Host nation support means civil and military assistance rendered in peace, emergencies, crisis and conflict by a Host Nation to Allied Forces and organisations which are located on, operating in or in transit through the Host Nation's territory. Arrangements concluded between the appropriate authorities of Host Nations and the "Sending Nations" and/or NATO form the basis of such assistance.

Host Nation support is crucial to the sustainability of all types and categories of forces. Bilateral or multilateral agreements which take into account NATO's operational requirements contribute to the protection of the forces as well as providing the required logistic support and infrastructure for their reception, movement and employment.

The flexibility needed by multinational forces calls for the involvement of NATO military commanders in formulating requirements for Host Nation support, in negotiating Memoranda of Understanding on behalf of NATO and in coordinating the development of the relevant Host Nation Support agreements. Moreover the increasingly varied nature of deployment options means that the planning of Host Nation support arrangements now has to be based on a more generic approach than in the past.

Medical Support

Medical services make a major contribution to military operations through the prevention of disease, the rapid evacuation and treatment of the sick, injured and wounded, and their early return to duty. Medical capabilities in an area where forces are deployed need to be commensurate with the force strength and their risk of exposure to sickness or injury. Medical support capabilities also need to be in place and operational prior to the start of military operations. The Committee of the Chiefs of Military Medical Services in NATO advises the Military Committee and provides the focus for cooperation in this field. Civil-military coordination is provided by a Joint Medical Committee (JMC).

Logistics Interoperability and Standardisation

Operational interoperability directly influences the combat effectiveness of NATO forces, particularly those involving multinational formations. Standardisation of equipment, supplies and procedures is thus an overall force multiplier which has to be taken into account in the design and production of systems and equipment. The minimum objectives needed to obtain combat effectiveness are interoperability of the principal equipment, interchangeability of supplies and commonality of procedures. These requirements have a direct bearing on logistic support for standardised equipment. Sufficient flexibility also has to be provided in order to facilitate the participation of non-NATO nations in NATO-led operations.

Consumer Logistics and Partnership for Peace

Most consumer logistic activities in the Partnership Work Programme and Individual Partnership Programmes and in nationally-approved bilateral programmes come into the following categories:

- team visits to the Partner country to consider the scope of possible cooperation on logistic issues and the organisation of logistic courses;

- information exchange, expert advice, technical assistance, logistic courses, logistic input into peacekeeping courses, and logistic exercises;

- formal contacts, such as staff talks, seminars and workshops;

- harmonisation and standardisation of concepts, policies, materiel, procedures and other aspects of logistic structures and systems.

The above activities are all supported by meetings of the principal NATO forums dealing with the participation of Partner countries. This applies, for example, to the Senior NATO Logisticians' Conference, the Movement and Transportation Advisory Group, the NATO Pipeline Committee and the Committee of the Chiefs of Military Medical Services in NATO, all of which meet with Partner countries on a regular basis. Further details relating to the above can be found in Chapter 14.

Logistics Courses for Partners

A NATO Logistics Course takes place three times a year, open to participants from both NATO and Partner countries. Various other courses are offered by NATO and by Partner nations relating to NATO logistics, UN and NATO peacekeeping, medical planning, participation in a Multinational Joint Logistic Centre, and civil-military cooperation in the field of Civil Emergency Planning. In the medical field, a PfP Medical Planner's Course has become an integral part of the educational programme at the NATO SHAPE School. 34 students from 17 nations attended the course in April 2000 and there are plans to increase this to 80 students per course. The class content is continually being modified by lessons learned in NATO-led operations in the Balkans.

Other related activities include Host Nation Support Seminars for Partners, designed to introduce civil and military staff officers from Partner nations to the host nation concept and to NATO planning procedures and arrangements in this field. They also provide an opportunity for participants to address regional matters, especially with regard to host nation support for the nations contributing forces to NATO-led operations in Bosnia and Herzegovina and Kosovo.

Exercise Cooperative Support

This is an annual exercise designed to introduce Partner nations to the Alliance's concept for the logistic support of multinational operations. Initially limited to maritime operations only, the exercise now involves land, air and maritime activities with the aim of familiarising participants with the full spectrum of multiservice logistic support.

Technical Support to PfP Countries

The NATO Maintenance and Supply Agency (NAMSA) is authorised to render technical assistance, on a reimbursable basis, to Partnership for Peace countries. Initially consultative in nature, such assistance will involve logistics management and operations in the longer term.

In addition to these multinational activities, there are extensive bilateral logistic contacts between individual NATO and Partnership nations.

CONSUMER LOGISTICS AND PEACE SUPPORT OPERATIONS

The monitoring and enforcement operations undertaken by NATO in support of United Nations peacekeeping initiatives in Bosnia and Herzegovina as well as in Kosovo highlighted the importance of consumer logistics in relation to Crisis Response Operations. The demands of future multinational Alliance operations, possibly involving non-NATO nations, also point to the need for the multinational management of logistic support based on agreed logistics principles and policies. The likely benefits include a reduction in the degree of logistic support that individual nations need to provide, improved cost-effectiveness, better coordination, increased interoperability and greater flexibility.

PRODUCTION AND LOGISTICS ORGANISATIONS

The North Atlantic Council has created a number of NATO Production and Logistics Organisations (NPLOs) to carry out specific tasks (see Chapter 14). Those dealing specifically with consumer logistics are the NATO Maintenance and Supply Organisation (NAMSO) and the Central Europe Pipeline Management Organisation (CEPMO).

Further information on consumer logistics within NATO can be found in the "NATO Logistics Handbook", issued by the secretariat of the Senior NATO Logisticians' Conference and available from Logistics (IS Element), SILCEP Division, NATO, 1110 Brussels. The handbook is not a formally agreed document but has proved to be a useful guide to the broad spectrum of issues covered by the term "logistics".

ARMAMENTS COOPERATION, PLANNING AND STANDARDISATION

Armaments Cooperation

Cooperation between NATO countries in the armaments field is the responsibility of the Conference of National Armaments Directors (CNAD), which meets on a regular basis to consider political, economic and technical aspects of the development and procurement of equipment for NATO forces. Army, Air Force and Naval Armaments Groups support the work of the Conference and are responsible to it in their respective fields. A Research and Technology Board, which is an integrated NATO body responsible for defence research and technological development, provides advice and assistance to the CNAD and to the Military Committee. It conducts a programme of collaborative activities across a broad range of defence research and technology issues. Assistance on industrial matters is provided by a NATO Industrial Advisory Group (NIAG), which enables the CNAD to benefit from industry's advice on how to foster government-to-industry and industry-to-industry cooperation and assists the Conference in exploring opportunities for international collaboration. Other groups under the Conference, formerly known as Cadre Groups and renamed "CNAD Partnership Groups", are active in fields such as defence procurement policy and acquisition practices, codification, quality assurance, test and safety criteria for ammunition, and materiel standardisation.

Within the above structure, working groups and ad hoc groups are established to promote cooperation in specific fields. The overall structure enables member countries to select the equipment and research projects in which they wish to participate. At the same time, it facilitates exchange of information on national equipment programmes and on technical and logistics matters where cooperation can be of benefit to individual nations and to NATO as a whole.

In 1993, the North Atlantic Council approved revised policies, structures and procedures for NATO armaments cooperation. These were designed to strengthen cooperative activities in the defence equipment field; to streamline the overall CNAD committee structure in order to make it more effective and efficient; and to direct the work of the CNAD towards the following key areas:

- harmonisation of military requirements on an Alliance-wide basis;

- promotion of essential battlefield interoperability;

- pursuit of cooperative opportunities identified by the CNAD and the promotion of improved transatlantic cooperation;

- the development of critical defence technologies, including expanded technology sharing.

In 1994, the CNAD agreed on a series of practical cooperation measures with the Western European Armaments Group (WEAG)[3], providing a means of expanding the dialogue on transatlantic armaments issues between European and North American allies.

Armaments Planning

In 1989 the North Atlantic Council approved the establishment of a Conventional Armaments Planning System (CAPS). The aims of this system are to provide guidance to the CNAD and orientation to the nations on how the military requirements of the Alliance can best be met by armaments programmes, individually and collectively; to harmonise longer-term defence procurement plans; and to identify future opportunities for armaments cooperation on an Alliance-wide basis.

The outcome of this planning process is a series of recommendations issued every two years by the NATO Conventional Armaments Review Committee under the authority of the CNAD. The recommendations are designed to eliminate unnecessary duplication of effort in meeting the military needs of the Alliance; to provide a framework for the exchange of information and the harmonisation of operational requirements within the CNAD's armaments groups; and to establish more rational and cost-effective methods of armaments cooperation and defence procurement.

A review of NATO's armaments planning procedures is being undertaken, focusing in particular on structures and procedures within the CNAD.

Standardisation

Standardisation amongst NATO forces makes a vital contribution to the combined operational effectiveness of the military forces of the Alliance and enables opportunities to be exploited for making better use of economic resources. Extensive efforts are therefore made in many different spheres to improve cooperation and eliminate duplication in research, development, pro-

---

3   From 1976 to 1992, the Independent European Programme Group (IEPG) provided a forum through which European member nations of NATO could discuss and formulate policies designed to achieve greater cooperation in armaments procurement. The IEPG was dissolved at the end of 1992 when its functions were transferred to the Western European Union (WEU). Subsequently, these matters have been handled by the Western European Armaments Group (WEAG) within the framework of the WEU.

duction, procurement and support of defence systems. NATO Standardisation Agreements for procedures and systems and for equipment components, known as STANAGs, are developed and promulgated by the NATO Military Agency for Standardisation in conjunction with the Conference of National Armaments Directors and other authorities concerned.

By formulating, agreeing, implementing and maintaining standards for equipment and procedures used throughout NATO, a significant contribution is made to the cohesion of the Alliance and to the effectiveness of its defence structure. While standardisation is of relevance in many different areas, the principal forum for standardisation policy issues is the NATO Standardisation Organisation (NSO), which aims to incorporate standardisation as an integral part of Alliance planning and acts as a coordinator between senior NATO bodies confronting standardisation requirements. The NSO was established in 1995 to give renewed impetus to Alliance work aimed at improving the coordination of allied policies and programmes for standardisation in the materiel, technical and operational fields. Further details about the NATO Standardisation Organisation and related bodies are given in Chapter 14.

COMMUNICATIONS AND INFORMATION SYSTEMS

Consultation, Command and Control matters are known within NATO under the collective name of "C3". The NATO Consultation, Command and Control Organisation (NC3O) is responsible for the provision of a NATO-wide, cost-effective, interoperable and secure capability to ensure high level political consultation and command and control of military forces. This is accomplished by a number of Communications and Information Systems (CIS) which also interface with national fixed and mobile networks to cover the whole NATO area, linking the NATO Headquarters in Brussels, all Headquarters of the Integrated Military Command Structure, national capitals and the highest levels of national military command. Secure connections are also being established for political consultation with nations participating in the Euro-Atlantic Partnership Council (EAPC).

The NC3O comprises the NATO C3 Board (NC3B), acting as the Board of Directors of the NC3O; the Group of National C3 Representatives (NC3REPS), acting as the NC3B in permanent session; a NATO C3 Agency (NC3A); and a NATO Communications and Information Systems Operating and Support Agency (NACOSA). The NC3B is the senior multinational body acting on behalf of and responsible for advising the North Atlantic Council and Defence Planning Committee on all C3 policy matters, including the interoperability of NATO and national C3 systems, as well as advising the CNAD on C3 cooperative programmes.

The NC3 Agency performs central planning, engineering, design, integration, technical support and configuration control for NATO C3 systems. The Agency also provides scientific and technical advice and support to the Strategic Commanders and others on matters pertaining to Operations Research, surveillance, air command and control and provides technical support for exercises and operations and other projects assigned to it.

NACOSA and subordinate elements operate, control and maintain NATO Communication and Information systems assigned to them and provide appropriate support and training for these systems. Operational policy prioritisation and procedural direction are decided jointly by both Strategic Commanders. Non-operational direction is provided by the NC3B.

CIVIL/MILITARY COORDINATION OF AIR TRAFFIC MANAGEMENT

The North Atlantic Council established the Committee for European Airspace Coordination (CEAC) in 1955. In 1998 the Committee was reconstituted as the NATO Air Traffic Management Committee (NATMC).

The Committee is responsible for ensuring that all civil and military airspace requirements over the territory of the 19 NATO nations are fully coordinated. This includes the conduct of major air exercises, the harmonisation of air traffic control systems and procedures, and the sharing of communications frequencies. Observers from the International Civil Aviation Organisation, the International Air Transport Association and the European Organisation for the Safety of Air Navigation (EUROCONTROL) also assist the Committee. In the context of new Alliance missions, such as peacekeeping, the Committee is therefore able to provide a unique link between the NATO Military Authorities responsible for the coordination of large-scale military aircraft movements and the civil organisations managing the airspace.

In recent years, the surge in civilian air traffic and delays caused by insufficient capacity of air traffic control and airport structures in many parts of Europe to cope with peak-time traffic have highlighted the need for effective coordination between civil and military authorities in order to ensure that the airspace can be shared by all users on an equitable basis. Moreover, there is also a need to ensure, on a technical level, that military operators are able to maintain the required degree of compatibility with the different elements of the air traffic management system which the civil agencies plan to introduce in the future. Consequently, and in particular in view of current efforts to achieve pan-European integration of air traffic management, the Committee is represented in a number of international forums. It is a participant in the Programme approved by the Transport Ministers of the European Civil Aviation Conference.

Since exchanges of views on airspace management constitute part of the developing partnership between the NATO Alliance and its Partners, the Committee is also actively engaged in cooperation activities. Since 1991, meetings on civil/military coordination of air traffic management have been held periodically with high-level participation by NATO members and other European countries. In May 1992, the Central and East European and Central Asian states which were members of the North Atlantic Cooperation Council (later replaced by the Euro-Atlantic Partnership Council) took part in a seminar on this issue, together with representatives from NATO countries, as well as the NATO Military Authorities and five international organisations with responsibilities in this field.

From November 1992, Cooperation Partners were invited to take part in plenary sessions of the Committee addressing the civil/military dimension of the integration of Central and Eastern Europe in Western European air traffic management strategies. Early in 1994, other European neutral countries were also invited to participate in its activities. This established the Committee as a unique forum for coordination between civil and military users of the entire continental European airspace, as acknowledged by the European Civil Aviation Conference.

The Partnership for Peace initiative is further increasing concrete cooperation in this area, notably with regard to coordination of air exercises. Regular plenary and working level meetings now constitute part of the cooperation activities related to air traffic management foreseen in the PfP Partnership Work Programme. With the enhancement of the Partnership for Peace there is a considerable broadening and deepening of the Committee's activities in this area in the coming years.

Airspace Management and Control is included in the section of the EAPC Action Plan for 2000-2002 which lists agreed areas of cooperation within the Partnership for Peace programme. Cooperation in relation to air safety and airspace management and control is also foreseen in the context of the NATO-Russia relationship, NATO's partnership with Ukraine and the South East Europe Initiative.

AIR DEFENCE

The NATO Air Defence Committee (NADC) is responsible for advising the North Atlantic Council and Defence Planning Committee on all aspects of air defence, including tactical missile defence. It enables member countries to harmonise their national efforts with international planning related to air command

and control and air defence weapons. The air defence of Canada and the United States is coordinated within the North American Air Defence system (NORAD).

In 1994, the NADC began a dialogue with Cooperation Partners under the aegis of the North Atlantic Cooperation Council (NACC) in order to foster mutual understanding and confidence in air defence matters of common interest. Developments under the Partnership for Peace initiative which are further enhancing cooperation in this area include fact finding meetings of air defence experts, air defence seminars and the maintenance of a Cooperative Air Defence Programme. The dialogue is continuing within the framework of the Euro-Atlantic Partnership Council (EAPC), which replaced the NACC, and in the context of the Enhanced Partnership for Peace programme.

Effective air defence is fundamental to Alliance security. It is provided by a complex system which enables aircraft and tactical missiles to be detected, tracked and intercepted, either by maritime and ground-based weapons systems, or by interceptor aircraft. The command and control structure which facilitates air defence comprises the NATO Air Defence Ground Environment (NADGE) which includes sites stretching from Northern Norway to Eastern Turkey, the Improved United Kingdom Air Defence Ground Environment (IUKADGE) and the Portuguese Air Command and Control System (POACCS). These systems integrate the various sites which are equipped with modern radars, data processing and display systems and are linked by modern digital communications. Weapon systems and the command and control system form together the so-called NATO Integrated Air Defence System (NATINADS).

Multinationality is a key principle of the system. Much of the existing air defence structure has therefore been commonly financed through the NATO Security Investment Programme (NSIP) (formerly called the Infrastructure Programme) and a significant part of the successor system, known as the Air Command and Control System (ACCS), is similarly funded. The ACCS is designed to combine the tactical planning, tasking and execution of all air defence, offensive air and air support operations. Its scope is therefore much broader than just air defence. It is being implemented under the supervision of the NATO ACCS Management Organisation (NACMO) and will provide an initial operational capability within the next few years. During the late 1980s, early warning capability was enhanced through the acquisition of a fleet of E-3A NATO Airborne Early Warning and Control (NAEW&C) aircraft. The fleet is currently being improved through modernisation programmes managed by the NATO AEW&C Programme Management Organisation. These NATO-owned and operated aircraft, together with E-3D aircraft owned and operated by the United Kingdom, comprise the NATO Airborne Early Warning Force. The

French and United States Air Forces also have E-3 aircraft, which can interoperate with the NATO air defence structure.

NATO is also studying improvements for the rapid dissemination of early warning information on Tactical Ballistic Missile launches. Moreover the NATO Air Defence Committee (NADC) has revised the Alliance Air Defence Programme, now known as the Alliance Extended Air Defence Programme. This includes measures to adapt NATO's air defence structures in order to take account of the changed security situation and of corresponding changes in the Alliance's crisis management requirements. It also includes provisions for taking multinational training into account and for examining the potential contribution of maritime assets to air defence, as well as possible reinforcements by readily transportable air defence elements. In addition, since tactical missiles are now part of the weapons inventory of many countries, the Alliance is also examining ways of applying countermeasures to such systems.

Work is being undertaken within the CNAD on the development of an Alliance Ground Surveillance capability to complement the NATO Airborne Early Warning capability and to provide an effective system to assist military operations in the context of extended air defence (e.g. conventional counterforce operations), peacekeeping and crisis management. Furthermore, on the basis of Council approved policy, the CNAD is launching studies on layered missile defence to address the active defence part of the all encompassing Extended Air Defence Programme.

CIVIL EMERGENCY PLANNING

The aim of Civil Emergency Planning in NATO is to coordinate national planning activity to ensure the most effective use of civil resources in collective support of Alliance strategic objectives. Civil Emergency Planning is a national responsibility and civil assets remain under national control at all times. However, at the NATO level, national intentions and capabilities are harmonised to ensure that jointly developed plans and procedures will work and that necessary assets are available. These assets include ships, aircraft, trains, medical facilities, communications, disaster response capabilities and other civil resources.

The main roles of Civil Emergency Planning in NATO reflect the fundamental security tasks of the Alliance and consist of civil support for military and crisis response operations, support for national authorities in civil emergencies and the protection of civilian populations. Beneath these very broad headings, Civil Emergency Planning has a role to play in managing the availability of civil assets and facilities and the maintenance of normal life during emergency situations such as war, crises and disasters. Increasingly, this work is carried out in close cooperation with Partner countries, who now play an active part in Civil Emergency Planning in NATO.

All of this is brought together by the Senior Civil Emergency Planing Committee (SCEPC), which reports directly to the North Atlantic Council. The SCEPC meets at least twice a year in Plenary session and eight times a year in Permanent session. The Secretary General is Chairman of plenary sessions, but in practice these are chaired by the Assistant Secretary General for Security Investment, Logistics and Civil Emergency Planning while Permanent sessions are chaired by the Director of Civil Emergency Planning. Country representation at Plenary level is drawn from heads of national Civil Emergency Planning organisations in capitals. At Permanent level, members of national delegations at NATO Headquarters normally attend but may be reinforced from capitals. Reflecting the deep involvement of Civil Emergency Planning in PfP activities, SCEPC's twice-yearly Plenary meetings are also held in EAPC format, with attendance open to all Partner nations, and Permanent meetings with Partners are held at least four times a year.

Under the direction of the SCEPC, a number of technical Planning Boards and Committees bring together national government and industry experts and military representatives to coordinate planning in several areas of civil activity, namely;

- European Inland Surface Transport

- Ocean Shipping

- Civil Aviation

- Food and Agriculture

- Industrial production and supply

- Post and telecommunications

- Medical matters

- Civil protection

- Petroleum production and supply (although this is currently in dormant status).

These bodies meet regularly and provide the vital link between NATO policy and the means to carry it out. They are supported in their work by smaller, flexible working groups or specialised technical committees.

Overall direction of Civil Emergency Planning, at NATO and national level, is by Foreign Ministers, who decide priorities. However, the very wide range of

Civil Emergency Planning requires careful coordination in capitals of contributions from the many ministries and national agencies involved in Civil Emergency Planning today.

Civil Emergency Planning Activities Under Partnership for Peace

On the basis of plans developed and agreed individually by Partners with NATO, the Alliance and Partners are working together in support of shared ideals of democratic control of national institutions, including the armed forces, and towards addressing the many risks facing nations and described in the Alliance's Strategic Concept. Allies and Partners undertake joint planning and exercises to improve their ability to work together in support of the Alliance's broad approach to security. Civil Emergency Planning continues to be the largest non-military programme of cooperation activities and has included seminars, workshops, exercises, training courses and exchanges of information. All Partners have been involved from different levels of local, regional and national governments as well as from non-governmental organisations.

The programme directly addresses the political objectives of Partnership and is now focusing more and more on concrete cooperation by Partner participation in the work of the Planning Boards and Committees. This practical involvement in NATO Civil Emergency Planning will deepen the role of Partners and contribute to the development of an enhanced and more operational Partnership, in line with decisions taken by Ministers and Heads of State and Government.

At the same time, a large number of other international organisations also participate in Civil Emergency Planning activities. These include the Council of Europe, the European Union, the International Atomic Energy Agency, the International Federation of the Red Cross and Red Crescent Societies (IFRC), the International Committee of the Red Cross (ICRC), the UN Office for the Coordination of Humanitarian Affairs (UNOCHA), the United Nations Educational, Scientific and Cultural Organisation (UNESCO) and the UN High Commissioner for Refugees (UNHCR).

Disaster preparedness and protection of the population have been common elements in many PfP Civil Emergency Planning activities. Attention has been directed on avalanches, chemical accidents, earthquakes, floods, nuclear accidents and the transport of dangerous goods. Much of this has been done in cooperation with UNOCHA and its project on the Use of Military and Civil Defence Assets in Disaster Assistance (MCDA).

Responding to a mutual wish for more concrete cooperation in disaster relief, SCEPC in EAPC format developed plans for a Euro-Atlantic Disaster Response Capability comprising a Euro-Atlantic Disaster Response Coordination Centre (EADRCC) and a Euro-Atlantic Disaster Response Unit (EADRU). EAPC Ministers endorsed the establishment of the EADRCC in May 1998 and it opened the next month. It has done valuable work in coordinating international response to the floods in Ukraine and the earthquakes in Turkey and Greece. It also contributed substantially to the UNHCR relief operations in Albania and the former Yugoslav Republic of Macedonia[4] and was an invaluable asset in the coordination of humanitarian support in the Kosovo crisis.

The EADRU will be a non-standing resource, made up from assets and resources which nations might be prepared to make available in response to a request for assistance from a nation struck by disaster. Its existence will greatly help the development of responsive and flexible help.

NATO-Russia Cooperation

NATO-Russia cooperation in this field began in December 1991 when the North Atlantic Council tasked the Senior Civil Emergency Planning Committee to assist in coordinating the transportation of humanitarian assistance to the then Soviet Union. Over the next few months, NATO-Russia cooperation in humanitarian activities in the various successor states of the former Soviet Union provided a solid foundation for subsequent activities between NATO and Russia. Cooperation has been established between NATO's Civil Emergency Planning structures and the Ministry of the Russian Federation for Civil Defence, Emergencies and Elimination of Consequences of Natural Disasters (EMERCOM of Russia), both of which have been major supporters of the UN Office for the Coordination of Humanitarian Affairs and of its MCDA Project. An initial workshop in this field took place at NATO Headquarters in December 1992. Since then, considerable follow-up work has been undertaken by both NATO and Russia.

On 20 March 1996, in Moscow, EMERCOM of Russia and NATO signed a Memorandum of Understanding on Civil Emergency Planning and Disaster Preparedness. This commits both parties to increasing their efforts and support for practical cooperation and mutual assistance in disaster preparedness and response. Both parties are now considering proposals for cooperation in assisting UNOCHA operations in the event of a major disaster.

---

4   Turkey recognises the Republic of Macedonia with its constitutional name.

From 22-23 April 1997, a high level Civil Emergency Planning symposium on the Humanitarian Challenge for the Next Century was organised under the framework of Partnership for Peace (PfP), hosted by EMERCOM of Russia. This event took place in conjunction with a SCEPC Plenary meeting with Cooperation Partners held in Moscow on 24-25 April, marking the first occasion that a SCEPC Symposium has been conducted outside a NATO Country. This was also the first time that a Senior NATO Committee held a formal meeting in the Russian Federation.

Following the signing of the Founding Act on Mutual Relations, Cooperation and Security between NATO and the Russian Federation in Paris on 27 May 1997 and the creation of the NATO Russia Permanent Joint Council (PJC), an Expert Group on Civil Emergency Preparedness and Disaster Relief was created, which identified areas for future work. The Group oversees the implementation of the NATO-Russia Memorandum of Understanding. The PJC Pilot Project on the Use of Satellite Technology in Disaster Management is one example of follow-on work which has since been initiated.

NATO-Ukraine Cooperation

NATO-Ukraine cooperation in Civil Emergency Planning began in 1995, following heavy rains and the flooding of the Ouda and Donets Rivers in eastern Ukraine. The floods incapacitated and partially destroyed the sewage plant of the town of Kharkov, resulting in severe contamination of the water supplies for a city of approximately two million people. NATO's Civil Emergency Planning Directorate coordinated assistance from NATO and Partner countries to overcome these problems.

In 1996 Ukraine hosted the first meeting of a Civil Emergency Planning Board outside NATO. In conjunction with the exercise "Carpathian Safety '96", NATO's Civil Protection Committee with Cooperation Partners held a meeting in Lvov. Successful cooperation between NATO's Civil Emergency Planning Directorate and the Ministry of Emergencies and Protection of the Population from the Consequences of the Chernobyl Catastrophe paved the way for a Seminar on "Aeromedical Evacuation and Rescue Operations in Emergencies", conducted in September 1997 in Kyiv.

Cooperation in the area of Civil Emergency Planning and Disaster Preparedness is a key component of the NATO-Ukraine Charter signed in Madrid in July 1997. A Memorandum of Understanding with NATO in this area was signed on 16 December 1997.

The MOU aims at improving capabilities in the field of civil emergency preparedness and disaster management, as well as further enhancing good cooperation between the parties. Accordingly, it focuses on areas of mutual interest, including regional disaster preparedness and emergency management, civil-military cooperation, transport, aero-medical evacuation arrangements and enhancement of the overall response capability to nuclear accidents.

SCIENTIFIC COOPERATION

Science Programme Activities

Scientific cooperation in NATO falls within the ambit of the NATO Science Committee. The Science Committee is responsible for the NATO Science Programme, under which support is available for collaboration in civil science between NATO-country scientists and scientists in NATO's EAPC Partner countries.

The Science Programme is structured in four sub-programmes encompassing a variety of collaborative support mechanisms to achieve different objectives:

Science Fellowships: The objective of the Science Fellowships sub-programme is to prepare for the long-term future by training young researchers. Administered in a decentralised manner, the fellowships offer opportunities for Partner scientists to continue their studies or pursue their research for a period in a NATO country and vice-versa.

Cooperative Science and Technology: The objective of this sub-programme is to initiate cooperation and to establish enduring personal links between scientists of the NATO and Partner or Mediterranean Dialogue countries. Support is offered for Collaborative Linkage Grants (CLG) and Expert Visits (EV) to fund collaboration on research projects, and funding to organise high-level tutorial Advanced Study Institutes (ASI) and intensive brain-storming Advanced Research Workshops (ARW).

All scientific areas are eligible for support under this sub-programme, and applications from individuals in the scientific community are examined by Advisory Panels on Physical and Engineering Sciences and Technology (PST), Life Science and Technology (LST), Environmental and Earth Science and Technology (EST) and Security-Related Civil Science and Technology (SST).

Research Infrastructure Support: The objective of this sub-programme is to support Partner countries in structuring the organisation of their research programmes and creating required basic infrastructure. In contrast to the co-operative nature of the previous sub-programmes, support here is directed from NATO towards Partner countries. Different activities are open to support in two areas - 1) Computer Networking and 2) Science and Technology Policy and Organisation.

Science for Peace: The objective of this sub-programme is to strengthen research for application to industrial activities or to environmental problems in Partner countries. It brings together scientists of research laboratories, industry, or user services, from NATO and Partner countries, for three to five years' work on applied R&D projects.

The origins of scientific cooperation in NATO can be traced to the 1956 recommendations of the Committee of Three on Non-Military Cooperation in NATO. This Committee of "Three Wise Men" - Foreign Ministers Lange (Norway), Martino (Italy) and Pearson (Canada) - observed that progress in science and technology was so crucial to the future of the Atlantic community that NATO members should ensure that every possibility of fruitful cooperation be examined. In accepting the report of a subsequent Task Force on Scientific and Technical Cooperation, the Heads of Government of the Alliance, at a meeting in December 1957, approved the establishment of a NATO Science Committee. The Science Committee met for the first time in March 1958.

The Science Programme developed over thirty years on the two pillars of scientific excellence and Alliance solidarity, and was designed from the outset to support collaboration between individual scientists in NATO countries, rather than to finance research work or institutions. During recent years the Programme has provided increasing opportunities for collaboration with NATO's Partners in the Euro-Atlantic Partnership Council. At the beginning of 1999 the Programme was completely transformed to provide assistance only for collaboration between NATO-country scientists and scientists in NATO's Partner countries or, for activities of the sub-programme Cooperative Science & Technology, countries of the Mediterranean Dialogue. Collaboration between NATO-country scientists exclusively is no longer supported.

Today about 10 000 scientists from NATO and Partner countries are involved in the NATO Science Programme each year, as grantees and meeting participants, or as referees and Advisory Panel members. Some examples of the diverse topics supported are: "Industrial Mineral Exploration in Albanian Ophiolite Complexes" (Environment CLG - Albania and UK); "Calcium and Transmitter Release in Vascular Nerves" (Life Sciences CLG - Russia and Denmark); "Magnetic Accretion in Young Stars" (Physics CLG - Uzbekistan, Kazakhstan, Armenia, France, USA and Germany); "Application of Gun and Rocket Propellants in Commercial Explosives" (Security-Related Civil Science ARW - Russia, USA); "Scientific Issues of Environmentally-

Acceptable Reclamation and Pollution Endpoints" (Environment ASI - Ukraine and USA)[5].

The Science Committee meets three times a year, and annually with Partners in the Euro-Atlantic Partnership Council. The Committee is assisted in its work of assessing and selecting applications for support by Advisory Panels whose members are appointed by the Committee from among the scientists of NATO and Partner countries.

NATO-Russia Cooperation

Guided by the provisions of the NATO-Russia Founding Act, a Memorandum of Understanding on Scientific and Technological Cooperation between NATO and the Ministry of Science and Technology of the Russian Federation was signed at a meeting of the NATO-Russia Permanent Joint Council at Ministerial Level, in Luxembourg in May 1998. The purposes of the Memorandum are (a) to encourage and promote scientific and technological cooperation between NATO and the Russian Federation in areas of mutual interest, and (b) to support scientific research and development activities which further the advancement of science and technology.

The Memorandum provides for the setting up of a Joint NATO-Russia Scientific and Technological Cooperation Committee (JSTC), which carries out its work under the authority of the Permanent Joint Council. The Committee is scheduled to meet once a year, alternatively in the Russian Federation and at NATO Headquarters.

A first meeting of the JSTC was held in November 1998, at which time the committee identified three areas for cooperation under the Memorandum of Understanding: Plasma Physics, Plant Biotechnology, and the Forecast and Prevention of Catastrophes.

NATO-Ukraine Cooperation

Cooperation with Ukraine under the NATO Science Programme began in 1991, and is being intensified under the provisions of the NATO-Ukraine Charter. A special NATO-Ukraine Working Group on Scientific Cooperation has been set up through an exchange of letters between Ukrainian and NATO offi-

---

5   CLG: Collaborative Linkage Grant
     ARW: Advanced Research Workshop
     ASI: Advanced Study Institute

cials. This working group will assess the level of participation by Ukrainian scientists in the NATO Science Programme, and identify means to foster increased participation.

Cooperation under the Mediterranean Dialogue

The NATO Science Committee also pursues a special initiative with the Mediterranean Dialogue countries, and scientists from Mediterranean Dialogue countries may now prepare applications with NATO-country colleagues for support of Collaborative Linkage Grants, Expert Visits, Advanced Study Institutes and Advanced Research Workshops. Particular attention is being paid to identifying topics of regional interest among the Mediterranean Dialogue countries, and encouraging applications for scientific cooperation in these area.

ENVIRONMENT AND SOCIETY

CCMS - Challenges of Modern Society

The environmental challenges facing the international community were recognised by the Alliance in 1969 with the establishment of the Committee on the Challenges of Modern Society (CCMS), created to respond to concerns about environmental issues. Member countries have participated through this Committee in numerous initiatives to take advantage of the potential offered by the Alliance for cooperation in tackling problems affecting the environment and the quality of life.

Under the auspices of the Committee, projects have been undertaken in fields such as environmental pollution, noise, urban problems, energy and human health, and, in particular, defence-related environmental issues. Examples include pilot studies on Environmental Aspects of Re-Using Former Military Lands, to assist Partners in converting former military bases to civilian use; Environmental Security in an International Context; Environmental Management Systems in the Military Sector; Clean Products and Processes; Ecosystem Modelling of Coastal Lagoons for Sustainable Management; and Environmental Impact Assessment.

The Committee provides a unique forum for the sharing of knowledge and experiences on technical, scientific and policy aspects of social and environmental matters both in the civilian and military sectors among NATO and EAPC Partner countries. The work of the Committee is carried out on a decentralised basis and participation by nations to the pilot studies, projects, workshops and seminars, which are nationally funded, is voluntary. The NATO Civil Budget provides some funding for CCMS to award grants to enable experts to participate in CCMS activities.

For each project embarked upon, one or more nations volunteer to assume a pilot role, which includes taking responsibility for planning and financing the work, coordinating its execution, preparing the necessary reports and promoting follow-up action. In 1993 it became possible for a Partner country to assume the role of co-director of a pilot study, working with a co-director from a NATO country. At least two other Alliance countries must be participants.

Since 1996 the Committee has introduced new tools for cooperation within the framework of the CCMS Programme. These include ad hoc 6-18 month projects focused on specific topics; and workshops to disseminate information in well-defined areas. In this context, two projects are ongoing: "Development of an Integrated Coastal Zone Management Programme (INCOM) through Coastal and Shelf Monitoring and Modelling in the Black Sea" and "Sustainable Building for Military Infrastructure".

In accordance with the EAPC Action Plan for 2000-2002, the Committee on the Challenges of Modern Society is broadening its work to include joint meetings with NATO's Partners and workshops on defence-related environmental issues, as well as new pilot studies on topics of particular interest to Partner countries. As examples of the types of environmental conferences sponsored by CCMS, two conferences were organised in 1999, the first one within the framework of the EAPC Action Plan on "Environmental Security of Oil Pipeline in Georgia" (Tbilisi, Georgia, October 1999) and the second one in the framework of the NATO-Ukraine Charter on "Ecological Problems from Defence Activities in the Black Sea and Azov Sea" (Sevastopol, Ukraine, October 1999).

Meetings of the CCMS in EAPC format take place annually. Activities initiated or under discussion include pilot studies on clean-up methodology for contaminated former military sites; environmental management in the military sector; environmental security; and work on the interrelationship of defence, the environment and economic issues, designed to identify environmentally sound approaches to the operations of armed forces both in Alliance and Partner countries.

NATO-Russia Cooperation

A Memorandum of Understanding is in preparation between the Russian Federation and NATO on Environmental Protection.

NATO-Ukraine Cooperation

Cooperation with Ukraine in CCMS is pursued under the provisions of the NATO-Ukraine Charter and has focused particularly on defence-related environmental problems.

Cooperation under the Mediterranean Dialogue

The Mediterranean Dialogue countries are encouraged to participate in the projects of the Committee on the Challenges of Modern Society.

CHAPTER 9

COMMON-FUNDED RESOURCES: NATO BUDGETS AND FINANCIAL MANAGEMENT

The Principles of Common Funding

Cost Sharing

The Civil Budget

The Military Budget

The NATO Security Investment Programme

Resource Management

Financial Management

Financial Control

COMMON-FUNDED RESOURCES: NATO BUDGETS AND FINANCIAL MANAGEMENT

THE PRINCIPLES OF COMMON FUNDING

NATO is an intergovernmental organisation to which member nations allocate the resources needed to enable it to function on a day-to-day basis and to provide the facilities required for consultation, decision-making and the subsequent implementation of agreed policies and activities. It serves a political Alliance supported by an essential military structure which provides for the common defence of the member countries, cooperation with NATO's Partner countries and implementation of Alliance policies in peacekeeping and other fields.

In the military context, apart from a limited number of permanent headquarters and small standing forces, the vast majority of military forces and assets belonging to NATO member countries remain under national command and control until such time as some or all of these, depending on the country, may be assigned to NATO for the purposes of undertaking specific military tasks. The forces of NATO countries contributing to the Stabilisation Force led by NATO in Bosnia and Herzegovina (SFOR) and to the Kosovo Force (KFOR) are thus assigned to NATO temporarily in order to fulfil the Alliance's mandates but are trained, equipped, maintained and financed by the individual defence budgets of member nations.

In order to facilitate consultation and joint decision-making in the framework of their Alliance, each member country maintains a diplomatic and military presence at NATO headquarters as well as civil and/or military representation at the headquarters of the various NATO agencies and military commands. The costs of maintaining and staffing their national delegations and military missions are also a national responsibility, financed in accordance with the different accounting principles and practices of each country.

The two examples given above - the costs of maintaining military forces and the costs of civil and military representation in Alliance forums - illustrate expenditures which would have to be taken into account in any analysis of the total cost to each nation of its NATO membership. Such expenditures would have to be offset by a similar analysis of the economic benefits obtained by each member country as a result of its participation in the Alliance.

However, the rationale for NATO membership extends far beyond the confines of a financial balance sheet drawn up on the above basis and embraces political, economic, scientific, technological, cultural and other factors which do not lend themselves readily to translation into financial terms. Moreover, to arrive at a meaningful conclusion each member country would have to factor into the calculation the costs which it would have incurred, over time, in making provision for its national security independently or through alternative forms of international cooperation.

The purpose of this chapter is not to attempt any such theoretical calculation, which must remain a matter for each nation to address in accordance with its own procedures and practices. The aim of the chapter is rather to describe the principles of common-funding and cost-sharing which apply throughout the Alliance and the major budgets used to manage the Alliance's financial resources. Taken together, these expenditures represent less than half of one percent of the total defence expenditures of NATO countries (see Table 3).

NATO funds are devoted essentially to those expenditures which reflect the interests of all member countries. The common funding structure is diverse and decentralised. Certain multinational cooperative activities relating to research, development, production and logistic support do not involve all and, in some instances, may only involve a small number of member countries. These activities, most of which are managed by NATO Production and Logistics Organisations, are subject to the general financial and audit regulations of NATO but otherwise operate in virtual autonomy under charters granted by the North Atlantic Council. Reference is made to them below (see Financial Management).

With few exceptions, NATO funding does not therefore cover the procurement of military forces or of physical military assets such as ships, submarines, aircraft, tanks, artillery or weapon systems. Military manpower and materiel are assigned to the Alliance by member countries, which remain financially responsible for their provision. An important exception is the NATO Airborne Early Warning and Control Force, a fleet of radar-bearing aircraft jointly procured, owned, maintained and operated by member countries and placed under the operational command and control of a NATO Force Commander responsible to the NATO Strategic Commanders. NATO also finances investments directed towards collective requirements, such as air defence, command and control systems or Alliance-wide communications systems which cannot be designated as being within the responsibility of any single nation to provide. Such investments are subject to maintenance, renewal and ultimately replacement in accordance with changing requirements and technological developments and the expenditures this requires also represent a significant portion of NATO funding.

The starting point for the process of seeking and obtaining approval for common funding of a given project is the identification and recognition of the need for expenditure and a determination that the responsibility for that expenditure cannot reasonably be attributed to a single country and that it will serve the interests of all contributing countries. The requirement must be duly generated, stated and authenticated and this in itself calls for a complex interaction of national and international administrative processes. Once recognised, the requirement for expenditure must be judged eligible for common funding by member countries on a defined scale. The determination of whether the requirement is eligible for common funding is made by consensus of the member countries which would be liable to support the cost.

Over the years since the establishment of the Alliance, the application of these principles has given rise to the elaboration of complex rules involving scales of integral or partial funding support and the exclusion of various cost elements, for example, national or local taxes. Another major and perhaps surprising exclusion dating from the time of NATO's establishment is the remuneration of military personnel serving at NATO Headquarters or at any of the international headquarters forming part of the military structure of the Alliance. This remains a charge to the assigning nation. Some 15 000 military personnel are routinely posted to international headquarters, all of whom are paid for by their nations. Remuneration of the international civilian staff at NATO Headquarters in Brussels and at NATO military headquarters is financed respectively by NATO's common-funded civil and military budgets. Significant areas of NATO-related funding are subject to conventions of this nature accepted by all the member countries.

The criteria for common funding are held under constant review and changes may be introduced as a result of new contingencies - for example, the need to develop clear definitions of those parts of NATO's peacekeeping costs which should be imputed to international budgets and those which should be financed by national budgets. Other changes in existing conventions relating to common funding may result from organisational or technological developments or simply from the need to control costs in order to meet requirements within specific funding limitations. Despite these challenges, the principle of common funding on the basis of consensus remains fundamental to the workings of the Alliance. It continues to be upheld by all the member countries and can be seen as a reflection of their political commitment to NATO and of the political solidarity which is the hallmark of the implementation of agreed NATO policies.

COST SHARING

As a general rule, all member countries participate in the expenditures which are accepted for common funding. Thus, all member countries contribute to financing the expenditures of the International Staff, the International Military Staff and Military Committee agencies and to the common-funded elements of

Peace Support Operations and Partnership for Peace activities. The expenditures of the NATO Airborne Early Warning and Control Force, however, are financed by the 13 countries participating in the Force. Expenditure relating to other parts or entities within the international military structure and expenditure under the NATO Security Investment Programme are shared according to the nature of the nations' participation in NATO's integrated command arrangements.

By convention, the agreed cost sharing formulae which determine each member country's contributions are deemed to represent each country's "ability to pay". However the basis for the formulae applied is as much political as it is economic. The formulae applied to the Civil and Military Budgets and to the NATO Security Investment Programme were originally negotiated in the early 1950s. They have subsequently been adapted, largely proportionally, to reflect new membership and differing degrees of participation in the integrated command arrangements. Their relationship to current measurements of relative economic capacity such as GDP or purchasing power parities is consequently imprecise.

Currently, the Civil Budget is financed under a single 19-nation formula. The greater part of the Military Budget covering the international military structure is financed under a slightly different 19-nation formula and two 18-nation formulae. The NATO Security Investment Programme is similarly financed under two different 19 and 18-nation cost-sharing formulae. The part of the military budget which funds the NATO Airborne Early Warning and Control Force is governed by a 13-nation and a 14-nation formula which reflect the industrial/commercial orientation of the cost sharing arrangements for the related procurement organisation, NAPMO (see Chapter 14).

Tables 1 and 2 show the range of member countries' cost shares under the civil and military budgets and for the NATO Security Investment Programme.

THE CIVIL BUDGET

The Civil Budget is established and executed under the supervision of the Civil Budget Committee and is primarily funded from the appropriations of Ministries of Foreign Affairs. It covers the operating costs of the International Staff at the NATO Headquarters in Brussels; the execution of approved civilian programmes and activities; and the construction, running and maintenance costs of facilities including the personnel costs associated with providing conference services for all meetings of NATO committees and subordinate groups, security services, etc. During recent years, a growing portion of budgetary resources has been devoted to funding activities with Partner countries. The total budget approved for 2000 amounts to approximately US$ 133 million[1]. Personnel costs absorb approximately 61 percent (US$ 80 million). Special programme costs such as those for the NATO Science Programme or for information activities consume approximately 26 percent (US$ 35 million). The balance (13 percent or approximately US$ 18 million) covers other operating and capital costs.

THE MILITARY BUDGET

The Military Budget, established and executed under the supervision of the Military Budget Committee, is largely financed from the appropriations of Ministries of Defence. It covers the operating and maintenance costs and, with the exception of major construction and system investments financed by the NATO Security Investment Programme, the capital costs of the international military structure. This includes the Military Committee, the International Military Staff and associated Agencies, the two NATO Strategic Commands (ACE and ACLANT) and associated command, control and information systems, research and development agencies, procurement and logistics agencies, and the NATO Airborne Early Warning and Control Force.

Currently, the budget also supports the operating costs of the NATO command structure for peacekeeping activities in Bosnia and Herzegovina and Kosovo. The total budget approved for 2000 amounts to approximately US$ 751.5 million. It should be noted that this figure excludes the very substantial costs of assignment of military personnel, which are borne by the respective contributing countries. Of the common-funded total, mission operating and maintenance expenses absorb approximately 43 percent or US$ 323 million; civilian personnel costs approximately 30 percent or US$ 225 million; general administrative expenses approximately 22 percent or US$ 166 million; and capital investment approximately 5 percent or US$ 37.5 million.

THE NATO SECURITY INVESTMENT PROGRAMME (NSIP)

The NATO Security Investment Programme is implemented under the supervision of the Infrastructure Committee within annual contribution ceilings approved by the North Atlantic Council. The ceiling agreed for 2000 is approx-

---

1   Caution should be exercised when comparing figures given in this chapter with figures published in earlier editions of the Handbook. Changes may be due to fluctuations in the rate of the dollar.

imately equivalent to US$ 688 million. The Programme finances the provision of the installations and facilities needed to support the roles of the NATO Strategic Commands recognised as exceeding the national defence requirements of individual member countries. The investments cover such installations and facilities as communications and information systems, radar, military headquarters, airfields, fuel pipelines and storage, harbours, and navigational aids. As is the case for the military budget, the NSIP Programme also covers the eligible requirements for Peace Support Operations such as SFOR and KFOR including Communications, Information Systems, Local Headquarters Facilities, Power Systems, and Repairs to Airfields, Rail, and Roads. The introduction of Partnership for Peace in 1994 added a new cooperative dimension to the programme. More recently, the Defence Capabilities Initiative, launched at the Washington Summit in 1999 has provided additional guidance on the future development of the programme.

RESOURCE MANAGEMENT

Since the mid 1990s, under pressures to optimise the allocation of military common-funded resources, member countries have reinforced NATO's management structure by promoting the development of "capability packages" and by establishing the Senior Resource Board (SRB) which has responsibility for overall resource management of NATO's military resources (i.e. excluding resources covered by the Civil Budget). The capability packages identify the assets available to and required by NATO military commanders to fulfil specified tasks. They are a prime means of assessing common-funded supplements (in terms of both capital investment and recurrent operating and maintenance costs) as well as the civilian and military manpower required to accomplish the task. These packages are reviewed by the Senior Resource Board composed of national representatives, representatives of the Military Committee and the NATO Strategic Commanders and the Chairmen of the Military Budget, Infrastructure and NATO Defence Manpower Committees. The Board endorses the capability packages from the point of view of their resource implications prior to their approval by the North Atlantic Council. It also annually recommends for approval by the North Atlantic Council a comprehensive Medium Term Resource Plan which sets financial ceilings for the following year and planning figures for the four subsequent years. Within these parameters the Military Budget and Infrastructure and Defence Manpower Committees oversee the preparation and execution of their respective budgets and plans. The Board further produces an Annual Report which allows the North Atlantic Council to monitor the adequacy of resource allocations in relation to requirements and to review the military common-funded resource implications for NATO's common-funded budgets of new Alliance policies.

FINANCIAL MANAGEMENT

Financial management within NATO is structured to ensure that the ultimate control of expenditure rests with the member countries supporting the cost of a defined activity and is subject to consensus among them. Control may be exercised, at all levels of decision-making, either in terms of general limitations or by specific restrictions. Examples of general limitations are the allocation of fixed resources or ceilings for operating costs and capital investment (as agreed by the Senior Resource Board) or civilian and military manpower complements, within which financial managers (the Secretary General, NATO Strategic Commanders and Subordinate Commanders and other designated Heads of NATO bodies) have relative discretion to propose and execute their budgets. Specific restrictions may take many forms, ranging from the imposition of specific economy measures to the temporary immobilisation of credits for a given purpose or the restriction of credit transfers. Such restrictions or controls may be stipulated in the terms in which approval of the budget is given or exercised by contributing countries through exceptional interventions in the course of the execution of the budget. Approval of the respective budgets can be seen as the translation into concrete measures of policies - political, organisational or financial - which contributing member countries wish to implement. Such policies evolve over time in response to the changing international environment and the requirement for corresponding adaptation of the Organisation's structures and tasks.

This dynamic process of adjustment over the five decades of the Alliance's existence largely explains the diversity and decentralisation of the financial management structure of NATO. No single body exercises direct managerial control over all four of the principal elements of the Organisation's financial structure, namely the International Staff (financed by the Civil Budget); the international military structure (financed by the Military Budget); the Security Investment Programme; and specialised Production and Logistics Organisations. The latter fall into two groups: those which are financed under arrangements applying to the international military structure; and those which operate under charters granted by the North Atlantic Council, with their own Boards of Directors and finance committees and distinct sources of financing within national treasuries.

The financial management of the organisational budgets (i.e. the Civil and Military Budgets) differs from that of the Security Investment Programme. The diversity and decentralisation of the financial management structure of the organisational budgets is sanctioned by Financial Regulations approved by the North Atlantic Council. The Regulations, which are complemented by rules and procedures adapting them to the particular requirements of the various NATO bodies and programmes, provide basic unifying principles around which the overall financial structure is articulated.

The Regulations prescribe that each NATO body shall have its own budget, expressed in the currency of the host country, with exchange counter-values being determined via a common accounting unit. The budget is annual, coinciding with the calendar year. It is prepared under the authority of the Head of the respective NATO body, reviewed and recommended for approval on the basis of consensus by a finance committee composed of representatives of contributing member countries, and approved for execution by the North Atlantic Council. Failure to achieve consensus before the start of the financial year entails non-approval of the budget and the financing of operations, under the supervision of the finance committee, through provisional allocations limited to the level of the budget approved for the preceding year. This regime may last for six months, after which the Council is required to decide either to approve the budget or to authorise continuation of interim financing. This contingency measure, though rarely applied, reinforces the principle of collective intergovernmental control of expenditure implicit in the requirement for unanimous approval of the budget by all contributing member countries.

When the budget has been approved, the Head of the NATO body has discretion to execute it through the commitment and expenditure of funds for the purposes authorised. This discretion is limited by different levels of constraint prescribed by the Financial Regulations regarding such matters as recourse to restricted or full international competitive bidding for contracts for the supply of goods and services, or transfers of credit to correct over or under-estimates of the funding required. Discretionary authority to execute a budget may be further limited by particular obligations to seek prior approval for commitments and expenditure. These may occasionally be imposed by the finance committee in the interests of ensuring strict application of new policies or of monitoring the implementation of complex initiatives such as organisational restructuring.

While budgetary credits must be committed, to the extent justified by actual requirements, during the financial year for which they are approved, the liquidation of commitments by expenditure is permitted during the two succeeding financial years.

Implementation of the NATO Security Investment Programme has its starting point in the capability packages. Once these have been approved, authorisation of individual projects can commence under the responsibility of the Infrastructure Committee. The Host Nation (usually the nation on whose territory the project is to be implemented) prepares an authorisation request which includes the technical solution, the cost, a specification of eligibility for common-funding, and the bidding procedure to be followed. Particular arrangements apply with regard to international competitive bidding procedures designed to facilitate maximum participation by member countries. If a nation wishes to carry out any type of bidding procedure other than international competitive bidding, it must request exemption from the Infrastructure Committee. When the Committee has agreed to the project, the Host Nation can proceed with its physical implementation.

The financial management system which applies to the Security Investment Programme is based on an international financial clearing process. Nations report on the expenditure foreseen on authorised projects within their responsibility. Nations will in most cases have expenditure either exceeding or below their agreed contribution to the budget. With international financial clearing these inequalities are balanced out by the transfer of funds between nations. Once a project has been completed, it is subject to a Joint Final Acceptance Inspection to ensure that the work undertaken is in accordance with the work authorised. Only when this report is accepted by the Infrastructure Committee does NATO formally take responsibility for the work and for the capability which it provides.

Currently, there are several levels of financial reporting. Twice a year the International Staff prepares for each Host Nation Semi-Annual Financial Reports. These report on projects under implementation. Quarterly, the prepaysheet and paysheet are published. These reports refer to the transfer of funds between host nations. An NSIP Expenditure Profile is prepared every spring. This report covers the NSIP expenditure levels for the next 10 years. It focuses on resource allocation and serves as the basis for the NSIP portion of the Senior Resource Board's Medium Term Resource Plan. The NSIP Financial Statements are prepared in the spring of each year. The financial statements portray the financial situation of the NSIP as at 31 December of each year and the summary of activity during the year in a manner similar to that in private enterprise. The focus in this latter report is on financial reporting and it serves as the baseline for Infrastructure Committee discussion on the state of the NSIP.

FINANCIAL CONTROL

Although the Head of the respective NATO body is ultimately responsible for the correct preparation and execution of the budget, the administrative support for this task is largely entrusted to his Financial Controller. The appointment of this official is the prerogative of the North Atlantic Council, although the latter may delegate this task to the relevant finance committee. Each Financial Controller has final recourse to the finance committee in the case of persistent disagreement with the Head of the respective NATO body regarding an intended transaction.

The Financial Controller is charged with ensuring that all aspects of execution of the budget conform to expenditure authorisations, to any special controls imposed by the finance committee and to the Financial Regulations and their associated implementing rules and procedures. He may also, in response to internal auditing, install such additional controls and procedures as he deems necessary for maintaining accountability. A major task of the Financial Controller is to ensure that the funds required to finance execution of the budget are periodically called up from contributing member countries in accordance with their agreed cost shares and in amounts calculated to avoid the accumulation of excessive cash holdings in the international treasury. The outcome of all these activities is reflected in annual financial statements prepared and presented for verification to the International Board of Auditors.

The International Board of Auditors is composed of representatives of national audit institutions. It operates under a Charter guaranteeing its independence, granted by the North Atlantic Council to which it reports directly. It has powers to audit the accounts of all NATO bodies, including the Production and Logistics Organisations, and the NATO Security Investment Programme. Its mandate includes not only financial but also performance audits. Its role is thus not confined to safeguarding accountability but extends to a review of management practices in general.

Table 1
PERCENTAGE COST SHARES OF NATO MEMBER COUNTRIES CIVIL AND MILITARY BUDGETS

NATO Member Country	Civil Budget	Military Budget (Headquarters, Agencies and Programmes)		Military Budget (NATO Airborne Early Warning & Control Force)	
PARTICIPATING COUNTRIES	"19"	"19"	"18"	"14"	"13"
Belgium	2.76	2.8	3.3	2.5869	3.2821
Canada	5.35	5.33	5.95	7.1994	9.1343
Czech Republic	0.9	0.9	1.08	0	0
Denmark	1.47	1.68	1.94	1.5282	1.9389
France	15.35	15.25	0	0	0
Germany	15.54	15.54	18.2	21.4886	27.2638
Greece	0.38	0.38	0.46	0.4728	0.5999
Hungary	0.65	0.65	0.78	0	0
Iceland	0.05	0.04	0.05	0	0
Italy	5.75	5.91	7.08	5.5485	7.0397
Luxembourg	0.08	0.08	0.1	0.0825	0.1045
Netherlands	2.75	2.84	3.28	2.8625	3.6317
Norway	1.11	1.16	1.36	1.1146	1.4142
Poland	2.48	2.48	2.97	0	0
Portugal	0.63	0.63	0.75	0.5323	0.6754
Spain	3.5	3.5	4.19	2.77	3.1
Turkey	1.59	1.59	1.9	1.2419	1.5757
United Kingdom	17.25	16.09	19.12	20.8558	0
United States	22.41	23.15	27.49	31.716	40.239
Total	100	100	100	100	100

Table 2
PERCENTAGE COST SHARES OF NATO MEMBER COUNTRIES
NATO SECURITY INVESTMENT PROGRAMME

NATO Member Country	Expenditures shared at 18	Expenditures shared at 19
Belgium	4.24	3.72
Canada	4.025	3.22
Czech Republic	1.0333	0.9
Denmark	3.44	3
France	0	12.9044
Germany	23.135	20.254
Greece	1.05	1
Hungary	0.7463	0.65
Iceland	0	0
Italy	9.1	7.745
Luxembourg	0.2	0.1845
Netherlands	4.74	4.14
Norway	2.895	2.6
Poland	2.8474	2.48
Portugal	0.392	0.345
Spain	3.7793	3.2916
Turkey	1.13	1.04
United Kingdom	11.7156	10.1925
United States	25.5311	22.333

Table 3*
Defence Expenditures of NATO Countries (1980-2000)
(Based on current prices and exchange rates. Currency unit = millions)

Member Country (Currency)	1980	1985	1990	1995	1996	1997	1998	1999	2000 (Est.)
Belgium (Belgian francs)	115 754	144 183	155 205	131 156	131 334	131 796	133 007	136 252	140 256
Czech Republic (Czech koruny)	//	//	//	//	//	//	//	41 167	44 022
Denmark (Danish kroner)	9 117	13 344	16 399	17 468	17 896	18 521	19 079	19 428	19 349
France (French francs)	110 514	186 715	231 911	238 432	237 375	241 103	236 226	239 488	243 936
Germany (DM)	48 518	58 650	68 376	58 986	58 671	57 602	58 327	59 854	59 617
Greece (Drachmas)	96 975	321 981	612 344	1 171 377	1 343 276	1 510 684	1 724 621	1 853 189	1 981 984
Hungary (Forint)	//	//	//	//	//	//	//	187 672	218 023
Italy (1000 Italian lire)	7 643	17 767	28 007	31 561	36 170	38 701	40 763	43 062	4 3002
Luxembourg (Lux. francs)	1 534	2 265	3 233	4 194	4 380	4 797	5 197	5 330	5 468
Netherlands (Dutch guilder)	10 476	12 901	13 513	12 864	13 199	13 345	13 561	14 534	14 192
Norway (Norw. kroner)	8 242	15 446	21 251	22 224	22 813	23 010	25 087	25 809	25 675
Poland (Zlotys)	//	//	//	//	//	//	//	12 599	14 065
Portugal (Escudos)	43 440	111 375	267 299	403 478	401 165	418 772	420 654	452 843	475 178
Spain (Pesetas)	350 423	674 883	922 808	1 078 751	1 091 432	1 123 046	1 124 054	1 180 075	1 266 429
Turkey (1000 Turkish lira)	203	1 235	13 866	302 864	611 521	1 183 327	2 289 430	4 167 636	6 998 960
United Kingdom (Pounds sterling)	11 593	18 301	22 287	21 439	22 330	21 612	22 551	22 548	22 823
Total NATO Europe (US dollars)	**111 981**	**92 218**	**186 189**	**184 352**	**186 821**	**172 732**	**175 306**	**179 671**	**164 559**
Canada (Canadian dollars)	5 788	10 332	13 473	12 457	11 511	10 831	11 168	12 360	11 948
United States (US dollars)	138 191	258 165	306 170	278 856	271 417	276 324	274 278	280 969	296 373
Total North America (US dollars)	**143 141**	**265 731**	**317 717**	**287 933**	**279 860**	**284 146**	**281 806**	**289 288**	**304 441**
Total NATO (US dollars)	**255 122**	**357 949**	**503 906**	**472 284**	**466 681**	**456 879**	**457 112**	**468 960**	**468 999**

The figures given in Table 3 represent payments actually made or to be made during the course of the fiscal year. They are based on the definition of defence expenditures used by NATO. In view of the differences between this and national definitions, the figures shown may diverge considerably from those which are quoted by national authorities or given in national budgets. For countries providing military assistance, this is included in the expenditures figures. For countries receiving assistance, figures do not include the value of items received. Expenditures for research and development are included in equipment expenditures and pensions paid to retirees in personnel expenditures.

France is a member of the Alliance without belonging to the integrated military structure and does not participate in collective force planning. The defence data relating to France are indicative only.

Iceland has no armed forces. The Czech Republic, Hungary and Poland joined the Alliance in 1999.

* Source: Financial and Economic Data Relating to NATO Defence, M-DPC-2(2000)107 published on 5.12.2000.

Table 4
DEFENCE EXPENDITURES OF NATO COUNTRIES AS % OF GROSS DOMESTIC PRODUCT (1980-2000)
(Based on current prices) (averages)

MEMBER COUNTRY (CURRENCY)	1980-1984	1985-1989	1990-1994	1995-1999	1996	1997	1998	1999	2000 (EST.)
Belgium (Belgian francs)	3.2	2.8	2.0	1.5	1.6	1.5	1.5	1.4	1.4
Czech Republic (Czech koruny)	//	//	//	//	//	//	//	2.2	2.3
Denmark (Danish kroner)	2.4	2.0	1.9	1.7	1.7	1.7	1.6	1.6	1.5
France (French francs)	4.0	3.8	3.4	2.9	3.0	2.9	2.8	2.7	2.7
Germany (DM)	3.3	3.0	2.1	1.6	1.6	1.6	1.5	1.5	1.5
Greece (Drachmas)	5.3	5.1	4.4	4.6	4.5	4.6	4.8	4.8	4.9
Hungary (Forint)	//	//	//	//	//	//	//	1.6	1.7
Italy (1000 Italian lire)	2.1	2.3	2.1	1.9	1.9	1.9	2.0	2.0	1.9
Luxembourg (Lux. francs)	1.0	1.0	0.9	0.8	0.8	0.8	0.8	0.8	0.7
Netherlands (Dutch guilder)	3.0	2.8	2.3	1.8	1.9	1.8	1.7	1.8	1.6
Norway (Norw. kroner)	2.7	2.9	2.8	2.2	2.2	2.1	2.3	2.2	1.9
Poland (Zlotys)	//	//	//	//	//	//	//	2.0	2.0
Portugal (Escudos)	2.9	2.7	2.6	2.3	2.4	2.4	2.2	2.2	2.2
Spain (Pesetas)	2.3	2.1	1.6	1.4	1.4	1.4	1.3	1.3	1.3
Turkey (1000 Turkish lira)	4.0	3.3	3.8	4.4	4.1	4.1	4.4	5.4	6.0
United Kingdom (Pounds sterling)	5.2	4.5	3.8	2.8	3.0	2.7	2.7	2.5	2.4
Total NATO Europe (US dollars)	**3.5**	**3.2**	**2.6**	**2.2**	**2.2**	**2.2**	**2.1**	**2.1**	**2.1**
Canada (Canadian dollars)	2.0	2.1	1.9	1.4	1.4	1.2	1.3	1.3	1.2
United States (US dollars)	5.6	6.0	4.7	3.3	3.5	3.3	3.1	3.0	3.0
Total North America (US dollars)	**5.3**	**5.6**	**4.4**	**3.2**	**3.3**	**3.2**	**3.0**	**2.9**	**2.9**
Total NATO (US dollars)	**4.5**	**4.5**	**3.5**	**2.7**	**2.8**	**2.7**	**2.6**	**2.6**	**2.5**

CHAPTER 10

CIVILIAN ORGANISATION AND STRUCTURES

NATO Headquarters

Permanent Representatives and National Delegations

The Secretary General

The International Staff

The Private Office

The Office of the Secretary General

The Executive Secretariat

The Office of Information and Press

The NATO Office of Security

The Division of Political Affairs

The Division of Defence Planning and Operations

The Division of Defence Support

NATO Headquarters Consultation, Command and Control Staff
(NHQC3S)

The Division of Security Investment, Logistics
and Civil Emergency Planning

The Division of Scientific and Environmental Affairs

Office of Management

Office of the Financial Controller

Office of the Chairman of the Senior Resource Board

Office of the Chairman of the Budget Committees

International Board of Auditors

NATO Production and Logistics Organisations

Civilian Organisation and Structures

NATO Headquarters

The NATO Headquarters in Brussels is the political headquarters of the Alliance and the permanent home of the North Atlantic Council. It houses Permanent Representatives and national delegations, the Secretary General and the International Staff, national Military Representatives, the Chairman of the Military Committee and the International Military Staff. It also accommodates the diplomatic missions of Partner countries, the NATO Headquarters Consultation, Command and Control (C3) Staff and a number of NATO agencies.

There are approximately 3 150 people employed at NATO Headquarters on a full-time basis. Of these, some 1 400 are members of national delegations and national military representatives to NATO. There are approximately 1 300 civilian members of the International Staff or agencies and 350 members of the International Military Staff including about 80 civilian personnel. Officials representing the diplomatic missions or liaison offices of Partner countries also have offices at NATO Headquarters.

Permanent Representatives and National Delegations

Each member nation is represented on the North Atlantic Council by an Ambassador or Permanent Representative supported by a national delegation composed of advisers and officials who represent their country on different NATO committees. The delegations are similar in many respects to small embassies. Their collocation within the same headquarters building enables them to maintain formal and informal contacts with each other, as well as with NATO's international staffs, and with the representatives of Partner countries, easily and without delay.

The Secretary General

The Secretary General is a senior international statesman nominated by the member governments as Chairman of the North Atlantic Council, the Defence Planning Committee, and the Nuclear Planning Group; as titular Chairman of other senior NATO committees; and as Secretary General and chief executive of NATO. He is also Chairman of the Euro-Atlantic Partnership Council and of the Mediterranean Cooperation Group, and Joint Chairman (together with the representative of Russia and the representative of the NATO country acting as Honorary President) of the NATO-Russia Permanent Joint Council. He is also Joint Chairman, together with the Ukrainian representative, of the NATO-Ukraine Commission.

The Secretary General is responsible for promoting and directing the process of consultation and decision-making throughout the Alliance. He may propose items for discussion and decision and has the authority to use his good offices in cases of dispute between member countries. He is responsible for directing the International Staff and is the principal spokesman for the Alliance, both in its external relations and in communications and contacts with member governments and with the media. The Deputy Secretary General assists the Secretary General in the exercise of his functions and replaces him in his absence. He is Chairman of the High Level Task Force on Conventional Arms Control, the Executive Working Group, the NATO Air Defence Committee, the Joint Consultative Board, the Joint Committee on Proliferation and a number of other Ad Hoc and Working Groups.

The Secretary General is responsible for the direction of the International Staff as a whole and has under his direct authority a Private Office and the Office of the Secretary General. The International Staff is drawn from the member countries and serves the Council and the Committees and Working Groups subordinate to it as well as the Euro-Atlantic Partnership Council, the NATO-Russia Permanent Joint Council, the NATO-Ukraine Commission and the Mediterranean Cooperation Group. It acts as a secretariat as well an advisory political and operational staff and works on a continuous basis on a wide variety of issues relevant to the Alliance and to its Partner countries.

THE INTERNATIONAL STAFF

The work of the North Atlantic Council and its subordinate committees is supported by an International Staff consisting of personnel from member countries, either recruited directly by the Organisation or seconded by their governments. The members of the International Staff are responsible to the Secretary General and owe their allegiance to the Organisation throughout the period of their appointment.

The International Staff comprises the Office of the Secretary General, five operational Divisions, the Office of Management and the Office of the Financial Controller. Each of the Divisions is headed by an Assistant Secretary General, who is normally the chairman of the main committee dealing with subjects in his field of responsibility. Through their structure of Directorates, Sections and

Services, the Divisions support the work of the committees in the various fields of activity described in other sections.

The International Staff supports the process of consensus-building and decision-making between member and Partner countries and is responsible for the preparation and follow-up of the meetings and decisions of NATO committees, as well as those of the institutions created to manage the different forms of bilateral and multilateral partnership with non-member countries established since the end of the Cold War. In addition, there are a number of civil agencies and organisations located in different member countries, with responsibilities in fields such as communications and information systems and logistic support (see Chapter 14).

THE PRIVATE OFFICE

The Private Office supports the Secretary General and Deputy Secretary General in all aspects of their work. Its staff includes a Legal Adviser and a Special Adviser for Central and East European Affairs.

THE OFFICE OF THE SECRETARY GENERAL

The Office of the Secretary General consists of the Private Office and the Executive Secretariat, the Office of Information and Press and the NATO Office of Security.

THE EXECUTIVE SECRETARIAT

The Executive Secretariat is responsible for the smooth functioning of the North Atlantic Council (NAC), the Euro-Atlantic Partnership Council (EAPC), the NATO-Russia Permanent Joint Council (PJC), the NATO-Ukraine Commission (NUC), the Mediterranean Cooperation Group (MCG), the Defence Planning Committee (DPC) and the Nuclear Planning Group (NPG), as well as the work of the whole structure of committees and working groups set up to support those bodies. It is also responsible for the planning and organisation of all Ministerial and Summit meetings, both at NATO Headquarters and abroad. The Executive Secretariat is, furthermore, responsible for the administrative arrangements concerning the EAPC and other bodies meeting in the EAPC or Partnership for Peace formats, and for the coordination of arrangements for the accreditation of diplomatic missions of Partner countries to NATO. Members of the Executive Secretariat act as Committee

Secretaries and Minute Writers, providing administrative and secretarial backup to the Council and its senior committees. They prepare agendas, decision sheets, summary records and documents of a procedural nature required by the bodies concerned and act as advisers to committee chairmen and points of contact for the committees themselves.

The Executive Secretary, as the Secretary of all Ministerial and Ambassadorial level bodies, is responsible to the Secretary General for ensuring that the work of the different divisions of the International Staff is carried out in accordance with the directives given. Through the Information Systems Service, his office ensures information technology support to both the International Staff and the International Military Staff and office communications for NATO Headquarters. He is also responsible for the implementation of the NATO-wide Information Management Policy and for the declassification, release to the public and archiving of NATO documents, in accordance with agreed procedures, when authorised by member countries.

THE OFFICE OF INFORMATION AND PRESS

The Office of Information and Press consists of a Press and Media Service and an Information Service divided into a Planning and Productions Section, a NATO Country Relations Section and an Outreach and Partner Relation Section. The Office has an Information and Documentation Centre in Kyiv. The Director of Information and Press is Chairman of the Committee on Information and Cultural Relations.

The Press Spokesman and Press and Media Service issue official statements on behalf of the Alliance and the Secretary General and arrange on the record and background briefings for journalists. The Press and Media Service arranges accreditation for journalists; issues written communiqués and speeches by the Secretary General; and provides a daily press review and press cutting service for the staff of the NATO Headquarters in Brussels. It organises media interviews with the Secretary General and other NATO officials and provides technical assistance and facilities for radio and television transmissions.

The Office of Information and Press assists member governments and Partner countries to widen public understanding of NATO's role and policies through a variety of programmes and activities. These make use of periodical and non-periodical publications, video production, photographs and exhibitions, group visits, conferences and seminars and research fellowships. The Office includes a Library and Documentation Service, a Media Library and a Distribution Unit.

The Office maintains close contacts with national information authorities and non-governmental organisations and undertakes activities designed to explain the aims and achievements of the Alliance to public opinion in each member country. It also organises or sponsors a number of multinational programmes involving citizens of different member countries and, in conjunction with NATO's Partner countries, undertakes information activities designed to enhance public knowledge and understanding of the Alliance in the countries represented in the Euro-Atlantic Partnership Council and in the Mediterranean Cooperation Group.

THE NATO OFFICE OF SECURITY

The NATO Office of Security coordinates, monitors and implements NATO security policy. The Director of Security is the Secretary General's principal adviser on security issues and is Chairman of the NATO Security Committee. He directs the NATO Headquarters Security Service and is responsible for the overall coordination of security within NATO.

THE DIVISION OF POLITICAL AFFAIRS

The Division of Political Affairs comes under the responsibility of the Assistant Secretary General for Political Affairs who chairs the Senior Political Committee and is acting chairman of a number of other committees (see Chapter 13). The Division has a Political Directorate and an Economics Directorate. The Director of the Political Directorate is Deputy Assistant Secretary General for Political Affairs, Deputy Chairman of the Senior Political Committee and Acting Chairman of the Political Committee. The Director of the Economics Directorate is Chairman of the Economic Committee.

The day-to-day work of the *Political Directorate* is handled by seven sections:

- The NATO *Multilateral and Regional Affairs Section* focuses on the development of NATO's relations with other European security institutions, notably the EU and the WEU; preparation of NATO Foreign Ministers' and Summit meetings; NATO-related political developments in member countries; NATO-related developments in a number of other countries which are not participants in the Euro-Atlantic Partnership Council or Partnership for Peace (notably Japan and some European states); the development of NATO's Mediterranean Dialogue; and the preparation and follow-up to meetings of working groups of experts from capitals on regional questions.

- The *Policy Planning and Speechwriting Section* is responsible for the drafting of relevant speeches, articles and notes for the Secretary General and other leading Alliance officials; the preparation of policy planning papers; and giving briefings on NATO's political agenda. It maintains contacts with the academic community and think tanks and undertakes the preparatory work and follow-up for the Atlantic Policy Advisory Group (APAG). Assisting with the preparation of communiqués and other texts and contributing to the drafting process which takes place in the context of meetings of NATO Foreign Ministers and meetings at Summit level also form part of the Section's work.

- The *Eastern European Partners Section* covers NATO's relations with Russia and Ukraine; the implementation of the NATO-Russia Founding Act and the NATO-Ukraine Charter; overall coordination of annual work programmes and the preparation and follow-up to Summit, Foreign Ministerial and Ambassadorial meetings of the NATO-Russia Permanent Joint Council (PJC) and the NATO-Ukraine Commission (NUC).

- The *Euro-Atlantic Partnership and Cooperation Section* covers bilateral relations between NATO and all other Partner countries as well as issues relating to NATO enlargement and the implementation and overall guidance of all activities under the Membership Action Plan (MAP). The Section prepares Summit, Foreign Ministerial and Ambassadorial meetings of the Euro-Atlantic Partnership Council, and deals with PfP issues in support of the Division of Defence Planning and Operations; coordinates NATO's South East Europe Initiative and its contribution to the Stability Pact on South East Europe, and NATO's overall political relations with the former Yugoslav Republic of Macedonia[1] in the light of NATO's KFOR commitment.

- The *Cooperative Security and Political Crisis Management Section* is responsible for cooperative security issues (including the EAPC Ad Hoc Group on Peacekeeping and the NATO/Russia Peacekeeping Working Group); overall relations between NATO and the Organisation for Security and Cooperation in Europe (OSCE); political aspects of crisis management exercise (CMX) planning; and peacekeeping aspects of NATO/United Nations relations. The section is the principal focus for political crisis management issues within the Political Affairs Division, and is responsible for day-to-day representation of the Division on the Balkans Task Force[2].

---

1   Turkey recognises the Republic of Macedonia with its constitutional name.

2   The Balkans Task Force is a coordinating body bringing together representatives of the International Staff and International Military Staff involved in the day to day coordination of matters relating to NATO's role in the Balkans.

- The *Conventional Arms Control and Coordination Section* is responsible for arms control policy and implementation issues related to the CFE Treaty; the Vienna Document; the Dayton Agreement; regional conventional arms control and Confidence and Security Building Measures (CSBMs); Small Arms and Light Weapons (SALW) and Anti-Personnel Landmines (APLs); the organisation of NATO multinational CFE inspection teams; management and development of the NATO verification data base (VERITY) and management, on behalf of the Verification Coordinating Committee (VCC), of cooperation with 14 Central and Eastern European signatory states to the CFE Treaty.

- The *Weapons of Mass Destruction Centre* was launched in May 2000 as a result of the Initiative on Weapons of Mass Destruction (WMD) that was approved at the April 1999 Washington Summit. The Centre is a section of the Political Directorate and includes a number of personnel from the International Secretariat as well as National Experts. The Centre's role is to improve coordination of WMD-related activities, as well as strengthen consultations on non-proliferation, arms control, and disarmament issues. The Centre also supports defence efforts to improve the preparedness of the Alliance to respond to the risks of WMD and their means of delivery.

The *Economics Directorate* provides advice concerning economic developments that have defence and security implications for NATO. It undertakes studies of economic trends and defence economic issues for the attention of the Secretary General; carries out studies on security-related economic issues on behalf of the Economic Committee; prepares economic assessments relating to NATO countries for the Defence Review Committee, in the context of NATO defence planning; and maintains contacts with international economic organisations. The Economics Directorate also has responsibility for implementing cooperation activities with Partner Countries in the framework of the Euro-Atlantic Partnership Council, the NATO-Russia Permanent Joint Council and the NATO-Ukraine Commission. These activities are focused on security-related economic questions, including defence budgeting, defence restructuring and economic problems in the area of defence policy.

THE DIVISION OF DEFENCE PLANNING AND OPERATIONS

The Division of Defence Planning and Operations comes under the responsibility of the Assistant Secretary General for Defence Planning and Operations, who is Chairman of the Defence Review Committee (the senior defence planning body in NATO under the authority of the Defence Planning

Committee) and Vice-Chairman of the Executive Working Group. He is Chairman of the Policy Coordination Group (PCG). The Division also supports the Political-Military Steering Committee on Partnership for Peace (PMSC/PfP) in the coordination and development of Partnership for Peace (PfP) activities. The Division has a Defence Policy and Force Planning Directorate, a Defence Partnership and Cooperation Directorate, a Crisis Management and Operations Directorate and a Nuclear Policy Directorate. The Directorate provides staff support to the Deputy Secretary General in his capacity as Chairman of the High Level Steering Group (HLSG), which oversees the implementation of the Alliance's Defence Capabilities Initiative.

The *Defence Policy and Force Planning Directorate* consists of a *Defence Policy Section and a Force Planning Section.* It is responsible for defence policy issues and for most matters of a politico-military nature considered by the Council or the Policy Coordination Group, as well as for the preparation, in collaboration with national delegations, of all papers and business concerned with the Defence Review, including the analysis of national defence programmes; for other matters of a politico-military nature considered by the Defence Planning Committee; for the preparation of studies of general or particular aspects of NATO defence planning and policy on behalf of the Executive Working Group and Defence Review Committee; for supporting the PfP programme and managing the PfP Planning and Review Process (PARP); for developing the Combined Joint Task Forces (CJTF) concept; for the maintenance of a computerised data base of information on NATO forces; and for the organisation and direction of statistical studies required to assess the NATO defence effort. The Director for Defence Policy and Force Planning is the Deputy Assistant Secretary General and is also Vice-Chairman of the Defence Review Committee.

The *Crisis Management and Operations Directorate* includes the Crisis Management Section, the Council Operations Section, and the Peacekeeping Staff. The Director of Crisis Management and Operations is also responsible on behalf of the Secretary General for the development and control of the NATO Situation Centre (SITCEN).

The *Crisis Management Section* provides staff support to the Secretary General, the Council and Defence Planning Committee, and relevant subordinate groups on major politico-military crisis management policy issues. It is responsible for implementing, monitoring and reporting on Council decisions associated with crisis management and the preparation and conduct of NATO operations. It also has a liaison and coordination function with NATO and non-NATO nations and appropriate international organisations such as the United Nations, the Organisation for Security and Cooperation in Europe, the

European Union, the Western European Union, the Office of the High Representative and the United Nations High Commissioner for Refugees.

The *Council Operations Section* supports NATO crisis management by the development and improvement of procedures, organisation and facilities to support the needs of the Council and Defence Planning Committee and to facilitate consultation in periods of tension and crisis. This includes coordinating and updating NATO's two crisis management manuals, developing an annual crisis management exercise, reviewing crisis management communications requirements, supporting the development of ADP support for crisis management, and conducting activities with PfP Partners to enhance their capacity to undertake crisis management and to improve cooperation in the crisis management field.

The *Peacekeeping Staff* supports the crisis management process by providing conceptual and technical advice on peace support operations. The Peacekeeping Staff also support other aspects of NATO's work in the field of peacekeeping, including the development of Alliance peacekeeping policy, the development of CIMIC (Civil-Military Cooperation) policy, and support for the PMSC Ad Hoc Group on Peacekeeping.

The *Situation Centre*, known as the SITCEN, has three specific roles: to assist the North Atlantic Council, the Defence Planning Committee and the Military Committee in fulfilling their respective functions in the field of consultation; to serve as a focal point within the Alliance for the receipt, exchange, and dissemination of political, military, and economic intelligence and information; and to act as a link with similar facilities of member nations and of the NATO Strategic Commands. The Situation Centre is supported by a Communication Centre or "COMCEN".

The *Defence Partnership and Cooperation Directorate* was established in 1997. It is responsible for PfP policy and implementation. It chairs the Politico-Military Steering Committee on Partnership for Peace (PMSC) and contributes to the work of other NATO bodies on issues relating to the EAPC, military cooperation in the context of PfP, NATO-Russia and NATO-Ukraine relations and the Mediterranean Dialogue. In the context of PfP implementation, the Directorate stays in close contact with all PfP Partner countries and chairs meetings of the NATO teams established to help Partner countries to develop their Individual Partnership Programmes (IPPs).

The *Nuclear Policy Directorate* provides staff support to the Secretary General, the Nuclear Planning Group and its senior body, the High Level Group (HLG), and to the Senior Defence Group on Proliferation. Its main functions are to assist in the development of all matters of nuclear policy and strategy, including the development of nuclear planning and procedures, exercises and training activities; and to assist in the coordination of NATO's defence-related activities in response to risks stemming from the proliferation of weapons of mass destruction and their associated delivery means. Part of the latter function will in future be fulfilled by the new WMD Centre, which has been established within the Division of Political Affairs. The Directorate is also responsible for the preparation of meetings of the Nuclear Planning Group at Ministerial, Permanent Representative and Staff Group levels, and for the development of public information on NATO's nuclear posture and defence-related response to proliferation risks.

THE DIVISION OF DEFENCE SUPPORT

The Division of Defence Support, under the responsibility of the Assistant Secretary General for Defence Support, has the following tasks:

- advising the Secretary General, the North Atlantic Council, the Defence Planning Committee and other NATO bodies on all matters relating to armaments research, development, production, procurement, and extended air defence;

- promoting the most efficient use of the resources of the Alliance for the equipment of its forces.

The Division provides liaison with NATO production and logistics organisations concerned with cooperative equipment projects and liaison with NATO military agencies dealing with defence research and related issues. It participates in all aspects of the NATO defence planning process within its responsibility and competence. The Assistant Secretary General for Defence Support serves as the permanent Chairman of the Conference of National Armaments Directors (CNAD) and of the NATO C3 Board and as Co-Chairman of the NATO Committee for Standardisation. The Division consists of two Directorates:

The *Armaments Planning, Programmes and Policy Directorate* supports the Assistant Secretary General in addressing broad policy and programming issues related to defence equipment procurement and Alliance armaments cooperation. Its Director is Deputy Assistant Secretary General for Defence Support. The Directorate is responsible for the formulation of policy initiatives in the armaments field designed to help to orient CNAD activities towards the accomplishment of the Alliance's missions. It is also responsible for the harmonisation of NATO armaments planning with other aspects of the Alliance's overall defence planning process.

The Directorate provides support to the Army, Navy and Air Force Armaments Groups and their subordinate bodies. Their role is to facilitate the exchange of information and the harmonisation of materiel concepts and operational requirements for future Alliance land, maritime, and air capabilities in order to promote cooperative solutions based on the programming steps and milestones of the Phased Armaments Programming System, and in order to achieve a high level of equipment standardisation in implementing the NATO Standardisation Programme.

In addition, the Directorate is responsible for the implementation of the Enhanced Partnership for Peace programme within the area of responsibility of the CNAD, including the Partnership Planning and Review Process; the management of the CNAD's contribution to the work led by the Senior Defence Group on Proliferation (DGP) in regard to the defence dimension of NATO's Proliferation policy; the support of CNAD's activities in the field of Extended Air Defence and Theatre Missile Defence and their coordination with parallel activities by the NATO Military Authorities, the NATO Air Defence Committee and the DGP; and the oversight of CNAD's work on the defence equipment aspects of peace support operations. The Directorate maintains liaison with external bodies such as the Western European Armaments Group (WEAG), and agencies such as the NATO EF 2000 and Tornado Development, Production and Logistics Management Agency (NETMA), the NATO Helicopter Design, Development, Production and Logistics Management Agency (NAHEMA) and the SACLANT Undersea Research Centre (SACLANTCEN).

A section of the Staff of the Research and Technology Agency (RTA) is co-located with the Armaments Planning, Programmes and Policy Directorate within the Division of Defence Support. The NATO Research and Technology Agency, which has its headquarters in Paris, supports the activities of the NATO Research and Technology Board (RTB). The RTA and RTB together form the NATO Research and Technology Organisation (RTO). The Director of the RTA reports to the Assistant Secretary General for Defence Support, as well as to the Director of the International Military Staff.

The *Air Defence and Airspace Management Directorate* (formerly the Air Defence Systems Directorate), has responsibility for the important relationship between air defence and military, as well as civil, airspace and air traffic management. The Directorate provides support to the NATO Air Defence Committee (NADC), whose role is to advise the Council and Defence Planning Committee on all aspects of air defence programme development. It does this in close cooperation with the NATO Military Authorities. The NADC is responsible for promoting and coordinating efforts to assure the continuing adequacy, effectiveness and efficiency of NATO's Air Defence System from a policy point of view and the extension of the system to provide capabilities that enable

NATO's Integrated Air Defence System (NATINADS) to fulfil its role in the new missions and responsibilities of the Alliance. The extension of NATINADS and its related concept address the need for more flexibility in collective defence, functional integration of maritime air capabilities, extended air defence to include missile defence, enlargement and Peace Support Operations/Crisis Response Operations.

The Directorate's other major area of responsibility is support of the NATO Air Traffic Management Committee (NATMC) (formerly Committee for European Airspace Coordination or "CEAC"). The NATMC's role is to ensure the coordination of civil and military airspace requirements for the Alliance. It also plays an important role in the cooperative efforts being undertaken with Partner countries in relation to the improvement of air traffic management. The Committee's role has been expanded to ensure, at the technical level, that military operators are able to maintain the required degree of compatibility with the different elements of the air traffic management system which the civil agencies are introducing now and in the future. In the context of current efforts towards future pan European integration of Air Traffic Management, the Directorate represents the Air Traffic Management Committee in a number of international forums.

Within the framework of NATO's cooperation activities, the Directorate also has responsibility for providing advice and assistance on air defence and airspace management matters to aspirant nations participating in the Membership Action Plan (MAP) and to other Partner countries. Analytical work in this context is carried out by the NATO Analytical Air Defence Cell (NAADC) established within the Directorate for this purpose.

The Directorate also provides liaison with the agencies responsible for the implementation of air defence related systems, the NATO Airborne Early Warning Programme, the NATO Air Command and Control System Programme, the improved HAWK Surface to Air Missile System, and the Medium Extended Air Defence System (MEADS).

NATO HEADQUARTERS CONSULTATION, COMMAND AND CONTROL STAFF (NHQC3S)

The NHQC3S combines the former C3 elements of both the International Staff and the International Military Staff in a single integrated staff. The main task of the NHQC3S is to develop policies and guidance for planning, implementation, operation and maintenance of NATO's Communication and Information System (CIS) and to monitor their application. The staff provides support to the NATO Consultation, Command and Control Board and to its substructure. It also provides support to the North Atlantic Council, the Military Committee, the Conference of National Armaments Directors, the Senior Resource Board and other committees with responsibilities relating to C3 matters. The Staff is organised in six Branches: Requirements and Concepts Branch (RCB); the Interoperability Branch (IOB); Frequency Management Branch (FMB); Information Security Branch (ISB); Information Systems and Technology Branch (ISTB); and the Communication, Navigation and Identification Systems Branch (CNISB). It operates under the coordinated management of the Assistant Secretary General for Defence Support and the Director of the International Military Staff. The Director of the NHQC3S is a Co-Vice Chairman of the NC3 Board and Chairman of the National C3 Representatives (NC3 Reps).

THE DIVISION OF SECURITY INVESTMENT, LOGISTICS AND CIVIL EMERGENCY PLANNING

The Division of Security Investment, Logistics and Civil Emergency Planning comes under the responsibility of the Assistant Secretary General for these matters. He is the Chairman of the Senior Civil Emergency Planning Committee in Plenary Session, and Co-Chairman of the Senior NATO Logisticians' Conference. He is also the Chairman of the Infrastructure Committee. The Division consists of the Security Investment and Civil Emergency Planning Directorates, the Logistics (IS Element) and the Resource Policy Coordination Unit.

The *Security Investment Directorate* comes under the direction of the Controller, Security Investment Programme, who is Deputy Assistant Secretary General and permanent Chairman of the Infrastructure Committee. The Security Investment Directorate supports the Senior Resource Board, the Infrastructure Committee and the Military Budget Committee by:

- screening Capability Packages from the technical, financial, economic and political points of view (Capability Packages set out the military requirements of the NATO Strategic Commanders in terms of capital investment, operation and maintenance costs and manpower);

- providing policy support and technical and financial supervision of the NATO Security Investment Programme;

- screening, from a technical and financial point of view, requests to the Infrastructure Committee for authorisations of scope and funds for projects which may be eligible for common-funding;

- providing technical and financial screening, as requested, on military common funded issues under discussion in the Military Budget Committee;

- providing technical and financial support to other NATO committees (SPC(R), PCG, PMSC) that touch on NSIP issues specifically and on resource issues in general.

The *Logistics (IS Element)* comes under the direction of the Head of Logistics, who is the Chairman of the NATO Pipeline Committee and Deputy Co-Chairman of the Senior NATO Logisticians' Conference. The Logistics (IS Element) is responsible for:

- the development and coordination of plans and policies designed to achieve a coherent approach on consumer logistics matters within the Alliance and through the Partnership for Peace Programme, in order to increase the effectiveness of forces by achieving greater logistical readiness and sustainability;

- providing staff support to the Senior NATO Logisticians' Conference and its subsidiary bodies;

- providing technical staff support to the NATO Pipeline Committee;

- supporting, coordinating and maintaining liaison with NATO military authorities and with NATO and other committees and bodies dealing with the planning and implementation of consumer logistics matters;

- maintaining liaison, on behalf of the Secretary General, with the directing bodies of the Central Europe Pipeline System (CEPS) and the NATO Maintenance and Support Organisation (NAMSO).

The *Civil Emergency Planning Directorate*, under the direction of the Director of Civil Emergency Planning who is the Chairman of the Senior Civil Emergency Planning Committee in Permanent Session, is responsible for:

- the coordination and guidance of planning aimed at the rapid transition of peacetime economies of the nations of the Alliance to an emergency footing;

- development of the arrangements for the use of civil resources in support of Alliance defence and for the protection of civil populations;

- providing staff support to the Senior Civil Emergency Planning Committee and the nine civil emergency planning boards and committees responsible for developing crisis management arrangements in the areas of civil sea, land and air transport; energy; industry; food and agriculture; civil communications; medical care; and civil protection;

- supervision of the Euro-Atlantic Disaster Response Coordination Centre (EADRCC) which coordinates international responses to requests for assistance from or on behalf of a nation stricken by disaster.

The Director of Civil Emergency Planning also oversees civil emergency planning activities undertaken in the context of the EAPC, Partnership for Peace, the NATO-Russia Permanent Joint Council, the NATO-Ukraine Commission, and the Mediterranean Cooperation Group.

The *Resource Policy Coordination Unit* is responsible for:

- developing, in coordination with the relevant bodies, policy proposals and planning documents on overall resource issues affecting the Alliance;

- coordinating across all elements of the staff on such issues;

- providing support to the Senior Resource Board on the development of resource policy and resource planning documents.

THE DIVISION OF SCIENTIFIC AND ENVIRONMENTAL AFFAIRS

The Division of Scientific and Environmental Affairs comes under the responsibility of the Assistant Secretary General for Scientific and Environmental Affairs, who is Chairman of the NATO Science Committee and Chairman of the Committee on the Challenges of Modern Society. He is assisted by a Deputy Assistant Secretary General and has the following responsibilities:

- advising the Secretary General on scientific and technological matters of interest to NATO;

- implementing the decisions of the Science Committee; directing the activities of the sub-committees and advisory panels created by it; and developing ways to promote collaboration in science and technology between scientists in Alliance countries and those in Partner and Mediterranean Dialogue countries, thereby strengthening the scientific and technological capabilities of the countries;

- supervising the development of pilot studies, short-term projects and workshops initiated by the Committee on the Challenges of Modern Society;

- ensuring liaison in the scientific field with the International Staff of NATO, with NATO agencies, with agencies in the member countries responsible for implementation of science policies and with international organisations engaged in scientific, technological and environmental activities;

- overseeing activities designed to enhance the participation of scientists from Partner countries in the NATO Science Programme and in projects of the Committee on the Challenges of Modern Society.

OFFICE OF MANAGEMENT

The Office of Management comes under the responsibility of the Director of Management who is responsible for all matters pertaining to the organisation and structure of the International Staff, and for advising the Secretary General on civilian staff policy and emoluments throughout the Organisation. He is charged with the preparation, presentation and management of the International Staff budget. He supervises a Coordination and Policy Section (which addresses management matters relating to the Organisation as a whole); a Budgets and Financial Analysis Section; and a Management Advisory Unit, which has responsibility for advising the Secretary General on matters related to organisation, work methods, procedures and manpower.

The Deputy Director of Management is responsible for the general administration of the International Staff including personnel services, the maintenance of the headquarters, the provision of conference, interpretation and translation facilities and the production and distribution of internal documents.

OFFICE OF THE FINANCIAL CONTROLLER

The Financial Controller is appointed by the Council and is responsible for the call-up of funds and the control of expenditures within the framework of the Civil and Military Budgets and in accordance with NATO's financial regulations. His Office consists of a Budget and Treasury Service and an Internal Control Service.

OFFICE OF THE CHAIRMAN OF THE SENIOR RESOURCE BOARD

The Senior Resource Board (SRB) is the principal advisory body to the Council on the requirements for, and availability of, military common-funded resources. The SRB is chaired by a national Chairman selected by the nations. The Chairman is supported by a small staff provided by the International Staff.

OFFICE OF THE CHAIRMAN OF THE BUDGET COMMITTEES

The Chairman of the Budget Committees is provided by one of the member countries. His position is nationally funded in order to maintain the independence of the Budget Committees. He has a small staff provided by the International Staff.

INTERNATIONAL BOARD OF AUDITORS

The accounts of the various NATO bodies and those relating to expenditure under NATO's common-funded Infrastructure programme are audited by an International Board of Auditors. The Board is composed of government officials from auditing bodies in member countries. They have independent status and are selected and remunerated by their respective countries. They are appointed by and are responsible to the Council.

NATO PRODUCTION AND LOGISTICS ORGANISATIONS

There are a number of NATO Production and Logistics Organisations (NPLOs) established by NATO and responsible to the North Atlantic Council for carrying out specific tasks. While there are differences in their mandates, funding, financial authority and management, they all report to a Board of Directors or Steering Committee responsible for supervising their activities. Further details are given in Chapter 14.

CHAPTER 11

MILITARY ORGANISATION AND STRUCTURES

The Military Committee

Strategic Commanders

International Military Staff

Partner Country Representation

MILITARY ORGANISATION AND STRUCTURES

THE MILITARY COMMITTEE

Earlier chapters have described the NATO Headquarters in Brussels, which is the political headquarters of the Alliance and is where the Permanent Representatives, at Ambassadorial level, meet in the North Atlantic Council under the Chairmanship of the Secretary General to discuss and approve NATO policy. At regular intervals the Council and other senior level policy committees (principally the Defence Planning Committee (DPC) and the Nuclear Planning Group (NPG)) meet in Brussels, or in other Alliance capitals, at higher levels involving Foreign or Defence Ministers and from time to time, when Summit meetings are convened, Heads of State and Government.

The decisions taken by each of these bodies have the same status and represent the agreed policy of the member countries, irrespective of the level at which they are taken. Subordinate to these senior bodies are specialised committees also consisting of officials representing their countries. It is this committee structure which provides the basic mechanism giving the Alliance its consultation and decision-making capability, ensuring that each member nation can be represented at every level and in all fields of NATO activity.

In a similar fashion, in order to assist and advise the North Atlantic Council, DPC and NPG on military matters, senior military officers serve as national Military Representatives to NATO and as members of the Military Committee in permanent session, under the chairmanship of an elected Chairman (CMC). Like the political decision-making bodies, the Military Committee also meets regularly at a higher level, namely at the level of Chiefs of Defence (CHODs). Iceland, which has no military forces, is represented at such meetings by a civilian official. The Committee is the highest military authority in NATO, working under the overall political authority of the Council, DPC and NPG.

On a day-to-day basis, the work of the Military Committee is undertaken by the Military Representatives, acting on behalf of their Chiefs of Defence. They work in a national capacity, representing the best interests of their nations while remaining open to negotiation and discussion so that consensus can be reached. This often involves reaching agreement on acceptable compromises, when this is in the interests of the Alliance as a whole and serves to advance its overall objectives and policy goals. The Military Representatives therefore have adequate authority to enable the Military Committee to discharge its collective tasks and to reach prompt decisions.

The Committee is responsible for recommending to NATO's political authorities those measures considered necessary for the common defence of the NATO area. Its principal role is to provide direction and advice on military policy and strategy. It provides guidance on military matters to the NATO Strategic Commanders, whose representatives attend its meetings, and is responsible for the overall conduct of the military affairs of the Alliance under the authority of the Council, as well as for the efficient operation of Military Committee agencies (see Chapter 14).

The Committee assists in developing overall strategic concepts for the Alliance and prepares an annual long term assessment of the strength and capabilities of countries and areas posing a risk to NATO's interests. Its additional responsibilities in times of crises, tension or war are to advise the Council and Defence Planning Committee of the military situation and to make recommendations on the use of military force, the implementation of contingency plans and the development of appropriate rules of engagement.

The Military Committee meets every Thursday, following the regular Wednesday meeting of the Council, so that it can follow up promptly on Council decisions. In practice, meetings can also be convened whenever necessary and both the Council and the Military Committee often meet much more frequently. As a result of the Alliance's role in Bosnia and Herzegovina and Kosovo, the internal and external adaptation of Alliance structures, the development of partnership and cooperation with other countries and of the new institutions to oversee these developments, the frequency of meetings of all the decision-making bodies of the Alliance has greatly increased.

The Military Committee in Chiefs of Defence Session (CHODS) normally meets three times a year. Two of these Military Committee meetings occur in Brussels and one is hosted by NATO nations, on a rotational basis.

In the framework of the Euro-Atlantic Partnership Council (EAPC) and Partnership for Peace (PfP), the Military Committee meets regularly with EAPC/PfP Partner countries at the level of national Military Representatives (once a month) and at CHODS level (twice a year) to deal with military cooperation issues. Further details are given in Chapter 12, together with details of meetings of the Military Committee with Russia and with Ukraine.

The Chairman of the Military Committee

The Chairman of the Military Committee (CMC) is selected by the Chiefs of Defence and appointed for a three year term of office. He acts exclusively in an international capacity and his authority stems from the Military Committee, to which he is responsible in the performance of his duties. He normally chairs all meetings of the Military Committee. In his absence, the Deputy Chairman of the Military Committee (DCMC) takes the chair.

The Chairman of the Military Committee is both its spokesman and representative. He directs its day-to-day business and acts on behalf of the Committee in issuing the necessary directives and guidance to the Director of the International Military Staff (see below). He represents the Military Committee at high level meetings, such as those of the North Atlantic Council, the Defence Planning Committee and the Nuclear Planning Group, providing advice on military matters when required.

By virtue of his appointment, the Chairman of the Committee also has an important public role and is the senior military spokesman for the Alliance in contacts with the press and media. He undertakes official visits and representational duties on behalf of the Committee, both in NATO countries and in countries with which NATO is developing closer contacts in the framework of the Partnership for Peace programme, the Euro-Atlantic Partnership Council, the NATO-Russia Permanent Joint Council, the NATO-Ukraine Commission, the Mediterranean Cooperation Group and the South East Europe Initiative. The Chairman is also ex-officio Chairman of the NATO Defense College Academic Advisory Board. The role of the Defense College is described in Chapter 14.

STRATEGIC COMMANDERS

The Strategic Commanders (SCs), namely the Supreme Allied Commander Europe (SACEUR) and the Supreme Allied Commander Atlantic (SACLANT), are responsible to the Military Committee for the overall direction and conduct of all Alliance military matters within their areas of command. They also provide advice to the Military Committee. They each have representatives at NATO of General or Flag Officer rank, who assist them by maintaining close links with both the political and military staffs within the headquarters and by ensuring that the flow of information and communications in both directions works efficiently. The SC Representatives attend meetings of the Military Committee and provide advice on Military Committee business relating to their respective Commands.

INTERNATIONAL MILITARY STAFF

The International Military Staff (IMS) is headed by a General/Flag officer, selected by the Military Committee from candidates nominated by member nations for the position of Director of the International Military Staff (DIMS). The IMS, under his direction, is responsible for planning, assessing and recommending policy on military matters for consideration by the Military Committee, as well as ensuring that the policies and decisions of the Committee are implemented as directed.

The IMS consists of military personnel who have been sent by their nations to take up staff appointments at NATO Headquarters, to work in an international capacity for the common interest of the Alliance rather than on behalf of their nation. Some posts within the International Military Staff are filled by civilian personnel, who work in clerical and support roles. The International Military Staff supports the work of the Military Committee, preparing and following up its decisions, and is also actively involved in the process of cooperation with the countries of Central and Eastern Europe under the Partnership for Peace (PfP) initiative.

Coordination of staff action, and controlling the flow of information and communications both within the IMS and between the IMS and other parts of the NATO Headquarters, is the responsibility of the Executive Coordinator located within the Office of the Director of the IMS. The Executive Coordinator and his staff also provide secretarial support to the Military Committee as well as procedural advice. The Director of the International Military Staff is also supported by five Assistant Directors, each of whom heads a separate functional Division.

The **Plans and Policy Division** develops and coordinates the Military Committee contribution to NATO defence policy and strategic planning. This includes contributing to the development of politico-military concepts, studies, assessments and related documents, NATO force planning, the Force Goal process, the annual defence review, the PfP Planning and Review Process (PARP) and long term conceptual thinking. The Division also participates on behalf of the Military Committee in NATO's overall defence planning process and develops and represents the views of the Military Committee and of the NATO Strategic Commanders on military policy matters in various NATO bodies.

The **Operations Division** supports the Military Committee in the development of current operational plans and in addressing questions relating to the NATO force posture and military management issues relating to NATO's role in international crises. The Division promotes and coordinates multinational training and exercises, including those involving PfP nations; and coordinates efforts relating to the development of an effective NATO electronic warfare operational capability and associated training and exercises. It is responsible for monitoring and assessing Electronic Warfare programmes and requirements. It provides support for the NATO Air Defence Committee and has responsibility within the International Military Staff for air defence matters. The Division also acts as the point of contact for the NATO Liaison Officer to the United Nations, a position which is filled by a serving member of the

International Military Staff, on behalf of the Organisation as a whole, when required.

The **Intelligence Division** provides day-to-day strategic intelligence support to the Secretary General, the North Atlantic Council/Defence Planning Committee, the Military Committee, and other NATO bodies such as International Military Staff elements, the Political Committee and WMD Proliferation Centre. It relies on the NATO nations and NATO Commands for its basic intelligence needs since it has no independent intelligence gathering function or capacity. On the basis of these contributions, it acts as a central coordinating body for the collation, assessment and dissemination of intelligence within NATO Headquarters and to NATO commands, agencies, organisations and nations. In addition to providing routine staff intelligence support, the Intelligence Division manages and coordinates the production and dissemination of NATO strategic intelligence estimates, intelligence policy documents and basic intelligence documents, as well as the maintenance of selected data bases and digital intelligence information services. It also performs strategic warning and crisis management functions and conducts liaison with other NATO and national bodies performing specialised intelligence functions and related activities. In sum, the Intelligence Division, supported by NATO nations and Commands, keeps the Alliance's senior bodies continually informed, facilitates the Military Committee's formulation of military advice to political authorities, provides an intelligence foundation for guiding the composition, organisation and operations of NATO forces, and performs a broad range of tasks in support of NATO defence and political functions.

The **Cooperation and Regional Security Division** serves as the focal point for military contacts and cooperation with Euro-Atlantic Partnership Council (EAPC), Partnership for Peace (PfP) countries, Russia within the framework of the NATO-Russia Founding Act, and Ukraine within the framework of the NATO-Ukraine Charter. It is responsible for the development and coordination of all IMS staff work on EAPC, PfP, NATO-Russia and NATO-Ukraine rélated issues, as well as the Mediterranean Dialogue. Its Cooperation Policy and Arms Control Branch produces and coordinates IMS PfP policy staff work, while the Russia-Ukraine Branch plans, develops and implements MC policy in relation to these two countries. In addition the Arms Control Section of the Cooperation Policy and Arms Control Branch coordinates and develops military advice on NATO involvement in different aspects of disarmament, arms control and cooperative security issues. It is also the channel for the Military Committee's focus on issues dealt with by the Organisation for Security and Cooperation in Europe (OSCE) in the field of disarmament, arms control and cooperative security. A section of the Division is located in the Western Consultation Office (WCO) in Vienna, in order to facilitate and enhance NATO's cooperation with the OSCE. The IMS PfP Staff element (PSE) is integrated within the Division as a separate branch, in which Partner officers work side-by-side with NATO colleagues as the focal point in the IMS for all elements of Partner country expertise related to the military aspects of PfP. It acts as the IMS' primary liaison with Partner Military Representatives and Partner Liaison Officers at NATO Headquarters.

The **Logistics, Armaments and Resources Division (LA&R)**, in co-operation with the SILCEP Division of the International Staff, is responsible for the development of logistics principles and policies, including medical support and transport and movement. It provides staff support to the Senior NATO Logisticians' Conference (SNLC) and Committee of the Chiefs of Military Medical Services (COMEDS), the deputy military co-chairman of the SNLC, and the military co-chairman/chairman of its two subordinate bodies. The Division also has a major responsibility within the area of logistic aspects of crisis management, humanitarian assistance and disaster relief, and provides the IMS representative to the Senior Civil Emergency Planning Committee (SCEPC) and COMEDS. The Division provides military advice to the Military Committee on issues relating to development of military policies and procedures for armaments planning, including research and technology matters. It represents the Military Committee at the CNAD, Major Armament Groups (MAGs), the Research and Technology bodies and Air/Ground Surveillance (AGS) Steering Committee, as well as within Western European Armaments Group (WEAG) and EUROLONGTERM groups. When required, the Division also supports the NATO Industrial Advisory Group (NIAG). It is also responsible for development of military policies and procedures for management of resources, including NATO common military budgets, infrastructure and manpower in cooperation with the International Staff and the two Strategic Commanders. It represents the Military Committee on the NDMC, SRB, IC and MBC. The Management Advisory Unit/NATO Defence Manpower Committee (NDMC) is an independent entity within the Division working directly for the NDMC, providing the expertise and staff nucleus to carry out management surveys, audits, validations and consultations.

The **NATO Situation Centre** assists the North Atlantic Council, the Defence Planning Committee and the Military Committee in fulfilling their respective functions in the field of consultation. It serves as the focal point within the Alliance for the receipt, exchange and dissemination of political, military and economic information. It monitors political, military and economic matters of interest to NATO and to NATO member countries on a 24 hour basis. The NATO Situation Centre also provides facilities for the rapid expansion of consultation during periods of tension and crises and maintains and updates relevant background information during such periods.

The **Public Information Adviser** (PIA) advises the Chairman of the Military Committee, the Deputy Chairman of the Military Committee and the Director of the IMS on public information matters and acts as a public enquiry and news media coordinator, as well as spokesperson for the Military Committee and IMS. The PIA's office coordinates public information activities with the NATO Office of Information and Press, and the counterpart public information organisations within the Strategic Commands and national Ministries of Defence.

The **Financial Controller** of the IMS is responsible for advising the Chairman of the Military Committee, the Deputy Chairman of the Military Committee and the Director of the IMS on all financial and fiscal matters related to the group of budgets administered by the IMS. He is responsible to the Military Budget Committee (MBC) for the financial management of the IMS budget. He is also responsible for preparing, justifying, administering and supervising all budget-related matters for presentation to the Military Budget Committee. Among other supervisory functions, he assumes financial control of the NATO bodies whose budgets are administered by the IMS, namely the NATO Standardisation Agency (NSA), NATO Defense College (NADEFCOL), and the Research and Technology Agency (RTA). He is responsible for conducting internal audits of accounts and activities with financial repercussions within his area of responsibility. Further details about the management of the Military Budget are to be found in Chapter 9.

The **NATO HQ Consultation, Control and Communications Staff (NHQC3S)** is a single integrated organisation composed of personnel from both the International Staff and the International Military Staff. The Director, NHQC3S, reports directly to Director of the International Military Staff and the Assistant Secretary General for Defence Support in meeting the requirements of the IMS and IS. As one of the co-Vice Chairmen of the NATO C3 Board, the Director is also the MC's representative to the Board. Members of the NATO C3 Staff support the NC3B through maintenance of key positions on the Board's eight sub committees and in turn support the provision of NC3B advice to the MC on C3/CIS Capability Packages from a C3 Policy, Plans and Architecture point of view. See further details in Chapters 10 and 14.

PARTNER COUNTRY REPRESENTATION

Since 1994 a number of Partner countries have opened Liaison Offices and, since 1997, permanent diplomatic missions, at NATO Headquarters. Military links with Partner nations are being further strengthened by the establishment of "Partnership for Peace Staff Elements". Currently eight of these elements, which consist of officers from NATO and PfP Partner countries, are located within the IMS at NATO HQ and at the first and second levels of the NATO integrated military structure. A new PfP Staff element was recently established at the NATO (SHAPE) School as a potentially important element in facilitating collaboration with PfP Training Centres and other PfP institutes. Officers from Partner countries filling such posts work alongside officers from NATO nations in an international capacity, participating in the preparation of policy discussions and the implementation of policy decisions dealing with relevant Partnership for Peace military matters. Since 1998, PfP Partner officers have also been part of the PCC staff and participate fully in its work.

CHAPTER 12

THE MILITARY COMMAND STRUCTURE

The Role of Integrated Military Forces

Evolution of the New Military Structure

Implications of the Development of the European Security and Defence Identity

The Combined Joint Task Force Concept (CJTF)

Internal Adaptation of Alliance Forces

New Command and Control Concepts

The Military Structure

NATO Enlargement and the Accession of New NATO Members

Partnership for Peace Activities and Initiatives

Wider Consultation and Cooperation

THE MILITARY COMMAND STRUCTURE

THE ROLE OF INTEGRATED MILITARY FORCES

All nations opting to be members of the military part of NATO contribute forces which together constitute the integrated military structure of the Alliance. In accordance with the fundamental principles which govern the relationship between political and military institutions within democratic states, the integrated military structure remains under political control and guidance at the highest level at all times.

The role of the integrated military structure is to provide the organisational framework for defending the territory of member countries against threats to their security and stability, in accordance with Article 5[1] of the North Atlantic Treaty. Within this integrated military structure, the Alliance maintains the necessary military capabilities to accomplish the full range of NATO's missions. With respect to collective defence under Article 5 of the Washington Treaty, the combined military forces of the Alliance must be capable of deterring any potential aggression against it, of stopping an aggressor's advance as far forward as possible should an attack nevertheless occur, and of ensuring the political independence and territorial integrity of its member states. They must also be prepared to contribute to conflict prevention and to conduct non-Article 5 crisis response operations. The Alliance's forces have essential roles in fostering cooperation and understanding with NATO's Partners and other states, particularly in helping Partners to prepare for potential participation in NATO-led Partnership for Peace operations. Thus they contribute to the preservation of peace, to the safeguarding of common security interests of Alliance members, and to the maintenance of the security and stability of the Euro-Atlantic area. The first significant example of this new extended role was the unprecedented deployment of NATO military forces alongside those of other countries in Bosnia and Herzegovina, where NATO was given responsibility by the United Nations, at the end of 1995, for implementing the military aspects of the Dayton Peace Agreement.

At the end of 1996, the Implementation Force (IFOR), created to undertake this task was replaced by a NATO-led multinational Stabilisation Force (SFOR), also consisting of forces drawn from NATO countries working alongside those of other countries participating in the effort to create the conditions for peace in the former Yugoslavia. At the end of 1997, member governments announced that from mid 1998, subject to a new mandate from the UN Security

---

1   See footnote 2 on page 158.

Council, NATO would organise and lead a further multinational force to consolidate the achievements to date, retaining the name SFOR.

In 1999, following the end of the Alliance's air campaign to end the repression and ethnic cleansing directed against the Kosovar Albanians by the Serb leadership, a Kosovo Force (KFOR) was created in accordance with the decision of the UN Security Council, with NATO at its core, to implement the Military Technical Agreement concluded on 10 June by the KFOR Commander and Yugoslav representatives. The first elements entered Kosovo on 12 June. As agreed in the Military Technical Agreement, the deployment of the security force was synchronised with the departure of Serb security forces from the province. By 20 June, the Serb withdrawal was complete and KFOR was well established in Kosovo.

At its full strength KFOR comprised some 50 000 personnel. It is a multinational force under unified command and control with substantial NATO participation, and arrangements for participation by the Russian Federation. More than 12 other non-NATO nations participated in the initial troop contributions to KFOR.

These decisions and the political process leading up to them are described in other chapters, as well as other aspects of the new roles and responsibilities of the Alliance including the implementation of the Partnership for Peace programme and the development of the European Security and Defence Identity within the Alliance (ESDI). Together, they have made extensive demands on NATO's existing military command structure and have exercised a major influence on its further adaptation and on the continuing implementation of the new command structure, whose activation began on 1 September 1999.

The reorganisation of its forces has changed the Alliance's overall defence posture. Adjustments relating to the availability and readiness of NATO forces continue to reflect the strictly defensive nature of the Alliance. However, the former concept of forward defence no longer applies in continental Europe, although regional differences remain with regard to the challenges which the forces may be required to face and their respective needs for forward deployment. United States forces in Europe have been cut by about two-thirds, and the majority of Allied forces previously stationed in Germany have left. These manifestations of the transformation of the defence posture are described more fully in Chapter 2.

Other aspects have also played an important part in the transformation. For example, the flexibility and mobility of the current overall defence posture includes provisions to ensure that NATO has the means to address challenges and risks posed by weapons of mass destruction (nuclear, biological and chemical weapons) and their means of delivery. Increased attention is devoted to ensuring that these challenges are reflected in Alliance defence capabilities.

Increased «multinationality» has also been an important factor in the development of the new defence posture. It has provided enhanced opportunities for multinational task sharing among Allies, allowing military capabilities available to NATO to be maintained or enhanced and ensuring that the most effective use can be made of resources allocated for defence purposes. The principle of "multinationality" is applied throughout Alliance structures and is of key importance for NATO's solidarity and cohesion, for the conduct of Alliance missions, and as a disincentive for the renationalisation of defence policy.

The principle of collective effort in Alliance defence is embodied in practical arrangements that enable the Allies to enjoy the crucial political, military and resource advantages of collective defence, and prevent the renationalisation of defence policies, without depriving the Allies of their sovereignty. These arrangements also enable NATO's forces to carry out non-Article 5 crisis response operations and constitute a prerequisite for a coherent Alliance response to all possible contingencies. They are based on procedures for consultation, an integrated military structure, and on cooperation agreements. Key features include collective force planning; common funding; common operational planning; multinational formations, headquarters and command arrangements; an integrated air defence system; a balance of roles and responsibilities among the Allies; the stationing and deployment of forces outside home territory when required; arrangements, including planning, for crisis management and reinforcement; common standards and procedures for equipment, training and logistics; joint and combined doctrines and exercises when appropriate; and infrastructure, armaments and logistics cooperation. The inclusion of NATO's Partners in such arrangements or the development of similar arrangements for them, in appropriate areas, is also instrumental in enhancing cooperation and common efforts in Euro-Atlantic security matters.

EVOLUTION OF THE NEW MILITARY STRUCTURE

The evolution towards NATO's new military command structure has been influenced by many factors, of which the most significant are the development of the European Security and Defence Identity within the Alliance; the implementation of the Combined Joint Task Force concept; the reductions and restructuring of Allied military forces as a whole, rendered possible by the transformation of the security environment following the end of the Cold War; and the assumption by the Alliance of new tasks and responsibilities, in particular in the sphere of peace support operations and crisis management. The influence of each of these factors on the military structure of the Alliance is described below.

IMPLICATIONS OF THE DEVELOPMENT OF THE EUROPEAN SECURITY AND DEFENCE IDENTITY

The rationale for the decision made by NATO governments to strengthen the European Security and Defence Identity (ESDI) within the Alliance is described in Chapter 4, together with the implications of that decision and the resulting interaction between NATO and the Western European Union (WEU) and the European Union (EU).

The emergence of a more clearly identifiable and strengthened European role within NATO has both political and military significance and has played a significant role in defining the parameters of the Alliance's transformation. The process is a continuing one which has been influenced at different stages over the past decade by decisions taken by the European Union, those taken by the Western European Union, and those taken by the Alliance itself. While these decisions have been interlinked and form part of the adaptation of European and Euro-Atlantic institutions to the changed security environment brought about by the end of the Cold War, other factors have also played a key role. Three factors should be mentioned in particular.

The first of these has been the intensification of cooperation in the security field between the European and North American democracies represented in NATO and the newly independent states of the former Soviet Union and of Central and Eastern Europe, as well as European countries which adopted a neutral or non-aligned political position during the Cold War period. With the end of the division of Europe, the former opposition between East and West ceased to be relevant and allowed a broader, inclusive concept of security to be developed, in the interests of the Euro-Atlantic area as a whole. The second essential factor in this context has been the growing importance of crisis management, peacekeeping and peace support operations, thrown into sharp relief above all by the conflicts in the former Yugoslavia.

The third fundamental series of developments after the end of the Cold War began with the wish expressed by a significant number of Central and Eastern European countries to become members of the Alliance, followed by the decision by NATO countries to open the Alliance to new members in accordance with Article 10 of the North Atlantic Treaty, and finally the historic decision taken in July 1997 to invite three countries to begin accession negotiations. The military impact of this development is described later in this Chapter.

These developments taken together have provided the context in which the discussion of the European Security and Defence Identity within the Alliance has taken place.

In the political sphere, the development of the ESDI is aimed at strengthening the European pillar of the Alliance while reinforcing the transatlantic link. It is designed to enable European allies to assume greater responsibility for their common security and defence and to enable a more coherent contribution to be made by the European Allies to the security of the Alliance as a whole.

In the military sphere, the development of the ESDI calls for assets of the Alliance together with the forces of non-NATO countries, in agreed circumstances, to be placed under the authority of the Western European Union for operations in which the Alliance itself may not be directly involved.

One of the central requirements of ESDI is accordingly for arrangements which enable the necessary elements of the NATO command structure to be used to assist in the conduct of operations led by the Western European Union[2]. These elements have therefore been described as "separable, but not separate", since they could be placed under the authority of the Western European Union while remaining integral parts of the Alliance's own military structure.

A further central aspect in the development of the European Security and Defence Identity is the concept known as "Combined Joint Task Forces" or "CJTFs". This concept and its significance for the adaptation of NATO's military structure are described below.

THE COMBINED JOINT TASK FORCE (CJTF) CONCEPT

A CJTF is a multinational (combined) and multi-service (joint) task force, task-organised and formed for the full range of the Alliance's military missions requiring multinational and multi-service command and control by a CJTF Headquarters. It may include elements from non-NATO Troop Contributing Nations.

---

2   The role of the Western European Union (WEU) with respect to the development of the European Security and Defence Identity has been progressively assumed by the European Union (EU), in accordance with decisions taken by the Council of the European Union in Helsinki in December 1999 and in Feira, Portugal, in June 2000. In November 2000, in Marseilles, corresponding decisions were taken by the WEU Council of Ministers: the operational role of the WEU was formally transferred to the EU and arrangements were put in place for the WEU's residual functions and structures. See also Chapter 4 and Chapter 15.

The CJTF concept was launched in late 1993 and was endorsed at the Brussels Summit of January 1994. On that occasion, Alliance Heads of State and Government directed that the further developments of the concept should reflect their readiness to make NATO assets available, on the basis of case-by-case decisions by the North Atlantic Council, for operations led by the Western European Union (WEU), thereby supporting the building of the European Security and Defence Identity. In addition, they linked the development of the CJTF concept to practical political-military cooperation in the context of the Partnership for Peace (PfP).

The need which the concept was created to fulfil arose from the changing security situation in Europe and the emergence of smaller but diverse and unpredictable risks to peace and stability. In particular, it was agreed that future security arrangements would call for easily deployable, multinational, multi-service military formations tailored to specific kinds of military tasks. These included humanitarian relief, peacekeeping and peace enforcement, as well as collective defence. The forces required would vary according to the circumstances and would need to be generated rapidly and at short notice.

At the core of the CJTF concept which was evolved to meet these needs are the command and control arrangements essential to allow such forces to operate effectively. The wide variety of circumstances under which CJTFs might operate places considerable demands on the command and control arrangements for such operations. The role of CJTF headquarters is therefore crucial. A CJTF headquarters will be formed around core elements (the "nuclei") from selected "parent" headquarters of the command structure. It will be augmented from other NATO headquarters and by nations and contributing Partner countries as necessary, using a modular approach, in order to meet the requirements of the specific mission.

A number of trials of the CJTF concept have been completed, for example, in the context of the Exercise Allied Effort in November 1997, in which a number of Partner countries participated as observers; and in the context of the Exercise Strong Resolve in March 1998, in which Partner countries participated and were integrated throughout the structure of the CJTF. The aim of the trials was to validate the evolving CJTF Headquarters concept.

Based on these trials and other relevant staff analyses, the Alliance began the full implementation of the CJTF concept in 1999. This process, which includes the acquisition of necessary headquarters support and command, control and communications equipment is scheduled for completion in late 2004. The implementation process is taking fully into account lessons learned from NATO-led operations in former Yugoslavia. Work also continues in the training and equipping of the headquarters contributing to CJTF. The final phase of implementation of the Concept will provide the Alliance with an important tool for crisis management in the 21st century.

INTERNAL ADAPTATION OF ALLIANCE FORCES

The internal adaptation of the Alliance's military forces is a further development of the reductions and restructuring undertaken in recent years to enable the Alliance to confront more effectively the circumstances of the changed security environment.

This process can be traced back to the London Declaration of July 1990, when Heads of State and Government of NATO nations called for a process of adaptation commensurate with the changes that were reshaping Europe. The London Summit was a decisive turning point in the history of the Alliance and led to the adoption, in November 1991, of a new Strategic Concept, reflecting a much broader approach to security than had been envisaged hitherto. This was reflected in the evolution in the European security situation in 1992 and 1993 and, in January 1994, NATO Heads of State and Government called for a further examination of how the Alliance's political and military structures and procedures might be developed and adapted to conduct the Alliance's missions, including peacekeeping, more efficiently and flexibly.

In September 1994, the Military Committee launched the NATO Long Term Study (LTS) to examine the Alliance's Integrated Military Structure and to put forward "*proposals for change to the Alliance's Force Structures, Command Structures and Common Infrastructure*". As work continued on the Study, Foreign Ministers provided further crucial guidance at their meeting in Berlin in June 1996, defining the scope of missions for NATO for which the new command structure would need to be equipped.

At their meeting in Berlin in June 1996, NATO Foreign Ministers affirmed that an essential part of the Alliance's adaptation is to build a European Security and Defence Identity within NATO, to enable all European allies to make a more coherent and effective contribution to the missions and activities of the Alliance as an expression of shared responsibilities; to act themselves as required; and to reinforce the transatlantic partnership. They also called for the further development of the Alliance's ability to carry out new roles and missions relating to conflict prevention and crisis management and efforts against the proliferation of weapons of mass destruction and their means of delivery, while maintaining the capability for collective defence. This was to be complemented by enhancing the Alliance's contribution to security and stability throughout the Euro-Atlantic area by broadening and deepening cooperation with NATO Partner countries.

This essential impetus for the Military Committee's work on internal adaptation resulted from decisions taken collectively by all 16 member countries. In December 1997, Spain announced its intention to join the new military structure. France, which participates in the Military Committee's work on internal adaptation, has indicated that it is not in a position to participate fully in NATO's integrated structures, but has expressed its continued positive attitude towards the continuing process of internal adaptation and selective participation in NATO-led operations.

The Alliance's efforts to improve its capability to fulfil all its roles and missions called for three fundamental objectives to be achieved. The Alliance's military effectiveness had to be ensured; the transatlantic link preserved; and the European Security and Defence Identity (ESDI) developed within the Alliance.

The overriding imperative in developing any new structure was that it must be "mission oriented". It needed to provide NATO with the capability to cope with the full range of Alliance roles and missions, ranging from its traditional task of undertaking collective defence, to fulfilling new roles in changing circumstances, including "non-Article 5" missions such as peace support operations. Furthermore, factors such as flexibility, force effectiveness, Alliance cohesion, the principle of multinationality, affordability and incorporation of ESDI and CJTF requirements all had to be taken into account.

The new structure also had to have growth potential and the flexibility to accommodate new member nations without the need for major restructuring. In this context, it was determined that the accession of the Czech Republic, Hungary and Poland would not require any additional NATO command structure headquarters. Finally, the structure had to afford adequate opportunity for the participation of Partner countries.

NEW COMMAND AND CONTROL CONCEPTS

In its internal adaptation work, NATO has developed new concepts of command interrelationships designed to ensure effective coordination between the different levels of command established under the new military structure. These new concepts reflect a more flexible approach to the conduct of Alliance missions and the fulfilment of mission requirements. They are based on a streamlined, multi-functional approach to the whole command structure. They include the following characteristics:

- A "supported/supporting" command relationship. This is one of the mainstays of the interrelationship concept which has shaped the development of the new structure. It is designed to give the North Atlantic

Council, the Military Committee, and military commanders at all levels greater flexibility in transferring the weight of emphasis to where it may be most required.

- Greater emphasis on the conduct of Alliance activities and operations at the regional level. This also takes into account the increased interdependency among regions. Work on the new command structure has accentuated the need for regionally-based headquarters able both to receive forces and to support inter- and intra-regional reinforcement.

- A flexible approach with respect to command and control (C2) measures, such as boundaries, coordination lines and phasing which will greatly facilitate the conduct of exercises and operations. For example, in Allied Command Europe, only those command and control measures necessary for the conduct of strategic and regional level daily peacetime operations need to be permanently employed or established. The requirement for permanently established boundaries below regional level in Allied Command Europe is thus eliminated and under the new structure there are no permanently activated Joint Sub-Regional Command (JSRC) Joint Operations Areas.

- Increased focus on the principle of "multinationality" with regard to the manning of the new military headquarters. This allows scope for representation of all member nations at the Strategic Command level. It also facilitates representation across the command structure of nations whose territory is adjacent to other Regional Commands, enhancing initial reinforcement capabilities; and resulting in wider participation at the JSRC-level, allowing nations whose territory is adjacent to a country in which a JSRC is located to be equitably represented.

This adaptation was carried forward under the Terms of Reference of the Long Term Study launched in 1994. The type, number and location of the headquarters which would constitute the command structure was agreed by Defence Ministers in 1997. With this decision as a basis, the North Atlantic Council approved activation requests for the headquarters in March 1999, paving the way for the full implementation of the new NATO Military Command Structure which began in September 1999.

THE MILITARY STRUCTURE

The integrated military structure includes forces made available to NATO by the member nations participating in the structure, in accordance with prescribed conditions. These forces are currently organised in three main categories, namely **Immediate and Rapid Reaction Forces, Main Defence Forces,** and **Augmentation Forces.**

Reaction Forces are versatile, highly mobile ground, air and maritime forces maintained at high levels of readiness and available at short notice for an early military response to a crisis. **Immediate Reaction Forces** consist of land, maritime and air components such as the Alliance's Standing Naval Forces in the Atlantic and Mediterranean and the Allied Command Europe (ACE) Mobile Force (Land) (AMF(L)) Headquarters. **Rapid Reaction Forces** are composed of other land, air and maritime components such as the ACE Rapid Reaction Corps Headquarters and the Multinational Division (Central) Headquarters (MND(C)).

Main Defence Forces include active and mobilisable ground, air and maritime forces able to deter and defend against coercion or aggression. These forces comprise multinational and national formations at varying levels of readiness which include four multinational main defence corps: one Danish-German, one Dutch-German and two German-United States. Some of these forces could also be employed for sustaining "non-Article 5 operations".

In addition to these forces, an agreement is in place setting out arrangements under which the European Corps (Eurocorps), consisting of units from Belgium, France, Germany, Luxembourg and Spain, can be made available to NATO in times of crisis for employment under the framework of both Main Defence Forces and Reaction Forces. In April 2000, similar arrangements resulted in the transfer of the operational command of the Kosovo Force (KFOR) to the Eurocorps as part of the command rotation, under the overall command of NATO.

Augmentation Forces consist of other forces at varying degrees of readiness and availability which can be used to reinforce any NATO region or maritime area for deterrence, crisis management or defence.

These forces are further delineated between those which come under the **operational command** or **operational control** of a Strategic Commander when required, in accordance with specified procedures or at prescribed times; and those which member states have agreed to assign to the operational command of a Strategic Commander at a future date, if required.

Some of the above terms have precise military definitions. The terms "command" and "control", for example, relate to the nature of the authority exercised by military commanders over the forces assigned to them. When used internationally, these terms do not necessarily have the same implications as they do when used in a purely national context. In assigning forces to NATO, member nations assign operational command or operational control as distinct from full command over all aspects of the operations and administration of those forces. These latter aspects continue to be a national responsibility and remain under national control.

In general, most NATO forces remain under full national command until they are assigned to the Alliance for a specific operation decided upon at the political level. Exceptions to this rule are the integrated staffs in the various NATO military headquarters; parts of the integrated air defence structure, including the Airborne Early Warning and Control Force (AWACS); some communications units; and the Standing Naval Forces as well as other elements of the Alliance's Reaction Forces.

The Supreme Allied Commander Europe (SACEUR)

The primary task of SACEUR is to contribute to preserving the peace, security and territorial integrity of Alliance member states. Should aggression occur, or be considered imminent, SACEUR, as Supreme Commander, is responsible for executing all military measures within his capability and authority, to demonstrate Alliance solidarity and preparedness to maintain the integrity of Alliance territory, safeguard freedom of the seas and economic lifelines, and to preserve or restore the security of his Area of Responsibility (AOR).

SACEUR conducts military planning, including the identification and requesting of forces required for the full range of Alliance missions, which include the promotion of stability, contribution to crisis management and provision for effective defence. He makes recommendations to NATO's political and military authorities on any military matter which might affect his ability to carry out his responsibilities. SACEUR has direct access to national Chiefs of Staff and may communicate with appropriate national authorities, as necessary, to facilitate the accomplishment of his missions.

Like the Chairman of the Military Committee, the Supreme Allied Commander, Europe, also has an important public profile and is the senior military spokesman for the Supreme Headquarters Allied Powers Europe (SHAPE). Through his own activities and those of his public information staff he maintains regular contacts with the press and media and undertakes official visits within NATO countries and in the countries with which NATO is developing dialogue, cooperation and partnership. He is also responsible for developing military contacts with NATO's PfP Partners.

Allied Command Europe (ACE)

SACEUR is the senior military commander for NATO's Strategic Command (SC) Europe. He is a United States (US) Flag or General officer. His command is exercised from the Supreme Headquarters Allied Powers Europe (SHAPE) at Casteau, Mons, Belgium.

The task of Allied Command Europe is to safeguard the area extending from the northern tip of Norway to Southern Europe, including the whole of the Mediterranean, and from the Atlantic coastline to the eastern border of Turkey, and includes an area around the Canary Islands and its associated airspace. This equates to nearly two million square kilometres of land, more than three million square kilometres of sea, and a population of about 320 million people. In the event of crisis, the Supreme Allied Commander Europe becomes responsible for implementing military measures to defend, preserve the security, or restore the integrity, of Allied Command Europe's Area of Responsibility within the framework of the authority given to him by the Alliance's political authorities.

Within Allied Command Europe, there are two Regional Commands responsible to the Supreme Allied Commander Europe:

Allied Forces North Europe (AFNORTH): Brunssum, the Netherlands.

Allied Forces South Europe (AFSOUTH): Naples, Italy.

Allied Forces North Europe (AFNORTH)

Brunssum, the Netherlands

The AFNORTH area includes Belgium, the Czech Republic, Denmark, Germany, Luxembourg, the Netherlands, Norway, Poland and the United Kingdom. It also includes the North Sea, Irish Sea, English Channel, Skagerrak, the Kattegat, the Sound and Belts and the Baltic Sea. The Commander is a German or United Kingdom four-star Flag or General officer. His subordinate commands are composed of:

- Two Component Commands:

    - Allied Air Forces North in Ramstein, Germany;

    - Allied Naval Forces North in Northwood, United Kingdom.

- Three Joint Sub-Regional Commands:

    - Joint Command Centre in Heidelberg, Germany;

    - Joint Command Northeast in Karup, Denmark;

    - Joint Command North in Stavanger, Norway.

Allied Forces South Europe (AFSOUTH)

Naples, Italy

AFSOUTH covers an area of some four million square kilometres including Greece, Hungary, Italy, Spain and Turkey. It also includes the Black Sea, the Sea of Azov, the whole of the Mediterranean and the Atlantic Approaches to the Strait of Gibraltar east of longitude 7° 23' 48" W, and an area around the Canary Islands and its associated airspace. The region is physically separated from the AFNORTH region by non-NATO countries (Switzerland and Austria). The Commander of AFSOUTH is a United States four-star Flag or General Officer. His subordinate commands are composed of:

- Two Component Commands:

    - Allied Air Forces South in Naples, Italy;

    - Allied Naval Forces South in Naples, Italy.

- Four Joint Sub-Regional Commands:

    - Joint Command South in Verona, Italy;

    - Joint Command Southcentre in Larissa, Greece;

    - Joint Command Southeast in Izmir, Turkey;

    - Joint Command Southwest in Madrid, Spain.

Other Staffs and Commands Responsible to SACEUR

The staffs or commands responsible to the Supreme Allied Commander Europe and dealing principally with Reaction Forces consist of :

- Reaction Forces Air Staff (RF(A)S): Kalkar, Germany;

- NATO Airborne Early Warning Force (NAEWF) : Geilenkirchen, Germany;

- ACE Rapid Reaction Corps (ARRC): Rheindahlen, Germany;

- Multinational Division (Central)(MND(C)): Rheindahlen, Germany;

- Multinational Division (South) (MND(S)) (yet to be activated; location to be determined);

- Standing Naval Force Mediterranean (STANAVFORMED);

- ACE Mobile Forces, Land (AMF(L)): Heidelberg, Germany;

- Mine Counter Measures Force North (MCMFORNORTH);

- Mine Counter Measures Force Mediterranean (MCMFORMED).

The Reaction Forces (Air) Staff (RF(A)S)

The RF(A)S was created to facilitate detailed planning for Reaction Forces Air. The staff of approximately 80 personnel is located at Kalkar, Germany and is headed by a three-star German Air Force general as Director.

NATO Airborne Early Warning Force (NAEWF)

The NATO Airborne Early Warning Force was established following a NATO Defence Planning Committee decision in December 1978 to acquire a NATO-owned Airborne Early Warning air defence capability to provide air surveillance and command and control for all NATO commands. The NATO AEW Force (NAEWF) is the largest commonly funded acquisition programme undertaken by the Alliance.

The NAEWF is a fully operational, multinational force consisting of two components: the E-3A component, which comprises 18 NATO E-3A aircraft and operates from a Main Operating Base (MOB) at Geilenkirchen in Germany and the E-3D component which consists of seven UK-owned and operated E-3D aircraft based at RAF Waddington in the United Kingdom. The NAEWF provides an air surveillance and early warning capability which greatly enhances effective command and control of NATO forces by enabling data to be transmitted directly from Airborne Warning and Control System (AWACS) aircraft to command and control centres on land, sea or in the air. Each aircraft is equipped with sophisticated radar systems capable of detecting aircraft at great distances over large expanses of territory.

The ACE Rapid Reaction Corps (ARRC)

The ARRC is the land component of the ACE Rapid Reaction Forces. Its role is to be prepared for employment throughout Allied Command Europe (ACE) in order to augment or reinforce local forces whenever necessary. Its peacetime planning structure includes 10 assigned divisions plus corps troops from 14 NATO nations, allowing a rapid response to a wide range of eventualities. Its broad spectrum of capabilities enables forces to be tailored appropriately to multi-faceted and unpredictable risks.

The operational organisation, composition and size of the ARRC would depend on the type of crisis, area of crisis, its political significance, and the capabilities and availability of regional and local forces. The transportability of components, the availability of lift assets, the distances to be covered and the infrastructure capabilities of the receiving member nation also play a significant, determining role. The ARRC Headquarters could deploy up to four divisions and corps troops. The major units available to the ARRC consist of:

- national divisions from Germany, Greece, Turkey, and the United States, as well as the Spanish Rapid Reaction Division made available under special coordination agreements;

- framework divisions under the lead of one nation: one British with an Italian component; one British with a Danish component; and one Italian with a Portuguese component;

- the Multinational Division Central (MND(C)) including Belgian, Dutch, German and British units;

- the Multinational Division South (MND(S)) (yet to be activated; location to be determined);

- corps troop units - predominantly British but with significant contributions from other participating Allies.

The Headquarters of the ARRC is multinational. It is located in Rheindahlen, Germany. The Headquarters of the ARRC is under the command and control of the Supreme Allied Commander Europe (SACEUR) in peacetime, with the Headquarters of MND(C) under operational command of Commander, ARRC. The remaining divisions and units come under SACEUR's operational control only after being deployed. The commander of the ARRC is a British three-star general.

The Headquarters of the ARRC assumed, for the first time, command of the land component of the NATO-led Peace Implementation Forces (IFOR) in Bosnia and Herzegovina on 20 December 1995.

Immediate Reaction Forces (Maritime)

There are three Maritime Immediate Reaction Forces operating in ACE. The Standing Naval Force Mediterranean (STANAVFORMED) consists of destroyer or frigate ships and provides the core of SACEUR's multinational maritime force in periods of tension or crisis. Two Standing Naval Forces for mine countermeasures, MCMFORNORTH and MCMFORMED, provide a continuous NATO Mine Countermeasures (MCM) capability, primarily for regional use in the AFNORTH and AFSOUTH Areas or Responsibility. They are under the operational command of SACEUR and can be deployed NATO-wide, when required.

These forces provide NATO with a continuous naval presence and are a constant and visible reminder of the solidarity and cohesiveness of the

Alliance. They are an immediately available deterrent force and make an important contribution to the Alliance's operational capabilities.

The Standing Naval Force Mediterranean (STANAVFORMED) was established in April 1992, replacing the former Naval On-Call Force for the Mediterranean (NAVOCFORMED) created in 1969. It is composed of destroyers and frigates contributed by those nations operating naval forces in Allied Command Europe (ACE). Ships of other NATO nations participate from time to time.

The MCMFORNORTH replaced the Standing Naval Force Channel (STANAVFORCHAN) in 1998 and is composed of units primarily from countries in the Northern Region. The naval forces of other nations also join the force from time to time.

The ACE Mobile Force (AMF)

The AMF was created in 1960 as a small multinational force which could be sent at short notice to any threatened part of Allied Command Europe. The Headquarters of the AMF is at Heidelberg, Germany. Its role is to demonstrate the solidarity of the Alliance and its ability and determination to resist all forms of aggression against any member of the Alliance. The AMF was deployed for the first time in a crisis role in January 1991, when part of its air component was sent to south-east Turkey during the Gulf War, as a visible demonstration of NATO's collective solidarity in the face of a potential threat to Allied territory. The land component of the force, consisting of a brigade-sized formation of about 5 000 men, is composed of units assigned to it by 14 NATO nations.

The composition of the AMF has been adapted to meet the requirements of its new role as part of NATO's Immediate Reaction Forces (IRF). It consists of air and land elements (IRF(A) and IRF(L)) to which most NATO Allies contribute.

The Supreme Allied Commander Atlantic (SACLANT)

The primary mission of SACLANT, under the overall political authority of the North Atlantic Council and/or the Defence Planning Committee, is to contribute to the military capability required to preserve the peace, security and territorial integrity of Alliance member states. Should aggression occur, or be considered imminent, SACLANT, as Supreme Commander, is responsible for executing all military measures within his capability and authority, to demonstrate Alliance solidarity and preparedness to maintain the integrity of Allied territory; safeguard freedom of the seas and economic lifelines; and preserve or restore the security of his Area of Responsibility. As the NATO strategic commander located in North America, SACLANT also plays an important role in maintaining the transatlantic link between Europe and North America. Like SACEUR, he advises NATO's political and military authorities on military matters and has direct access to the Chiefs of Defence, Defence Ministers and Heads of Government of NATO member countries when circumstances require.

The Headquarters of the Supreme Allied Commander, Atlantic (HQ SACLANT) is located in Norfolk, Virginia, USA.

Allied Command Atlantic (ACLANT)

The ACLANT Area of Responsibility (AOR) extends from the North Pole to the Tropic of Cancer and from the East Coast of North America to the West Coast of Africa and Europe (including Portugal, but not the English Channel, the British Isles or the Canary Islands).

NATO is an Atlantic Alliance, dependent on vital sea lines for economic well-being in peacetime and survival in war. The primary task of ACLANT is therefore to contribute to security in the Atlantic area by safeguarding the Allies' sea lines of communication, supporting land and amphibious operations, and protecting the deployment of the Alliance's sea-based nuclear deterrent.

The Alliance's Strategic Concept, approved by Heads of State and Government at the Washington Summit in April 1999, reflects a broad approach to security which places increased emphasis on conflict prevention and crisis management. In keeping with this approach, NATO's maritime force structures have been adapted to meet the needs of today's security environment in order to provide the range of options needed to respond to peacetime, crisis or conflict situations.

NATO's new military command structure eliminates the need for permanently established boundaries between commands below the strategic level. There are five major subordinate commands, including three Regional Headquarters, which report directly to SACLANT. Each of the Regional Headquarters is responsible to SACLANT for planning and executing Alliance military activities and arrangements, in peace, crisis or conflict, including undertaking tasks which may be delegated to them within the ACLANT Area of Responsibility or beyond it if required.

The five major subordinate commands are as follows:

Regional Headquarters, Eastern Atlantic (RHQ EASTLANT)

Northwood, United Kingdom

The primary mission of RHQ EASTLANT is to contribute to preserving the peace, security and territorial integrity of Alliance member states throughout the ACLANT Area of Responsibility. The Commander-in-Chief Eastern Atlantic (CINCEASTLANT) is a British four-star admiral.

CINCEASTLANT is "dual-hatted", serving both as a regional commander within the Allied Command Europe (ACE) structure in his capacity as CINCEASTLANT, and as a component commander under CINCNORTH in his capacity as Commander, Allied Naval Forces North (COMNAVNORTH). Operating within the chain of command of both NATO Strategic Commanders enables the headquarters to be a focus for military movements and seamless maritime operations involving both Strategic Commands.

CINCEASTLANT is also responsible for the administration and operation of the Standing Naval Force Atlantic (STANAVFORLANT), on behalf of the Supreme Allied Commander, Atlantic.

Standing Naval Force Atlantic (STANAVFORLANT)

The Standing Naval Force Atlantic (STANAVFORLANT) is a permanent peacetime multinational naval squadron composed of destroyers, cruisers and frigates from the navies of various NATO nations. The Force operates, trains and exercises as a group, providing day-to-day verification of current NATO maritime procedures, tactics and effectiveness.

Created in 1967, the Force has since involved a total of over 500 ships and more than 150 000 serving men and women. It participates annually in a series of scheduled NATO and national exercises designed to maintain readiness and foster interoperability. It provides a visible, practical example of Allied solidarity and transatlantic cooperation. Recent exercises have also demonstrated the capacity of the Force to undertake peace support and humanitarian operations outside the traditional area of responsibility of the Alliance, in line with NATO's policy of extending security throughout the Euro-Atlantic area.

Regional Headquarters, Western Atlantic (RHQ WESTLANT)

Norfolk, Virginia

The primary mission of RHQ WESTLANT is to contribute to preserving the peace, security and territorial integrity of Alliance member states throughout the ACLANT Area of Responsibility. The Commander-in-Chief Western Atlantic (CINCWESTLANT) is an American four-star admiral.

WESTLANT's most significant role in crisis or war is to ensure the safe transit of critical reinforcement and resupply from North America to Europe, in support of the full spectrum of NATO forces operating anywhere in or beyond NATO's area of responsibility.

In peacetime, CINCWESTLANT sponsors joint multinational exercises and Partnership for Peace (PfP) activities, as well as maintaining operational control and providing support for the NATO forces assigned to the headquarters.

Regional Headquarters, Southern Atlantic (RHQ SOUTHLANT)

Lisbon, Portugal

The primary mission of RHQ SOUTHLANT is to contribute to preserving the peace, security and territorial integrity of Alliance member states throughout the ACLANT Area of Responsibility. The Commander-in-Chief Southern Atlantic (CINCSOUTHLANT) is a Portuguese three-star admiral.

As the ACLANT commander bordering the southern portion of Allied Command Europe, CINCSOUTHLANT is the focus for military movements and seamless maritime operations across much of the southeast boundary between the European and Atlantic Regional Commands.

Striking Fleet Atlantic (STRIKFLTLANT)

Norfolk, Virginia

The Commander, Striking Fleet Atlantic (COMSTRIKFLTLANT) is the Supreme Allied Commander, Atlantic's major subordinate commander at sea. As such, his primary mission is to deter aggression by establishing and maintaining maritime superiority in the Atlantic and ensuring the integrity of NATO's sea lines of communication. COMSTRIKFLTLANT is an American three-star admiral.

The composition of the Force can be tailored to manage crisis situations as they evolve, providing support to aviation forces as well as amphibious and marine forces, and directly supporting Allied Command Europe land and air operations. Forces from Belgium, Canada, Denmark, Federal Republic of Germany, the Netherlands, Norway, Portugal, United Kingdom and United States contribute to the Force. STRIKFLTLANT has a potential wartime complement of three to four carrier battle groups, one or two anti-submarine task forces, an amphibious task force and approximately 22 000 Dutch, British and American marines.

NATO exercises are conducted periodically to ensure the interoperability of the forces assigned to the fleet under realistic environmental conditions and to strengthen command and control procedures.

Submarine Allied Command Atlantic (SUBACLANT)

Norfolk, Virginia

The Commander Submarine Allied Command Atlantic (COMSUBACLANT) is the principal adviser to the Supreme Allied Commander, Atlantic on submarine matters and undersea warfare. COMSUBACLANT is an American three-star admiral.

SUBACLANT provides a coordination capability for Allied Command Atlantic as well as direct liaison with Allied Command Europe for the management of Alliance submarine policy and doctrine. It is essentially a coordinating authority and is the principal source of submarine operational and tactical doctrine to both strategic commands.

Saclant undersea research centre (SACLANTCEN)

La Spezia, Italy

The role and structure of the SACLANT Undersea Research Centre, which forms an integral part of the major subordinate command structure of ACLANT, is described in Chapter 14 (Research and Technology).

Canada - United States Regional Planning Group (CUSRPG)

The Canada-United States Regional Planning Group (CUSRPG) is composed of military representatives of Canada and the United States. Its function is to coordinate the defence efforts of NATO in the Canada-United States (CANUS) region. There is no overall NATO commander for the region. Command arrangements therefore depend on the existing structures of the

Canadian and United States armed forces and the North American Aerospace Defence Command (NORAD), unless the respective military and national authorities determine that the formation of other combined headquarters is required to exercise such command.

The mission of the CUSRPG is to undertake the military planning required to preserve the peace, security and territorial integrity of the CANUS region. This includes arrangements for the basing and protection of strategic nuclear forces in this area; early warning and air defence; protection of industrial mobilisation and military potential; and defence against military actions which pose a threat to the security of the region.

The CUSRPG is composed of a Chiefs of Staff Committee (COSC), a Regional Planning Committee (RPC), a Regional Planning Committee Working Team (RPC WT), and a Secretariat located in Washington. Observers from the NATO International Military Staff (IMS) and the NATO Strategic Commanders (SCs) may be invited to attend RPC meetings.

The Chief of the Defence Staff of Canada and the United States Chairman of the Joint Chiefs of Staff are responsible to the NATO Military Committee (MC) for the coordination of NATO matters in the CANUS region. This includes the preparation and approval of plans for the defence of the CANUS region which are forwarded to the Chairman of the NATO Military Committee; maintaining liaison with the Chairman of the Military Committee, the NATO Strategic Commanders and other NATO agencies as required; and overseeing NATO and Partnership for Peace (PfP) training and exercise activities in the CANUS region.

NATO ENLARGEMENT AND THE ACCESSION OF NEW NATO MEMBERS

The underlying objective of opening up the Alliance to new members is to enhance stability in Europe as a whole, not to expand NATO's military influence or capabilities or to alter the nature of its basic defence posture. NATO's collective security guarantees and its dependence on multinational force structures offer the best means of achieving the above objective, on the basis of shared risks, shared responsibilities and shared costs. The opening up of the Alliance and the accession of three new members in 1999, combined with the influence of partnership and cooperation in the framework of the Partnership for Peace programme, allows the military focus to be directed towards current and future needs. This implies more mobile and flexible capabilities, designed to facilitate rapid response, reinforcement and other requirements in the crisis management field. New member countries participate in the full range of NATO missions and tasks. They are actively involved, along with the other countries participating in the integrated military command structure, in the planning, development and manning of NATO's force structures.

At the Madrid Summit in July 1997, the Czech Republic, Hungary and Poland were invited to begin accession negotiations with the Alliance. These were completed and Protocols of Accession were signed by the end of 1997. The three new member countries acceded to the Alliance in March 1999. In the intervening period, in parallel with the political process, intensive work was undertaken both in the countries themselves and within NATO to enable Czech, Hungarian and Polish forces to adapt their future role so that the process of joining the military structures of the Alliance could be managed efficiently. Pre-accession briefings and discussions took place to prepare each country for the obligations which they would assume on becoming members of the Alliance and to familiarise them with the procedures and practices which apply. These preparations helped to define each new member country's participation in NATO structures, to establish the methods by which their integration would be achieved, and to facilitate their involvement in Alliance activities during the accession period.

PARTNERSHIP FOR PEACE ACTIVITIES AND INITIATIVES

Within the general framework of the Partnership for Peace initiative, and particularly in the context of the Partnership Planning and Review Process (PARP), a wide range of military activities and initiatives have been introduced to further strengthen links between NATO and its Partner countries. These are not limited to participation in military exercises but also include, for example, opportunities to attend courses at the NATO Defense College in Rome and at the NATO (SHAPE) School in Oberammergau. PfP nations have also been invited to put forward candidates for posts under the arrangements mentioned earlier for Partnership for Peace Staff Elements located at different NATO military headquarters, participating fully in the planning and conduct of PfP activities.

Officers from Partnership countries have also assumed international functions within NATO's International Military Staff at the Partnership Coordination Cell (PCC) (see Chapter 3). The scope for involvement of personnel from Partner countries in CJTF exercise planning, concept and doctrine development and operations, as well as in CJTF headquarters, is also being examined.

Progress in implementing many of these measures has been rapid. Some 20 Partnership countries participated in the NATO-Crisis Management Exercise held from 12-18 February 1998. This command post exercise (i.e. not involving actual troop deployments) was designed to test and practice actions to be taken by NATO, in association with its Partners, in implementing a UN-mandated peace support operation in a hypothetical crisis situation. Another part of the exercise focused on NATO and Partner country involvement in responding to material disasters.

Throughout these activities as well as through cooperation in relation to other topics and activities identified as PfP Areas of Cooperation, emphasis is being placed on increasing transparency in relation to military activities and enhancing consultation and cooperation.

In conducting NATO/PfP exercises, for example in the context of search and rescue missions and humanitarian or peace support operations, emphasis is placed on contributing to the capabilities and readiness of participating countries to undertake such operations. Simultaneously, mutual understanding of different military systems and procedures is being enhanced and strengthened.

There is also a strong focus on multinationality within the military headquarters as well as in the forces taking part in exercises. This has facilitated the transition to more complex forms of NATO/PfP exercises involving higher levels of military units. The process has proven to be mutually beneficial to NATO and Partner countries, allowing valuable lessons to be learned from the experience of working together in combined exercises.

WIDER CONSULTATION AND COOPERATION

Following the Madrid Summit in July 1997, as part of the process of enhancing consultation and cooperation and introducing measures to increase transparency, a number of new institutions were created in both the political and military spheres.

In addition to the Euro-Atlantic Partnership Council (EAPC), NATO-Russia Permanent Joint Council (PJC), and NATO-Ukraine Commission (NUC), which operate in the civilian, political dimension and are described in earlier chapters, meetings take place in various formats to manage the military side of these multilateral and bilateral cooperative institutions. A Euro-Atlantic Partnership Military Committee (EAPMC) now meets to discuss and exchange views among all EAPC countries on military issues. In the same way, to facilitate closer links in support of the special relationship between NATO and Russia, meetings of Military Representatives and Chiefs of Staff have been established under the auspices of the PJC (PJC-MR/CS). Similar meetings are held with Ukraine at the Military Representatives' level (MC/PS with Ukraine) and at the Chiefs of Staff level (MC/CS with Ukraine).

Meetings of the Euro-Atlantic Partnership Military Committee (EAPMC) are held either in Plenary Session, with all Partner countries, or in Limited Session, in order to focus on functional or regional matters such as joint participation in Peace Support Operations. Alternatively, they may be held in Individual Session with a single Partner country. These meetings take place . either at the level of Chiefs of Defence (CHODs), normally held twice a year to coincide with the other CHODs meetings taking place in Brussels, or every month at the level of Permanent Military Representative. These arrangements limit the frequency and costs of the journeys to Brussels which each Chief of Defence needs to make. All meetings are chaired by the Chairman of the NATO Military Committee.

The NATO-Russia Permanent Joint Council (PJC) in Chiefs of Staff/Chiefs of Defence Session (PJC-CS) normally meets at least twice a year, to coincide with the meeting of the Military Committees in Chiefs of Staff Session in the spring and autumn of each year.

Each meeting is attended by NATO Chiefs of Defence, the NATO Strategic Commanders and military representatives of Russia. Meetings of the PJC-MR in Permanent Session, attended by military representatives based in Brussels, may take place more frequently.

Both meetings in Chiefs of Defence Session and meetings in Permanent Session are chaired jointly by three representatives, namely the Chairman of the Military Committee, a NATO Chief of Defence or a NATO Military Representative based at NATO headquarters in Brussels, and the Russian Military Representative. The NATO representation at the above meetings rotates among NATO countries for periods of three months.

During meetings at both the Chiefs of Defence and Permanent Representative levels, the three joint chairmen also share the lead for each agenda item. The agenda for each meeting is prepared on the basis of agreement established bilaterally between the NATO International Military Staff and the Russian representation, and is subsequently approved by each of the three chairmen.

The Military Committee with Ukraine meets in Chiefs of Defence session at least twice a year, and is also scheduled to coincide with other meetings taking place at the same level. The meeting includes NATO Chiefs of Defence, the NATO Strategic Commanders and the Ukrainian Representative, and is chaired by the Chairman of the Military Committee. Meetings of the Military Committee with Ukraine at Military Representative level are also convened twice a year.

CHAPTER 13

KEY TO THE PRINCIPAL NATO COMMITTEES AND TO THE INSTITUTIONS OF COOPERATION, PARTNERSHIP AND DIALOGUE

KEY TO THE PRINCIPAL NATO COMMITTEES AND TO THE INSTITUTIONS OF COOPERATION, PARTNERSHIP AND DIALOGUE

KEY TO THE PRINCIPAL NATO COMMITTEES

The principal forums for Alliance consultation and decision-making are supported by a committee structure which ensures that each member nation is represented at every level in all fields of NATO activity in which it participates. Some of the committees were established in the early days of NATO's development and have contributed to the Alliance's decision-making process for many years. Others have been established more recently in the context of the Alliance's internal and external adaptation, following the end of the Cold War and the changed security environment in Europe.

The following section summarises the membership, chairmanship, role, levels, subordinate structure and principal source of staff support of the principal NATO Committees. It should be noted that the Secretary General is titular chairman of a number of policy committees which are chaired or co-chaired on a permanent basis by senior officials responsible for the subject area concerned. The committees are grouped in accordance with their normal, permanent chairmanship. The list does not therefore follow any rigid hierarchical or structural pattern.

The main source of support shown under the respective committees is the Division or Directorate of the International Staff with the primary responsibility for the subject matter concerned. Most committees receive administrative, procedural and practical support from the Executive Secretariat. Many of the committees are also supported by the International Military Staff.

The summaries should not be confused with the detailed terms of reference for each committee which are approved by its parent body at the time of its establishment.

All NATO committees take decisions or formulate recommendations to higher authorities on the basis of exchanges of information and consultations leading to consensus. There is no voting or decision by majority.

NB: The NATO Military Committee is subordinate to the North Atlantic Council and Defence Planning Committee but has a special status as the senior military authority in NATO. The role of the Military Committee is described in Chapter 11.

The Military Committee and most of the Committees listed below also meet regularly together with representatives of Partner states included in the Euro-Atlantic Partnership Council (EAPC) and Partnership for Peace (PfP) to deal with EAPC/PfP issues.

1. North Atlantic Council (NAC)

2. Defence Planning Committee (DPC)

3. Nuclear Planning Group (NPG)

4. Military Committee (MC)

5. Executive Working Group (EWG)

6. High Level Task Force on Conventional Arms Control (HLTF)

7. Joint Committee on Proliferation (JCP)

8. Political-Military Steering Committee on Partnership for Peace (PMSC/PfP)

9. NATO Air Defence Committee (NADC)

10. NATO Consultation, Command and Control (C3) Board (NC3B)

11. NATO Air Command and Control System (ACCS)

12. Political Committee at Senior Level (SPC)

13. Atlantic Policy Advisory Group (APAG)

14. Political Committee (PC)

15. Mediterranean Cooperation Group (MCG)

16. Senior Politico-Military Group on Proliferation (SGP)

17. Verification Coordinating Committee (VCC)

18. Policy Coordination Group (PCG)

19. Defence Review Committee (DRC)

20. Conference of National Armaments Directors (CNAD)

21. NATO Committee for Standardisation (NCS)

22. Infrastructure Committee

23. Senior Civil Emergency Planning Committee (SCEPC)

24. Senior NATO Logisticians' Conference (SNLC)

25. Science Committee (SCOM)

26. Committee on the Challenges of Modern Society (CCMS)

27. Civil and Military Budget Committees (CBC/MBC)

28. Senior Resource Board (SRB)

29. Senior Defence Group on Proliferation (DGP)

30. High Level Group (NPG/HLG)

31. Economic Committee (EC)

32. Committee on Information and Cultural Relations (CICR)

33. Council Operations and Exercises Committee (COEC)

34. NATO Air Traffic Management Committee (NATMC)

35. Central Europe Pipeline Management Organisation Board of Directors (CEPMO BOD)

36. NATO Pipeline Committee (NPC)

37. NATO Security Committee (NSC)

38. Special Committee

39. Archives Committee

1. North Atlantic Council (NAC)

Members	All member countries.
Chairman	Secretary General.
Role	Principal decision-making authority of the North Atlantic Alliance. The only body formally established by the North Atlantic Treaty, invested with the authority to set up "such subsidiary bodies as may be necessary" for the purposes of implementing the Treaty.
Levels	Permanent (Permanent Representatives/Ambassadors). Ministerial (Foreign and/or Defence Ministers). Summit (Heads of State and Government).
Principal Subordinate Committees	The Council is supported by a large number of committees covering the whole range of Alliance activities.
International Staff Support	All Divisions and Independent Offices of the International Staff support the work of the Council directly or indirectly. The Council's role as the body responsible for fulfilling the objectives of the Treaty has included the creation of a number of agencies and organisations which also support its work in specialised fields.

2. Defence Planning Committee (DPC)

Members	Member countries participating in NATO's integrated military structure (all member countries except France).
Chairman	Secretary General.
Role	Principal decision-making authority on matters relating to the integrated military structure of NATO.
Levels	Permanent (Permanent Representatives/Ambassadors) Ministerial (Defence Ministers).
Principal Subordinate Committees	Defence Review Committee.
International Staff Support	Division of Defence Planning and Operations; Executive Secretariat.

3. Nuclear Planning Group (NPG)

Members	All member countries except France.
Chairman	Secretary General.
Role	Principal decision-making authority on matters relating to Alliance nuclear policy.
Levels	Defence Ministers, Permanent Representatives.
Principal Subordinate Committees	High-Level Group (HLG), NPG Staff Group.
International Staff Support	Division of Defence Planning and Operations; Executive Secretariat.

4. Military Committee (MC)

Members	All member countries.
Chairman	Chairman of the Military Committee.
Role	Senior military authority in NATO under the overall authority of the North Atlantic Council and Defence Planning Committee.
Levels	Chiefs of Staff/Chiefs of Defence, National Military Representatives.
Principal Subordinate Committees	Military Committee Working Groups. A number of joint civil and military bodies also report to the Military Committee as well as to the Council and Defence Planning Committee.
International Staff Support	International Military Staff.

5. Executive Working Group (EWG)

Members	All member countries.
Chairman	Deputy Secretary General. Permanent Chairman: Assistant Secretary General, Defence Planning and Operations.
Role	Senior advisory body to the North Atlantic Council on defence matters concerning the 19 member countries and relations with other organisations such as the Western European Union (WEU).
Levels	Defence Counsellors of national delegations.
Principal Subordinate Committees	N/A.[1]
International Staff Support	Division of Defence Planning and Operations; Executive Secretariat.

6. High Level Task Force on Conventional Arms Control (HLTF)

Members	All member countries.
Chairman	Deputy Secretary General; Acting Chairman: Assistant Secretary General for Political Affairs.
Role	Consultative and advisory body to Foreign and Defence Ministers on conventional arms control issues.
Levels	Experts from Ministries of Foreign Affairs and Ministries of Defence at the level of Political Directors; Political Advisers to NATO delegations.
Principal Subordinate Committees	HLTF at Deputies level.
International Staff Support	Division of Political Affairs (Conventional Arms Control and Coordination Section); Executive Secretariat.

---

1   N/A: not applicable.

7. Joint Committee on Proliferation (JCP)

Members	All member countries.
Chairman	Deputy Secretary General.
Role	Senior advisory body providing coordinated reports to the North Atlantic Council on politico-military and defence aspects of the proliferation of weapons of mass destruction.
Levels	Members of the Senior Politico-Military Group on Proliferation (SGP) and the Senior Defence Group on Proliferation (DGP) meeting in joint session.
Principal Subordinate Committees	N/A.
International Staff Support	Division of Political Affairs; Executive Secretariat.

8. Political-Military Steering Committee on Partnership for Peace (PMSC/PfP)

Members	All member countries.
Chairman	Deputy Secretary General. Permanent Chairmen: Assistant Secretary General for Political Affairs; Assistant Secretary General for Defence Planning and Operations/Director, Defence Partnership and Cooperation Directorate (DPAO).
Role	Principal policy-making body and advisory body to the North Atlantic Council for all aspects of the Partnership for Peace including the PfP Planning and Review Process (PARP).
Levels	Representatives of national delegations (two members per delegation); membership frequently changes depending on the subjects being discussed.
Principal Subordinate Committees	N/A.
International Staff Support	Division of Political Affairs; Division of Defence Planning and Operations; Executive Secretariat.

9. NATO Air Defence Committee (NADC)

Members	All member countries.
Chairman	Deputy Secretary General.
Role	Advises the North Atlantic Council and the EAPC on all aspects of air defence, including tactical missile defence. Promotes harmonisation of national efforts with international planning related to air command and control and air defence weapons.
Levels	Senior national military or executive officers involved in the management and policy relating to air defence or air command and control systems.
Principal Subordinate Committees	Air Defence Representatives (ADREPS); Panel on Air Defence Weapons (PADW); Panel on Air Defence Philosophy (PADP): Early Warning Inter-Staff Group (EWISG); Partner Air Defence Representatives (PADREPS).
International Staff Support	Division of Defence Support (Air Defence and Airspace Management Directorate); Executive Secretariat.

10. NATO Consultation, Command and Control Board (NC3B)

Members	All member countries.
Chairman	Deputy Secretary General.
Permanent Chairman	Assistant Secretary General for Defence Support
Co-Vice Chairmen	Director, NATO Headquarters C3 Staff and an elected Co-Vice Chairman.
Role	Senior multinational body acting on behalf of and responsible to the North Atlantic Council and Defence Planning Committee on all matters relating to Consultation, Command and Control (C3) throughout the Organisation.
Levels	The C3 Board brings together 2 senior representatives from each nation involved in management and policy of Communication and Information Systems (CIS) in support of C3, able to take into account the wide ranging functional responsibilities of the Board; 1 representative from the Military Committee; 1 representative from each Strategic Command; 1 representative from the following NATO committees: CNAD, SCEPC/CCPC, COEC, NADC, NACMO BOD, NAPMO BOD, NSC, SRB, PMSC, NCS and RTB; the General Manager, NC3A and the Controller, NACOSA.
Principal Subordinate Committees	Group of National C3 Representatives acting as the Board in permanent session, working groups and sub-committees + 8 sub-committees with their sub-structure of working groups, ad hoc working groups, sub-groups and ad hoc groups (Joint C3 Requirements and Concepts (JRCSC-SC/1); Interoperability (ISC-SC/2); Frequency Management (FMSC-SC/3); INFOSEC (INFOSECSC-SC/4); Information Systems (ISSC-SC/5); Communications Network (CNSC-SC/6); Identification (IDENTSC-SC/7); and Navigation (NAVSC-SC/8)).
International Staff Support	NATO Headquarters C3 Staff (NHQC3S); Executive Secretariat.

11. NATO Air Command and Control System (ACCS) Management Organisation (NACMO) Board of Directors

Members	17 participating NATO countries (NATO member countries excluding Iceland and Luxembourg).
Chairman	Deputy Secretary General. National Chairman (Vice Chairman of the NATO Air Defence Committee (NADC)).
Role	Ensures the planning and implementation of NATO's Air Command and Control System Programme.
Levels	Senior national military or executive officers involved in the management of air defence or air command and control systems.
Principal Subordinate Committees	ACCS Advisory Committee.
International Staff Support	Division of Defence Support (Air Defence and Airspace Management Directorate); Executive Secretariat.

12. Political Committee at Senior Level (SPC)

Members	All member countries.
Chairman	Assistant Secretary General for Political Affairs.
Role	Senior advisory body of the North Atlantic Council on political and specific politico-military questions. Reinforced with experts when dealing with some issues (SPC(R)).
Levels	Deputy Permanent Representatives.
Principal Subordinate Committees	N/A.
International Staff Support	Division of Political Affairs; Executive Secretariat and other IS Divisions/Offices as required.

13. Atlantic Policy Advisory Group (APAG)

Members	All member countries.
Chairman	Assistant Secretary General for Political Affairs.
Role	Advisory body to the North Atlantic Council, charged with examining relevant security policy projections in the longer term.
Levels	National representatives at the level of Political Directors, acting in an individual expert capacity. The APAG meets annually, with Partner country participation.
Principal Subordinate Committees	N/A.
International Staff Support	Division of Political Affairs.

14. Political Committee (PC)

Members	All member countries.
Chairman	Assistant Secretary General for Political Affairs.
Role	Advisory body to the North Atlantic Council on political questions.
Levels	Political Advisers to national delegations, reinforced as required by experts.
Principal Subordinate Committees	N/A.
International Staff Support	Division of Political Affairs; Executive Secretariat.

15. Mediterranean Cooperation Group (MCG)

Members	All member countries.
Chairman	Assistant Secretary General for Political Affairs. Acting Chairman: Deputy Assistant Secretary General and Director, Political Directorate.
Role	Advisory body to the North Atlantic Council on Mediterranean Dialogue issues.
Levels	Political Advisers to NATO delegations. Also meets with representatives of Mediterranean Dialogue Countries.
Principal Subordinate Committees	N/A.
International Staff Support	Division of Political Affairs; Executive Secretariat.

16. Senior Politico-Military Group on Proliferation (SGP)

Members	All member countries.
Chairman	Assistant Secretary General for Political Affairs.
Role	Senior advisory body on politico-military aspects of the proliferation of weapons of mass destruction.
Levels	Senior national officials responsible for political and security issues related to non-proliferation.
Principal Subordinate Committees	Also meets with Senior Defence Group on Proliferation (DGP) becoming the Joint Committee on Proliferation (JCP).
International Staff Support	Division of Political Affairs; Executive Secretariat.

17. Verification Coordinating Committee (VCC)

Members	All member countries.
Chairman	Assistant Secretary General for Political Affairs. Acting Chairman: Head, Verification and Implementation Coordination Section.
Role	Principal body for decisions on matters of conventional arms control implementation and verification coordination.
Levels	Plenary sessions, Working Groups, Expert Groups, Seminars/ Workshops with experts from Ministries of Foreign Affairs and Ministries of Defence, experts from Verification Units, Secretaries of Delegations.
Principal Subordinate Committees	N/A.
International Staff Support	Division of Political Affairs (Conventional Arms Control Coordination Section); Executive Secretariat.

18. Policy Coordination Group (PCG)

Members	All member countries.
Chairman	Assistant Secretary General for Defence Planning and Operations.
Role	Principal forum for consultation and advisory body to the North Atlantic Council on politico-military matters (including peacekeeping operations, development of the Combined Joint Task Force (CJTF) concept, and review of NATO's Strategic Concept).
Levels	Deputy Permanent Representatives and national Military Representatives.
Principal Subordinate Committees	N/A.
International Staff Support	Division of Defence Planning and Operations; Executive Secretariat.

19. Defence Review Committee (DRC)

Members	All member countries except France.
Chairman	Assistant Secretary General for Defence Planning and Operations.
Role	Senior advisory committee to the Defence Planning Committee on force planning and other issues relating to the integrated military structure.
Levels	Defence Counsellors of national delegations.
Principal Subordinate Committees	DRC Working Group.
International Staff Support	Division of Defence Planning and Operations; Executive Secretariat.

20. Conference of National Armaments Directors (CNAD)

Members	All member countries.
Chairman	Secretary General. Permanent Chairman: Assistant Secretary General for Defence Support.
Role	Senior body under the North Atlantic Council dealing with production logistics. Promotes NATO armaments co-operation and considers political, economic and technical aspects of the development and procurement of equipment for NATO forces.
Levels	National Armaments Directors.
Principal Subordinate Committees	National Armaments Directors' Representatives (NADREPS); NATO Army Armaments Group (NAAG); NATO Air Force Armaments Group (NAFAG); NATO Navy Armaments Group (NNAG); NATO Industrial Advisory Group (NIAG).
International Staff Support	Division of Defence Support (Armaments Planning, Programmes and Policy Directorate); Executive Secretariat.

21. NATO Committee for Standardisation (NCS)

Members	All member countries.
Chairman	Secretary General.
Permanent Co-Chairman	Assistant Secretary General for Defence Support and Director of the International Military Staff.
Role	Senior authority of the Alliance responsible for providing coordinated advice to the North Atlantic Council on overall standardisation matters.
Levels	Senior officials from capitals representing coordinated national positions on standardisation.
Principal Subordinate Committees	Group of NCS Representatives (NCSREPs); NATO Standardisation Staff Group (NSSG).
International Staff Support	Executive Secretariat; NATO Standardisation Agency (NSA).

22. Infrastructure Committee

Members	All member countries.
Chairman	Assistant Secretary General for Security Investment, Logistics and Civil Emergency Planning. Permanent Chairman: Controller for Security Investment Programme.
Role	Responsible for the implementation of the NATO Security Investment Programme, as screened and endorsed by the Senior Resource Board and approved by the North Atlantic Council or Defence Planning Committee.
Levels	Infrastructure advisers of national delegations; representatives of the Military Committee, NATO Strategic Commanders and NATO Agencies.
Principal Subordinate Committees	N/A.
International Staff Support	Division of Security Investment, Logistics and Civil Emergency Planning.

23. Senior Civil Emergency Planning Committee (SCEPC)

Members	All member countries.
Chairman	Secretary General. Permanent Chairmen: Assistant Secretary General for Security Investment, Logistics and Civil Emergency Planning/Director, Civil Emergency Planning Directorate.
Role	Senior policy and advisory body to the North Atlantic Council on civil emergency planning and disaster relief matters. Responsible for policy direction and coordination of Planning Boards and Committees.
Levels	Senior officials from capitals with responsibility for coordination of civil emergency activities/representatives from national delegations.
Principal Subordinate Committees	Planning Boards and Committees (Ocean Shipping, European Inland Surface Transport, Civil Aviation, Food and Agriculture, Industrial Preparedness, Petroleum Planning (dormant), Civil Communications Planning, Civil Protection, Medical Planning).
International Staff Support	Division of Security Investment, Logistics and Civil Emergency Planning (Civil Emergency Planning Directorate); Executive Secretariat.

24. Senior NATO Logisticians' Conference (SNLC)

Members	All member countries.
Chairman	Secretary General. Permanent Chairmen: Assistant Secretary General for Security Investment, Logistics and Civil Emergency Planning and Deputy Chairman of the Military Committee.
Role	Senior body advising the North Atlantic Council, Defence Planning Committee and Military Committee on consumer logistics matters. Joint civil/military body responsible for assessment of Alliance consumer logistics requirements and ensuring adequate logistics support of NATO forces. The SNLC has the primary responsibility on behalf of the Council, for the coordination of issues across the whole logistics spectrum with other NATO logistics bodies.
Levels	Senior national, civil and military officials with responsibilities for consumer logistics matters in member countries.
Principal Subordinate Committees	SNLC Logistic Staff Meeting; Movement and Transportation Advisory Group.
International Staff Support	Division of Security Investment, Logistics and Civil Emergency Planning (Logistics (IS Element)). Logistics, Armaments and Resources Division (IMS).

25. Science Committee (SCOM)

Members	All member countries.
Chairman	Assistant Secretary General for Scientific and Environmental Affairs.
Role	Principal decision-making authority for the NATO Science Programme.
Levels	National experts in Science Policy appointed from government or independent bodies in member countries.
Principal Subordinate Committees	The Science Committee appoints a variety of sub-committees, advisory panels and steering groups to carry out special tasks.
International Staff Support	Division of Scientific and Environmental Affairs.

26. Committee on the Challenges of Modern Society (CCMS)

Members	All member countries.
Chairman	Assistant Secretary General for Scientific and Environmental Affairs.
Role	Principal decision-making authority for the NATO programme on the Challenges of Modern Society.
Levels	National representatives with expertise and/or responsibilities for environmental programmes in member countries.
Principal Subordinate Committees	Nations appoint representatives to a subcommittee responsible for CCMS fellowships.
International Staff Support	Division of Scientific and Environmental Affairs.

27. Civil and Military Budget Committees (CBC/MBC)

Members	All member countries.
Chairman	National Chairman appointed on a rotational basis by the North Atlantic Council.
Role	Responsible to the North Atlantic Council for the assessment and recommendation of the annual budgets for the International Staff, International Military Staff, Major NATO Commands, and the NAEW&C Force; and for review of budgetary execution.
Levels	Financial Counsellors from national delegations.
Principal Subordinate Committees	The Budget Committees establish working groups as required.
International Staff Support	Office of the Chairman of the Budget Committees, Office of the Financial Controller, Office of Management.

28. Senior Resource Board (SRB)

Members	All member countries.
Chairman	National Chairman selected on rotational basis.
Role	Senior advisory body to the North Atlantic Council on the management of military common-funded resources.
Levels	National representatives, representatives of the Military Committee, NATO Strategic Commanders, Chairmen of the Military Budget Committee, Infrastructure Committee and NATO Defence Manpower Committee.
Principal Subordinate Committees	N/A.
International Staff Support	Office of the Chairman of the SRB; Division of Security Investment, Logistics and Civil Emergency Planning; Executive Secretariat.

29. Senior Defence Group on Proliferation (DGP)

Members	All member countries.
Chairman	Co-Chairmanship: one North American and one European representative.
Role	Senior advisory body to the North Atlantic Council on the proliferation of weapons of mass destruction and associated delivery systems.
Levels	Senior NATO officials concerned with defence matters.
Principal Subordinate Committees	DPG Steering Committee (composed of working-level experts); other temporary ad hoc bodies as required. Also meets with Senior Politico-Military Group on Proliferation (SGP), becoming the Joint Committee on Proliferation (JCP).
International Staff Support	Division of Political Affairs; Executive Secretariat.

30. High Level Group (NPG/HLG)

Members	All member countries except France.
Chairman	National Chairman (United States).
Role	Advisory body to the Nuclear Planning Group (NPG). Meets several times per year to consider aspects of NATO's nuclear policy and planning and matters concerning the safety, security, and survivability of nuclear weapons. NB: The HLG has taken over the functions of the former Senior Level Weapons Protection Group (SLWPG) referred to in Chapter 7.
Levels	National experts from NATO capitals.
Principal Subordinate Committees	N/A.
International Staff Support	Division of Defence Planning and Operations (Nuclear Policy Directorate).

31. Economic Committee (EC)

Members	All member countries.
Chairman	Director of Economics Directorate.
Role	Advisory body to the North Atlantic Council on economic issues.
Levels	Representatives from NATO delegations (Economic Counsellors). Reinforced meetings attended by experts from capitals.
Principal Subordinate Committees	N/A.
International Staff Support	Division of Political Affairs, Economics Directorate; Executive Secretariat.

32. Committee on Information and Cultural Relations (CICR)

Members	All member countries.
Chairman	Director of Information and Press.
Role	Advisory body to the North Atlantic Council on information and press issues.
Levels	Representatives from NATO delegations. Reinforced meetings attended by experts from capitals.
Principal Subordinate Committees	N/A.
International Staff Support	Office of Information and Press; Executive Secretariat.

33. Council Operations and Exercises Committee (COEC)

Members	All member countries.
Chairman	Director, Crisis Management and Operations Directorate, Division of Defence Planning and Operations.
Role	Principal forum for consultation and coordination of crisis management arrangements, procedures and facilities, including communications issues, questions relating to the NATO Situation Centre (SITCEN), and the preparation and conduct of crisis management exercises.
Levels	Political and military representatives from national delegations concerned with crisis management and exercises.
Principal Subordinate Committees	N/A.
International Staff Support	Division of Defence Planning and Operations (Council Operations Section); Executive Secretariat.

34. NATO Air Traffic Management Committee (NATMC)

(formerly Committee on European Airspace Coordination (CEAC))

Members	All member countries.
Chairman	Elected (currently the Director for Air Defence and Airspace Management, NATO International Staff).
Role	Senior advisory body on matters related to civil/military coordination of air traffic management.
Levels	Senior civil and military air traffic managers from national capitals.
Principal Subordinate Committees	Communications and Navigation Group; Surveillance and Identification Group; Air Traffic Management Group.
International Staff Support	Division of Defence Support (Air Defence and Airspace Management Directorate); Executive Secretariat.

35. Central Europe Pipeline Management Organisation Board of Directors (CEPMO BOD)

Members	Seven participating member countries (Belgium, Canada, France, Germany, the Netherlands, United Kingdom, United States).
Chairman	National representative.
Role	Senior directing body for the Central Europe Pipeline System (CEPS).
Levels	Representatives of participating countries plus representatives of the Central Europe Pipeline Management Agency (CEPMA).
Principal Subordinate Committees	N/A.
International Staff Support	Division of Security Investment, Logistics and Civil Emergency Planning (Logistics (IS Element)); Executive Secretariat; NATO Military Authorities (CINCNORTH, AFNORTH).

36. NATO Pipeline Committee (NPC)

Members	All member countries.
Chairman	Head, Logistics (IS Element).
Role	Senior advisory body in NATO on consumer logistics relating to military petroleum supplies.
Levels	Government experts on military petroleum matters.
Principal Subordinate Committees	Working Group on Special Tasks, Fuels and Lubricants Working Group. Petroleum Handling Equipment Working Group.
International Staff Support	Division of Security Investment, Logistics and Civil Emergency Planning (Logistics (IS Element)); Executive Secretariat; NATO Military Authorities (SHAPE, SACLANT).

37. NATO Security Committee (NSC)

Members	All member countries.
Chairman	Director of the NATO Office of Security (NOS).
Role	Advisory body to the North Atlantic Council on matters relating to NATO Security Policy.
Levels	National representatives and national delegation security officers.
Principal Subordinate Committees	Working Group on ADP Security.
International Staff Support	NATO Office of Security.

38. Special Committee

Members	All member countries.
Chairman	Annual rotating chairmanship amongst member nations.
Role	Advisory body to the North Atlantic Council on matters of espionage and terrorist or related threats which might affect the Alliance.
Levels	Heads of Security Services of member countries.
Principal Subordinate Committees	N/A.
International Staff Support	NATO Office of Security.

39. Archives Committee

Members	All member countries.
Chairman	Deputy Executive Secretary.
Role	In keeping with the adaptation of NATO to the new international security environment following the end of the Cold War, and in a spirit of promoting greater transparency, the Alliance has established a policy of declassification and public disclosure of NATO documents of historical importance for research purposes. The role of the Archives Committee is to continue and expand the archival programme (including provision of facilities for public access) and to manage and preserve archives held by civilian and military bodies of the Alliance.
Levels	Deputy Permanent Representatives reinforced by national archivists.
Principal Subordinate Committees	N/A.
International Staff Support	Executive Secretariat, Office of Management (Archives Section).

KEY TO THE INSTITUTIONS OF COOPERATION, PARTNERSHIP AND DIALOGUE

The following section summarises the membership, chairmanship, status or role, levels and associated structures, as well as the principal source of staff support, of the institutions of Cooperation and Partnership.

Further details relating to these institutions are to be found in Chapter 3.

- Euro-Atlantic Partnership Council (EAPC)
- NATO-Russia Permanent Joint Council (PJC)
- NATO-Ukraine Commission (NUC)
- Mediterranean Cooperation Group (MCG)

Euro-Atlantic Partnership Council (EAPC)

Members	Forty-six countries (19 member countries of NATO + 27 partner countries).
Chairman	Secretary General.
Role	Established in accordance with the EAPC Basic Document of May 1997. The overarching framework for political and security consultations and for enhanced cooperation under the Partnership for Peace (PfP) programme.
Levels	Ambassadorial (Permanent Representatives of NATO member countries and Ambassadors of Partner countries). Ministerial (Foreign and Defence Ministers). Summit (Heads of State and Government).
Principal Related Committees	Subordinate committees of the North Atlantic Council meeting with Partner countries participating in the EAPC/PfP.
Staff Support	Supported by Diplomatic Missions and Liaison Offices of EAPC countries and by NATO staffs. Many Divisions and Offices of the International Staff and International Military Staff support the work of the EAPC, directly or indirectly.

NATO-Russia Permanent Joint Council (PJC)

Members	All member countries of NATO and the Russian Federation.
Chairman	Secretary General, the Representative of the Russian Federation and a Representative of a NATO member country on a three-monthly rotational basis.
Role	Established in accordance with the NATO-Russia Founding Act of 27 May 1997. Forum for consultation, cooperation and consensus-building between NATO and Russia.
Levels	Ambassadorial. Ministerial (Foreign and Defence Ministers). Summit (Heads of State and Government).
Principal Related Committees	No formal substructure. However, Chiefs of Staff/Chiefs of Defence meet under the auspices of the PJC no less than twice a year. Military representatives meet monthly The PJC is also supported by a number of expert working groups.
Staff Support	Supported by Russian and NATO staffs. Many Divisions and Offices of the NATO International Staff and International Military Staff support the work of the PJC directly or indirectly.

NATO-Ukraine Commission (NUC)

Members	All member countries of NATO, and Ukraine.
Chairman	Secretary General.
Role	In accordance with the NATO-Ukraine Charter of July 1997, the North Atlantic Council meets periodically with Ukraine as the NATO-Ukraine Commission, as a rule not less than twice a year, to assess the implementation of the relationship and consider its further development.
Levels	Ambassadorial. Ministerial (Foreign and Defence Ministers). Summit (Heads of State and Government).
Principal Related Committees	A number of senior NATO committees meet regularly with Ukraine, including the Military Committee in Permanent or Chiefs of Staff session. The NUC is also supported by expert working groups such as the Joint Working Group on Defence Reform.
Staff Support	Supported by Ukrainian and NATO staffs. Many Divisions and Offices of the International Staff and International Military Staff support the work of the Commission, directly or indirectly.

Mediterranean Cooperation Group (MCG)

Members	All member countries of the Alliance with Algeria, Egypt, Israel, Jordan, Mauritania, Morocco, Tunisia.
Chairman	Assistant Secretary General for Political Affairs. Acting Chairman Deputy Assistant Secretary General and Director, Political Directorate.
Role	Consultative body on Mediterranean issues.
Levels	Meetings are held at the level of Political Counsellors with representatives of Mediterranean Dialogue Countries.
Principal Subordinate Committees	N/A.
Staff Support	Supported by staffs of participating countries and NATO staffs. Many Divisions and Offices of the International Staff and International Military Staff support the work of the Group, directly or indirectly.

CHAPTER 14

KEY TO ORGANISATIONS AND AGENCIES AND OTHER SUBORDINATE BODIES

Introduction

Consumer Logistics

Production Logistics and Equipment

Standardisation

Civil Emergency Planning

Air Traffic Management and Air Defence

Airborne Early Warning

Communication and Information Systems

Electronic Warfare

Meteorology

Military Oceanography

Research and Technology

Education and Training

KEY TO ORGANISATIONS AND AGENCIES AND OTHER SUBORDINATE BODIES

INTRODUCTION

In general, subordinate bodies established by the North Atlantic Council, Defence Planning Committee, Nuclear Planning Group or NATO Military Committee act in an advisory capacity, undertaking studies of particular topics on the basis of mandates passed on to them by their parent body. Their role consists primarily of formulating policy recommendations which can be used as the basis for decision-making.

However, a number of organisations and agencies have been established at different times to undertake more specific tasks. Located within the NATO Headquarters in Brussels or in different member countries of the Alliance, they form an integral part of the overall NATO structure. They provide a focus for specialised research and advice, for the implementation of Alliance decisions, for the management and operation of cooperative programmes and systems, and for education and training.

Some of the above bodies are directly responsible to one parent body, such as the North Atlantic Council or the Military Committee. Others report to both, or have wider responsibilities which may involve them in managing or supervising systems or services which respond to the needs of the Alliance as a whole. In such cases their "tasking authorities" may include the NATO Strategic Commanders or other parts of the NATO structure.

Many of the organisations referred to in this section come into the category of NATO Production and Logistics Organisations known as "NPLOs". These are subsidiary bodies created within the framework of the implementation of the North Atlantic Treaty. Each NPLO is granted organisational, administrative and financial independence by the North Atlantic Council. Their tasks are to establish the collective requirements of participating nations in relevant fields of design and development, production, operational or logistic support, and management, in accordance with their individual Charters.

Membership of NPLOs is open to all NATO countries on the basis of Memoranda of Understanding (MOUs) signed by each participating country.

Typically, an NPLO consists of a senior policy committee, a Board or Board of Directors (sometimes called Steering Committee) which acts as its directing body and is responsible for promoting the collective interests of the member nations; subordinate committees or working groups established by the Board, with responsibility for particular aspects of the task; and an executive agency, which is the management arm of the NPLO, normally headed by a General Manager.

The title used to describe the overall organisational structure of individual NPLOs normally concludes with the word "Organisation" and the management body with the word "Agency". This is reflected in the corresponding acronyms, resulting in names such as "NAMSO", describing the NATO Maintenance and Supply Organisation as a whole, and "NAMSA" describing the NATO Maintenance and Supply Agency.

In addition to the above, there are a number of NATO Project Steering Committees (NPSCs) and Project Offices. A "NATO Project" is a formal status, conferred on an armaments or equipment cooperation project involving two or more NATO nations, by the Conference of National Armaments Directors (CNAD). The CNAD is the senior body in NATO responsible for cooperation in the field of production logistics.

Each Project Steering Committee is the subject of an intergovernmental agreement between participating countries, relating to the coordination, execution and supervision of an equipment procurement programme. Established in accordance with agreed NATO procedures for cooperation in the research, development and production aspects of military equipment, NPSCs report to the CNAD, which reviews progress and decides on the continuation, adaptation or curtailment of the project, and where appropriate, on the establishment of a Project Office.

There are currently some 20 NATO Project Steering Committees/Project Offices. These are listed at the end of the chapter[1].

The following sections provide more detailed information on the policy committees, organisations and agencies described above in their respective fields of specialisation, grouped within the following categories:

- Consumer Logistics;

- Production Logistics and Equipment;

- Standardisation;

- Civil-Emergency Planning;

- Air Traffic Management, and Air Defence;

- Airborne Early Warning;

---

1   In addition to NATO Production and Logistics Organisations, Project Steering Committees, Agencies and other organisations, this chapter describes the role of a number of policy committees dealing with technical matters.

- Communication and Information Systems;

- Electronic Warfare;

- Meteorology;

- Military Oceanography;

- Research and Technology;

- Education and Training.

CONSUMER LOGISTICS

Senior NATO Logisticians' Conference (SNLC)

The principal committee dealing with consumer logistics, the SNLC, meets under the Chairmanship of the NATO Secretary General twice per year, in joint civil and military sessions. It has two permanent co-chairmen, namely the Assistant Secretary General for Security Investment, Logistics and Civil Emergency Planning, and the Deputy Chairman of the Military Committee. The Conference reports jointly to both the Council and the Military Committee, reflecting the dependence of consumer logistics on both civil and military factors.

Membership of the Conference is drawn from senior national civil and military representatives of Ministries of Defence or equivalent bodies with responsibility for consumer aspects of logistics in member countries. Representatives of the Strategic Commands, the NATO Maintenance and Supply Agency (NAMSA), the NATO Standardisation Agency (NSA), the Committee of the Chiefs of Military Medical Services in NATO (COMEDS) and other sectors of the NATO Headquarters Staff also participate in the work of the conference. The overall mandate of the SNLC is to address consumer logistics matters with a view to enhancing the performance, efficiency, sustainability and combat effectiveness of Alliance forces and to exercise, on behalf of the Council, an overarching coordinating authority across the whole spectrum of logistics vis-à-vis the other logistic committees and bodies of NATO.

NATO Maintenance and Supply Organisation (NAMSO)

The NATO Maintenance and Supply Organisation provides the structure for the logistics support of selected weapons systems in the national inventories of two or more NATO nations, through the common procurement and supply of spare parts and the provision of maintenance and repair facilities.

NATO Maintenance and Supply Agency (NAMSA)

The NATO Maintenance and Supply Agency is the executive arm of NAMSO. Its task is to provide logistic services in support of weapon and equipment systems held in common by NATO nations, in order to promote materiel readiness, to improve the efficiency of logistic operations and to effect savings through consolidated procurement in the areas of supply, maintenance, calibration, procurement, transportation, technical support, engineering services and configuration management. Modern materiel management and procurement techniques developed by NAMSA include the Stock Holding and Assets Requirements Exchange scheme, known as SHARE (see Chapter 8) and Common Item Materiel Management (COMMIT). NAMSA also provides support for the Group of National Directors on Codification, which manages the NATO Codification System (NCS) on behalf of the Conference of National Armaments Directors (CNAD); and logistics support for the NATO forces deployed in Bosnia and Herzegovina (SFOR) and Kosovo (KFOR).

Further information can be obtained from:

NATO Maintenance and Supply Agency (NAMSA)
8302 Capellen
Luxembourg
Tel: 352 30 631
Fax: 352 30 87 21

NATO Pipeline System (NPS)

The NATO Pipeline System consists of nine separate military storage and distribution systems for fuels and lubricants, and is designed to ensure that NATO's requirements for petroleum products and their distribution can be met at all times. The system consists of a number of single nation pipeline systems covering Italy, Greece, Norway, Portugal, Turkey (two separate systems, East and West), and the United Kingdom; and two multinational systems, namely the Northern European Pipeline System (located in Denmark and Germany) and the Central European Pipeline System, covering Belgium, France, Germany, Luxembourg and the Netherlands. The NPS as a whole runs through twelve NATO nations and provides some 11 500 kilometres of pipeline, linking together storage depots, air bases, civil airports, pumping stations, refineries and entry points.

Central Europe Pipeline System (CEPS)

The Central European Pipeline System is the largest of the NATO Pipeline systems and is used by eight host country or user nations (Belgium, Canada, France, Germany, Luxembourg, the Netherlands, the United Kingdom and the United States).

NATO Pipeline Committee (NPC)

Chaired by the Head, Logistics (IS-Element), the NPC is the main advisory body on consumer logistics relating to petroleum. It acts on behalf of the North Atlantic Council, in consultation with the NATO Military Authorities and other relevant bodies, on all matters relating to overall NATO interests in connection with military fuels, lubricants and associated products and equipment, and in overseeing the NATO Pipeline System.

The Central Europe Pipeline Management Organisation (CEPMO)

The CEPMO comprises its governing body, the Board of Directors on which each NATO member country participating in the system is represented, and the Central Europe Pipeline System (CEPS) itself. Representatives of the NATO Military Authorities as well as the General Manager of the Central Europe Pipeline Management Agency also participate in the Board.

Central Europe Pipeline Management Agency (CEPMA)

CEPMA is responsible for the 24-hour operation of the Central Europe Pipeline System and its storage and distribution facilities.

Further information on the organisation and management structure of the Central Europe Pipeline System can be obtained from:

Central Europe Pipeline Management Agency (CEPMA)
BP 552
78005 Versailles
France
Tel: 33 1 3924 4900
Fax: 33 1 3955 6539

The Committee of the Chiefs of Military Medical Services in NATO (COMEDS)

The Committee of the Chiefs of Military Medical Services in NATO is composed of the senior military medical authorities of member countries. It acts as the central point for the development and coordination of military medical matters and for providing medical advice to the NATO Military Committee.

Historically, medical matters within NATO were regarded strictly as a national responsibility. For the greatest part of the Alliance's existence, there was therefore no requirement for the establishment of a high level military medical authority within NATO.

New NATO missions and concepts of operations place increased emphasis on joint military operations, enhancing the importance of coordination of medical support in peacekeeping, disaster relief and humanitarian operations. The Committee of the Chiefs of Military Medical Services in NATO was established in 1994 for this purpose. The Chairman and the Secretary of COMEDS are provided by Belgium, and the Secretariat is located within the Belgian Surgeon General's Office in Brussels.

Comprised of the Surgeons General of the Alliance nations plus the Medical Advisers of the NATO Strategic Commands (SHAPE and ACLANT), a representative of the NATO Standardisation Agency , the chairman of the Joint Medical Committee, a representative from the Military Committee, and a representative from the International Military Staff, the COMEDS meets biannually in Plenary Session and reports annually to the Military Committee. From 2001, the Surgeons Generals of Partner Nations have been invited to participate in the COMEDS Plenary Meeting in EAPC format.

The objectives of the COMEDS include improving and expanding arrangements between member countries for coordination, standardisation and interoperability in the medical field; and improving the exchange of information relating to organisational, operational and procedural aspects of military medical services in NATO and Partner countries. Since 1997, PfP countries have been invited to participate fully in the work of most COMEDS Working Groups, and since 1996, in the annual COMEDS/PfP medical seminar. This is now incorporated into COMEDS Plenary Meetings.

The work of the COMEDS is coordinated with other NATO bodies with responsibilities in the medical field, including the NATO Agency for Standardisation (NSA), the Joint Medical Committee (JMC), the Medical Advisers of the NATO Strategic Commanders, the Human Factors and Medicine Panel of the Research and Technology Organisation (HFM/RTO), the Weapons of Mass Destruction (WMD) Centre and the IMS medical staff officer.

The Chairman of the JMC and the Chairman of the MAS General Medical Working Group attend plenary sessions of the COMEDS as observers.

To assist in carrying out its tasks, the COMEDS has the following nine subordinate working groups, each of which meets at least annually:

Military Medical Structures, Operations and Procedures;
Military Preventive Medicine;
Emergency Medicine;
Military Psychiatry;
Dental Service;
Medical Materiel and Military Pharmacy;
Cooperation and Coordination in Military Medical Research;
Food Hygiene, Food Technology, and Veterinary Medicine;
Medical Training.

Further information can be obtained from:

COMEDS
c/o Medical Staff Officer
Logistics, Armaments
and Resource Division
International Military Staff
NATO
1110 Brussels - Belgium
Tel: 32 2 707 5551
Fax: 32 2 707 4117

COMEDS
Etat-major du Service Médical
Quartier Reine Elisabeth
Rue d'Evere
1140 Brussels
Belgium

Fax: 32 2 701 3071

PRODUCTION LOGISTICS AND EQUIPMENT

Conference of National Armaments Directors (CNAD)

The major part of the collaborative work undertaken within NATO to identify opportunities for collaboration in the research, development and production of military equipment and weapon systems for the armed forces takes place under the auspices of the CNAD. The Conference meets in plenary session twice a year under the Chairmanship of the Secretary General. The Assistant Secretary General for Defence Support is the permanent Chairman. The CNAD brings together the senior officials with responsibility for defence acquisition in member nations, representatives from the Military Committee and NATO Strategic Commands, the Chairmen of the CNAD Main Groups, and other civil and military authorities responsible for different aspects of production logistics.

The CNAD organisation

Representatives of the National Armaments Directors (NADREPS), within the national delegations of member countries, undertake the routine tasks of the CNAD and direct the work of its Groups.

The CNAD substructure consists of:

- groups, subgroups and working groups responsible to three CNAD Main Armaments Groups (the NATO Naval Armaments Group (NNAG); NATO Air Force Armaments Group (NAFAG); the NATO Army Armaments Group (NAAG)); and the NATO Group on Acquisition Practices;

- the NATO Industrial Advisory Group - (NIAG);

- CNAD Ad Hoc Groups responsible for special armaments projects (e.g. Alliance Ground Surveillance Steering Committee);

- CNAD Partnership Groups (Group of National Directors on Codification; Group of National Directors for Quality Assurance; Group of Experts on the Safety Aspects of Transportation and Storage of Military Ammunition and Explosives; Group on Standardisation of Material and Engineering Practices; and Group on Safety and Suitability for Service of Munitions and Explosives);

- the NATO Conventional Armaments Review Committee (NCARC) composed of representatives from the staffs of the National Armaments Directors and Chiefs of Defence as well as representatives of the NATO Military Authorities. It is responsible to the CNAD for the management of the Conventional Armaments Planning System (CAPS).

NATO Medium Extended Air Defence System Design and Development, Production and Logistics Management Agency (NAMEADSMA)

Further information:

NAMEADSMA
Building 1
620 Discovery Drive
Suite 300
Huntsville, AC 35806, USA
Tel: 1 205 922 3972
Fax: 1 205 922 3900

NATO EF 2000 and TORNADO Development Production and Logistics Management Agency (NETMA)

NETMA replaces the former NATO Multirole Combat Aircraft Development and Production Management Agency (NAMMA) and the NATO EFA Development Production and Logistics Management Agency (NEFMA), and is responsible for the joint development and production of the NATO European Fighter Aircraft and the NATO MRCA (Tornado).

Further information:

NETMA
Insel Kammerstr. 12 + 14
Postfach 1302
82008 Unterhaching
Germany
Tel: 49 89 666 800
Fax: 49 89 666 80555\6

NATO Helicopter Design and Development Production and Logistics Management Agency (NAHEMA)

Further information:

NAHEMA
Le Quatuor
Bâtiment A
42 Route de Galice
13082 Aix-en-Provence Cedex 2
France
Tel: 33 42 95 92 00
Fax: 33 42 64 30 50

NATO HAWK Management Office (NHMO)

NHMO is responsible for improvement programmes for the HAWK surface-to-air missile system.

Further information:

NHMO
26 rue Galliéni
92500 Rueil-Malmaison
France
Tel: 33 147 08 75 00
Fax: 33 147 52 10 99

STANDARDISATION

The NATO Standardisation Organisation (NSO)

The NATO Standardisation Organisation (NSO) comprises the NATO Committee for Standardisation, the NATO Standardisation Staff Group, and the NATO Standardisation Agency.

Its role is to enhance interoperability and to contribute to the ability of Alliance forces to train, exercise and operate effectively together, and when appropriate, with forces of Partner and other nations, in the execution of their assigned tasks. It undertakes this by harmonising and coordinating standardisation efforts throughout the Alliance and providing support for standardisation activities.

In accordance with Alliance policy, national and NATO authorities are encouraged to develop, agree and implement concepts, doctrines, procedures and designs which will enable them to achieve and maintain interoperability. This requires the establishment of the necessary levels of compatibility, interchangeability or commonality in operational, procedural, materiel, technical and administrative fields.

The NSO was established by the North Atlantic Council in January 1995 and was restructured in 2000 as a result of a Standardisation Review carried out to meet the requirements of the 1999 Washington Summit and the challenges posed by the Defence Capabilities Initiative launched at the Summit.

NATO Committee for Standardisation (NCS)

The NATO Committee for Standardisation is the senior NATO authority on overall standardisation matters and reports to the Council.

It is supported by the Group of NCS Representatives (NCSREPs), which provides harmonisation and guidance at delegate level, under the overall direction and management of the Committee. The focus of the work undertaken by the NCSREPs is on the harmonisation of standardisation between NATO and national bodies and promoting interaction between them in the standardisation field.

The NCS is chaired by the Secretary General, normally represented by two permanent co-chairmen, namely the Assistant Secretary General for Defence Support and the Director of the International Military Staff. Since September 2000, Partner nations have become actively involved in NCS activities.

NATO Standardisation Staff Group (NSSG)

The NATO Standardisation Staff Group is a staff group subordinate to the NATO Committee for Standardisation. Its principal task is to harmonise standardisation policies and procedures and to coordinate standardisation activities. It is responsible for staff liaison and for the preparation of related documentation, contributing, inter alia, to the formulation of Military Standardisation Requirements by the Strategic Commands and the drafting of Standardisation Objectives for the NATO Standardisation Programme. It includes representatives from the Strategic Commands and staff representatives from the International Military Staff and the International Staff supporting the Standardisation Tasking Authorities. These are senior NATO bodies with the authority to task their subordinate groups to produce Standardisation Agreements (STANAGs) and Allied Publications (APs), namely the Military Committee (MC), the Conference of National Armaments Directors (CNAD), the Senior NATO Logisticians Conference (SNLC) and the NATO Consultation, Command and Control Board (NC3B). Staff representatives of other bodies and organisations also participate in the work of the NSSG.

NATO Standardisation Agency (NSA)

The NATO Standardisation Agency is a single, integrated body set up by the North Atlantic Council and composed of military and civilian staff. It is responsible to the NATO Standardisation Committee for the coordination of issues between all fields of standardisation. It sets out procedures, planning and execution functions related to standardisation for application throughout the Alliance. It is responsible for the preparation of the work for the NCS, NCSREPs and NSSG meetings and the overall administration of all Standardisation Agreements (STANAGs) and Allied Publications (APs).

The NSA also supports the Joint and the Single Service Boards, each of which acts as a Tasking Authority for Operational Standardisation, including doctrine, as delegated by the Military Committee. The Service Boards are responsible for the development of operational and procedural standardisation among member nations. Like other Tasking Authorities, they do this by developing applicable STANAGs and APs with the member nations and NATO Military Commands.

The Director of the NSA is responsible for the day to day work of five Branches, namely Policy and Requirements, Joint, Naval, Army and Air Branches. The Service Branches provide staff support to their related Boards and are responsible for monitoring and harmonising standardisation activities in their area of responsibility.

The Boards, with one member per nation, are in permanent session and meet formally once a month. Decisions are normally reached on the basis of unanimity. However, as standardisation is a voluntary process, agreements may also be based on majority decisions of the nations that are participating in any particular Standardisation Agreement. The Strategic Commanders have a staff representative on each Board.

Further information:

NATO Standardisation Agency
NATO
1110 Brussels
Belgium
Tel: 32 2 707 5576
Fax: 32 2 707 5718
E-mail: NSA@hq.nato.int

CIVIL EMERGENCY PLANNING

Senior Civil Emergency Planning Committee (SCEPC)

The Senior Civil Emergency Planning Committee meets twice a year in plenary session with representatives from capitals and monthly in Permanent Session, with representatives from national delegations at NATO. The Committee is chaired by the Assistant Secretary General for Security Investment, Logistics and Civil Emergency Planning.

Civil Emergency Planning Boards and Committees

The SCEPC coordinates and provides guidance for the activities of nine subordinate Planning Boards and Committees, namely: Planning Board for Ocean Shipping (PBOS); Planning Board for European Inland Surface Transport (PBEIST); Civil Aviation Planning Committee (CAPC); Food and Agriculture Planning Committee (FAPC); Industrial Planning Committee (IPC); Petroleum Planning Committee (PPC) (dormant); Joint Medical Committee (JMC); Civil Communications Planning Committee (CCPC); and Civil Protection Committee (CPC).

EuroAtlantic Disaster Response Coordination Centre (EADRCC)

On 29 May 1998, a Euro-Atlantic Disaster Response Coordination Centre (EADRCC) was established at NATO Headquarters, headed by the Director of the Civil Emergency Planning Directorate with staff from the CEP Directorate and NATO and Partner countries. The EADRCC also has a liaison officer from the United Nations. It is responsible for coordinating, in close consultation with the UN Office for the Coordination of Humanitarian Affairs (UNOCHA), the response of EAPC countries to a disaster occurring within the EAPC's geographical area.

In consultation with nations, the EADRCC is also developing a Euro-Atlantic Disaster Response Unit. This will be a non-standing resource, comprising personnel and equipment which nations have earmarked as potentially available in response to a request for assistance from a nation struck by a major disaster.

AIR TRAFFIC MANAGEMENT AND AIR DEFENCE

The NATO Air Traffic Management Committee (NATMC)

(Formerly Committee on European Airspace Coordination - CEAC)
(See Chapter 8).

The NATO Air Defence Committee (NADC)

Advises the Council and the Defence Planning Committee on all aspects of air defence programme development. It meets twice per year under the chairmanship of the NATO Deputy Secretary General. (See Chapter 8).

Military Committee Air Defence Study Working Group (MC-ADSWG)

The Military Committee Air Defence Study Working Group (MC-ADSWG) is a multinational body, working in support of the Military Committee. It is tasked with reviewing, advising and making recommendations on air defence issues which affect NATO's integrated air defence system.

NATO Air Command and Control System (ACCS) Management Organisation (NACMO)

The NATO Air Command and Control System Management Organisation provides the structure for the planning and implementation of the command and control system supporting NATO air operations. It replaces the former Air Defence Ground Environment System known as NADGE. Its headquarters are in Brussels, Belgium. (See Chapter 8).

Further information:

NATO Air Command Control System (ACCS) Management Agency
NACMA
8 rue de Genève
1140 Brussels, Belgium
Tel: 32 2 707 4111
Fax: 32 2 707 8777

AIRBORNE EARLY WARNING

The initial AEW programme involved the acquisition by NATO of its own collectively operated and maintained aircraft fleet as well as the modification and upgrading of 40 existing NATO Air Defence Ground Environment (NADGE) sites, to enable them to interoperate with the Airborne Early Warning System. These sites are located in nine different countries, stretching from northern Norway to eastern Turkey.

The largest element of the programme was the acquisition of 18 NATO E3A aircraft over the period 1982-85. The E-3A was based on the US Air Force (USAF) Airborne Warning and Control System (AWACS) in service since 1977. Based on the Boeing 707-320B airframe, it is distinguished by the 30 feet diameter rotodome mounted on top of the fuselage, housing the surveillance and IFF radars.

Subsequently, both near-term and mid-term modernisation programmes have been undertaken. The mid-term programme will cover NATO's AEW requirements from 1998 to 2004.

NATO Airborne Early Warning and Control Programme Management Organisation (NAPMO)

NAPMO is responsible for all aspects of the management and implementation of the NATO AEW&C Programme and reports directly to the North

Atlantic Council. The Organisation consists of a Board of Directors (BOD), supported by a Programme Management Agency (NAPMA) which is located at Brunssum, in the Netherlands, and by a Legal, Contracts and Finance (LCF) Committee; an Operations, Technical and Support (OTS) Committee; and a Depot Level Maintenance (DLM) Steering Group.

Each participating nation is represented on the Board of Directors and its committees. Representatives of the NATO Secretary General, the NATO Strategic Commanders, the NATO AEW Force Commander and other NATO bodies also attend meetings of the Board of Directors and Committee meetings. The Board of Directors normally meets twice a year.

The day-to-day management of the Programme is the responsibility of the NAPMA General Manager. The NATO AEW Force Command Headquarters is co-located with Supreme Headquarters Allied Powers Europe (SHAPE) at Mons, Belgium. Both NAPMA and the Force Command are manned by personnel from the participating nations.

The Main Operating Base is at Geilenkirchen in Germany and is also manned by personnel from the participating NAPMO nations. Airbases in Norway, Italy, Greece and Turkey have been extensively modified to provide forward operating support for NATO E-3A aircraft operations.

The NAPMO's current member nations are Belgium, Canada, Denmark, Germany, Greece, Italy, Luxembourg, the Netherlands, Norway, Portugal, Spain, Turkey and the United States. The Czech Republic, Hungary and Poland are observers. The United Kingdom provides seven E-3D aircraft to the NATO AEW Force. France attends NAPMO meetings in an observer role, based on its acquisition of four national E-3F aircraft.

From August 1990 to March 1991, in response to Iraq's invasion of Kuwait, aircraft of the NATO E-3A Component were deployed to eastern Turkey to reinforce NATO's southern flank in order to monitor air and sea traffic in the eastern Mediterranean and to provide continuous airborne surveillance along the Turkey/Iraq border.

Since July 1992 the NAEW Force, comprising both the E-3A Component and the UK E-3D Component, has been extensively deployed in the area of the former Republic of Yugoslavia to support NATO's actions relating to the monitoring and implementation of United Nations Security Council resolutions, and subsequently to support the Implementation Force (IFOR) and Stabilisation Force (SFOR) and Kosovo Force (KFOR) operations. Aircraft of the French E-3F force have also taken part in these operations

Further information:

NATO Airborne Early Warning and Control Programme
Management Agency (NAPMA)
Akerstraat 7
6445 CL Brunssum
The Netherlands
Tel: 31 45 526 + Ext.
Fax: 31 45 525 4373

COMMUNICATIONS AND INFORMATION SYSTEMS

NATO C3 Organisation

The NATO C3 Organisation (NC3O) was created in 1996 to ensure the provision of a NATO-wide cost-effective, interoperable and secure C3 capability, meeting the NATO users' requirements by making use of common funded, multinational and national assets. The NC3O also ensures the provision of services and support in the field of C3 to NATO users. The NATO C3 Board (NC3B) oversees the NC3O.

The Board is the senior multinational policy body, advising the Council and Defence Planning Committee on collective interests of all the member states acting as the Board of Directors of the NC3O. It is composed of senior national representatives from capitals; representatives of the Military Committee and Strategic Commanders and NATO committees with an interest in C3, the General Manager of the NATO C3 Agency (NC3A), and the Controller of the NATO CIS Operating and Support Agency (NACOSA). The Board is chaired by the Deputy Secretary General and has a Permanent Chairman (the Assistant Secretary General for Defence Support) and two Co-Vice Chairmen (Director NHQC3S and a Co-Vice Chairman elected from national nominees). It is assisted by the Group of National C3 Representatives (NC3REPS), which acts as the NC3B in permanent session. These National C3 Representatives are normally attached to their national delegations or to their military representatives at NATO.

The NC3B is supported by a NATO C3 Subordinate Structure of multinational bodies composed of eight sub-Committees (Joint C3 Requirements and Concepts, Interoperability, Frequency Management, Information Systems, Information Security Systems, Communications Network, Identification and Navigation). Each of these has its own substructure. The NC3B, NC3REPS and the NC3B Substructure is supported by the NATO Headquarters C3 Staff (NHQC3S), a single integrated civilian and military staff directed by the Assistant Secretary General for Defence Support, IS and the Director of the

IMS. The NHQC3S provides support to the Council, Military Committee, CNAD, SRB and other NATO committees on C3 matters.

The Board also oversees the work of the two NC3O agencies, the NC3A and NACOSA. The NC3A performs central planning, system integration design, system engineering, technical support and configuration control. It also provides scientific and technical advice and support in the field of C3 sensor systems and operational research, and procures and implements projects assigned to it. The NC3A is located in Brussels, Belgium and in The Hague, the Netherlands. NACOSA exercises operating control and supports the in-service NATO CIS and installations assigned to it. The NACOSA central staff is located in Mons, Belgium.

NATO Consultation, Command and Control Agency (NC3A)

In July 1996, the NATO C3 Agency came into being as part of NATO's strategy to restructure its C3 activities within the Alliance. This action brought together the planning, scientific and development and acquisition functions of NATO's Communications and Information Systems, and some C3 functions, thereby enhancing the Alliance's capability to carry out its new crisis management tasks, while preserving its collective defence capabilities. The NC3 Agency provides central planning, systems integration, design, systems engineering, technical support and configuration control for NATO C3 systems and installations. The Agency procures and implements projects assigned to it and provides scientific and technical advice and support to the Strategic Commanders and other customers on matters pertaining to operational research, surveillance, air command and control (including theatre missile defence, electronic welfare and airborne early warning and control) and communications and information systems.

The NC3A has its headquarters in Brussels, Belgium but operates from split locations in Brussels (Planning and Acquisition) and the The Hague, the Netherlands (Scientific Support). It currently employs about 450 civilian and military personnel.

Further information can be obtained from:

NATO HQ C3 Staff	NC3A Brussels	NC3A The Hague
- NATO Headquarters	(HQ, Planning &	(Scientific &
1110 Brussels	Acquisition)	technical matters)
Belgium	8 rue de Genève	P.O. Box 174
Tel: 32 2 707 4358	1140 Brussels	Oude Waalsdorperweg 61
Fax: 32 2 707 5709	Belgium	2501 CD The Hague
	Tel: 32 2 707 8267	The Netherlands
	Fax: 32 2 708 8770	Tel: 31 70 3142329
		Fax: 31 70 3142111

NATO Headquarters Consultation, Command and Control Staff (NHQC3S)

The NATO Headquarters C3 Staff provides support on C3 matters to the North Atlantic Council, the Military Committee, the NC3 Board, the Conference of National Armaments Directors, the Senior Resource Board, to other committees with responsibilities relating to C3 matters, and to Divisions and Directorates of the International Staff and International Military Staff.

The NATO Frequency Management SubCommittee (FMSC)

NATO's specialised body in this area is the NATO Frequency Management Sub-Committee (FMSC). The NATO FMSC acts as the NATO Frequency Authority of the Alliance and is the successor body to the Allied Radio Frequency Agency, or ARFA.

Frequency management cooperation in NATO

Through the NATO FMSC, Alliance nations cooperate in many areas of frequency management. This includes the establishment of overall policy for all parts of the radio frequency spectrum used by the military and the establishment of a specific policy for the military management of the 225400 MHz band, which is widely used for military aircraft, naval and satellite communications and is therefore a particular responsibility of the NATO FMSC. Close liaison also takes place with the civil aviation community through the NATO Air Traffic Management Committee (formerly Committee for European Airspace Coordination (CEAC)). In addition, the NATO FMSC meets regularly with representatives of the Civil Administrations of the member nations to ensure adequate military access to common and reserved parts of the spectrum. In this context, a NATO Joint Civil/Military Frequency Agreement was concluded in 1995.

At the Command level, the two NATO Strategic Commands, Allied Command Europe (ACE) and Allied Command Atlantic (ACLANT), are responsible for detailed bilateral military radio frequency issues with host nations and for preparing plans based on approved radio frequencies.

Since 1994 cooperation in radio frequency management has been extended to NATO Partner countries in the framework of Partnership for Peace.

The NATO FMSC is working actively with Partner countries to address the need for harmonisation. The NATO Joint Civil/Military Frequency Agreement is being used as the basis for this, both in the NATO FMSC and in the Conference of European Postal and Telecommunications Administrations, in which Partner countries also participate.

Further information:

NATO Frequency Management Sub-Committee
NATO Headquarters C3 Staff
1110 Brussels
Belgium
Tel: 32 2 707 5528

NATO Headquarters Information Systems Service (ISS)

The NATO Headquarters Information Systems Service forms part of the Information Systems Directorate within the Executive Secretariat. The latter comes under the Office of the Secretary General. Although managerially an International Staff body, the ISS is staffed by both International Staff and International Military Staff personnel. It provides information systems support to the North Atlantic Council, the Defence Planning Committee and the Military Committee as well as to subordinate committees and supporting staff. In addition, the ISS supplies systems design, development and maintenance support to the International Staff and to the Military Agency for Standardisation. It provides support for tasks such as crisis management, as well as registry and document control services, financial and personnel management information systems, and force planning. It has responsibility for the operation of centralised computer facilities at NATO headquarters, for developing and maintaining software for specific user applications, for providing training and user assistance, maintaining NATO headquarters information systems, and advising staff officials on information systems matters.

NATO CIS Operating and Support Agency (NACOSA)

The NATO CIS Operating and Support Agency (NACOSA) and its subordinate elements manage, operate and control on behalf of all users, the Communications and Information System (CIS) and installations assigned to it by the NC3B. In addition, NACOSA and its subordinate elements provide operational support comprising hardware and software maintenance, personnel training, installation and associated services including security for assigned CIS and authorised users. In cooperation with other NATO bodies, commercial firms and national agencies, NACOSA and its subordinate elements monitor the quality of services to authorised users. To support political consultation and command and control for all NATO operations, the management, control, operating and support activities undertaken by NACOSA and its subordinate elements apply both to fixed headquarters and to mobile forces.

NACOSA is composed of a Central Staff located in Mons, Belgium and is supported by the NATO CIS School in Latina, Italy, the Integrated Software Support Centre, the ACE COMSEC and the Operating and Control Organisation. NACOSA is managed by the Controller, NACOSA, who also exercises the functions of ACOS CIS SHAPE. Operational policy prioritisation and procedural matters are decided jointly by the Strategic Commanders. Non-operational direction is provided by the NC3B.

ELECTRONIC WARFARE

NATO Electronic Warfare Advisory Committee (NEWAC)

The NATO Electronic Warfare Advisory Committee was established in 1966 to support the Military Committee, the NATO Strategic Commanders and the nations by acting as a joint, multinational body to promote an effective NATO Electronic Warfare (EW) capability. It monitors progress achieved nationally and within the Integrated Military Command Structure in implementing agreed EW measures. It is responsible for the development of NATO's EW policy, doctrine, operations and educational requirements and contributes to the development of command and control concepts. Electronic warfare capabilities are a key factor in the protection of military forces and in monitoring compliance with international agreements and are essential for peacekeeping and other tasks undertaken by the Alliance. NEWAC also assists in introducing NATO's EW concepts to Partner countries in the framework of Partnership for Peace.

NEWAC is composed of representatives of each NATO country and of the NATO Strategic Commanders. Members are senior military officials in national electronic warfare organisations. The Chairman and Secretary of the Committee are permanently assigned to the Operations Division of the International Military Staff. There are a number of subordinate groups dealing with electronic warfare data base support, training and doctrine.

Further information:

NATO Electronic Warfare Advisory Committee (NEWAC)
Operations Division
International Military Staff
1110 Brussels
Belgium
Tel: 32 2 707 5627

METEOROLOGY

Military Committee Meteorological Group (MCMG)

The Military Committee Meteorology Group is a specialist forum, composed of national representatives and representatives of NATO Strategic Commanders, that provides meteorological policy guidance to the Military Committee, the Strategic Commanders and the NATO nations. It is responsible for ensuring the most efficient and effective use of national and NATO assets in providing accurate and timely meteorological information to NATO forces. The MCMG is supported by two permanent working groups, namely the Working Group on Operations, Plans and Communications and the Working Group on Battle-area Meteorological Systems and Support.

The Working Group on Operations, Plans and Communication addresses planning and operational issues relating to meteorological support for NATO exercises and operations. It also develops meteorological communications capabilities and standard procedures for communications and exchange of meteorological data.

The Working Group on Battle-area Meteorological Systems and Support encourages cooperation in research, development and transition of new meteorological equipment, techniques, and software to operational capability. It provides technical advice on meteorological matters to other NATO groups and undertakes studies of issues such as flood forecasting and artificial fog dissipation. Basic weather forecasts are often inadequate for tactical planning or mission execution. The Group therefore maintains an inventory of meteorological Tactical Decision Aids (TDAs) developed by the nations. To further standardise the use of Tactical Decision Aids and enhance operability, the Group has developed a library of approved TDAs that are available to all NATO nations.

The MCMG holds annual meetings with Partner countries in the framework of the Partnership for Peace Programme and has developed a Meteorological Support Manual for Partner countries. The Working Group on Battle-area Meteorological Systems and Support also welcomes the participation of PfP nations.

Further information:

MCMG Operations Division (IMS)
NATO-1110 Brussels,
Belgium
Tel: 32 2 707 5538
Fax: 32 2 707 5988
E-mail: imssmo@hq.nato.int

MILITARY OCEANOGRAPHY

The Military Oceanography (MILOC) Group

Military oceanography is the study of oceanographic conditions, ranging from temperature and salinity to tidal movements and coastal features, which can have a bearing on maritime operations. The subject is relevant to many aspects of maritime operations and is particularly relevant to Anti-Submarine Warfare (ASW), Mine Warfare (MW) and Amphibious Warfare (AW) operations. Work undertaken by the MILOC Group focuses on obtaining the maximum military advantage for NATO forces from oceanographic effects.

The MILOC Group is composed of national representatives, representatives of those NATO Commanders with a particularly maritime focus and representatives from the SACLANT Undersea Research Centre. It provides advice to the Supreme Allied Commander Atlantic (SACLANT), who has overall responsibility for military oceanographic issues throughout NATO. A permanent MILOC Sub Group supports the Group.

The MILOC Group ensures that military oceanographic activity is consistent with Alliance strategy. Routine activities of the Group include supporting NATO operations and exercises; developing plans and policies applicable to the field of military oceanography; promoting research and development in the oceanographic field; and undertaking liaison with other NATO and national groups, including those with responsibilities in the meteorological and geographic spheres.

The MILOC Group actively encourages new concepts in the field of environmental support and is responsible for originating NATO's concept of maritime Rapid Environmental Assessment (REA). This is a new methodology which uses developing technologies such as computer modelling, state-of-the-art sensors, Tactical Decision Aids (TDA) and network systems to provide timely forms of support adapted to the needs of the military user.

The work of the Group also takes into account requirements stemming from the development of the European Security and Defence Identity (ESDI); the enhancement of the Partnership for Peace; and NATO's enlargement process, and helps to strengthen transatlantic cooperation as a whole.

The MILOC Sub Group examines issues as tasked by the MILOC Groups and formulates recommendations and reports as appropriate.

The MILOC Group meets annually. NATO Partner countries are encouraged to participate within the framework of the Partnership for Peace (PfP) programme.

Further Information:

MILOC Group
Strategy Division
HQ SACLANT
7857 Blandy Road, Suite 1000
Norfolk, Virginia 23551-2490 USA
Tel: 1 757 445 3431
Fax: 1 757 445 3271
Website: http://www.saclant.nato.int

RESEARCH AND TECHNOLOGY

Research and Technology Organisation (RTO)

The NATO Research and Technology Organisation (RTO) is responsible for integrating the direction and coordination of NATO defence research and technology; conducting and promoting cooperative research and technical information exchange among national defence research activities; developing a long term NATO Research and Technology strategy; and providing advice on research and technology issues.

The RTO builds upon earlier cooperation in defence research and technology under the former Advisory Group for Aerospace Research and Development (AGARD) and the Defence Research Group (DRG), both of which have been brought together to form the new Organisation. The mission of the RTO is to conduct and promote cooperative research and information exchange, to support the development and effective use of national defence research and technology to meet the military needs of the Alliance, to maintain a technological lead and to provide advice to NATO and national decision makers. It is supported by an extensive network of national experts and coordinates its activities with other NATO bodies involved in research and technology.

The RTO reports both to the Military Committee and to the Conference of National Armament Directors. It comprises a Research and Technology Board (RTB) and a Research and Technology Agency (RTA), with its headquarters in Neuilly, France. The full range of research and technology activities is covered by six Panels, dealing with the following subjects:

- Studies, Analysis and Simulation (SAS);

- Systems Concepts and Integration (SCI);

- Sensors and Electronics Technology (SET);

- Information Systems Technology (IST);

- Applied Vehicle Technology (AVT);

- Human Factors and Medicine (HFM).

Each Panel is made up of national representatives including highly qualified scientific experts. The Panels maintain links with military users and other NATO bodies. The scientific and technological work of the RTO is carried out by Technical Teams, created for specific activities and with a specific duration. The Technical Teams organise workshops, symposia, field trials, lecture series and training courses and ensure the continuity of the expert networks. They also play an important role in formulating longer term plans.

In order to facilitate contacts with the military users and other NATO activities, part of the RTA staff is located in the Technology Studies and Coordination Office at NATO Headquarters in Brussels. This staff provides liaison with the International Military Staff and with the Defence Support Division of the International Staff. The coordination of efforts directed towards Partner countries is also mainly undertaken from Brussels.

The coordination of research and technology activities with other parts of the NATO structure is facilitated by the participation of RTO representatives on relevant Boards and in the meetings of directing bodies such as the NATO C3 Board and the NATO Science Committee. Similarly, the General Manager of the NATO C3 Agency and the Director of the SACLANT Undersea Research Centre, to take another example, are ex-officio members of the Research and Technology Board. Coordination of research and technology activities with the member nations is handled through National Coordinators, who also assist in the organisation of activities such as symposia, Board meetings, lecture series and Consultant Missions.

In the context of the Partnership for Peace programme, contacts with NATO's Partner countries initiated under the former AGARD Outreach programme are being extended, with particular emphasis on the countries which are aspirants for NATO membership.

Further information:

Research and Technology Agency (RTA)
BP 25
F-92201 Neuilly sur Seine
France
Tel: 33 1 5561 22 00
Fax: 33 1 5561 22 99
      33 1 5561 22 98
E-mail: mailbox@rta.nato.int
Website: http://www.rta.nato.int

EDUCATION AND TRAINING

NATO Defense College (NDC)

The NATO Defense College, located in Rome, is under the direction of the Military Committee. An independent Advisory Board advises the Commandant and submits recommendations on academic programmes and curricula to the Military Committee. The College runs strategic level courses on politico-military issues designed to prepare selected personnel for NATO and NATO-related appointments as well as undertaking other programmes and activities in support of NATO. Officers and officials from the Alliance's Cooperation Partner countries participate in the programme of the College. The Commandant of the College is an officer of at least Lieutenant General rank, or equivalent, who is appointed by the Military Committee for a three-year period. He is assisted by a civilian Deputy Commandant and a military Deputy Commandant provided by the host nation, Italy. The Chairman of the Military Committee chairs the College's Academic Advisory Board. The Faculty of the College is composed of military officers and civilian officials normally from the Ministries of Foreign Affairs and Defence of Member countries.

The College was established in Paris in 1951 and transferred to Rome in 1966. It organises nine or ten different courses and seminars a year on security issues relevant to the Euro-Atlantic security situation, catering for a wide variety of senior officers from the armed forces, high-level government servants, academics and parliamentarians. Virtually all the College's activities are open to participants from both NATO and Partnership for Peace countries. Participants are selected and funded by their respective national authorities. A number of activities have also recently been opened to participants from countries participating in NATO's Mediterranean Dialogue.

The core activity of the College is a Senior Course, which is held twice a year and lasts five and a half months. It is attended by up to 84 course members selected by their own Governments on a national quota basis. Its members are either military officers holding the rank of Colonel or Lieutenant Colonel, or civilian officials of equivalent status from Ministries of Foreign Affairs or Defence and other relevant government departments or national institutions. Most course members go on to staff appointments in NATO Commands or national NATO related posts in their own countries. The Course Curriculum covers the developments in international politics in general and politico-military issues on security and stability affecting the Member and Partner Nations. At the beginning of each Course, participants are assigned to multinational, multiservice Committees guided by a member of the College Faculty. Daily lectures are given by visiting academics, politicians, high ranking military and civil servants. The focus of the preparations and discussions undertaken by participants is on achieving consensus.

In 1991 the College introduced a two-week Course for senior officers and civilians from the then CSCE countries. The following year, the Course was integrated into the regular Senior Course as an Integrated PfP/OSCE Course. Its aim is to analyse the mission, policies and security functions of the NATO Alliance and its structures and organisation and to discuss current security issues within the context of the changing Euro-Atlantic security situation.

Two General Flag Officers' Courses are organised every year. Their aim is to enhance the understanding of current politico-military issues of the Alliance. One of these takes place both at the Defense College and in Brussels during a two-week period in October and is open to officers and officials from NATO and PfP countries. A second General Flag Officer Course was introduced in April 1998 for participants from NATO member countries and representatives of countries participating in NATO's Mediterranean Dialogue. The Course is designed to contribute to the strengthening of regional stability by promoting dialogue, understanding and confidence building.

A Conference of Commandants is held every year, bringing together the Commandants of senior national defence colleges of NATO and PfP countries to exchange views on academic philosophies and educational methods. The Conference is chaired by the Commandant of the NATO Defense College.

The College participates as a full member in the Secretariat of the Consortium of Defence Academies and Security Studies Institutes, a non-NATO cooperative educational body. In this capacity, the College provides the focal point of contact within NATO to this Consortium.

Every other year, a NATO Reserve Officers' Course takes place. The aim of the course is to familiarise Reserve Officers from NATO and Partner countries with the recent organisational, structural and procedural developments of relevance to the Alliance and to enhance their understanding of the politico-military environment in which NATO operates.

The College organises an International Research Seminar on Euro-Atlantic Security every year, in cooperation with an academic institution from one of the PfP countries. Its objective is to bring together security experts from NATO and Partner countries and to debate topics of importance to the Euro-Atlantic security situation.

An International Research Seminar with Mediterranean Dialogue Countries also takes place annually.

The College offers a Fellowship twice a year in the field of security studies to nationals of Partnership for Peace countries.

The Fellowship is designed to promote individual scholarly research on topics of particular interest to PfP countries, primarily dealing with Euro-Atlantic and Eurasian security issues. Papers presented and discussed as an integral part of the international Research Seminars and research papers by recipients of fellowships are frequently published in the NATO Defense College's Monograph series.

The College generates a strong corporate spirit among its graduates and organises an annual seminar for its alumni. In 1999 the NATO Defense College moved into new purpose-built premises in Rome, designed to accommodate larger courses and to equip the College for its expanded tasks.

For further information contact:

NATO Defense College
Via Giorgia Pelosi 1
00143 Roma
Italy
Tel: 39 06 505 259 (Switchboard)
Fax: 39 06 50525799

The NATO (SHAPE) School - *Oberammergau, Germany*

The NATO (SHAPE) School (Oberammergau) acts as a centre for training military and civilian personnel serving in the Atlantic Alliance, as well as for Partner countries. Its courses are continually revised and updated to reflect current developments in Allied Command Europe and Allied Command Atlantic. Each year a wide range of courses are taught on topics such as weapons employment, nuclear, biological and chemical defence, electronic warfare, command and control, mobilisable forces, multinational forces, peace-keeping, environmental protection, crisis management, and basic NATO orien-tation. The School is under the operational control of the Supreme Allied Commander, Europe (SACEUR) but operates as an operational facility for both NATO Strategic Commands. A Board of Advisers, consisting of members of the SHAPE and School staffs, provides assistance and guidance. Germany and the United States contribute facilities and logistic support, but the School relies on tuition fees from students to offset its operating costs and is essentially self-supporting.

The NATO (SHAPE) School has its origins in the early years of the Alliance's history but received its charter and present name in 1975. For many years its principal focus was on the issues relating to NATO's collective defence. More recently, following the introduction of NATO's new Strategic Concept in 1991, the role of the School was fundamentally altered to include courses, training and seminars in support of NATO's current and developing strategy and policies, including cooperation and dialogue with military and civilian personnel from non-NATO countries. In addition, since the beginning of NATO operations in Bosnia in the context of IFOR and SFOR, the School provides indirect support to current NATO military operations.

In 1998, 47 courses were scheduled in the School's Academic Calendar, involving more than 5 500 students from up to 50 nations. Courses are organised in five fundamental NATO operational areas, namely technical procedures; NATO staff officer orientation; NATO operational procedures; NATO-led multinational operational procedures; and current operational policy forums. The School's Faculty includes staff from NATO countries supplemented by guest speakers from NATO commands and headquarters, NATO and Partnership for Peace countries and world humanitarian and commercial organisations. The focus of all courses is to develop NATO and non-NATO combined joint operational staff officers who can work together more effectively.

Non-military participation in courses has increased significantly during recent years, as have the School's contacts with international organisations such as the International Committee for the Red Cross (ICRC), the United Nations High Commissioner for Refugees (UNHCR), and the World Bank as well as international journalists and news agencies.

In 1994, the School introduced a course on Reserve Forces and Mobilisation which is attended by reserve officers from NATO and PfP countries.

The largest growth area in the School's curricula activity has been in support of the Partnership for Peace programme. An initial course on European Security Cooperation was offered in 1991. Additional courses were added in 1993-1994 on CFE Arms Control Verification Inspector/Escort Procedures; Responsibilities of Military Officers in Environmental Protection; Reserve Forces; and Mobilisation and Peacekeeping.

Further courses were developed in 1995-1996, in order to prepare PfP and NATO officers to work together on combined-joint staffs. These included Resource Management; NATO Orientation; Civil Emergency Planning/Civil-Military Cooperation; and Multinational Crisis Management.

In 1997 the first technical course open to PfP countries was introduced on NBC Defence Warning and Reporting System Procedures. In the same year the School initiated two NATO-sponsored courses for military and civilian leaders of the countries which are signatories to the General Framework Agreement for Peace in Bosnia and Herzegovina (Dayton Agreement). The courses focus on the role of professional officers in a democracy and on operational issues and procedures relevant to the implementation of the Agreement. In 1998, a NATO Partner Operational Staff Officers' Course was also introduced. This is designed to educate NATO and Partner Operational Staff Officers in NATO doctrine and procedures for use in NATO-led Combined Joint Headquarters for Peace Support Operations. NATO's core functions also continue to receive attention, for example with the 1998 introduction of a new course on Air Campaign Planning.

Further developments of the School's curriculum are being introduced to take account of lessons learned in the context of the NATO-led Stabilisation Force in Bosnia as well as other developments within the Alliance. For example, countries participating in NATO's Mediterranean Dialogue also periodically send students to participate in the School's multinational courses.

Further information:

NATO School (SHAPE)
Am Rainenbichl 54
82487 Oberammergau
Germany
Tel: 49 8822 4477 (student administration)
Fax: 49 8822 1035
E-mail: postmaster@natoschool-shape.de

NATO Communications and Information Systems (NCISS) School

The NATO Communications and Information Systems School provides advanced training for civilian and military personnel in the operation and maintenance of NATO's communications and information systems. The School also provides orientation courses and management training on NATO communications and information systems and conducts CIS Orientation Courses for Partner countries.

Originally established in 1959, the School has undergone a number of transformations since that time and has existed under its present name since 1989. In 1994, new courses were introduced in the context of Partnership for Peace. From 1995 the School has also provided courses to support NATO forces in the former Yugoslavia.

The School currently conducts over 50 courses lasting from one to 10 weeks and receives approximately 1 650 students per year.

The School is divided into two Branches, Training and Support. The Training Branch is itself divided into a Network Domain Section responsible for courses concerned with transmission systems, switching systems and network control; an User Domain Section responsible for courses concerned with Command and Control Information systems, software engineering project management and programming; and a Infosec Domain Section responsible for courses on the operation, maintenance and repair of cryptographic equipment. The Training Branch also conducts CIS Officer and Orientation courses, courses on Frequency Management and a CIS course for Partner countries.

The Support Branch is responsible for the logistical and administrative support of the Training Branch.

The Commandant of the School is a serving officer from a NATO member country with the rank of colonel or equivalent. A Principal Telecommunications Engineer acts as his technical adviser. A Training Management Office is responsible for management aspects such as developing the annual course schedule and training documentation and for monitoring statistics.

The School operates as a training establishment for both NATO Strategic Commands and receives administrative support from AFSOUTH. The NATO CIS School is responsible to the NATO Communications and Information Systems Operating and Support Agency (NACOSA).

The School is supported by the Italian Ministry of Defence through the Italian Air Force Training Brigade at Latina with which it is collocated.

Further information on the School can be obtained from:

NATO CIS School
04010 Borgo Piave
Latina
Italy
Tel: 39 0773 6771
Fax: 39 0773 662467

The NATO Training Group (NTG)

The NATO Training Group is responsible for the consolidation of individual training. Its objectives are to improve and expand existing training arrangements between member nations and to initiate new training activities. It reports to the Military Committee and maintains close contacts with the NATO Standardisation Agency (NSA).

The Group facilitates the exchange of information between member countries and NATO's military authorities on national training capabilities and provides a forum for discussion and exchange of views on individual training matters. By identifying and encouraging the use of training projects which lend themselves to bilateral or multilateral cooperation, it promotes qualitative improvements in training as well as cost and manpower savings, standardisation and interoperability. Participation in shared training projects by individual nations is undertaken on a case by case basis and does not duplicate or replace national training programmes. The Group encourages individual nations to assume responsibility for specific training projects on behalf of the Alliance as a whole or Alliance member countries with common requirements. The Group's activities have been extended to include common training projects for Partner countries.

Work is conducted through the medium of five Sub Groups (Joint, Navy, Army, Air Force and Financial) and specialist Working Groups, on which NATO and Partner nations are represented. The activities of the NTG are coordinated by a full time Staff Element located at HQ NATO.

For further information contact:

NATO Training Group Staff Element
IMS Operations Division
NATO
1110 Brussels, Belgium
Tel: 32 2 707 5750

Project Steering Committees/Project Offices

Area Defence;
Battlefield Information Collection and Exploitation System (BICES);
Communications Systems Network Interoperability;
Data Fusion;
F-16 Fighter Aircraft;
Ground Surveillance (Provisional Project Office);
Inertial Navigation Systems for Ships;
MILAN Anti-tank Weapon System;
Multifunctional Information Distribution (Low Volume Terminal);
Multiple Launch Rocket System;
NATO Continuous Acquisition and Life-Cycle Support (CALS) (Management Board);
NATO Improvement Link II;
NATO Insensitive Munitions Information Centre (NIMIC);
NATO Maritime Patrol Aircraft;
NATO Naval Forces Sensor and Weapons Accuracy Check Sites (FORACS);

NATO SEA SPARROW AT Defence Missile;
NATO SEA GNAT System;
OTO MELARA 76/62 Compact Gun;
Very Short and Short Range Air Defence Systems.

Further information on the above projects can be obtained from Defence Support Division, NATO, 1110 Brussels, or from the following Project Offices:

Alliance Ground Surveillance Capability
Provisional Project Office (AGS/PPO)
NATO, 1110 Brussels
Tel: 32 2 707 + Ext.
Fax: 32 2 707 7962

Battlefield Information Collection and Exploitation System (BICES)
8 rue de Genève
1140 Brussels
Tel: 32 2 707 + Ext.
Fax: 32 2 707 8811

NATO Continuous Acquisition and Life Cycle Support Office (CALS)
NATO
1110 Brussels
Tel: 32 2 707 + Ext.
Fax: 32 2 707 4190

NATO FORACS Office
NATO
1110 Brussels
Tel: 32 2 707 4244
Fax: 32 2 707 4103
E-Mail: Foracs@hq.nato.int

NATO Insensitive Munitions Information Centre (NIMIC)
NATO
1110 Brussels
Tel: 32 2 707 + Ext.
Fax: 32 2 707 5363
E-Mail: idnnim@hq.nato.int

CHAPTER 15

THE WIDER INSTITUTIONAL FRAMEWORK FOR SECURITY

The United Nations

The Organisation for Security and Cooperation in Europe

The European Union

The Western European Union

The Council of Europe

THE WIDER INSTITUTIONAL FRAMEWORK FOR SECURITY

THE UNITED NATIONS (UN)

The Charter of the United Nations was signed in San Francisco on 26 June 1945 by 50 nations. On 24 October 1945, the United Nations formally came into being.

Article 51 of the UN Charter establishes the inherent right of individual or collective self-defence of all UN member countries. It sanctions measures they might take in the exercise of this right until such time as the UN Security Council has taken the steps necessary to maintain international peace and security. It stipulates, in addition, that measures taken by member countries under the terms of this Article must be immediately reported to the UN Security Council and do not in any way affect the authority and responsibility of the Security Council to take what actions it deems necessary to maintain or restore international peace and security.

The relevance of the UN Charter to the North Atlantic Alliance is therefore twofold. First, it provides the juridical basis for the creation of the Alliance; and second, it establishes the overall responsibility of the UN Security Council for international peace and security. These two fundamental principles are enshrined in the North Atlantic Treaty signed in Washington on 4 April 1949. The preamble to the Treaty makes it clear from the outset that the UN Charter is the framework within which the Alliance operates. In its opening phrases, the members of the Alliance reaffirm their faith in the purposes and principles of the Charter. In Article 1 they also commit themselves both to settling international disputes by peaceful means in accordance with the goals of the Charter and to refraining from the threat or use of force in any manner inconsistent with the purposes of the UN. Article 5 of the Treaty makes explicit reference to Article 51 of the Charter in asserting the right of the signatories to take, individually or collectively, such action as they deem necessary for their self-defence, including the use of armed force; and, it commits the member countries to terminating the use of armed force in restoring and maintaining the security of the North Atlantic area when the UN Security Council has itself taken the measures necessary to restore and maintain international peace and security.

Further reference to the UN Charter is to be found in Article 7 of the North Atlantic Treaty, which reminds signatories of their rights and obligations under the Charter and reaffirms the primary responsibility of the UN Security Council for the maintenance of peace and security. And finally, in Article 12, a clause was included in the Treaty providing for it to be reviewed after ten years, if any of the Parties to it so requested. It stipulated that the review would take place in the light of new developments affecting peace and security in the North Atlantic area, including the development of universal and regional arrangements under the UN Charter.

The North Atlantic Treaty came into force on 24 August 1949. None of the Parties to it have requested a review of the Treaty under Article 12, although at each stage of its development the Alliance has kept the implementation of the Treaty under continuous review for the purpose of securing its objectives. The direct relationship between the Treaty and the Charter of the United Nations is and will remain a fundamental principle of the Alliance.

From 1949 to the present day, the formal link between the United Nations and the North Atlantic Alliance has remained constant and has manifested itself first and foremost in the juridical relationship between their respective founding documents. Contacts between the institutions of the United Nations and those of the Alliance were, for most of this period, extremely limited, both in scope and in content. In 1992, in the context of the conflict in the former Yugoslavia, the situation changed.

In July 1992, against the background of growing conflict, NATO ships belonging to the Alliance's Standing Naval Force Mediterranean, assisted by NATO Maritime Patrol Aircraft, began monitoring operations in the Adriatic in support of a United Nations arms embargo against all republics of the former Yugoslavia. In November 1992, NATO and the Western European Union (WEU) began enforcement operations in support of UN Security Council resolutions aimed at preventing the escalation of the conflict by movements of additional arms into the area.

The readiness of the Alliance to support peacekeeping operations under the authority of the UN Security Council was formally stated by NATO Foreign Ministers in December 1992. The measures already being taken by NATO countries, individually and as an Alliance, were reviewed and the Alliance indicated that it was ready to respond positively to further initiatives that the UN Secretary General might take in seeking Alliance assistance in this field.

A number of measures were subsequently taken, including joint maritime operations under the authority of the NATO and WEU Councils; NATO air operations; close air support for the United Nations Protection Force (UNPROFOR); air strikes to protect UN "Safe Areas"; and contingency planning for other options which the UN might take. These measures and the basis on which they were undertaken are described in Chapter 5.

In December 1995, following the signature of the Bosnian Peace Agreement in Paris on 14 December, NATO was given a mandate by the UN, on the basis of Security Council Resolution 1031, to implement the military aspects of the Peace Agreement. A NATO-led Implementation Force (IFOR) began operations to fulfil this mandate on 16 December. Details of the work of IFOR and its subsequent replacement by a NATO-led Stabilisation Force (SFOR) in December 1996, are also described in Chapter 5. Throughout their mandates both multinational forces have worked closely on the ground in Bosnia and Herzegovina with other international organisations and humanitarian agencies, including those of the United Nations, such as the UN High Commissioner for Refugees (UNHCR) and the UN International Police Task Force (IPTF).

In February 1998, after discussions with non-NATO contributors to SFOR, the North Atlantic Council announced that, subject to the necessary mandate from the UN Security Council, NATO was prepared to organise and lead a multinational force to continue the work in Bosnia and Herzegovina following the end of SFOR's mandate in June 1998. The new force retains the name "SFOR", reflecting the continuing need for stabilisation of the Bosnian situation and for laying the foundations for permanent peace in the region.

From the onset of the conflict in Kosovo in 1998 and throughout the crisis, close contacts were maintained between the Secretary General of the United Nations and the Secretary General of NATO. Actions taken by the Alliance in support of UN Security Council resolutions both during and after the conflict and the role of the Kosovo Force (KFOR) established on the basis of UN Security Council resolution 1244 of 12 June 1999, are described in Chapter 5.

Outside the context of the former Yugoslavia, in the face of other threats to world peace, NATO countries, while not directly involved as an Alliance, have lent their support and their voice to the efforts of the UN Security Council and the UN Secretary General to avert conflict and restore the rule of international law. In the early part of 1998, in the context of the implementation of UN Security Council resolutions relating to Iraq and of the international inspection régime established to ensure the identification and elimination of weapons of mass destruction and the capacity to produce such weapons, the Alliance called for full compliance by Iraq.

On 25 February 1998, the NATO Secretary General issued a statement welcoming the agreement between the Secretary General of the United Nations and Iraq on a diplomatic solution to the Iraq crisis. He paid tribute to the diplomatic efforts and determined stance of the international community, including the NATO Allies, and insisted on the need for full compliance with all the relevant UN Security Council Resolutions. When the North Atlantic Council discussed the situation in Iraq again, on 4 March 1998, it welcomed the unanimous adoption of UN Security Council Resolution 1154, relating to the implementation of the agreement between the UN Secretary General and Iraq. The Council expressed its support for the relevant UN decisions and emphasised the importance of stability in the Gulf region to the security of the Euro-Atlantic area.

Both juridical and strong practical links thus exist between the UN Charter and the North Atlantic Treaty on the one hand, and the institutions of the UN and those of the Alliance on the other. Both these elements contribute to the wider institutional framework within which the Alliance operates. Other institutional relationships contributing to this framework are described below.

THE ORGANISATION FOR SECURITY AND COOPERATION IN EUROPE (OSCE)[1]

The Organisation for Security and Cooperation in Europe (OSCE), formerly known as the Conference on Security and Cooperation in Europe (CSCE), was initially a political consultative process involving participating states from Europe, Central Asia and North America. It became an Organisation in January 1995.

Launched in 1972, the CSCE process led to the adoption of the Helsinki Final Act in 1975. This document encompassed a wide range of standards for international behaviour and commitments governing relations between participating states, measures designed to build confidence between them, especially in the politico-military field, respect for human rights and fundamental freedoms, and cooperation in economic, cultural, technical and scientific fields.

Institutionalisation of the OSCE

On 21 November 1990, the CSCE Summit Meeting of Heads of State and Government of the then 34 participating states adopted the Charter of Paris for a New Europe. The Charter established the Council of Foreign Ministers of the

---

1   List of participating states: Albania, Andorra, Armenia, Austria, Azerbaijan, Belarus, Belgium, Bosnia and Herzegovina, Bulgaria, Canada, Croatia, Cyprus, Czech Republic, Denmark, Estonia, Finland, France, Georgia, Germany, Greece, Holy See, Hungary, Ireland, Iceland, Italy, Kazakhstan, Kyrgyz Republic, Latvia, Liechtenstein, Lithuania, Luxembourg, Malta, Moldova, Monaco, the Netherlands, Norway, Poland, Portugal, Romania, Russian Federation, San Marino, Slovakia, Slovenia, Spain, Sweden, Switzerland, Tajikistan, the former Yugoslav Republic of Macedonia*, Turkmenistan, Turkey, Ukraine, United Kingdom, United States of America, Uzbekistan, the Federal Republic of Yugoslavia**.

*   Turkey recognises the Republic of Macedonia with its constitutional name.

**   Yugoslavia was suspended from the OSCE on 8 July 1992 because of the nature of its involvement in the conflict in Bosnia and Herzegovina. Following the election of Vojislav Kostunica as President in September 2000, the Federal Republic of Yugoslavia was admitted to the OSCE on 10 November 2000, as the 55th member state.

CSCE as the central forum for regular political consultations. It also established a Committee of Senior Officials to review current issues, prepare the work of the Council and carry out its decisions; and three permanent institutions of the CSCE: a secretariat in Prague (later subsumed into the general secretariat in Vienna), a Conflict Prevention Centre in Vienna, and an Office for Free Elections in Warsaw (subsequently renamed the Office for Democratic Institutions and Human Rights (ODIHR)).

On 19 June 1991, the first meeting of the Council of Foreign Ministers took place in Berlin. The Council adopted a mechanism for consultation and coop-eration with regard to emergency situations in the area covered by the CSCE. This mechanism has been used in the case of the former Yugoslavia and that of Nagorno-Karabakh.

At the conclusion of the Helsinki Follow-Up Meeting on 9 July 1992, the Heads of State and Government of the CSCE participating states adopted the Helsinki Summit Declaration entitled "The Challenges of Change". The Declaration reflected agreement on further strengthening CSCE institutions, establishing a High Commissioner on National Minorities and developing a structure for early warning, conflict prevention and crisis management, includ-ing fact-finding and rapporteur missions.

At the Stockholm meeting of the Council of Foreign Ministers on 14 December 1992, a Convention on Conciliation and Arbitration within the CSCE was adopted. It was also decided to establish the post of CSCE Secretary General.

The Council of Foreign Ministers endorsed new organisational changes at their meeting in Rome on 1 December 1993, including the establishment of the Permanent Committee - the first permanent body of the CSCE for political con-sultation and decision-making - and the creation of a single general secretariat, both located in Vienna. The Foreign Ministers also expressed their concern about the number and scale of regional conflicts and reaffirmed their commit-ment to the resolution of these conflicts, particularly in the former Yugoslavia. They took steps to improve the capabilities of the CSCE in crisis management and conflict prevention and agreed that relations with other "European and Transatlantic Organisations" should be developed.

A number of institutional decisions to strengthen the CSCE were intro-duced at the 1994 Budapest Summit. These included the renaming of the CSCE, which would in future be known as the Organisation for Security and Cooperation in Europe (OSCE); the scheduling of the next meeting of OSCE Heads of State and Government in Lisbon, in 1996; the replacement of the Committee of Senior Officials by the Senior Council, which would meet at least twice a year, as well as before the Ministerial Council Meeting, and would also convene as the Economic Forum; the establishment of the Permanent Council (formerly Permanent Committee), meeting in Vienna, as the regular body for political consultation and decision-making; and the scheduling of the review of implementation of all CSCE commitments at a meeting to be held in Vienna before each Summit.

At the Budapest Summit, CSCE states declared their political will to provide a multinational CSCE peacekeeping force following agreement among the parties for cessation of armed conflict in Nagorno-Karabakh.

At the OSCE Summit which took place in Istanbul in November 1999, it was decided to strengthen the political consultation process within the OSCE by establishing a Preparatory Committee under the OSCE Permanent Council as well as an Operations Centre, in order to plan and deploy OSCE field operations.

Security Dialogue, Arms Control, Disarmament and Confidence and Security Building Measures (CSBMs)

Significant landmarks in the evolution of the CSCE's work on Confidence and Security Building Measures (CSBMs) include the 1986 Stockholm Document, which was later expanded and improved in the Vienna 1990 and Vienna 1992 Documents. At the Helsinki Follow-up Meeting in July 1992 the participating states decided to establish the CSCE Forum for Security Cooperation (FSC) in Vienna, under whose auspices security dialogue is promoted and negotiations on arms control, disarmament and confidence and security building now take place.

The Forum was inaugurated on 22 September 1992. Over the next two years, in accordance with a mandate agreed upon at Helsinki entitled "Programme for Immediate Action", negotiations took place in the Forum on a series of documents addressing arms control issues, disarmament and confidence and security building measures, security enhancement and cooperation and conflict prevention.

In the light of the Programme for Immediate Action two further elements were agreed in December 1994 in the run-up to the CSCE's Budapest Summit: a new version of the Vienna Document (Vienna Document 1994), subsuming the earlier Stockholm and Vienna Documents and incorporating the Defence Planning and Military Contacts and Cooperation texts agreed in 1993; and a Document on the Global Exchange of Military Information. The Summit Document itself incorporated new Principles Governing Non-proliferation and took the important step of agreeing a Code of Conduct on Politico-Military

Aspects of Security, which included significant new commitments on the Democratic Control and Use of Armed Forces.

In the field of conventional arms control, the opening of the CSCE Summit in Paris on 19 November 1990 saw the signature by 22 members of NATO and the (then) Warsaw Treaty Organisation of the far-reaching Conventional Forces in Europe Treaty (CFE), which limits conventional forces in Europe from the Atlantic Ocean to the Ural Mountains. The Treaty entered into force on 9 November 1992. Its signature was followed by negotiation of the CFE-1A Concluding Act, which introduced limitations on military personnel as well as establishing additional stabilising measures. This was signed in the framework of the CSCE Helsinki Summit Meeting on 10 July 1992.

The 1995 Dayton Peace Agreement mandated negotiation of CSBMs amongst the entities of Bosnia and Herzegovina and of an Arms Control régime amongst the parties to the Dayton agreement itself. These were negotiated under OSCE auspices in 1996. Personal Representatives of the OSCE Chairman-in-Office (CIO) chaired the negotiations and have assisted with their implementation. A cell within the OSCE Secretariat in Vienna has responsibility for organising the necessary inspections, in which various OSCE participating states have taken part.

The OSCE Summit Meeting held in Istanbul in November 1999 saw the signing of an Adapted CFE Treaty, which now has 30 signatories, and a revised Vienna Document (Vienna Document 1999).

In 1999, the OSCE Forum for Security Cooperation also decided to explore methods to control trafficking of small arms and light weapons.

Conflict prevention and crisis management

In accordance with the 1992 Helsinki Summit Declaration, the OSCE has developed a number of methods of sending official missions and personal representatives of the Chairman-in-Office to areas of potential regional tension or conflict, for fact finding, rapporteur, monitoring and "good offices" purposes, in furtherance of its remit for crisis management and conflict prevention.

The Office of the OSCE Commissioner on National Minorities, for example, has a mandate to conduct on-site missions and to engage in preventative diplomacy at the earliest stages of tension. The role of the Office, which was established in 1992, is to seek early resolution of ethnic tensions that might endanger peace, stability and friendly relations between OSCE states.

Over the past several years such OSCE activities have been undertaken in Kosovo, Sandjak, Vojvodina, Skopje, Georgia, Estonia, Tajikistan, Moldova, Latvia, Nagorno-Karabakh and Chechnya. From September 1992, the CSCE operated Sanctions Assistance Missions (SAMs) in Albania, Bulgaria, Croatia, the former Yugoslav Republic of Macedonia[2], Hungary and Romania, to assist in monitoring the implementation of UN-Mandated sanctions against the Federal Republic of Yugoslavia (Serbia and Montenegro).

In 1996 the OSCE organised general elections in Bosnia and Herzegovina following the Dayton peace agreement and, in September 1997, it organised the ensuing municipal elections. In 1997 the OSCE Chairman-in-Office's Personal Representative assisted in finding a political solution to the crisis in Albania. The OSCE monitored the resulting elections.

The Kosovo conflict and international intervention to end the conflict and rebuild peace and stability combined to create one of the greatest challenges the OSCE has faced. Developments in the province continue to represent major demands on the Organisation in terms of resources, personnel and time. The growing relationship between the OSCE and NATO has been one of the important bi-products of the crisis, the consequences of which will remain high on the international agenda for many years to come.

From January to March 1998, the OSCE mounted a Kosovo Verification Mission to monitor compliance on the ground with the cease-fire agreements reached as a result of NATO intervention in support of UN Security Council Resolution 1199. NATO conducted a parallel aerial surveillance mission. Both missions were endorsed by UN Security Council Resolution 1203.

NATO established a special military task force to help with the emergency evacuation of the OSCE Kosovo Verification Mission, if renewed conflict placed the Mission at risk.

The OSCE Mission monitored human rights violations on both sides of the ethnic divide but concluded that there was overwhelming evidence of suffering on the Kosovo Albanian side at the hands of the Yugoslav and Serbian military and security apparatus.

At the beginning of 1999, the situation in Kosovo flared up again with acts of provocation on both sides. Some of these incidents were defused through the mediation efforts of the OSCE verifiers but the situation deteriorated further in mid January 1999, with the escalation of the Serbian offensive against the Kosovar Albanians. On 20 March 1999, the Kosovo Verification Mission was

---

2   Turkey recognises the Republic of Macedonia with its constitutional name.

forced to withdraw from the region, when obstruction by Serbian forces rendered it impossible for it to fulfil its task.

The OSCE Mission in Kosovo (OMIK) was established by the OSCE Permanent Council on 1 July 1999 to take the lead role, within the overall framework of the United Nations Mission to Kosovo (UNMIK), in matters relating to institution- and democracy-building and human rights. The OSCE Mission has since established a number of field offices and regional centres around Kosovo and is working together with other international and non-governmental organisations to build a democratic, stable future for Kosovo. Its work involves promoting the development of democratic political party training activities; building contacts with non-governmental and civil structures; addressing human rights issues and helping to integrate human rights training and protection into social structures; participating in development of judicial institutions and in police education and development; assisting in addressing the problems of civil and electoral registration; and helping to establish media and broadcasting structures which support freedom of press and information activities in Kosovo.

The OSCE's security model

At the Budapest Summit on 5-6 December 1994, Heads of State and Government of the CSCE launched a broad and comprehensive discussion on all aspects of security aimed at devising a concept of security for the 21st Century, taking into account the ongoing debates in participating states on this topic.

The 1996 Lisbon Summit Declaration on a Common and Comprehensive Security Model for Europe for the 21st Century reaffirmed that European security required the widest cooperation and coordination among participating states and European and transatlantic organisations, and identified the OSCE as a forum particularly well suited for enhancing cooperation and complementarity among such organisations and institutions. The Summit launched the development of a Charter on European Security, aimed at strengthening security and stability in the region and improving the operational capabilities of the OSCE. The declaration also expressed the intention of the OSCE to strengthen cooperation with other security organisations which are transparent and predictable in their actions, whose members individually and collectively adhere to OSCE principles and commitments, and whose membership is based on open and voluntary commitments.

The next step in the development of the Security Model was the OSCE Ministerial meeting in Copenhagen in December 1997, which issued guidelines for the development of a Document-Charter on European Security. At this meeting, a Common Concept for the development of cooperation between mutually reinforcing institutions[3] was also adopted.

The Charter on European Security was adopted at the OSCE Summit in Istanbul in November 1999. It reflected several policy initiatives including the development of the OSCE's role in peacekeeping operations; the adoption of a Platform for Cooperative Security; the creation of Rapid Expert Assistance and Cooperation Teams (REACT) to enable the OSCE to respond quickly to demands for civilian assistance and for large civilian field operations; the expansion of the OSCE ability to carry out police activities; the establishment of an Operations Centre in order to plan and deploy OSCE field operations; and the strengthening of the political consultation process within the OSCE by establishing a Preparatory Committee under the OSCE Permanent Council.

The Platform for Cooperative Security aims to further strengthen and develop reciprocal cooperation with competent organisations. At Istanbul, Heads of State and Government expressed readiness in principle to deploy the resources of international organisations and institutions of which they are members in support of the OSCE's work.

Alliance interaction with the OSCE

As the only forum which brings together all the countries of Europe, as well as Canada and the United States, the Organisation for Security and Cooperation in Europe (OSCE) represents a key component of Europe's security architecture. It provides a comprehensive framework for cooperation in the areas of human rights, fundamental freedoms, democracy, the rule of law, security and economic cooperation.

The Alliance has actively supported the CSCE/OSCE since its creation, and was among the proponents of the institutionalisation of the CSCE process agreed at the Paris CSCE Summit Meeting in 1990. At its Rome Summit in November 1991, the Alliance confirmed its commitment to the CSCE process and defined the roles of the CSCE and the Alliance, in the development of dialogue and cooperation in Europe, as complementary. Recognising that the

---

3   The concept of "mutually reinforcing institutions" in the security field, previously referred to as "interlocking institutions", can be traced back to the Rome Declaration on Peace and Cooperation issued at the NATO Summit Meeting in Rome in November 1991. The Declaration recognised that the challenges which would have to be faced in the new Europe could not be comprehensively addressed by one institution alone but only in a framework of interlocking institutions tying together the countries of Europe and North America. NATO countries would therefore work towards a new European security architecture in which NATO, the CSCE (later OSCE), the European Community (later the European Union), the WEU and the Council of Europe would complement each other and in which other regional frameworks of cooperation would also play an important role.

security of the Allies was inseparably linked to that of other states in Europe, the Alliance regarded dialogue and cooperation between the different institutions dealing with security as an important factor in helping to defuse crises and to prevent conflicts.

The importance ascribed to the CSCE by NATO was further underlined at Oslo, in June 1992. Foreign Ministers of the Alliance stated their preparedness to support peacekeeping activities under the responsibility of the CSCE, including by making available Allied resources and expertise. This important decision paved the way for increased NATO interaction with the OSCE, especially in the context of the Alliance's new tasks such as peacekeeping operations.

From December 1991 onwards, NATO's dialogue and cooperation with its Partner countries in Central and Eastern Europe and in the former Soviet Union took place in the framework of the North Atlantic Cooperation Council (NACC). The NACC obtained tangible results in a number of important areas, including the promotion of good neighbourly relations, disarmament and arms control, and cooperation in peacekeeping. The process provided a substantial contribution to the strengthening of cooperation among NATO Allies and Partner countries and in so doing supported the CSCE/OSCE role in these fields.

A stronger, more operational partnership between NATO and its NACC partners began to take shape in 1997, with the replacement of the NACC by the Euro-Atlantic Partnership Council (EAPC). The EAPC provides the overall framework for cooperation between NATO and its Partner countries, including Partnership for Peace (PfP) and raises it to a qualitatively new level. A body known as the Political-Military Steering Committee/Ad Hoc Group on Cooperation in Peacekeeping, working within the EAPC framework, provides an important institutional link to the OSCE. A representative of the OSCE Chairman-in-Office regularly attends its meetings and gives briefings on current OSCE issues of relevance to the Group. This formalised arrangement is particularly important in the field of peacekeeping. It provides evidence of the complementarity and transparency which characterises the development of cooperation in the field of peacekeeping which is now taking place in the EAPC and PfP framework.

Since its Budapest Summit in December 1994, the OSCE has been involved in a broad and comprehensive discussion on all aspects of security aimed at devising a concept of security for the 21st Century.

In December 1996, in their Lisbon Summit Declaration on a common and comprehensive security model for Europe for the 21st century, OSCE Heads of State and Government reaffirmed that European Security requires the widest cooperation and coordination among participating states and among European and transatlantic organisations. They also stated their intention to strengthen cooperation with other security organisations. The Alliance has contributed to OSCE discussion of the security model in this context.

In their 1997 Madrid Declaration on Euro-Atlantic security and coopera-tion, NATO Heads of State and Government recognised the OSCE as the most inclusive European-wide security organisation. They emphasised the essential role it plays in securing peace, stability and security in Europe and underlined the importance of the principles and commitments adopted by the OSCE as a foundation for the development of comprehensive and cooperative European security structures.

In Madrid, NATO also expressed its continued support both for the OSCE's work on a Common and Comprehensive Security Model for Europe for the 21st Century and for giving consideration to the idea of developing a Charter on European Security in accordance with the decisions taken at the 1996 Lisbon Summit of the OSCE.

The Common Concept for the Development of Cooperation between Mutually Reinforcing Institutions, as agreed at the OSCE Ministerial in Copenhagen in December 1997, features a list of principles and commitments for the development of cooperation between mutually reinforcing organisations and institutions within the Platform for Cooperative Security. Within the relevant organisations and institutions of which they are members, participating states commit themselves to work to ensure the organisations' and institutions' adher-ence to the Platform. As a first set of practical steps towards the development of cooperation between the OSCE and those organisations and institutions, the Common Concept prescribes regular contacts, including meetings, through a continuous framework for dialogue, increased transparency and practical cooperation. This includes the identification of liaison officers or points of con-tact, cross-representation at appropriate meetings, and other contacts intended to increase understanding of each organisation's conflict prevention tools. NATO and the OSCE have been developing their relations on the basis of the Common Concept.

The Alliance's commitment to promoting security, prosperity and democ-racy throughout the Euro-Atlantic region was underlined in the revised Strategic Concept and other documents issued by NATO Heads of State and Government at the Washington Summit in April 1999. NATO member countries are thus fully supportive of both the OSCE's fundamental principles and of its comprehensive and cooperative approach to security. This support has been made manifest in Alliance statements of its readiness to support OSCE efforts to strengthen European security and stability and, in particular, to support peacekeeping operations under the responsibility of the OSCE. Progress in defining the OSCE's contribution to peacekeeping operations is reflected in its Charter on European Security.

The emphasis given in the Charter to closer cooperation among international organisations has also been welcomed by the Alliance. Cooperation developed between NATO and the OSCE in recent years in the areas of conflict prevention, peacekeeping, crisis management and post-conflict rehabilitation, is entirely in keeping with the spirit of the Platform of Cooperative Security to be developed under the Charter.

Close practical cooperation between the two organisations is amplified in the context of international efforts to bring peace to the former Yugoslavia, specifically in relations between the OSCE and the NATO-led Stabilisation Force (SFOR) in Bosnia and Herzegovina, and between the OSCE and the Kosovo Force (KFOR) (see below).

Among the initiatives adopted at the Istanbul Summit is the creation of Rapid Expert Assistance and Cooperation Teams (REACT). This rapidly deployable capability will cover a wide range of civilian expertise to assist in conflict prevention, crisis management and post-conflict rehabilitation. The strengthening of the OSCE's ability to deploy quickly the civilian components of a peacekeeping operation facilitates cooperation with NATO-led peacekeeping forces working alongside these civilian teams.

At the OSCE Forum for Security Cooperation (FSC), NATO member states, in association with other participating states, tabled a number of substantive proposals addressing issues such as the exchange of information on defence planning; non-proliferation and arms transfers; military cooperation and contacts; global exchange of military information; and stabilising measures for localised crisis situations. Between 1993 and 1995 all of these proposals contributed to the development of a number of OSCE documents. The Alliance also made proposals for the updating of the Confidence and Security Building Measures (CSBMs) contained in the OSCE's Vienna Document and this contributed to the completion of a revised and improved version of the document, which was agreed in December 1994 (the Vienna Document 1994). The 1994 version has since been replaced by the Vienna Document 1999.

Areas of practical cooperation

Although the roles of the Atlantic Alliance, the OSCE, and other intergovernmental organisations contributing to the wider Euro-Atlantic security framework remain quite distinct, practical cooperation and support between them has become increasingly necessary.

In Bosnia and Herzegovina, the NATO-led Implementation Force (IFOR) and its successor SFOR have cooperated closely with the OSCE in the implementation of the Dayton Peace Agreement. IFOR supported the OSCE in its preparations for the September 1996 elections and it provided security and logistical support during the elections, which took place without any major incident. SFOR provided comparable support to the OSCE for the planning and conduct of the 1997 municipal elections.

IFOR and SFOR both supported the OSCE in a further practical way in the context of the implementation of Article II (CSBMs) and Article IV (Sub-Regional Arms Control Agreements) of the Dayton Agreement. Both IFOR and SFOR were able to assist the OSCE by providing relevant data on weapons cantonments. SFOR has also provided logistical support for arms control implementation, for example by transporting heavy weapons from cantonments to reduction sites.

The Kosovo crisis raised OSCE-NATO cooperation to new levels. The unique nature of cooperation between NATO and the OSCE's Kosovo Verification Mission in 1999 allowed the two organisations to work creatively together in very demanding circumstances. KFOR has subsequently continued to support the OSCE - and other organisations involved in the United Nations Mission in Kosovo - in particular by providing the secure environment necessary for them to carry out their work.

Further information about the OSCE can be obtained from the OSCE Secretariat, Kärntner Ring 5-7, 1010 Vienna, Austria. Tel: 43 1 514 360; Fax: 43 1 514 3696 (http://www.osce.org). The Secretariat also maintains an office in Prague: OSCE Secretariat Rytirska 31, 110 00 Prague 1, Czech Republic (http://www.osceprag.cz; E-Mail: webmaster@osceprag.cz).

THE EUROPEAN UNION (EU)

The European Union was established on the basis of the Treaty of Rome signed on 25 March 1957 by Belgium, France, Germany, Italy, Luxembourg and the Netherlands. In 1973 they were joined by Denmark, Ireland and the United Kingdom; in 1981 by Greece; in 1986 by Portugal and Spain; and in 1995 by Austria, Finland and Sweden. Accession negotiations were also successfully completed by Norway, but in a national referendum held in November 1994, 52.5 percent of Norwegian voters opposed membership of the European Union. Applications for membership of the EU have been submitted by Turkey and Cyprus, as well as the 10 associated countries of Central Europe (Bulgaria, the Czech Republic, Estonia, Hungary, Latvia, Lithuania, Poland, Romania, Slovakia, Slovenia).

At the Maastricht European Council on 9 and 10 December 1991, the Heads of State and Government adopted a Treaty on Political Union and a Treaty on Economic and Monetary Union, which together form the Treaty on

European Union. The Treaty came into force following ratification by all parties on 1 November 1993.

On 16 and 17 June 1997 in Amsterdam, EU Heads of State and Government agreed on a number of revisions to the Maastricht Treaty which have implications for the future Common Foreign and Security Policy of the Union. In particular it was agreed that:

- the Secretary General of the European Council would assume the functions of High Representative of the Common Foreign and Security Policy;

- a Policy Planning and Early Warning Unit would be established under his responsibility;

- the EU would draw up, together with the WEU, arrangements for enhanced cooperation between them within a year from the entry into force of the Treaty of Amsterdam;

- humanitarian and rescue tasks, peacekeeping tasks and tasks of combat forces in crisis management, including peacemaking (the so-called "Petersberg missions" of the WEU: see Chapter 4) would be included in the revised Treaty (Article J.7).

Conditional use of qualified majority voting was further elaborated in the context of the Common Foreign and Security Policy. According to the new structure of the Treaty, the European Council will decide on common strategies to be implemented by the European Union in areas where the member states have important interests in common. The European Council will implement them, in particular through undertaking joint actions and adopting common positions. These decisions will be by qualified majority, but include provision for a member state to take a position of "constructive abstention". This would signify that the member state concerned chooses not to participate in the decision, but does not impede action by the other member states. Alternatively, if there are important questions of national policy at stake, a member state may choose to block a qualified majority vote, leaving open the possibility of appeal by other member states to the European Council.

The role of the European Union in international relations extends far beyond the positions and actions adopted within the framework of the Common Foreign and Security Policy. The EU is the world's largest trade entity. It is one of the largest providers of funds for the developing countries, one of the biggest financial contributors in the context of the Middle East and the biggest financial contributor to international efforts aimed at laying the foundations for a lasting peace in the former Yugoslavia. Many other well-established EU policies, such as those on agriculture and fisheries, also have important external dimensions.

The Union's role in external relations will be further strengthened by the European Economic and Monetary Union and the establishment of a single currency.

Considerable importance is therefore attached to ensuring that the Common Foreign and Security Policy of the Union is in line with all its other external policies. The Council of Ministers and the European Commission both have the responsibility, within their respective mandates, for ensuring that the Union's external activities as a whole are consistent with its external relations, security, economic and development policies.

This approach has characterised policy development with regard to the enlargement of the EU, the EU pre-accession strategy towards the Central European candidate countries, EU-Russia relations and the EU's relations with the Mediterranean countries. The foundation for a future Euro-Mediterranean Partnership covering both political and economic relations, was laid at the Barcelona Conference in November 1995 (see Chapter 3).

Both political and economic elements were similarly included when the EU-Asian dialogue was launched at the March 1996 Bangkok Summit of Heads of State and Government of the 15 European and 10 Asian nations. At the mid-term revision of the Lomé Convention between the EU and the African, Caribbean and Pacific countries, the political elements of the convention were also reinforced. The European Union also maintains close cooperation with the Latin American countries. Furthermore, the Union maintains a continuing dialogue on political and economic issues of mutual interest and engages in direct negotiations on trade and investment issues with the United States, in the context of the General Agreement on Tariffs and Trade (GATT), and in the context of the EU-US Action Plan.

Since the outbreak of the conflict in the former Yugoslavia and the disintegration of the federal state of Yugoslavia, the European Union has been engaged in efforts to bring about peace to the region and to channel humanitarian aid to the war-stricken communities affected by the conflict. The London Conference on Yugoslavia held in August 1992, chaired jointly by the Secretary General of the United Nations and the Prime Minister of the United Kingdom (then President of the European Council), represented a new departure for the EU in the field of foreign policy. This was the first combined EU-United Nations international operation. A new European envoy to Bosnia, Ambassador Carlos Westendorp (Spain) was appointed in May 1997 following the resignation of his predecessor Carl Bildt, the former Prime Minister of Sweden. Carlos Westendorp was replaced in Summer 1999 by Wolfgang Petrisch, former Austrian ambassador and European Union envoy to Belgrade.

The structure of the European Union

The European Union is composed of three "pillars":

- the European Community is the legal framework for Community policies relating to the single market, international trade, development assistance, monetary policy, agriculture, fisheries, environment, regional development, energy, etc;

- the Common Foreign and Security Policy (CFSP);

- Justice and Home Affairs, covering cooperation within the Union in areas such as civil and criminal law, immigration and asylum policy, border control, drug trafficking, police cooperation and exchange of information.

All these three major components of the European Union are governed in part by a set of fundamental objectives and basic principles and in part by a single institutional framework.

The major overriding internal objective of the European Union is to promote economic and social progress, notably through the creation of a border-free area, through the promotion of economic and social cohesion, and through the establishment of economic and monetary union, including a single currency. Externally, the main overall objective of the Union is to assert its identity on the international scene, in particular through a Common Foreign and Security Policy, including the development of a common defence policy. The central basic principles governing the Union are respect for national identities, democracy and fundamental human rights.

As for the single institutional framework of the Union, the main EU institutions are as follows:

- The European Parliament represents the 370 million citizens of the European Union. Its role is to pass legislation and to subject to scrutiny and control the use of executive power by the institutions of the European Union. Until 1979, Members of the European Parliament (MEPs) were nominated by national legislative bodies from among their own members. Direct elections to the Parliament commenced in June 1979. The most important powers of the European Parliament fall into three categories: firstly, legislative power, where the Parliament's influence has been extended to amending and adopting legislation proposed by the Commission. Accordingly, the Parliament and Council now share power of decision in many areas; secondly, power over the budget, where the European Parliament approves the Union's budget each year; thirdly, supervision of the executive branch of the Union, through its power of appointment of the President and members of the Commission. The European Parliament may question individual

Commissioners and ultimately has the power to dismiss the Commission itself. Individually, or as a group, European citizens have the right to petition the Parliament. An Ombudsman is responsible for investigating allegations of maladministration brought by citizens.

- The Council of the European Union, known as the Council of Ministers, which acts on proposals from the Commission and is the Union's primary decision-making body. The Council's role is to define political objectives, coordinate national policies and resolve differences between its members or with other institutions. The Council's competence extends across all three pillars of the Union. It is composed of ministers of the governments of the Member States. Ministerial meetings are prepared by the Permanent Representatives of the Member States.

- The Commission, which is responsible for safeguarding the EU Treaties and for initiating and proposing community legislation and policy, as well as overseeing the implementation of such legislation. In addition, the Commission acts as the guardian of European Community law and can refer cases to the European Union's Court of Justice. The Commission is in effect the manager and executive authority of European Union policies and international trade relations. It is the Union's executive body and consists of 20 Commissioners nominated by the Member States and appointed for a period of five years.

- The Court of Justice, which is the final arbiter on Community law. Its judges (one from each Member State, one of whom is appointed President) settle disputes over the interpretation and application of Community law and have the power to overturn decisions deemed to be contrary to the Treaties establishing the Community. Its judgements are binding on the Commission, on national governments, and on firms and individuals. It thus provides the judicial safeguards necessary to ensure that the law is observed in the interpretation and implementation of the Treaties and in EU activities as a whole.

- The Court of Auditors completes the list of the main institutions of the European Union. Its job is to oversee the financial aspects of the Community, to ensure that money is not misspent and to highlight cases of fraud. The Court thus represents the interests of the taxpayer.

- The European Investment Bank is the European's Union's financing institution, which provides loans for capital investment promoting the Union's economic development.

- The Economic and Social Committee advises the Parliament, Council and Commission on economic and social activity in the Union, either on its own initiative or at the request of the institutions.

- The Committee of the Regions was created to protect regional and local identities in the regions of the European Union and to ensure that they are taken into account in the manner in which EU policies are implemented.

- The European Ombudsman represents the mechanism which enables victims of any improper administration by EU institutions to have recourse to appeal.

In 1999, decisions taken by the European Council meeting in Helsinki resulted in the establishment of a number of interim and permanent structures to further the development of a Common Foreign and Security Policy. These are described in Chapter 4, together with the evolution of the European Security and Defence Identity (ESDI), the development of relations between the European Union and the Western European Union (WEU), the establishment of contacts between the European Union and NATO. Further information on the role of the WEU in relation to these issues is provided later in this chapter.

The Common Foreign and Security Policy (CFSP)

The framework for the political development of the Union during the 1970s and 1980s was formally known as European Political Cooperation or "EPC". The establishment of a Common Foreign and Security Policy (CFSP) within the Treaty on the European Union which came into force in 1993 represented a substantive and qualitative leap forward. The main objectives of the CFSP, as set out in the Treaty, are as follows:

- to safeguard the common values, fundamental interests and independence of the Union;

- to strengthen the security of the Union and its Member States in all ways;

- to preserve peace and strengthen international security;

- to promote international cooperation; and

- to develop and consolidate democracy and the rule of law, and respect for human rights and fundamental freedoms.

The EU decision-making procedures in the field of foreign and security policy are essentially intergovernmental. The European Council defines the general guidelines for CFSP, and except for certain decisions on the implementation of joint actions described earlier, all subsequent decisions taken by the Council of Ministers are taken by unanimity.

As part of the continuing process of developing an effective CFSP, the EU has established a procedure for the nomination of special envoys to undertake specific tasks as representatives of the Union. This procedure has, for example, been used to appoint special EU envoys to Bosnia, to the Great Lakes region in Africa, and to the Middle East.

At the conclusion of the EU Intergovernmental Conference which took place during 1996 and 1997, the Heads of State and Government concluded the Treaty of Amsterdam. The implications of this Treaty for the future Common Foreign and Security Policy of the Union and for EU-WEU relations are described later in the chapter.

Further steps in the implementation of the CFSP and the CESDP were taken at subsequent European Council meetings, and in particular in Cologne in June 1999, in Helsinki in December 1999, and in Lisbon in March 2000.

The CFSP is intended to be comprehensive and to cover all areas of foreign and security policy. In the Treaty on the European Union, as well as the associated declaration by the Member States of the Western European Union (WEU), it was decided that the WEU should be an integral part of the development of the Union, and that the EU should be able to request the WEU to elaborate and implement CFSP decisions and actions which have defence implications. In order to ensure coherence between the EU, the WEU and NATO, members of the European Union were invited to accede to the WEU or to become observers, and other European members of NATO were invited to become associate members of the WEU.

In approving these measures, European Union leaders emphasised that NATO remained the foundation of the collective defence of its members and would continue to have an important role in crisis management. Moreover, the development of the CESDP would be without prejudice either to the commitments of member countries under Article 5 of the Washington (NATO) Treaty or to Article V of the Brussels (WEU) Treaty.

At Helsinki, in December 1999, in addition to the new permanent bodies and interim measures described above, the Council established a common European headline goal for readily deployable military capabilities and agreed to develop collective capability goals in the fields of command and control, intelligence and strategic transport, to enable the EU to carry out the full range of the "Petersberg" tasks. These goals would be achieved through voluntary, coordinated national and international efforts.

The headline goal for developing European military capabilities calls for an ability to deploy rapidly, within 60 days, and to sustain for at least one year, operationally capable forces of up to 60 000 troops. Targets for smaller rapid response elements at very high levels of readiness were also set.

In Lisbon, three months later, the European Council welcomed the fact that the interim bodies foreseen at Helsinki had been established and that a process had been elaborated for implementing the headline goal and identifying the national contributions which would be needed to meet the above military capability targets. A Capabilities Commitment Conference was scheduled for autumn 2000[4].

At the meeting of the European Council for Ministers in Santa Maria da Feira, Portugal, in June 2000, European Union leaders carried forward the CESDP process in a number of fields and in particular with respect to arrangements to be concluded by the Council with regard to contributions to EU military crisis management by third states.

These arrangements address the modalities of consultation and/or participation concerning non-EU European NATO members and other countries which are candidates for accession to the EU. The EU Council also agreed that Russia, Ukraine and other European states engaged in political dialogue with the Union, and other interested states might be invited to take part in EU-led operations. The Council welcomed the interest shown by Canada in this context.

Furthermore, the Council identified the principles on the basis of which consultation and cooperation with NATO should be developed. Specifically, they proposed to create four ad hoc working groups to address, respectively, security issues; capabilities goals; modalities enabling EU access to NATO assets and capabilities; and the definition of permanent arrangements for EU-NATO consultation.[5]

Further information can be obtained from the offices of the different institutions of the European Union described above, from regional information offices of the European Union, and from the European Commission.

The European Commission
73 rue Archimède
1040 Brussels
Belgium
Tel: 32 2 295 3844
Fax: 32 2 295 0166
Website: http://www.europa.eu.int

---

4   At the Capabilities Commitment Conference held in Brussels in November 2000, EU and Partner country Defence Ministers pledged substantial forces to the future European Rapid Reaction Force.

5   The Ad Hoc Working Groups began meeting in the summer. In December 2000, NATO ministers took stock of progress, welcoming the intensified NATO-EU dialogue and its contribution to increased understanding within the two organisations on how they might effectively cooperate.

THE WESTERN EUROPEAN UNION (WEU)[6]

The Western European Union has existed since 1954 and today includes 10 European countries: Belgium, France, Germany, Greece, Italy, Luxembourg, the Netherlands, Portugal, Spain and the United Kingdom. It has a Council and Secretariat formerly located in London and based in Brussels since January 1993, and a Parliamentary Assembly in Paris. The WEU has its origins in the Brussels Treaty of Economic, Social and Cultural Collaboration and Collective Self-Defence of 1948, signed by Belgium, France, Luxembourg, the Netherlands and the United Kingdom.

With the signature of the North Atlantic Treaty in 1949, the exercise of the military responsibilities of the Brussels Treaty Organisation or Western Union was transferred to the North Atlantic Alliance. Under the Paris Agreements of 1954, the Federal Republic of Germany and Italy acceded to the Brussels Treaty and the Organisation was renamed the Western European Union. The latter continued in being in order to fulfil the conditions and tasks laid down in the Paris Agreements.

The Western European Union was reactivated in 1984 with a view to developing a "common European defence identity" through cooperation among its members in the security field and strengthening the European pillar of the North Atlantic Alliance.

In August 1987, during the Iran-Iraq War, Western European Union experts met in The Hague to consider joint action in the Gulf to ensure freedom of navigation in the oil shipping lanes of the region; and in October 1987 WEU countries met again to coordinate their military presence in the Gulf following attacks on shipping in the area.

Meeting in The Hague in October 1987, the Ministerial Council of the Western European Union, made up of Foreign and Defence Ministers of the member countries, adopted a "Platform on European Security Interests" in which they affirmed their determination both to strengthen the European pillar of NATO and to provide an integrated Europe with a security and defence dimension. The Platform defined the Western European Union's relations with NATO and with other organisations, as well as the enlargement of the WEU and the conditions for the further development of its role as a forum for regular discussion of defence and security issues affecting Europe.

---

6   In November 2000, the WEU Council of Ministers meeting in Marseilles welcomed the progress made by the European Union in the field of European security and defence policy and the Atlantic Alliance's support for this process. The Council took a number of decisions relating to the transfer of its operational role to the European Union and arrangements to be put in place for the WEU's residual functions and structures.

Following the ratification of the Treaty of Accession signed in November 1988, Portugal and Spain became members of the Western European Union in 1990 in accordance with the decisions taken in 1987 to facilitate WEU enlargement. A further step was taken in November 1989 when the Council decided to create an Institute for Security Studies, based in Paris, with the task of assisting in the development of a European security identity and in the implementation of The Hague Platform.

A number of decisions were taken by the European Council at Maastricht on 9-10 December 1991 on the common foreign and security policy of the European Union and by the member states of the Western European Union on the role of the WEU and its relations with the European Union and the Atlantic Alliance (set out in the Maastricht Declarations). These decisions were welcomed by the North Atlantic Council when it met in Ministerial Session on 19 December 1991. They included extending invitations to members of the European Union to accede to the WEU or to seek observer status, as well as invitations to European member states of NATO to become associate members; agreement on the objective of the WEU of building up the organisation in stages, as the defence component of the European Union, and on elaborating and implementing decisions and actions of the Union with defence implications; agreement on the objective of strengthening the European pillar of the Atlantic Alliance and the role, responsibilities and contributions of WEU member states in the Alliance; affirmation of the intention of the WEU to act in conformity with positions adopted in the Alliance; the strengthening of the WEU's operational role; and the relocation of the WEU Council and Secretariat from London to Brussels. A number of other proposals were also examined including a new role for the WEU in armaments cooperation.

On 19 June 1992, the Foreign and Defence Ministers of WEU member states met near Bonn to strengthen further the role of the WEU and issued the "Petersberg Declaration". This declaration set out, on the basis of the Maastricht decisions, the guidelines for the organisation's future development. WEU member states declared their preparedness to make available military units from the whole spectrum of their conventional armed forces for military tasks under the authority of the WEU. These tasks, the so-called "Petersberg missions", consisted of humanitarian and rescue tasks; peacekeeping tasks; and tasks of combat forces in crisis management including peacemaking. In the Petersberg Declaration, WEU members pledged their support for conflict prevention and peacekeeping efforts in cooperation with the CSCE and with the United Nations Security Council.

The first application of provisions set out in the Maastricht Treaty with regard to the WEU (Article J.4.2 of the Treaty of European Union) occurred in November 1996. At that time the Council of the European Union adopted a decision requesting the WEU to examine urgently how it could contribute to the EU's humanitarian efforts in support of the refugees and displaced persons in the Great Lakes region in Africa. WEU-EU cooperation was also undertaken in relation to the planning of evacuation operations, supporting African peace-keeping efforts, and mine clearance.

Provisions established in accordance with the Maastricht Treaty were sub-sequently re-examined at the Inter-Governmental Conference (IGC) in 1996/97. At its Ministerial meeting in Madrid in 1995, the WEU agreed on a specific "WEU contribution to the European Union Intergovernmental Conference of 1996". This document assessed the organisation's development since Maastricht; set forth several options for the future EU-WEU relationship; and listed a number of agreed principles and guidelines to assist the IGC on European defence arrangements. It was formally submitted by the WEU to the Council of the European Union.

As a result of the Inter-Governmental Conference on 16 and 17 June 1997 in Amsterdam, EU Heads of State and Government agreed on revisions to the Maastricht Treaty with implications for the future Common Foreign and Security Policy of the Union and EU-WEU relations. In particular, the Petersberg missions, as defined by the WEU at the Ministerial meeting in June 1992, were included in the Treaty of Amsterdam.

The Amsterdam Treaty stipulated that the WEU is an integral part of the development of the European Union, providing the latter with access to an operational capability, notably in the context of the Petersberg missions. The WEU should support the EU in framing the defence aspects of the common for-eign and security policy; and the EU should, accordingly, foster closer institu-tional relations with the WEU *"with a view to the possibility of the integration of the WEU into the EU, should the European Council so decide"*.

The Amsterdam Treaty also states that the *"Union will avail itself of the WEU to elaborate and implement decisions and actions of the Union which have defence implications"*, giving the European Council competence to estab-lish guidelines in respect of the WEU for those matters for which the EU would avail itself of the WEU. In such cases, all EU member states, including those who are not full members of the WEU, would be entitled to participate fully in the tasks in question. In the same vein, the EU Council, in agreement with the institutions of the WEU, would adopt the necessary practical arrangements to allow all EU member states making a contribution to participate fully and on an equal footing in planning and decision-taking in the WEU.

The Protocol to Article 17 of the Amsterdam Treaty stated that the EU would draw up, together with the WEU, arrangements for enhanced coopera-tion between them within a year from the entry into force of the Treaty. The

WEU, in its "Declaration on the Role of Western European Union and its Relations with the European Union and with the Atlantic Alliance", adopted by WEU Ministers on 22 July 1997, took note of the parts of the Treaty of Amsterdam pertaining to the WEU. The Declaration also set out the WEU's understanding of its role and relations with the EU as well as with the Atlantic Alliance, describing the WEU as an integral part of the development of the European Union, providing it with access to operational capability, notably in the context of the Petersberg missions, and an essential element of the development of the ESDI within the Alliance, in accordance with the Paris Declaration and with the decisions taken by NATO Ministers in June 1996 in Berlin.

Following the Amsterdam and the WEU Declaration of 22 July 1997, further steps were taken in developing WEU-EU relations. In September 1997 the WEU Council introduced measures to harmonise as much as possible the six-monthly presidencies which rotate between members countries in both the WEU and the EU. At their meeting in Erfurt, Germany, in November 1997, EU Ministers endorsed a decision enhancing the operational role of WEU observer countries, in line with the provisions contained in Article 17.3 of the Amsterdam Treaty. In Erfurt Ministers also endorsed a decision concerning the participation modalities of associate members and observers in all WEU operations.

After 1991, the WEU developed a framework under which an increasing number of European countries became associated with its activities. In the second WEU Maastricht Declaration of 1991, the WEU invited states which were members of the EU to accede to WEU, on conditions to be agreed in accordance with Article XI of the modified Brussels Treaty, or to become observers. Simultaneously, other European members of NATO were invited to become associate members of WEU *"in a way which will give the possibility to participate fully in the activities of WEU"*. The Petersberg Declaration defined the rights and obligations of those states which are members of the European Union and NATO, as future members, observers or associate members. At the Rome Ministerial meeting on 20 November 1992, WEU members agreed to enlarge the organisation and invited Greece to become its tenth member, subject to parliamentary ratification.

On 9 May 1994, at their meeting in Luxembourg, the WEU Council of Ministers issued the "Kirchberg Declaration", according the nine Central and Eastern European countries which had signed "Europe Agreements" with the EU the status of "Associate Partners"[7] (as distinct from the Associate Membership of Iceland, Norway and Turkey). Slovenia became the tenth Associate Partner country in 1996.

---

7   Bulgaria, the Czech Republic, Estonia, Hungary, Latvia, Lithuania, Poland, Romania and Slovakia.

Greece joined the WEU formally in 1995. Iceland, Norway and Turkey, as member countries of NATO, were granted Associate Member status; and Denmark and Ireland, as members of the European Union, became Observers. Following their accession to the European Union on 1 January 1995, and after completion of parliamentary procedures, Austria, Finland and Sweden also became WEU Observers. On 23 March 1999, following their accession to NATO, the Czech Republic, Hungary and Poland became Associate Members.

These decisions thus created a system of variable geometry with three different levels of membership and affiliation, as well as observer status:

- Members (also members of both NATO and of the EU);

- Associate Members (NATO but not EU members);

- Associate Partners (neither NATO nor EU members), and;

- Observers (EU but not NATO members. Denmark also opted for Observer status).

Implementation of the Petersberg Tasks

During the 1990's, the WEU developed relations with a number of other countries and regions. A dialogue with Russia provided for political consultations and practical cooperation on subjects of mutual interest. This included, for example, the supply of Russian imagery to the WEU Satellite Centre. The WEU also developed a dialogue with Ukraine on the basis of a joint WEU/Ukraine communiqué of September 1996; and a dialogue with six non-WEU Mediterranean countries (Algeria, Egypt, Israel, Mauritania, Morocco and Tunisia). These dialogues have provided an opportunity to inform those countries about WEU activities and to exchange views on subjects of mutual interest, such as the experience gained from peacekeeping operations. In the context of efforts by the international community, the WEU has also undertaken work to assist African countries in developing effective peacekeeping capabilities.

Following the decisions taken at Maastricht and Petersberg, steps were undertaken to develop the WEU's operational capabilities in order to provide the organisation with the necessary tools to undertake the Petersberg missions. In this context, a WEU Planning Cell was set up, under the authority of the WEU Council, to carry out planning for possible WEU operations and to establish and to keep up-to-date the list of Forces Answerable to WEU (FAWEU). The WEU has no standing forces or command structures of its own. Accordingly, the military units and command structures designated by WEU members and associate members can be made available to WEU for its various possible tasks. They include both national units and several multinational formations, such as the Eurocorps; the Multinational Division Central; the UK/NL Amphibious Force; Eurofor and Euromarfor; the Headquarters of the First German-Netherlands Corps; and the Spanish-Italian Amphibious Force.[8]

Other measures aimed at developing the WEU's operational capabilities included the establishment of the Satellite Centre in Torrejon, Spain, inaugurated in April 1993, to interpret and analyse satellite data for the verification of arms control agreement, crisis monitoring and management in support of WEU operations; the creation of a Situation Centre (which became operational in June 1996) to monitor crisis areas designated by the WEU Council and the progress of WEU operations; and the creation of a Military Delegates Committee and the reorganisation of the military structure of the WEU headquarters in 1998, in accordance with decisions taken by WEU Ministers at their meetings in Paris and Erfurt in May and November of 1997.

Cooperation between the Western European Union and NATO underpinned the process of the reactivation of the WEU and became progressively more intensive and more frequent. On 21 May 1992, the Council of the Western European Union held its first formal meeting with the North Atlantic Council at NATO Headquarters. Subsequently, the Secretary General of the WEU regularly attended ministerial meetings of the North Atlantic Council, and the NATO Secretary General likewise participated in WEU ministerial meetings. The North Atlantic and WEU Councils began to meet four times a year, with the possibility of further meetings if necessary. A Security Agreement was agreed between NATO and WEU to facilitate the exchange of classified information. Other examples of enhanced practical cooperation included WEU access to NATO's integrated communications system on the basis of a NATO-WEU Memorandum of Understanding; and regular consultations between the secretariats and military staffs of both organisations.

An important further step towards closer cooperation between NATO and WEU was taken during the January 1994 NATO Summit in Brussels. The 16 member countries of the Alliance gave their full support to the development of a European Security and Defence Identity which would strengthen the European pillar of the Alliance while reinforcing the transatlantic link and would enable European Allies to take greater responsibility for their common security and defence. They expressed their support for strengthening this European pillar of the Alliance through the Western European Union, which was being

---

8   Eurocorps: Belgium, France, Germany, Luxembourg, Spain. The Multinational Division Central (MND(C)) forms part of the Reaction Forces available to the Supreme Allied Commander, Europe, within NATO's integrated military structure. The Eurofor (rapid deployment force) and Euromarfor (maritime force) include forces from France, Italy, Portugal and Spain.

developed as the defence component of the European Union. In order to avoid duplication of capabilities, NATO agreed to make its collective assets available, on the basis of consultations in the North Atlantic Council, *"for WEU operations undertaken by the European Allies in pursuit of their Common Foreign and Security Policy"*. In addition, Heads of State and Government endorsed the concept of Combined Joint Task Forces (CJTFs - see Chapter 12) as a means of facilitating contingency operations. They directed that the concept should be implemented in a manner that provided separable but not separate military capabilities that could be employed by NATO or the WEU and would respond to European requirements and contribute to Alliance security. At the same time, they reaffirmed that the Alliance remained the essential forum for consultation among its members and the venue for agreement on policies bearing on the security and defence commitments of Allies under the Washington Treaty.

At their meetings in June 1996, NATO Foreign and Defence Ministers decided that, as an essential part of the internal adaptation of NATO, the European Security and Defence Identity should be built within NATO. This would enable all European Allies to make a more coherent and effective contribution to the missions and activities of the Alliance as an expression of their shared responsibilities; to act themselves as required; and to reinforce the transatlantic partnership. Taking full advantage of the CJTF concept, this identity would be based on sound military principles, would be supported by appropriate military planning and would permit the creation of militarily coherent and effective forces capable of operating under the political control and strategic direction of the WEU, taking into account the full participation of all European Allies if they were so to choose. At the Summit meeting in Madrid in July 1997, NATO Heads of State and Government welcomed the major steps taken on the creation of the European Security and Defence Identity within the Alliance, implementing the important political decisions made by Foreign and Defence Ministers in June 1996, and tasked the North Atlantic Council in Permanent Session to complete its work expeditiously in cooperation with WEU.

A WEU/NATO Joint Crisis Management Exercise was held for the first time in February 2000, to test ESDI-related concepts and arrangements for handling WEU-led operations making use of NATO assets and capabilities, and a joint NATO-WEU Exercise Study (JES-01) was scheduled for 2001.

In the light of the decisions taken by the European Council in Helsinki in 1999, WEU Foreign and Defence Ministers recognised that the fulfilment by the EU of new responsibilities in the security field would have profound repercussions for the WEU as an organisation. At their meeting in Porto, Portugal, in May 2000, they instructed the Permanent Council of the WEU to examine the measures that would be needed at the appropriate time. Clarifications were also issued regarding the implications of the Common European Security and

Defence Policy on the Treaty of Brussels and the WEU. On the basis of the decisions taken at the Marseilles Ministerial meeting of the WEU, in November 2000, the incoming French Presidency of the WEU emphasised that Article V of the Brussels Treaty would continue to reflect the mutual commitment of the member countries with respect to their collective defence. Arrangements were put in place for carrying out the residual functions of the WEU, once the European Union had become operational.

Operational Tasks undertaken by the WEU

The WEU contributed to efforts undertaken by the international community in the context of the conflict in Bosnia and Herzegovina from 1992 on, and the crisis in Albania in 1997, both by mounting WEU operations and by conducting a joint operation with NATO to support the efforts of the United Nations to end the conflict in the former Yugoslavia.

In July 1992, the member countries of the WEU decided to make available naval forces for monitoring compliance in the Adriatic with UN Security Council Resolutions against the Federal Republic of Yugoslavia (Serbia and Montenegro). Similar measures were also taken by the North Atlantic Council in a Ministerial Session held on the margins of the OSCE Summit in Helsinki on 10 July 1992 in coordination with the WEU.

At a joint session on 8 June 1993, the North Atlantic Council and the Council of the Western European Union approved the concept of combined NATO/WEU embargo enforcement operations under the authority of the two Organisations. A single commander was appointed to head the combined NATO/WEU task force in the Adriatic. The implementation of this decision is described in more detail in Chapter 5.

On 5 April 1993, the WEU Council of Ministers decided to provide assistance to Bulgaria, Hungary and Romania in their efforts to enforce the UN embargo on the Danube. The assistance took the form of a civilian police and customs operation coordinated with other organisations and in particular with the EU and the CSCE. Following the termination of the UN sanctions, both the Adriatic and Danube operations were ended.

In early July 1994, the WEU responded to a request to provide support to the EU Administration being established in Mostar by dispatching a police contingent. The aim of the WEU police contingent was to assist the Bosnian and Croat parties in Mostar to set up a unified police force for Mostar. Following the termination of the EU Administration's mandate in July 1996, an EU Special Envoy was appointed until the end of the year. The WEU police contingent continued to provide assistance until the transfer of the Envoy's executive powers to the local authorities on 15 October 1996.

In 1997, the WEU Council, in the context of the Albanian crisis, decided to deploy a Multinational Advisory Police Element (MAPE) to complement the action of the Multinational Protection Force created and deployed by several European countries under the authority of the UN Security Council (Resolution 1101). The first WEU operation to be directed by the WEU Council with the support of the WEU Secretariat and Planning Cell on the role of the MAPE was to give the Albanian police authorities information and advice on appropriate aspects of policing and restoring order, as well as on their responsibilities in the electoral process. Deployment started in May 1997, with WEU Members, Associate Members, Observers and Associate Partners all contributing to this mission. In response to requests by the Albanian government, the MAPE's mandate was subsequently extended.

In May 1999, at the request of the European Union, the WEU initiated a Demining Assistance Mission to the Republic of Croatia. A decision was taken by the WEU Council of Ministers in Marseilles, in November 2000, that the mission should be undertaken within the WEU framework until its mandate expired in May 2001.

Further information on the Western European Union and on decisions relating to the transfer of the WEU's operational role to the EU and arrangements for the WEU's residual functions and structures can be obtained from:

Western European Union
Secretariat-General
4 rue de la Régence
Brussels, Belgium
Tel: 32 2 500 4455
Fax: 32 2 511 3519
E-mail: eo.presse@skynet.be
Website: http://www.weu.int

Western European Union Assembly
43 avenue du Président Wilson
75775 Paris Cedex 16,
France
Tel: 33 1 53 67 22 00
Fax: 33 1 47 20 45 43
E-Mail: 100315.240@compuserve.com
Website: http://www.weu.int/assembly

WEU Institute for Security Studies
43 Avenue du Président Wilson
75775 Paris Cedex 16
France
Tel 33 1 53 67 22 00
Fax: 33 1 47 20 81 78
E-Mail: weu.iss@csi.com
Website: http://www.weu.int/institut

THE COUNCIL OF EUROPE

The Council of Europe was established on 5 May 1949, *"to achieve a greater unity between its members for the purpose of safeguarding and realising the ideals and principles which are their common heritage and facilitating their economic and social progress"*. The Council's overall aim is to maintain the basic principles of human rights, pluralist democracy and the rule of law and to enhance the quality of life for European citizens[9].

The Council of Europe has 43 member countries (see below). The most recent new members are: Hungary (1990); Poland (1991); Bulgaria (1992); Estonia, Lithuania, Slovenia, the Czech Republic, Slovakia and Romania (1993); Andorra (1994); Latvia, Albania, Moldova, the former Yugoslav Republic of Macedonia[10] and Ukraine (1995); Russia and Croatia (1996); Georgia (1999), and Armenia and Azerbaijan (2001).

The Council is composed of a Committee of Ministers, in which agreements are reached on common action by governments, and a 291 member Parliamentary Assembly, which makes proposals for new activities and serves, more generally, as a parliamentary forum. Some of the Council of Europe's activities are open to non-member states. Bosnia and Herzegovina (since 28 January 1994) and the Federal Republic of Yugoslavia (since 22 January 2001) have special guest status with the Parliamentary Assembly. In 1997, Belarus' special guest status with the Parliamentary Assembly was suspended and the procedure for accession to the Council of Europe was frozen. Canada, Israel and Mexico are Observers to the Parliamentary Assembly and Canada, the Holy See, Japan, Mexico and the United States have observer status with the Committee of Ministers of the Council.

Some 165 inter-governmental conventions and agreements have been concluded by the Council, chief among which are the Convention for the Protection of Human Rights and Fundamental Freedoms; the European Cultural Convention; and the European Social Charter. At its Summit meeting in Vienna in 1993, the Council of Europe underlined its contribution to democratic security in Europe. The concept of democratic security has two aspects: first, absolute insistence on pluralistic and parliamentary democracy, on the indivisibility and universality of human rights, and on the rule of law and a common cultural heritage enriched by its diversity, as fundamental preconditions for security; and second, a strong emphasis on European cooperation on the basis of these values as a method of building networks of trust across the continent, which can simultaneously prevent conflicts and help find solutions to

---

9   The Statute of the Council of Europe, Chapter 1, Art. 1.

10   Turkey recognises the Republic of Macedonia with its constitutional name.

common problems. The promotion of democratic security contributes to the task of dealing with a significant range of security risks in Europe. Apart from diminishing the risks of any reversion to totalitarian rule, it responds to challenges stemming from: serious and massive violations of fundamental freedoms and human rights, including discrimination against a part of the population; major deficiencies in the structures for the rule of law; aggressive nationalism, racism and intolerance, as well as interethnic tensions and conflicts; terrorism and organised crime; and social disintegration, disparities and tension at local and regional level.

The Council of Europe held its second Summit Meeting in Strasbourg in October 1997, adopting an Action Plan for the main tasks of the Council in the period leading up to its 50th anniversary in May 1999 and beyond. The Action Plan addressed issues relating to democracy and human rights; social cohesion; security of citizens; and democratic values and cultural diversity. On 1 February 1998, the Council of Europe's Framework Convention for the protection of National Minorities entered into force. In addition, with effect from 1 November 1998, the Council approved the establishment of a new full-time Court of Human Rights, under the terms of the Protocol on the European Convention of Human Rights which establishes the Court.

The Action Plan also set in hand arrangements for appointing a Council of Europe Commissioner for Human Rights, the first of whom was appointed in 1999. Finally, a monitoring procedure has been set up to ensure that the commitments accepted by member states are effectively honoured. A confidential, constructive and non-discriminatory dialogue is carried out both at governmental level in the Committee of Ministers and at parliamentary level by the Parliamentary Assembly.

The significant extension of the membership of the Council of Europe since the end of the Cold War and the increasing number of conventions achieved represent a determination by the member governments to establish cooperative structures designed to avoid new rifts in the continent and to build a common European civilisation of democratic nations. The Council of Europe's efforts in these spheres are therefore complementary to those of the North Atlantic Alliance. The Council of Europe seeks implementation of its Action Plan in cooperation with European and other international organisations, notably the European Union and the OSCE.

Council of Europe - Member States

Albania
Andorra
Armenia
Austria
Azerbaijan
Belgium
Bulgaria
Croatia
Cyprus
Czech Republic
Denmark
Estonia

Finland
France
Georgia
Germany
Greece
Hungary
Iceland
Ireland
Italy
Latvia
Liechtenstein
Lithuania

Luxembourg
Malta
Moldova
Netherlands
Norway
Poland
Portugal
Romania
Russia
San Marino
Slovakia
Slovenia

Spain
Sweden
Switzerland
The former
Yugoslav
Republic
of Macedonia[11]
Turkey
Ukraine
United Kingdom

Applicant Members

Bosnia

Special Guest Status with the Parliamentary Assembly

Bosnia   The Federal
                Republic of
                Yugoslavia

Observer Status with the Committee of Ministers

Canada   Holy See   Japan   Mexico   United States

Observer Status with the Parliamentary Assembly
of the Council

Canada   Israel   Mexico

Further information:

Council of Europe,
67075 Strasbourg,
France
Tel: 33 3 88 41 20 00
Fax: 33 3 88 41 27 81/82/83
Website: http://www.coe.fr

---

11   Turkey recognises the Republic of Macedonia with its constitutional name.

CHAPTER 16

PARLIAMENTARY AND NON-GOVERNMENTAL ORGANISATIONS

NATO Parliamentary Assembly (NATO PA)

The Atlantic Treaty Association (ATA)

The Interallied Confederation of Reserve Officers (CIOR)

The Interallied Confederation of Medical Reserve Officers (CIOMR)

Parliamentary and Non-Governmental Organisations

NATO Parliamentary Assembly (NATO PA)

Alliance cohesion is substantially enhanced by the support of freely elected parliamentary representatives.

The NATO Parliamentary Assembly (NATO PA) (formerly known as the North Atlantic Assembly) is an interparliamentary organisation which, since 1955, has acted as a forum for legislators from the North American and West European member countries of the North Atlantic Alliance to meet together to consider issues of common interest and concern. In the past few years, in keeping with the major political changes which have occurred in the former Soviet Union and Central and Eastern Europe (CEE), the Assembly has significantly broadened both its membership and its mandate.

Seventeen of the Partner countries of the Alliance have associate delegation status in the NATO Parliamentary Assembly. This enables them to participate in the work of the Assembly and in its debates. These are focusing increasingly on the security of Europe as a whole, as well as on the specific economic, political, environmental and cultural problems of Central and Eastern Europe.

The countries which have associate delegation status in the NATO Parliament Assembly are as follows:

Albania, Austria, Bulgaria, Croatia, Estonia, Finland, Georgia, Latvia, Lithuania, Moldova, Romania, the Russian Federation, Slovakia, Slovenia, Switzerland, the former Yugoslav Republic of Macedonia[1], Ukraine.

The Assembly is completely independent of NATO but constitutes a link between national parliaments and the Alliance which encourages governments to take Alliance concerns into account when framing national legislation. It also acts as a permanent reminder that intergovernmental decisions reached within NATO are ultimately dependent on political endorsement in accordance with the due constitutional process of democratically elected parliaments. The Assembly was thus directly concerned with assisting in the process of ratification of the Protocols of Accession signed at the end of 1997, which culminated in the accession of the Czech Republic, Hungary and Poland to the Alliance in March 1999.

---

1   Turkey recognises the Republic of Macedonia with its constitutional name.

Delegates to the NATO Parliamentary Assembly are nominated by their parliaments according to their national procedures, on the basis of party representation in the parliaments. The Assembly therefore represents a broad spectrum of political opinion.

The Assembly meets twice a year in Plenary Session. Meetings are held in member and associate member countries on a rotational basis at the invitation of national parliaments. The Assembly functions through six committees: Political; Defence and Security; Economics and Security; Science and Technology; the Civilian Dimension of Security; and the Mediterranean Special Group. These are both study groups as well as major forums for discussion. The committees study and examine all major contemporary issues arising in their respective fields of interest. They meet regularly throughout the year and report to the Plenary Sessions of the Assembly. There is a Secretariat with a staff of 30 people, based in Brussels.

The primary purpose of the Assembly is educative and consensus-building. It allows Alliance legislators to convey national pre-occupations and concerns to their governments and to the decision-making bodies of the Alliance and to inform each other of the very different national and regional perspectives that exist on many key issues of mutual interest. Similarly, members of the Assembly are able to use the experience and information gained through participation in its activities when exercising their roles within national parliaments. This helps to ensure that Alliance interests and considerations are given maximum visibility in national discussions. The Assembly also constitutes an important touchstone for assessing parliamentary and public opinion on Alliance issues and, through its deliberations, provides a clear indication of public and parliamentary concerns regarding Alliance policies. In this sense the Assembly plays an indirect but important role in policy formation. Recommendations and Resolutions of the Assembly are forwarded to national governments, parliaments and other relevant organisations, and to the Secretary General of NATO, who formulates replies based on discussions within the North Atlantic Council.

Relations with Central and Eastern European countries have been co-ordinated under the so-called Rose-Roth Initiative, initiated in 1990 by US Congressman Charlie Rose, then President of the Assembly, and US Senator Bill Roth. The initiative has three aspects:

- the active participation of Central and Eastern European parliamentarians in the biannual meeting of the Assembly;

- the holding of special Rose-Roth seminars at regular intervals on subjects of specific interest to parliamentarians from CEE countries. These are organised in cooperation with member parliaments or the parliaments of CEE countries and ensure a regular dialogue among legislators on issues of common concern. Since the commencement of the initiative, more than 30 such seminars have been held;

- the programme also supports the development of parliamentary staff through two-week training programmes or short periods spent at the Assembly's Secretariat in Brussels. This programme is designed for parliamentary staff working for Foreign Affairs or Security Committees, or in other fields of international relations.

The aims of the Rose-Roth Initiative are:

- to integrate and involve parliamentarians from CEE countries in Assembly activities;

- to promote a sense of partnership and cooperation at the legislative level;

- to improve mutual understanding among legislators of their various problems and perspectives;

- to provide CEE parliamentarians with information on current issues;

- to promote the development of appropriate civil-military relations in CEE countries by helping CEE legislators to become more knowledgeable about security issues; and by demonstrating the relationship that exists in Alliance countries between parliamentarians, civil servants and military officials;

- to provide CEE legislators with practical expertise and experience in parliamentary practices and procedures;

- to help the development of a parliamentary staff structure in CEE parliaments in order to provide parliamentarians with the kind of assistance available to their Western counterparts.

The Assembly's role in developing relations with Central and Eastern European parliaments was recognised in the NATO-Russia Founding Act and the NATO-Ukraine Charter, both signed in 1997. These documents called for expanded dialogue and cooperation between the North Atlantic Assembly and the Federal Assembly of the Russian Federation and the Ukrainian Verkhovna Rada (parliament) respectively.

The Assembly's outreach programme is separate from, but reinforces, the work of the Euro-Atlantic Partnership Council (EAPC) and the Alliance's Partnership for Peace initiative (PfP). Particular emphasis is placed on helping to achieve a key PfP objective, namely the establishment of democratic control of armed forces. Assembly activities aim to provide the expertise, experience and information that will help CEE parliamentarians to become more effective in influencing the development of national defence policies and in ensuring that the control of their armed forces is fully democratic.

Further information on the NATO Parliamentary Assembly may be obtained from its International Secretariat:

Place du Petit Sablon 3
1000 Brussels
Tel: 32 2 513 2865
Fax: 32 2 514 1847
E-Mail: secretariat@naa.be
Website: http://www.naa.be

THE ATLANTIC TREATY ASSOCIATION (ATA)

The Atlantic Treaty Association created on 18 June 1954, brings together, as Members, national voluntary and non-governmental organisations in each of the Alliance's 19 member states to support the activities of NATO and promote the objectives of the North Atlantic Treaty.

Since the beginning of the 90's, the ATA regularly admits, as Associate Members, national voluntary and non-governmental organisations established in NATO's Partner countries. There are currently 18 associations which are Associate Members. In accordance with the constitution of the ATA, Associate Members may become full members of the Association when their countries become members of NATO and when their new position has been recognised by the ATA Assembly upon the proposal of the ATA Council.

Since 1999, following the amendment of the constitution, the ATA Assembly may also, on proposal by the Council, grant the position of Observer Member to non-governmental organisations created in the countries participating in NATO's Mediterranean Dialogue or in those which are directly or geographically concerned with Euro-Atlantic security problems, even if they have not signed Partnership for Peace agreements[2].

---

2   During its Assembly held in October-November 2000 in Budapest, the ATA admitted the Alliance for Security of Bosnia and Herzegovina as its first Observer Member association.

The objectives of the ATA and of its affiliated national organisations are:

- to inform the public concerning the missions and responsibilities of the North Atlantic Treaty Organisation;

- to conduct research into the various purposes and activities of NATO and their extension to countries of Central and Eastern Europe as well as the furtherance of NATO's Mediterranean Dialogue;

- to promote the solidarity of the people of the North Atlantic area and of those whose countries participate in NATO's Partnership for Peace Programme;

- to promote democracy;

- to develop cooperation between all its member organisations in order to promote the above objectives.

MEMBERS OF THE ATLANTIC TREATY ASSOCIATION

BELGIUM
Association Atlantique Belge
Quartier Reine Astrid
12 rue Bruyn
1120 Brussels
Tel: 32 2 264 40 17
Fax: 32 2 268 52 77
E-Mail: aabav.ata@skynet.be

CANADA
The Atlantic Council of Canada
6 Hoskin avenue (Trinity College)
Toronto
Ontario M5S 1H8
Tel: 1 416 979 1875
Fax: 1 416 979 0825
E-Mail: atlantic@idirect.com

CZECH REPUBLIC
Czech Atlantic Commission
Revolucni 26
110 00 Praha 1
Tel: 420 2 248 11417
Fax: 420 2 248 11239
E-mail: jitka.smolikova@eis.cuni.cz

DENMARK
Danish Atlantic Association
Ryvangs Allé 1 - Postboks 2521
2100 Copenhagen 0
Tel: 45 39 27 19 44
Fax: 45 39 27 56 26
E-Mail: atlant@atlant.dk

FRANCE
French Association for
the Atlantic Community
10 rue Crevaux
75116 Paris
Tel: 33 1 45 53 28 80
Fax: 33 1 47 55 49 63
E-Mail: afca@club-internet.fr

GERMANY
The German Atlantic
Association
Am Burgweiher 12
53123 Bonn
Tel: 49 228 62 50 31
Fax: 49 228 61 66 04
E-mail: DtAtlGes@aol.com

GREECE
Greek Association for Atlantic
and European Cooperation
160 A Ioannou Drossopoulou Str.
112 56 Athens
Tel: 30 1 865 5979
Fax: 30 1 865 4742
E-mail: gaaec@ath.fothnet.gr

HUNGARY
Hungarian
Atlantic Council
Margit Krt. 43-45
1024 Budapest
Tel: 36 1 326 8791 - 326 8792
Fax: 36 1 326 8793
E-Mail: mat@matavnet.hu

ICELAND
Association of Western Cooperation
PO Box 28
121 Reykjavik
Tel: 354 561 0015
Fax: 354 551 0015
E-mail: jonhakon@kom.is

ITALY
Italian Atlantic Committee
Piazza di Firenze 27
00186 Rome
Tel: 39 0 6 687 37 86
Fax: 39 0 6 687 33 76
E-mail: italata@iol.it

LUXEMBOURG
Luxembourg Atlantic Committee
BP 805
2018 Luxembourg
Tel: 352 463 563
Fax: 352 462 932

NETHERLANDS
Netherlands Atlantic Committee
Bezuidenhoutseweg 237-239
2594 AM Den Haag
Tel: 31 70 363 9495
Fax: 31 70 364 6309
E-Mail: atlcom@xs4all.nl

NORWAY
Norwegian Atlantic Committee
Fridtjof Nanssens Plass 6
0160 Oslo 1
Tel: 47 22 40 36 00
Fax: 47 22 40 36 10
E-Mail:
post@atlanterhavskomiteen.no

POLAND
Polish Atlantic Club
Al. 3 Maja 5/51
00-401 Warszawa
Tel/Fax: 48 22 625 47 49

Euro-Atlantic Association
Ul. Sienkiewicza 12/14
00-944 Warszawa
Tel: 48 22 828 11 45
Fax: 48 22 828 11 46

PORTUGAL
Portuguese Atlantic Committee
Av. Infante Santo 42, 6e
1350-174 Lisbon
Tel: 351 21 390 59 57
Fax: 351 21 397 84 93
E-Mail: cpa@mail.telepac.pt

SPAIN
Spanish Atlantic Association
Velasquez 78, 1°
28001 Madrid
Tel/Fax: 34 91 576 6572
Fax: 34 91 349 5392

TURKEY
Turkish Atlantic Committee
G.O. Pasa Kuleli Sokak 44/1
206700 Ankara
Tel: 90 312 446 34 23
Fax: 90 312 446 50 11

UNITED KINGDOM
The Atlantic Council of
the United Kingdom
185 Tower Bridge Road
London SEI 2UF
Tel: 44 20 7403 0640/0740
Fax: 44 20 7403 0901
E-mail:
acuk@atlanticcouncil.demon.co.uk

UNITED STATES
The Atlantic Council of
the United States
Suite 1000 - 910 17th Street, N.W.
Washington DC 20006
Tel: 1 202 463 7226
Fax: 1 202 463 7241
E-Mail: info@acus.org

ASSOCIATE MEMBERS OF THE ATLANTIC TREATY ASSOCIATION

ALBANIA
Albanian Atlantic
Association
Bul. Deshmoret e Kombit
Pallati I Kongresseve, Kati I Dyte
Tirana
Tel/Fax: 355 42 646 59
E-mail: amoisiu@abissnet.com.al

AZERBAIJAN
Azerbaijan Atlantic Cooperation
Association
Azerbaijan prospekti 37
Baku 370000
Tel: 994 12 983 176
Fax: 994 12 983 353
E-mail: peace@elkhan.baku.az

AUSTRIA
Euro-Atlantic Association
of Austria
Erlaufstrasse 7/1
2346 Maria Enzersdorf
Südstadt
Tel: 43 22236 41196
Fax: 43 2236 41196/9
E-mail: Institute@oeles.or.at

BELARUS
Belarussian Euro-Atlantic Association
77 Varvasheni Street - Suite 602
Minsk 220002
Fax: 375 17 221 32 20

BULGARIA
The Atlantic Club of Bulgaria
29 Slavyanska Street
Sofia 1000
Tel: 359 2 981 0699
Fax: 359 2 981 5782
E-Mail: passy@bulnet.bg

CROATIA
The Atlantic Council of Croatia
2Lepusiceva 6
10000 Zagreb
Tel:Tel: 385 1 4558 022
Fax: 385 1 4647 545

FINLAND
The Atlantic Council of Finland
C/o Karollina Honkanen
The Finnish Institute of
International Affairs
Mannerhelmintle 15A
00260 Helsinki
Tel: 358 9 434 207 25
Fax: 358 9 434 207 69
E-mail:
karollina.honkanen@upifila.fl

GEORGIA
Georgian Association of
Atlantic Collaboration
TMachabeli Str. 8
Tbilisi 380005
Tel: 995 32 92 33 40
Fax: 995 32 00 11 53
E-Mail: atlantic_geo@hotmail.com

LATVIA
The Latvian Transatlantic
Organisation
Elizabetes street 57
Riga 1050
Tel: 371 7286 302
Fax: 371 7 288 089
E-mail: lato@delfi.lv

LITHUANIA
Lithuanian Atlantic
Treaty Association
P.O. Box 2911
2000 Vilnius
Tel: 370 2 362 423
Fax: 370 2 362 519
E-Mail: lata_aslb@yahoo.com

MOLDOVA
Euro-Atlantic Association
of Moldova
8, N. Iorga str.
2009 Chisinau
Tel: 373 2 23 86 35
Fax: 373 2 362 519
E-Mail: magic@cni.md

ROMANIA
Euro-Atlantic Council of Romania
Kiseleff Av., 47
71268 Bucharest
20Tel/Fax: 40 1 222 71 62
TE-mail: euro_atl@rnc.ro

RUSSIAN FEDERATION
Association for Euro-Atlantic
Cooperation
3 Prechistenka St.
119034 Moscow
Tel: 7 095 203 62 71
Fax: 7 095 230 22 29

SLOVAK REPUBLIC
Slovak Atlantic Commission
C/o EuroAtlantic Centre
Kuzmanyho 3
974 01 Banska Bystrica
Tel/fax: 421 88 415 1689
E-Mail: eac@calipso.sk

SLOVENIA
The Atlantic Council of Slovenia
Kardeljeva pl. 16
1000 Ljubljana
Tel: 386 1 589 2327
Fax: 386 1 589 2290

THE FORMER YUGOSLAV
REPUBLIC OF MACEDONIA[3]
Euro-Atlantic Club
Parliament - Kancelarija 10020
"11 October" bb
91000 Skopje
Tel/Fax: 389 91 113 447
Fax: 389 91 111 675

SWEDEN
Atlantic Council of Sweden
Box 5434
114 84 Stockholm
Tel/Fax: 46 8 87 15 78
E-Mail:
Bo.hugemark@war-and-peace.se

UKRAINE
The Atlantic Council of Ukraine
Apt 122
36/1 Melnikov Str.
Kyiv 254119
Tel/Fax: 380 44 211 45 39
E-Mail: acu@gilan.uar.net

OBSERVER MEMBER OF THE ATLANTIC TREATY ASSOCIATION

BOSNIA AND HERZEGOVINA
Alliance for Security B&H
Obala Kulina bana 4
Sarajevo
Tel/Fax: 387 33 212 026/667 737
E-Mail: amv/fda@bih.net.ba

An **Atlantic Education Committee** (AEC) and an **Atlantic Association of Young Political Leaders** (AAYPL) are active in their own fields. A **Youth Atlantic Treaty Association** (YATA) was formed within the ATA in 1996.

Further information concerning the Atlantic Treaty Association may be obtained from:

ATA
10 rue Crevaux
75116 Paris
France
Tel: 33 145 53 28 80
Fax: 33 145 55 49 63
E-mail: ata-sg@wanadoo.fr

---

3   Turkey recognises the Republic of Macedonia with its constitutional name.

THE INTERALLIED CONFEDERATION OF RESERVE OFFICERS (CIOR)

The CIOR was founded in 1948 by the Reserve Officer Associations of Belgium, France and the Netherlands. The Confederation now brings together all existing Reserve Officer Associations in NATO countries - 18 in total.

The members of these Associations are active as civilians in business, industrial, academic, political and other fields of professional life, in addition to their role as Reserve Officers.

They are therefore in a position to contribute to a better understanding of security and defence issues in the population as a whole, as well as bringing civilian expertise and experience to the tasks and challenges facing reserve forces in NATO.

CIOR is the abbreviated title of the organisation and is derived from the full name in French "Confédération Interalliée des Officiers de Réserve". The Confederation is a non-political, non-governmental, non-profit-making organisation dedicated to cooperation between the national Reserve Officers Associations of NATO countries and to solidarity within the Atlantic Alliance.

The CIOR's principal objectives include working to support the policies of NATO and to assist in the achievement of the Alliance's objectives; maintaining contacts with NATO's military authorities and commands; and developing international contacts between Reserve Officers in order to improve mutual knowledge and understanding.

Delegates to the CIOR are elected by their national Reserve Officer Associations. The head of each delegation is a Vice-President of CIOR. The CIOR International President and Secretary General are elected by an Executive Committee. They serve for two years and are members of the same national association.

Apart from the President and Secretary General, the Executive Committee consists of the 18 Vice-Presidents and up to four other delegates from each national Association. Voting is on the basis of a single vote cast by each Vice-President on behalf of his delegation. The Executive Committee is the CIOR's policy body and decides which country will assume the presidency, where congresses will be held, what projects will be assumed by the various commissions and the final actions to be taken on these projects.

The CIOR is financed by annual subscriptions from its component national associations based on the size of the membership of each association and on subsidies, gifts and legacies.

Four permanent commissions and one legal committee work on behalf of the Executive Committee under the guidance of the President. The Commissions are as follows:

- Commission 1 - Defence Attitudes and Security Issues;
- Commission 2 - Civil/Military Cooperation;
- Commission 3 - Communication;
- Commission 4 - Competitions.

The Executive Committee may from time to time appoint a sub-committee or sub-commission to consider specific matters outside the terms of reference of permanent commissions or committees.

In order to accomplish its objectives, CIOR meets on an annual basis alternating the location among member countries. A mid-winter conference for the Executive Committee and Commissions is held at NATO Headquarters in Brussels, Belgium, usually during the first part of February.

THE INTERALLIED CONFEDERATION OF MEDICAL RESERVE OFFICERS (CIOMR)

The CIOMR (Confédération Interalliée des Officiers Médicaux de Réserve) was established in Brussels in 1947 as the official organisation of medical officers within NATO's reserve forces. Originally founded by Belgium, France and the Netherlands, the Confederation now includes all CIOR member countries. Its objectives include establishing close professional relations with the medical doctors and services of the reserve forces of NATO countries; studying issues of importance to medical reserve officers, including medico-military training; and promoting effective collaboration with the active forces of the Alliance.

The CIOMR is an associated member of CIOR. The CIOMR holds its sessions at the same time and place as the CIOR summer congress and winter conference but follows its own agenda for the discussion of medical matters.

Further information about the CIOR and CIOMR can be obtained from:

CIOR Liaison Office in NATO	Reserve Affairs Advisor	The Secretary General CIOMR
NATO/IMS/P1P/CIOR	Public Inform. Office	6 Boterdorpse
NATO HQ	7010 SHAPE	Verlaat
1110 Brussels	Belgium	3054 XL Rotterdam
Belgium	Tel: 32 65 44 33 89	The Netherlands
Tel: 32 2 707 5295		Fax: 31 10 4635307

Further information on national Reserve Officer associations can be obtained from the following addresses:

BELGIQUE
L'Union Royale Nationale des Officiers de Réserve de Belgique (URNOR-KNVRO)
24 rue des Petits Carmes
1000 Bruxelles
Tel: 32 2 701 3815

CANADA
The Conference of Defence Associations of Canada (CDA)
Suite 502
359 Kent Street
Ottawa, Ontario K2P OR7
Tel: 1 603 236 1552

CZECH REPUBLIC
Svaz Dustojnikua a Praporciku Armadycr
Vitezne Namesti, 4
16000 Praha 6
Tel: 420 2 20215393

DENMARK
Reserveofficersforeningen I Danmark (ROID)
Gl Hovedvagt
Kastellet 1
2100 Copenhagen - O
Tel: 45 33 14 16 01

FRANCE
L'Union Nationale des Officiers de Réserve de France (UNOR)
12 rue Marie Laurencin
75012 Paris
Tel: 33 1 43 47 40 16

GERMANY
Verband der Reservisten der Deutsche Bundeswehr. V. (VdRBw)
P.O. Box 14361
Bonn 1
Tel: 49 228 2590920

GREECE
The Supreme Pan-Hellenic Federation of Reserve Officers (SPFRO)
100 Solonos Street
10680 Athens
Tel: 30 1 362 50 21

HUNGARY
National Association of Reserve Soldiers (HUNGARY)
HUVOSH - Volgyi int 21/23
1026 Budapest

ITALY
Unione Nazionale Ufficiali in Congedo d'Italia (UNUCI)
Via Nomentana 313
00162 Roma
Tel: 39 068 414108

LUXEMBOURG
Amicale des Anciens Officiers de Réserve Luxembourgeois (ANORL)
124 A. Kiem
8030 Strassen

THE NETHERLANDS
Koninklijke Vereniging van Nederlandse Reserve Officieren (KVNRO)
Postbus 95395
2509 CJ's-Gravenhage
Tel: 31 70 316 29 40

NORWAY
Norway Norske Reserveoffiseres Forbund (NROF)
Oslo Mil. Akershus
0015 Oslo 1
Tel: 47 224 78260

PORTUGAL
Uniao Portuguesa de Officiais de Reserva
Estado Maior General das Forcas Armados
Av. Ilha da Madeira
1400-204 Lisbon
Tel: 351 21 301 00 01

SPAIN
Federacion de Organizaciones de la Reserva de Espana (FORE)
Mayor, 16
28013 Madrid
Tel: 34 91 661 6041

TURKEY
Turkiye Emekli
Subaylar Dernegi
Selanik Caddesi 34/6
Kizilay, Ankara
Tel: 90 312 418 77 61

UNITED KINGDOM
The Reserve Forces Association of the United Kingdom
Centre Block
Duke of York's Headquarters
Chelsea
London SW3 4SG
Tel: 44 207 4145588

UNITED STATES
The Reserve Officers Association of the United States (ROA)
1 Constitution Avenue, N.E.
Washington, D.C. 20002
Tel: 1 202 479 22 00

APPENDIX 1

ABBREVIATIONS IN COMMON USE

APPENDIX 1
ABBREVIATIONS IN COMMON USE[1]

AAP
Allied Administrative Publication

ABM
AntiBallistic Missile (Treaty 1972)

AC
Alliance Committee

ACCHAN
Allied Command Channel

ACCIS
Automated Command and Control
Information System

ACCS
Air Command and Control System

ACE
Allied Command Europe

ACLANT
Allied Command Atlantic

ADP
Automated Data Processing

AEW
Airborne Early Warning

AFCENT
Allied Forces Central Europe

AFNORTH
Allied Forces Northern Europe

AFNORTHWEST
Allied Forces Northwestern Europe

AFSOUTH
Allied Forces Southern Europe

AGARD
Advisory Group for Aerospace
Research and Development (reorganised under the NATO Research
and Technology Organisation (RTO)
as the Research & Technology
Agency)

AIRCENT
Allied Air Forces Central Europe

AIRNORTHWEST
Allied Air Forces Northwestern
Europe

AJP
Allied Joint Publication

ALMC
Air-Launched Cruise Missile

ALP
Allied Logistic Publication

AMF
ACE Mobile Force

AOR
Area of Responsibility

AP
Allied Publication

APAG
Atlantic Policy Advisory Group

AQAP
Allied Quality Assurance Publication

ARRC
ACE Rapid Reaction Corps

---

1   This list includes most acronyms which appear in the Handbook as well as others in current use.
However all acronyms used within NATO are not included.

ARW
Advanced Research Workshop
(NATO Science Programme)

ASG
Assistant Secretary General

ASI
Advanced Study Institute (NATO
Science Programme)

ASR
Alliance Standardisation
Requirements

ASW
Anti-Submarine Warfare

ATA
Atlantic Treaty Association

AWACS
Airborne Warning and Control
System

BALTAP
Allied Forces Baltic Approaches

BICES
Battlefield Information Collection and
Exploitation System

BMEWS
Ballistic Missile Early Warning
System

BTWC
Biological and Toxin Weapons
Convention

CALS
Continuous Acquisition and Life
Cycle Support

CAPC
Civil Aviation Planning Committee

CAPS
Conventional Armaments Planning
System

CAS
Close Air Support

CBC
Civil Budget Committee

CBM
Confidence Building Measure

CCC
Capabilities Coordination Cell

CCMS
Committee on the Challenges of
Modern Society

CCPC
Civil Communications Planning
Committee

CDE
Conference on Security and
Confidence Building Measures and
Disarmament in Europe

CEE
Central and Eastern Europe

CENTAG
Central Army Group, Central Europe

CEOA
Central Europe Operating Agency

CEP
Civil Emergency Planning

CEPMO(A)
Central Europe Pipeline
Management Organisation (Agency)

CEPS
Central Europe Pipeline System

CFE
Conventional Armed Forces in Europe (CFE of Treaty 1990)

CFE-IA
Concluding Act of the Negotiations on Personnel Strength of the Conventional Armed Forces in Europe Treaty (1992)

CFSP
Common Foreign and Security Policy

CHANCOM
Channel Committee

CIMIC
Civil/Military Cooperation

CINCEASTLANT
Commander-in-Chief Eastern Atlantic Area

CINCENT
Commander-in-Chief Allied Forces Central Europe

CINCHAN
Allied Commander-in-Chief Channel (position dissolved 1994)

CINCIBERLANT
Commander-in-Chief Iberian Atlantic Area

CINCNORTH
Commander-in-Chief Allied Forces Northern Europe

CINCSOUTH
Commander-in-Chief Allied Forces Southern Europe

CINCUKAIR
Commander-in-Chief United Kingdom Airforces

CINCWESTLANT
Commander-in-Chief Western Atlantic Area

CIO
Chairman-in-Office (OSCE)

CIS
Commonwealth of Independent States

CIS
Communications and Information Systems

CJTF
Combined Joint Task Force

C-M
Council Memorandum

CNAD
Conference of National Armaments Directors

COEC
Council Operations and Exercise Committee

COMEDS
Committee of the Chiefs of Military Medical Services in NATO

CONMAROPS
Concept of Maritime Operations

CP
Capability Package

CPC
Conflict Prevention Centre

CPC
Civil Protection Committee

CPSU
Communist Party of the Soviet Union

CPX
Command Post Exercise

CRG
Collaborative Research Grant (NATO Science Programme)

CSBM
Confidence and Security Building Measure

CSCE
Conference on Security and Cooperation in Europe (from January 1995, Organisation on Security and Cooperation in Europe or OSCE)

CST
Conventional Stability Talks

C3
Consultation, Command and Control

CUSRPG
Canada-US Regional Planning Group

CWC
Chemical Weapons Convention (1993)

DCA
Dual-Capable Aircraft

DCI
Defence Capabilities Initiative

DGP
Senior Defence Group on Proliferation

DIMS
Director International Military Staff (IMS)

DPAO
Division of Defence, Planning and Operations

DPC
Defence Planning Committee

DPQ
Defence Planning Questionnaire

DRC
Defence Review Committee

DRG
Defence Research Group (absorbed into the NATO Research and Technology Organisation (RTO))

DS
Division of Defence Support

EADRCC
Euro-Atlantic Disaster Response Coordination Centre

EADRU
Euro-Atlantic Disaster Response Unit

EAPC
Euro-Atlantic Partnership Council

ESA
European Space Agency

ESDI
European Security and Defence Identity

EU
European Union

EUROGROUP
Informal Group of NATO European Defence Ministers (dissolved 1993)

EV
Expert Visit (NATO Science Programme)

EW
Electronic Warfare

EWG
Executive Working Group

FAWEU
Forces Answerable to the Western European Union (WEU)

FORACS
NATO Naval Forces Sensors and Weapons Accuracy Check Sites

FRP
Financial Rules and Procedures

FSC
Forum for Security Cooperation (OSCE)

FSU
Former Soviet Union

GLCM
Ground-Launched Cruise Missile

GNW
Group on Nuclear Weapons

GSZ
Ground Safety Zone

HCNM
OSCE High Commission on National Minorities

HLG
High Level Group

HLTF
High Level Task Force

HNS
Host Nation Support

IATA
International Air Transport Association

ICAO
International Civil Aviation Organisation

ICB
International Competitive Bidding

ICBM
Intercontinental Ballistic Missile

ICRC
International Committee for the Red Cross

ICTY
International Criminal Tribunal for the former Yugoslavia

IEPG
Independent European Programme Group

IFOR
Implementation Force (for Bosnia and Herzegovina)

IGC
Inter-Governmental Conference

IISS
International Institute for Strategic Studies

IMS
International Military Staff

INF
Intermediate-Range Nuclear Forces (Treaty, 1987)

IO
Interoperability Objective

IPP
Individual Partnership Programme (PfP)

IPTF
United Nations International Police Task Force

IRBM
Intermediate-Range Ballistic Missile

IRF
Immediate Reaction Forces

IS
International Staff

JCP
Joint Committee on Proliferation

JSB
Joint Service Board (MAS)

JWG
Joint Working Group (NATO-Ukraine
Joint Working Group on Defence
Reform)

KFOR
Kosovo Force

LANDCENT
Allied Land Forces Central Europe

LANDSOUTH
Allied Land Forces Southern Europe

LANDSOUTHCENT
Allied Land Forces South Central
Europe

LANDSOUTHEAST
Allied Land Forces South Eastern
Europe

LCC
Logistics Coordination Centre

LG
Linkage Grant (NATO Science
Programme)

LTDP
Long-Term Defence Programme

MAG
Movement and Transportation
Advisory Group

MAP
Membership Action Plan

MARAIRMED
Maritime Air Forces Mediterranean

MAREQ
Military Assistance Requirement

MAS
Military Agency for Standardisation

MBC
Military Budget Committee

MBFR
Mutual and Balanced Force
Reductions

MC
Military Committee

MCD
Military and Civil Defence Assets

MCG
Mediterranean Cooperation Group

MCM
Mine Countermeasures

MCWG
Military Committee Working Group

MDF
Main Defence Forces

MEADS
Medium Extended Air Defence
System

MILREP
Military Representative (to the MC)

MLM
Military Liaison Mission

MLRS
Multiple Launch Rocket System

MNC
Major NATO Command/Commander
(renamed NATO Strategic
Command/Commander)

MOB
Main Operating Base

MOD
Ministry of Defence

MOU
Memorandum of Understanding

MRCA
Multi-Role Combat Aircraft
(TORNADO)

MSC
Major Subordinate Command/
Commander

MSU
Multinational Security Unit

MTRP
Medium Term Resources Plan

NAA
North Atlantic Assembly

NAADC
NATO Analytical Air Defence Cell

NAAG
NATO Army Armaments Group

NAC
North Atlantic Council

NACC
North Atlantic Cooperation Council

NACMA
NATO Air Command and Control
System (ACCS) Management
Agency

NACOSA
NATO CIS Operating and Support
Agency

NADC
NATO Air Defence Committee

NADEFCOL
NATO Defense College

NADGE
NATO Air Defence Ground
Environment

NAEWF
NATO Airborne Early Warning
Forces

NAFAG
NATO Airforce Armaments Group

NAHEMA
NATO Helicopter (NH90) Design,
Development, Production and
Logistics Management Agency

NAMEADSMA
NATO Medium Extended Air
Defence System Management
Agency

NAMFI
NATO Missile Firing Installation

NAMMA
NATO Multi-Role Combat Aircraft
Development and Production
Management Agency

NAMMO
NATO Multi-Role Combat Aircraft
Development and Production
Management Organisation

NAMP
NATO Annual Manpower Plan

NAMSA
NATO Maintenance and Supply
Agency

NAMSO
NATO Maintenance and Supply
Organisation

NAPMA
NATO Airborne Early Warning and Control (AEW&C) Programme Management Agency

NAPMO
NATO Airborne Early Warning and Control Programme Management Organisation

NAPR
NATO Armaments Periodic Review

NATO
North Atlantic Treaty Organisation

NAU
NATO Accounting Unit

NAVNORTHWEST
Allied Naval Forces North Western Europe

NAVOCFORMED
Naval On-Call Force, Mediterranean

NAVSOUTH
Allied Naval Forces Southern Europe

NBC
Nuclear, Biological and Chemical Weapons

NCARC
NATO Conventional Armaments Review Committee

NCCIS
NATO Command, Control and Information System

NCISS
NATO Communications and Information Systems School

NC3A
NATO Consultation, Command and Control Agency

NC3B
NATO Consultation, Command and Control Board

NC3O
NATO Consultation, Command and Control Organisation

NDC
NATO Defense College

NDMC
NATO Defence Manpower Committee

NDMP
NATO Defence Manpower Plan

NEFMA
NATO European Fighter Aircraft Development, Production and Logistics Management Agency

NEFMO
NATO European Fighter Aircraft (EFA) Development, Production and Logistics Management Organisation

NEPS
North European Pipeline System

NETMO(A)
NATO Eurofighter 2000 and TORNADO Development, Production and Logistics Management Organisation (Agency)

NFR
NATO Financial Regulations

NGO
Non-Governmental Organisation

NHMO
NATO HAWK Management Office

NHPLO
NATO HAWK Production and Logistics Organisation

NHQC3S
NATO Headquarters Consultation, Command and Control Staff

NIAG
NATO Industrial Advisory Group

NICS
NATO Integrated Communications System

NIDS
NATO Integrated Data Service

NIG
Networking Infrastructure Grant (NATO Science Programme)

NIMIC
NATO Insensitive Munitions Information Centre

NMA
NATO Military Authority

NMR
National Military Representative (to SHAPE)

NNAG
NATO Naval Armaments Group

NORAD
North American Air Defence System

NORTHAG
Northern Army Group, Central Europe

NPC
NATO Pipeline Committee

NPG
Nuclear Planning Group

NPLO
NATO Production and Logistics Organisation

NPS
NATO Pipeline System

NPSC
NATO Project Steering Committee

NPT
Treaty on the Non-Proliferation of Nuclear Weapons (1968)

NSC
NATO Supply Centre

NSIP
NATO Security Investment Programme

NSLB
NATO Standardisation Liaison Board

NSN
NATO Stock Number

NSO
NATO Standardisation Organisation

NTG
NATO Training Group

NUC
NATO-Ukraine Commission

OCC
Operational Capabilities Concept

ODIHR
Office for Democratic Institutions and Human Rights

OECD
Organisation for Economic Cooperation and Development

OHR
Office of the High Representative (Bosnia)

ONS
Office for NATO Standardisation

OPEC
Organisation of Petroleum Exporting Countries

OSCE
Organisation for Security and Cooperation in Europe (formerly CSCE)

OTAN
Organisation du Traité de l'Atlantique Nord

PA
Division of Political Affairs

PAPS
Periodic Armaments Planning System

PARP
(PfP) Planning and Review Process

PBEIST
Planning Board for European Inland Surface Transport

PBOS
Planning Board for Ocean Shipping

PC
Political Committee

PCC
Partnership Coordination Cell

PCG
Policy Coordination Group

PERM REP
Permanent Representative (to the NAC)

PfP
Partnership for Peace

PIC
Peace Implementation Council

PJC
Permanent Joint Council (NATO-Russia)

PMF
Political Military Framework

PMSC
Political-Military Steering Committee on Partnership for Peace

PMSC/AHG
Political-Military Steering Committee/AdHoc Group on Cooperation in Peacekeeping

PNET
Peaceful Nuclear Explosion Treaty (1976)

PO
Private Office

PPCG
Provisional Policy Coordination Group

PSC
Principal Subordinate Command/ Commander

PSE
Partnership for Peace Staff Element

PSO
Peace Support Operations

PTBT
Partial Test Ban Treaty

PWP
Partnership Work Programme (PfP)

R&D
Research and Development

RRF
Rapid Reaction Force

R&T
Research and Technology

RTO
Research and Technology
Organisation

SAC
Strategic Air Command

SACEUR
Supreme Allied Commander Europe

SACLANT
Supreme Allied Commander Atlantic

SACLANTCEN
SACLANT Undersea Research
Centre

SALT
Strategic Arms Limitation Talks

SAM
Sanctions Assistance Missions

SAM
Surface-to-Air Missile

SATCOM
Satellite Communications

SC
Strategic Commander

SCEPC
Senior Civil Emergency Planning
Committee

SCG
Special Consultative Group

SCMM
Standing Committee on Military
Matters (Bosnian Peace Agreement)

SCP
Security Cooperation Programme

SDI
Strategic Defence Initiative

SEEGROUP
South East Europe Security
Cooperation Steering Group

SEEI
South East Europe Initiative

SFOR
Stabilisation Force

SfP
Science for Peace

SG
Secretary General

SGP
Senior Political-Military Group on
Proliferation

SHAPE
Supreme Headquarters Allied
Powers Europe

SHARE
Stock Holding and Asset
Requirements Exchange

SLBM
Submarine-Launched Ballistic
Missile

SLCM
Sea-Launched Cruise Missile

SLWPG
Senior Level Weapons Protection
Group

SNF
Short-Range Nuclear Forces

SNLC
Senior NATO Logisticians'
Conference

SO
Standardisation Objective

SOFA
Status of Forces Agreements

SPC
Senior Political Committee

SPC(R)
Senior Political Committee
(Reinforced)

SRB
Senior Resource Board

STANAG
Standardisation Agreement

STANAVFORCHAN
Standing Naval Force Channel

STANAVFORLANT
Standing Naval Force Atlantic

STANAVFORMED
Standing Naval Force Mediterranean

START
Strategic Arms Reduction Talks

STC
SHAPE Technical Centre

STRIKFORSOUTH
Naval Striking and Support Forces

TEEP
Training and Education
Enhancement Programme

UNHCR
United Nations High Commissioner
for Refugees

UNMIK
United Nations Mission in Kosovo

UNOCHA
United Nations Office for the
Coordination of Humanitarian Affairs

UNPROFOR
United Nations Protection Force

UNSC
United Nations Security Council

VCC
Verification Coordinating Committee

WEAG
Western European Armaments
Group

WEU
Western European Union

WG
Working Group

WHO
World Health Organisation

WMD
Weapons of Mass Destruction

WP
Working Party

APPENDIX 2

SOURCES OF FURTHER INFORMATION

APPENDIX 2
SOURCES OF FURTHER INFORMATION

NATO Headquarters
NATO Office of Information and Press
NATO
1110 Brussels - Belgium
Tel: 32 2 707 4111
Fax: 32 2 707 1252
E-mail: natodoc@hq.nato.int
Website: http://www.nato.int

Further information on NATO's Science Programme and environmental
activities can be found at the following websites:
http://www.nato.int/science
http://www.nato.int/ccms

Regional Information Offices

NATO Information Office,
Box 28
121 Reykjavik
Iceland
Tel: 354 561 00 15
Fax: 354 551 00 15
E-mail: infonato@islandia.is

NATO Information and
Documentation Centre
36/1 Melnikov St.
Kyiv, 254 119
Ukraine
Tel: 380 44 246 86 16
Fax: 380 44 246 86 22

NATO Information Office
Mytnaya Street 3
117049 Moscow
Russia
Tel: 7 095 937 3640
      7 095 937 3641
      7 095 937 3676
Fax: 7 502 937 3809 (satellite line)
      7 095 937 3809
E-mail: nato@garnet.ru

Military Public Information Offices

Public Information Advisor
International Military Staff
NATO HQ
1110 Brussels
Tel: 32 2 707 5422
Fax: 32 2 707 5713
E-mail: pia@hq.nato.int
        dep.pia@hq.nato.int

SHAPE
7010 SHAPE/Mons - Belgium
Tel: 32 65 44 71 11
Fax: 32 65 44 35 44/74 42
E-mail: shapepio@shape.nato.int
Website: http://www.shape.nato.int

SACLANT
7857 Blandy Road - Suite 100
Norfolk VA 23551-2490, USA
Tel: 1 757 445 3400
Fax: 1 757 445 3234
E-mail: pio@saclant.nato.int
Website: http://www.saclant.nato.int

Addresses and points of contact for the following organisations are listed in Chapter 16:

NATO Parliamentary Assembly (NATO PA)

Atlantic Treaty Associations (ATA) and affiliated national Atlantic Associations, Atlantic Councils and Committees

Interallied Confederation of Reserve Officers (CIOR).

NATO Integrated Data Service (NIDS)

The NIDS facilitates computer access to NATO press releases, communiqués and official statements, speeches, printed reference books, and other documentation. Topics covered include political, military, economic and scientific issues as well as up-to-date information on NATO's role in the implementation of the Bosnia Peace Agreement (SFOR) and in the Kosovo Force (KFOR). The periodical "NATO Review" and other publications, providing information and analysis of NATO related issues, are also published through the NIDS.

The NIDS also provides access to information and documentation issued by NATO civilian and military agencies and by other related organisations such as the NATO Parliamentary Assembly and Atlantic Councils and Committees affiliated to the Atlantic Treaty Association.

The network of electronic contacts established by the NIDS with Ministries of Foreign Affairs and Defence, parliaments and academic institutes in NATO and EAPC countries is gradually being expanded, as are electronic information exchanges with other international organisations.

Information available through the NIDS can be accessed via the NATO website and is also available via electronic mail distribution.

To subscribe to E-mail distribution, send a request to listserv@listserv.cc.kuleuven.ac.be, mentioning one of the following references:

- SUB NATODATA (latest information from NATO and from NATO agencies and military commands, as well as other relevant international organisations);

- SUB NATOPRES (communications addressed primarily to journalists, including speeches, Ministerial communiqués and press advisories);

- SUB NATOSCI (data relating to NATO's Scientific and Environmental programme).

In each case, subscribers should give their first and last name.

APPENDIX 3

CHRONOLOGY

Chronology

This Chronology traces the principal developments in the evolution of NATO against the background of significant world events. It reflects the intensity of diplomatic contacts and exchanges in the early years following the end of the Cold War and the high level consultations which take place on a continuous basis in relation to key areas of Alliance policy. Numerous additional events which have taken place in the framework of Partnership for Peace and the Euro-Atlantic Partnership Council, including seminars and conferences, training courses, military and crisis management exercises, additional visits and exchanges and other activities are not recorded for reasons of space. Information about such events may be found in communiqués and press releases listed in NATO's Integrated Data Service on the Internet (http://www.nato.int).

References made in this chronology to the former Yugoslav Republic of Macedonia are marked with an asterisk (*) referring to the following footnote: Turkey recognises the Republic of Macedonia with its constitutional name.

1945

26 June	The United Nations Charter is signed at San Francisco.
6 August	Explosion of Hiroshima atomic bomb.

1946

5 March	Winston Churchill's "Iron Curtain" speech at Fulton, Missouri.

1947

19 January	The Soviet-sponsored Communist "Lublin-Committee" monopolises power in Poland.
12 March	President Truman urges the United States *"to support free peoples who are resisting attempted subjugation by armed minorities or by outside pressure"* (Truman Doctrine).
5 June	United States Secretary of State, George C. Marshall, announces plans for the economic rehabilitation of Europe (Marshall Plan).
22-27 September	Establishment of Cominform, the organisation for the ideological unity of the Soviet bloc, following rejection of Marshall Aid by the Soviet Union and its allies.

1948

22 January	Ernest Bevin, United Kingdom Secretary of State for Foreign Affairs, speaking in the House of Commons, proposes a form of Western Union. The Western Union Defence Organisation is subsequently established by the Defence Ministers of the Brussels Treaty Powers on 27-28 September 1948.
22-25 February	The Communist Party of Czechoslovakia gains control of the government in Prague through a coup d'état.
17 March	Signature of the Brussels Treaty of Economic, Social and Cultural Collaboration and Collective Self-Defence by the Foreign Ministers of Belgium, France, Luxembourg, the Netherlands and the United Kingdom.
11 June	The United States Senate adopts the "Vandenberg Resolution", establishing the basis for future US association with regional and other collective arrangements for security.
24 June	Beginning of the Berlin blockade by the Soviet Union.
28 June	Formal expulsion of Yugoslavia from Cominform.
6 July	Talks on North Atlantic defence begin in Washington between the United States, Canada and the Brussels Treaty Powers.
25-26 October	The Consultative Council of the Brussels Treaty Powers announces *"complete agreement on the principle of a defensive pact for the North Atlantic"*.
10 December	Negotiations on the North Atlantic Treaty open in Washington between the representatives of the Brussels Treaty Powers, Canada and the United States.

1949

15 March	The negotiating powers invite Denmark, Iceland, Italy, Norway and Portugal to adhere to the North Atlantic Treaty.
2 April	The governments concerned repudiate Soviet assertions that the North Atlantic Treaty is contrary to the United Nations Charter.
4 April	The North Atlantic Treaty is signed in Washington by Belgium, Canada, Denmark, France, Iceland, Italy, Luxembourg, the Netherlands, Norway, Portugal, the United Kingdom and the United States.
8 April	The Brussels Treaty Powers, Denmark, Italy and Norway request United States military and financial assistance.

4 May	The London Ten-Power Agreement sets up the Council of Europe. Inaugural meeting of the Council at Strasbourg takes place on 10 August.
9 May	The Berlin blockade is lifted.
24 August	The North Atlantic Treaty enters into force.
17 September	First session of the North Atlantic Council in Washington.
6 October	Mutual Defence Assistance Act of 1949 is signed by President Truman.

1950

27 January	President Truman approves the plan for the integrated defence of the North Atlantic area, releasing US$ 900,000,000 of military aid funds.
9 May	The French Government proposes the creation of a single authority to control the production of steel and coal in France and Germany, open for membership to other countries (Schuman Plan).
25 June	North Korean Forces attack the Republic of South Korea.
25 July	First meeting of NATO Council Deputies in London. Ambassador Charles M. Spofford, United States Representative to the North Atlantic Council, is elected Permanent Chairman.
24 October	French Prime Minister, René Pleven, outlines his plan for a European unified army, including German contingents, within the framework of NATO.
19 December	The North Atlantic Council appoints General Dwight D. Eisenhower to be the first Supreme Allied Commander Europe (SACEUR).
20 December	The Brussels Treaty Powers decide to merge the military organisation of the Western Union into the North Atlantic Treaty Organisation.

1951

15 February	Conference convened by French Government on the setting up of a European Army opens in Paris.
2 April	Allied Command Europe becomes operational with Supreme Headquarters Allied Powers Europe (SHAPE) located at Rocquencourt, near Paris.
18 April	Setting up of the European Coal and Steel Community by Belgium, France, Italy, Luxembourg, the Netherlands, and the Federal Republic of Germany.

3 May	Incorporation of the Defence Committee and the Defence Financial and Economic Committee into the North Atlantic Council.
19 June	The parties to the North Atlantic Treaty sign an agreement on the status of their forces.
20 September	The member countries sign an agreement in Ottawa on the Status of NATO, National Representatives and International Staff (Civilian Status Agreement).
9-11 October	First meeting of the Temporary Council Committee (TCC) in Paris, established by the North Atlantic Council to reconcile the requirements of collective security with the political and economic capabilities of the member countries.
17-22 October	Signature in London of the protocol to the North Atlantic Treaty on the accession of Greece and Turkey.
19 November	Inauguration of the NATO Defense College, Paris (transferred to Rome on October 10, 1966).

1952

30 January	Appointment of Vice-Admiral Lynde D. McCormick (United States) to be the first Supreme Allied Commander Atlantic (SACLANT).
18 February	Greece and Turkey accede to the North Atlantic Treaty.
20-25 February	The North Atlantic Council meeting in Lisbon reorganises the structure of the Alliance and NATO becomes a permanent organisation with its headquarters in Paris.
21 February	The Council establishes a Channel Command, and appoints Admiral Sir Arthur John Power as the first Commander-in-Chief Channel (CINCHAN).
12 March	Lord Ismay (United Kingdom) is appointed Vice-Chairman of the North Atlantic Council and Secretary General of the North Atlantic Treaty Organisation.
10 April	Allied Command Atlantic (ACLANT) becomes operational, with headquarters at Norfolk, Virginia, USA.
16 April	NATO opens its provisional headquarters at the Palais de Chaillot, Paris.
28 April	First meeting of the North Atlantic Council in permanent session in Paris.
27 May	Signature in Paris of the Treaty setting up the European Defence Community by Belgium, France, Italy, Luxembourg, the Netherlands and the Federal Republic of Germany. (Following the decision of the French National Assembly on 29 August 1954, the Treaty did not come into force).

| 28 August | Signature in Paris by member nations of the Alliance of a Protocol on the Status of International Military Headquarters. |

1953

5 March	Death of Stalin.
23 July	Korean Armistice signed at Panmunjon.
20 August	USSR issues a communiqué of its possession of the hydrogen bomb.
4-8 December	Conference in Bermuda of the Heads of Government of France, the United Kingdom and the United States, attended by Lord Ismay as observer for NATO.

1954

25 Jan./18 Feb.	Abortive Four-Power Conference in Berlin on German reunification.
7 May	The United Kingdom and the United States reject the USSR's bid to join the North Atlantic Treaty Organisation.
17-18 June	Meeting at The Hague of the Constituent Conference of the Atlantic Treaty Association sponsored by the International Atlantic Committee.
29 August	The French National Assembly decides against ratification of the Treaty setting up the European Defence Community (EDC).
6 September	Opening of Manila Conference which culminates in the signing of the treaties setting up SEATO (South-East Asia Treaty Organisation)[1].
28 Sept.-3 Oct.	Meeting in London of the Conference of Nine to seek an alternative to the EDC. (Participating countries: Belgium, Canada, France, Federal Republic of Germany, Italy, Luxembourg, the Netherlands, United Kingdom and United States).
23 October	Signature of the Paris Agreements. The Federal Republic of Germany is invited to join NATO, and Italy and the Federal Republic of Germany accede to the Western European Union (WEU).

1955

| 6 May | The Federal Republic of Germany becomes a member of NATO. |

---

[1] Member countries: Australia, France, New Zealand, Pakistan, Philippines, Thailand, United Kingdom and United States.

14 May	The USSR concludes the Warsaw Treaty with Albania, Bulgaria, Czechoslovakia, East Germany, Hungary, Poland and Romania.
18-23 July	First Conference of NATO Parliamentarians (since November 1966, the North Atlantic Assembly) in Paris.
30 December	The USSR signs a treaty with the régime in East Germany, granting it the prerogatives of a State.

1956

24 February	At the 20th Congress of the Soviet Communist Party, Khrushchev denounces Stalin in a "secret" speech.
18 April	Dissolution of Cominform.
28 June	Anti-régime riots erupt at Poznan in Poland.
26 July	Egypt nationalises the Suez Canal.
4 November	Soviet suppression of Hungarian people's rebellion.
13 December	The North Atlantic Council approves the recommendations contained in the Report of the Committee of Three on Non-Military Cooperation in NATO.

1957

25 March	Signature of the Rome Treaties setting up Euratom and the European Economic Community.
2-3 May	Ministerial meeting of the North Atlantic Council in Bonn. The Council decides to intensify its efforts in favour of German reunification by means of free elections.
16 May	Paul-Henri Spaak (Belgium) succeeds Lord Ismay as Secretary General of NATO.
29 July	Signing in Berlin of a declaration by the governments of France, the Federal Republic of Germany, the United Kingdom and the United States, affirming the identity of their policies with regard to the reunification of Germany and to European security.
14 September	The General Assembly of the United Nations condemns the Soviet intervention in Hungary.
4 October	The first Soviet Sputnik is launched.
31 October	Franco-British intervention in the Suez Canal area.
16-19 December	At a meeting of the North Atlantic Council in Paris, Heads of Government reaffirm the principles and purposes of the Atlantic Alliance.

1958

1 January	Entry into force of the Treaty of Rome setting up the European Economic Community.

26-29 March	First meeting of NATO Science Committee.
15-17 April	Defence Ministers of the NATO countries meeting in Paris reaffirm the defensive character of the NATO strategy.
10 November	Khrushchev announces that the USSR wishes to terminate the Four-Power Agreement on the status of Berlin. (The Plan was rejected by the Western Powers on December 31).
16-18 November	December Ministerial meeting of the North Atlantic Council. The Council associates itself with the views expressed by the governments of France, the United Kingdom and the United States on Berlin and on the right of the Western Powers to remain there.

1959

1 January	Overthrow of the Batista régime in Cuba by Fidel Castro.
11 June	Opening of Four-Power Meeting of Foreign Ministers in Geneva (France, the United Kingdom, the United States and the USSR) on the German question.
19 August	The Baghdad Pact signed on 24 February 1955 becomes the Central Treaty Organisation (CENTO). Full members: Iran, Iraq, Pakistan, Turkey and United Kingdom. Associate member: United States. Its headquarters is set up in Ankara. (Dissolved, 26 September 1979).
20 November	Austria, Denmark, Norway, Portugal, Sweden, Switzerland and the United Kingdom initial the Stockholm Convention establishing the European Free Trade Association (EFTA)[2].
15-22 December	Inauguration of the new NATO Headquarters at the Porte Dauphine in Paris.

1960

15 March	Opening of the United Nations Ten-Power Disarmament Committee negotiations in Geneva. Communist states withdraw on 27 June.
1 May	American U2 aircraft is shot down over Soviet territory.
19 May	French, United Kingdom and United States Foreign Ministers report to the North Atlantic Council on the break-

---

[2]   Finland became an associate member of EFTA in 1961. Iceland joined in 1970. Denmark and the United Kingdom withdrew from EFTA on joining the EEC on 1 January 1973. Portugal withdrew from EFTA on 1 January 1986.

	down of the Paris Summit meeting with the participation of the USSR on 16 May.
27 May	Military coup d'état in Turkey.
23 September	Khrushchev attends the General Assembly of the United Nations in New York.
10 November	Summit meeting in Moscow of the Communist leaders of 81 countries. Approval of Khrushchev's concept of peaceful coexistence.
14 December	Convention for the Establishment of the Organisation for Economic Cooperation and Development (OECD) in place of the OEEC signed by 18 European countries and the United States and Canada. Australia, New Zealand and Japan subsequently join the Organisation.

1961

12 April	Soviet Major Yuri Gagarin becomes the first man orbited in space.
21 April	Dirk U. Stikker (the Netherlands) succeeds Paul-Henri Spaak as Secretary General of NATO.
13 August	Erection of the Berlin Wall.
13-15 December	At a Ministerial meeting of the North Atlantic Council in Paris, the Alliance reaffirms its position on Berlin, strongly condemning the building of the Wall, and approves the renewal of diplomatic contacts with the Soviet Union to determine whether a basis for negotiation can be found. It also announces the establishment of a mobile task force.

1962

8-20 January	The "Alliance Convention" of citizens of NATO countries meets and endorses the "Declaration of Paris" in favour of strengthening the Alliance and the Atlantic Community.
18 March	The Evian agreements establish an independent Algeria.
29 March	Establishment of the European Organisation for the Development and Construction of Space Vehicle Launchers (ELDO). Member countries: Australia, Belgium, Federal Republic of Germany, France, Italy, the Netherlands and United Kingdom.
10 April	Macmillan and Kennedy appeal to Khrushchev for agreement on a test ban treaty.
4-6 May	Foreign Ministers and Defence Ministers of the North Atlantic Alliance review the circumstances in which the Alliance might be compelled to have recourse to nuclear weapons (Athens Guidelines).

14 June	Establishment of the European Space Research Organisation (ESRO). Member countries: Belgium, Denmark, France, Federal Republic of Germany, Italy, the Netherlands, Spain, Sweden, Switzerland, and United Kingdom. (ELDO and ESRO merged to become the European Space Agency (ESA) on 31 May 1975.)
22 Oct.-20 Nov.	Partial blockade of Cuba by the US following revelation of Soviet construction of missile bases on the island; lifted following Soviet agreement to dismantle the bases.
18-20 December	President Kennedy and Prime Minister Macmillan confer at Nassau, Bahamas. They agree to contribute part of their strategic nuclear forces to NATO.

1963

16 January	Following a statement by the French Representative, the Council notes that insofar as the former Algerian Departments of France are concerned, the relevant clauses of the North Atlantic Treaty became inapplicable as of 3 July 1962.
20 June	Agreement on a 'hot line' between Washington and Moscow is signed in Geneva by the United States and the Soviet Union.
15-25 July	The United States, the United Kingdom and the Soviet Union initial an agreement banning nuclear tests in the atmosphere, in outer space and underwater.
10 October	The Moscow Treaty on a partial nuclear test ban, signed on 5 August, comes into force.
22-23 October	In a military exercise (Operation "Big Lift"), 14 500 American soldiers are flown from the United States to Germany to demonstrate the ability of the United States to reinforce NATO forces in Europe rapidly in an emergency.
22 November	President Kennedy is assassinated in Dallas, Texas.

1964

1 August	Manlio Brosio (Italy) succeeds Dirk Stikker as Secretary General of NATO.
14 October	Khrushchev is removed from office. He is replaced by Leonid Brezhnev as General Secretary of the CPSU and by Alexei Kosygin as Prime Minister.
16 October	China explodes its first atomic bomb.

1965

6 April	The world's first commercial satellite "Early Bird" is launched by the United States. Successfully tested as first global communications system for telephone, TV and telegraphic communications.
7 April	Soviet and East German authorities block land access to Berlin at intervals for one week when the Parliament of the Federal Republic of Germany holds its plenary session in West Berlin's Congress Hall.
23 April	Soviet Union launches its first communications satellite.
31 May-1 June	Meeting of NATO Defence Ministers in Paris pays special attention to the defence problems of Greece and Turkey, and agrees to consider a proposal for improving consultation and extending participation in the planning of nuclear forces.
9 September	At a press conference President de Gaulle announces that French military integration within NATO would end by 1969.
20 October	The North Atlantic Council approves the revised missions of the Major NATO Commanders and the Canada-US Regional Planning Group.
14-16 December	The North Atlantic Council meeting in Ministerial session in Paris accepts new procedures designed to improve the annual process of reviewing the defence efforts of member countries and agreeing upon their force contributions.

1966

10 March	President de Gaulle formally announces France's intention of withdrawing from the integrated military structure of the Alliance.
14 December	The Defence Planning Committee establishes the Nuclear Defence Affairs Committee and the Nuclear Planning Group.

1967

18 January	Inauguration of NATO Defense College in Rome.
31 March	Official opening ceremony of SHAPE at Casteau, near Mons, Belgium.
6-7 April	First meeting of the Nuclear Planning Group in Washington.
21 April	Military régime takes over power in Greece.

14 June	The North Atlantic Council meeting in Luxembourg reviews the Middle East situation following the Six-Day War between Israel and its Arab neighbours.
16 October	Official opening of new NATO Headquarters in Brussels.
12 December	The Nuclear Defence Affairs Committee holds a meeting in Brussels to examine the Report of the Nuclear Planning Group on strategic nuclear forces, antiballistic missiles, the tactical use of nuclear weapons, and national participation in nuclear planning.
13-14 December	The North Atlantic Council approves the Harmel Report on the Future Tasks of the Alliance. The Defence Planning Committee adopts NATO's new strategic concept of flexible response and approves the establishment of a Standing Naval Force Atlantic (STANAVFORLANT).

1968

19 January	The United States and the Soviet Union table a draft nuclear non-proliferation treaty at the Geneva Disarmament Conference.
24-25 June	The Ministerial meeting of the North Atlantic Council in Reykjavik, Iceland reviews current measures affecting access routes to Berlin and issues a Declaration on Mutual and Balanced Force Reductions.
20-21 August	Soviet, Polish, East German, Bulgarian and Hungarian troops invade Czechoslovakia.
12 September	Albania renounces its membership of the Warsaw Treaty Organisation.
13-14 November	Formation of the Eurogroup.
15-16 November	The North Atlantic Council denounces Soviet actions in Czechoslovakia as contrary to the basic principles of the United Nations Charter and issues a warning to the USSR.

1969

| 28 May | Establishment of the naval on-call force in the Mediterranean (NAVOCFORMED). |
| 8-10 December | First meeting of the Committee on the Challenges of Modern Society (CCMS), established by the North Atlantic Council on 6 November, on the basis of a proposal by recently-elected US President Nixon. |

1970

| 5 March | Nuclear Non-Proliferation Treaty signed on 1 July 1968 comes into force. |

20 March	First NATO communications satellite launched from Cape Kennedy.
16 April	Opening in Vienna of US-USSR negotiations on strategic arms limitations (SALT).
11 June	The Defence Planning Committee in Ministerial session discusses the continuing expansion of the Soviet presence in the Mediterranean and welcomes the activation of the naval on-call force for the Mediterranean.
2-4 December	At Ministerial meetings of the Council and Defence Planning Committee (DPC) in Brussels the United States announces that it will not reduce US forces in Europe except in the context of reciprocal East-West action. The DPC adopts the study on "Alliance Defence in the '70s." Ten European countries adopt a special European Defence Improvement Programme.

1971

2 February	Second NATO communications satellite launched from Cape Kennedy.
1 October	Joseph Luns (the Netherlands) succeeds Manlio Brosio as Secretary General of NATO.
5-6 October	Former NATO Secretary General, Manlio Brosio is appointed to conduct exploratory talks on mutual and balanced force reductions with the Soviet and other interested governments.

1972

26 May	Signature in Moscow of interim agreement on strategic arms limitations (SALT) and anti-ballistic missile systems (ABM).
30-31 May	At its Ministerial meeting in Bonn, the North Atlantic Council agrees to start multinational preparatory talks for a Conference on Security and Cooperation in Europe (CSCE). Multilateral explorations on mutual and balanced force reductions (MBFR) are proposed by the countries participating in NATO's integrated military structure.
3 June	Quadripartite Agreement on Berlin signed by Foreign Ministers of France, United Kingdom, United States and the USSR.
21 November	Opening of SALT II negotiations in Geneva.
22 November	Opening in Helsinki of multilateral preparatory talks on a CSCE.

| 21 December | Signature in East Berlin of the "Basic Treaty" between the Federal Republic of Germany and the German Democratic Republic. |

1973

1 January	Denmark, Ireland and the United Kingdom join the European Economic Community (EEC).
31 Jan.-29 June	Multilateral exploratory talks on MBFR in Vienna.
11 May	Inauguration of Standing Naval Force Channel (STANAVFORCHAN).
3-7 July	Opening of Conference on Security and Cooperation in Europe (CSCE) in Helsinki.
6-24 October	Arab-Israeli Yom Kippur War.
30 October	Negotiations on Mutual and Balanced Force Reductions (MBFR) open in Vienna.

1974

25 April	Military coup d'état in Portugal.
26 June	NATO Heads of Government meeting in Brussels sign a Declaration on Atlantic Relations approved and published by the North Atlantic Council in Ottawa on 19 June.
23 July	Konstantinos Karamanlis becomes Prime Minister of Greece following the resignation of the military government.
14 August	Withdrawal of Greek forces from integrated military structure of NATO.
23-24 November	President Ford and General Secretary Brezhnev, meeting in Vladivostok, agree on steps towards limitation of US-USSR strategic nuclear arms.

1975

| 31 May | ELDO and ESRO merge to become the European Space Agency (ESA). Member countries: Belgium, Denmark, France, Federal Republic of Germany, Italy, Ireland, the Netherlands, Spain, Sweden, Switzerland and United Kingdom. |
| 31 July-1 August | The Heads of State and Government of the 35 participating states sign the CSCE Helsinki Final Act. |

1976

| 21-22 January | At the meeting of the Nuclear Planning Group (NPG) in Hamburg, NATO Defence Ministers discuss the continuing |

increase in Soviet strategic nuclear capabilities and review prospects for stabilisation through SALT.

2 February	Establishment of the Independent European Programme Group with the participation of all European member countries of NATO to provide cooperation in the research, development and production of equipment.
20-21 May	At the North Atlantic Council in Oslo, Foreign Ministers review East-West relations and progress towards implementation of Final Act of CSCE and discuss prospects for MBFR.
9-10 December	The North Atlantic Council rejects proposals by Warsaw Treaty countries to renounce first use of nuclear weapons and to restrict Alliance membership and calls for all CSCE states to renounce the threat or use of force including all types of weapons in accordance with the UN Charter and Helsinki Final Act.

1977

10-11 May	North Atlantic Council meeting in London with participation of newly-elected US President Carter and other Heads of State and Government. Initiation of a long-term defence programme.
4 October	CSCE Follow-up Meeting in Belgrade (4 October 1977 - 9 March 1978).
12 October	Establishment of NPG High Level Group on theatre nuclear force modernisation.

1978

30-31 May	Meeting of the North Atlantic Council with participation of Heads of State and Government in Washington.
31 Oct.-11 Dec.	CSCE Experts' Meeting on the Peaceful Settlement of Disputes, Montreux.
18 November	Third NATO communications satellite launched from Cape Canaveral, Florida.
5-6 December	Approval of Airborne Early Warning and Control System (AWACS).

1979

13 Feb.-26 March	CSCE Experts' Meeting on Mediterranean Cooperation, Valleta.
11 April	Establishment of Special Group to study arms control aspects of theatre nuclear systems. (The Special Group concluded its work on 11 December 1979).

18 June	SALT II agreement signed in Vienna by President Carter and General Secretary Brezhnev. (The agreement was not ratified by the United States).
4 November	Seizure of the United States Embassy in Teheran and 53 hostages by Islamic revolutionaries.
12 December	Special Meeting of Foreign and Defence Ministers in Brussels. "Double-track" decision on theatre nuclear force modernisation including the deployment in Europe of US ground-launched Cruise and Pershing II systems and a parallel and complementary arms control effort to obviate the need for such deployments.
25-26 December	Soviet invasion of Afghanistan.
29 December	Special meeting of North Atlantic Council following Soviet invasion of Afghanistan on 25-26 December.

1980

24 January	Members of the Alliance participating in the 12 December 1979 Special Meeting establish the Special Consultative Group on arms control involving theatre nuclear forces.
18 Feb.-3 March	CSCE Forum on Scientific Cooperation, Hamburg.
4 May	Death of President Tito of Yugoslavia.
31 August	Gdansk Agreements, leading to establishment and official recognition of independent Polish trade union "Solidarity".
12 September	Turkish military leadership takes over the administration of the country.
22 September	War breaks out between Iraq and Iran.
20 October	Reintegration of Greek forces into the integrated military structure of the Alliance.
11 November	Opening of CSCE Follow-up Meeting in Madrid.
9-12 December	Ministerial meetings of the Council and Defence Planning Committee reflect concern over the situation with regard to Poland and the continuing Soviet occupation of Afghanistan.

1981

1 January	Greece becomes the 10th member of the European Economic Community.
23 February	Abortive attempt by rebel civil guards to overthrow Spanish caretaker government.
6 October	Assassination of Egyptian President Sadat.
27 October	Soviet submarine grounded in Swedish territorial waters.

18 November	President Reagan announces new arms control initiatives including intermediate-range nuclear force (INF) negotiations and strategic arms reduction talks (START).
30 November	The United States and the Soviet Union open Geneva negotiations on intermediate-range nuclear forces (INF).
10-11 December	Signature of the Protocol of Accession of Spain to the North Atlantic Treaty.
13 December	Imposition of martial law in Poland.

1982

11 January	Special Ministerial Session of the North Atlantic Council issues a Declaration on Events in Poland.
2 April-14 June	The Falklands Conflict.
30 May	Spain becomes the 16th member of the North Atlantic Treaty Organisation.
10 June	Summit Meeting of the North Atlantic Council in Bonn. Heads of State and Government issue the Bonn Declaration setting out the Alliance Programme for Peace in Freedom.
30 June	Opening of Strategic Arms Reduction Talks (START) in Geneva.

1983

23 March	President Reagan announces a comprehensive research programme aimed at eliminating the threat posed by strategic nuclear missiles (Strategic Defence Initiative).
22 July	Ending of martial law in Poland. New laws reinforce government controls.
1 September	A South Korean airliner with 269 people on board is shot down by Soviet air defence off the coast of Sakhalin.
9 September	Conclusion of CSCE Follow-up Meeting in Madrid.
25 October	Military intervention in Grenada by United States and East Caribbean forces.
25 Oct.-11 Nov.	Preparatory meeting in Helsinki for Stockholm Conference on Security and Confidence Building Measures and Disarmament in Europe (CDE).
27 October	The Montebello Decision. Defence Ministers meeting in the NATO Nuclear Planning Group in Montebello, Canada announce their decision to withdraw a further 1 400 warheads from Europe, bringing the total of such withdrawals since 1979 to 2 400.
23 November	Deliveries of Ground-Launched Cruise Missile components to the United Kingdom mark the beginning of

	NATO's intermediate range nuclear force deployments (INF). Decision by the Soviet Union to discontinue the current round of negotiations in Geneva on intermediate-range nuclear forces (INF).
8 December	Conclusion of the current round of US-Soviet Geneva negotiations on Strategic Arms Reductions (START) without a date being set by the Soviet side for their resumption.
8-9 December	Foreign Ministers meeting in the Ministerial Session of the North Atlantic Council issue the Declaration of Brussels expressing their determination to seek a balanced and constructive relationship with the East and calling on the Soviet Union and other Warsaw Treaty countries to respond.
13 December	Formation of a civilian government in Turkey following parliamentary elections under a new constitution.

1984

17 January	Opening of the Stockholm Conference on Security and Confidence Building Measures and Disarmament in Europe (CDE).
21 March-30 April	CSCE Experts' Meeting on the Peaceful Settlement of Disputes, Athens.
31 May	NATO Foreign Ministers issue the Washington Statement on East-West Relations.
7-9 June	Summit meeting in London. Heads of State and Government of the seven major industrialised countries issue a declaration on East-West Relations and Arms Control.
12 June	Foreign Ministers of the seven countries of the Western European Union meeting in Paris decide to reactivate the WEU.
25 June	Lord Carrington (the United Kingdom) succeeds Joseph Luns as Secretary General of NATO.
16-26 October	CSCE Seminar on Economic, Scientific and Cultural Cooperation in the Mediterranean, Venice.
26-27 October	Foreign and Defence Ministers of the member countries of the Western European Union publish the "Rome Declaration" announcing their decision to increase cooperation within the WEU.
7 December	Presentation by the Secretary General of NATO of the first Atlantic Award to Per Markussen (Denmark), for his contri-

bution over many years to the objectives of the Atlantic Alliance.

1985

11 March	Mikhail Gorbachev becomes General Secretary of the Communist Party of the Soviet Union following the death of Konstantin Chernenko.
12 March	The United States and the USSR begin new arms control negotiations in Geneva, encompassing defence and space systems, strategic nuclear forces and intermediate-range nuclear forces.
26 April	The 1955 Treaty of Friendship, Cooperation and Mutual Assistance, establishing the Warsaw Treaty Organisation, is extended for 20 years by leaders of the seven member states.
7 May-17 June	CSCE Experts' Meeting on Human Rights, Ottawa.
15 Oct.-25 Nov.	CSCE Cultural Forum in Budapest.
12 November	Professor van der Beugel (the Netherlands) becomes the second recipient of NATO's Atlantic Award for outstanding services to the Atlantic Alliance.
19-21 November	At the Geneva Summit, United States President Ronald Reagan and Soviet leader Mikhail Gorbachev agree in principle on a reduction of strategic nuclear forces by 50 percent and on an interim INF agreement.
21 November	President Reagan reports on his Geneva talks with Soviet leader Mikhail Gorbachev at a special meeting of the North Atlantic Council with the participation of Heads of State and Government and Foreign Ministers.

1986

1 January	Portugal and Spain become members of the European Economic Community (EEC).
12 March	In a referendum organised by Prime Minister Felipe Gonzalez, Spanish voters support the continued membership of Spain in the Atlantic Alliance without participation in NATO's integrated military structure.
15 April	In response to terrorist attacks attributed to Libya, United States forces attack targets in Tripoli and Benghazi.
15 April-26 May	CSCE Experts' Meeting on Human Contacts, Berne.
26 April	Nuclear accident at the Chernobyl power station in the Soviet Union.
29-30 May	Foreign Ministers issue a Statement on the Ministerial meeting of the North Atlantic Council in Halifax, Canada,

calling on the Soviet Union to join them in taking "bold new steps" to promote peace, security and a productive East-West dialogue. Ministers establish a High-Level Task Force on Conventional Arms Control.

22 September	End of Stockholm Conference on Confidence and Security Building Measures and Disarmament in Europe (CDE). Concluding document (dated 19 September) includes mandatory measures for notification, observation and on-site inspection of military manoeuvres of participating countries.
13 October	At a special session of the North Atlantic Council attended by Foreign and Defence Ministers in Brussels, US Secretary of State Schultz briefs the Council on the negative outcome of the Reykjavik Summit 11-13 October.
21-22 October	Ministerial meeting of NATO's Nuclear Planning Group in Gleneagles, Scotland. Defence Ministers express support for President Reagan's arms control programme.
4 November	The third CSCE Follow-up Conference opens in Vienna.
24 November	Professor Karl Kaiser (Federal Republic of Germany) receives the third Atlantic Award for services to the Alliance.
11 December	NATO Foreign Ministers issue the Brussels Declaration on Conventional Arms Control calling for negotiations on conventional stability, aimed at eliminating existing disparities from the Atlantic to the Urals and establishing conventional stability at lower levels; and on further confidence and security building measures.

1987

26 January	Spain resumes negotiations with its NATO partners on the future role of Spanish forces with the Alliance.
17 February	Talks open in Vienna between NATO and Warsaw Treaty countries on a mandate for negotiations on conventional forces in Europe from the Atlantic to the Urals.
27 March	NATO Secretary General Lord Carrington, following an emergency meeting of the North Atlantic Council, offers to use his good offices to help to resolve the dispute in the Aegean between Greece and Turkey.
4 June	The parliament of the Federal Republic of Germany formally endorses a proposal calling for the elimination of intermediate-range (INF) and shorter-range (SRINF) missiles in Europe.

5 June	The Canadian Government announces its decision to re-direct its commitment to the reinforcement of Europe from the Northern to the Central Region.
19 June	Chancellor of the Federal Republic Helmut Kohl proposes the formation of a joint Franco-German brigade as the first step towards a joint European fighting force.
22 July	Soviet leader Mikhail Gorbachev announces Soviet readiness to eliminate all intermediate-range nuclear weapons including those deployed in the 1987 Asian part of the Soviet Union in the context of a United States-Soviet INF treaty.
23 July	Soviet negotiators present a proposal at the United States-Soviet Geneva arms control negotiations accepting the principle of a "double-zero option" eliminating Soviet and US land-based intermediate range (LRINF and SRINF) missiles on a global basis.
20 August	Western European Union experts meeting in The Hague consider joint action in the Gulf to ensure freedom of navigation in the oil shipping lanes of the region.
28-30 August	United States inspectors attend military manoeuvres near Minsk, the first such inspection to take place under the provisions of the September 1986 Stockholm Document.
5-7 October	Soviet inspectors attend NATO exercises in Turkey, the first such inspection to take place in an Alliance country under the provisions of the September 1986 Stockholm Document.
27 October	Foreign and Defence Ministers of the seven member countries of the Western European Union adopt "The Hague Platform on European Security Interests".
25 November	Presentation of NATO's annual Atlantic Award to Pierre Harmel (Belgium), author of the 1967 Harmel Report.
8 December	US President Reagan and Soviet Leader Mikhail Gorbachev, meeting at the beginning of their three-day summit talks, sign the Washington Treaty on Intermediate Range Nuclear Forces (INF), eliminating on a global basis land-based intermediate-range nuclear missiles.
9 December	The United States and the Soviet Union reach agreement on measures allowing the monitoring of nuclear explosions at each other's test sites.
10 December	At the end of their 3-day summit meeting in Washington, US President Reagan and Soviet Leader Mikhail Gorbachev pledge deep cuts in strategic arms and instruct

negotiators in Geneva to draft an agreement in line with the 1972 ABM Treaty.

11 December	The North Atlantic Council marks the 20th anniversary of the Harmel report. The Secretary of State of the United States and the Foreign Ministers of Belgium, Federal Republic of Germany, Italy, the Netherlands and the United Kingdom sign bilateral agreements relating to the implementation of the INF Treaty and its on-site inspection and verification procedures.

1988

22 January	Establishment of a Joint Security Council by the Governments of the Federal Republic of Germany and of France. The two Governments also sign an agreement relating to the formation of a joint Franco-German Army Brigade.
2-3 March	Summit meeting of the North Atlantic Council in Brussels emphasises Allied unity and reasserts the common objectives and principles and the continuing validity of Alliance policies. A Statement on Conventional Arms Control is issued calling for significant steps to bring about progress in eliminating conventional force disparities through negotiations on conventional stability.
15 May	Beginning of Soviet troop withdrawals from Afghanistan.
26-27 May	NATO Defence Ministers commission the Executive Working Group to conduct a review of roles, risks and responsibilities shared by member nations in the context of their efforts to sustain the credibility and effectiveness of collective security and defence.
31 May	During a five-day Summit meeting in Moscow, President Reagan and General Secretary Gorbachev exchange documents implementing the recently ratified December 1987 INF Treaty and sign bilateral agreements on nuclear testing and in other fields.
9-10 June	At the first Ministerial meeting of the North Atlantic Council to be held in Madrid, Foreign Ministers review the positive progress in East-West relations registered at the Moscow Summit meeting, and welcome the evolution of the Spanish contribution to the common defence.
24 June	Announcement of the formation of a NATO Composite Force to reinforce Northern Norway in periods of tension or hostility, to replace the Canadian CAST Brigade which

	will be reassigned to the Central Region in accordance with the plans of the Canadian Government.
28 June-1 July	The 19th CPSU Conference in Moscow sets in train a programme of political, constitutional and legal reforms.
1 July	Manfred Woerner, former Minister of Defence of the Federal Republic of Germany, succeeds Lord Carrington as Secretary General of NATO.
20 August	Entry into force of a ceasefire in the Gulf War between Iran and Iraq, in the framework of UN Security Council Resolution 598.
14 November	Portugal and Spain sign the Treaty of Accession to the Western European Union.
5 December	Paul Nitze, Special Adviser on Arms Control to President Reagan, receives the 1988 Atlantic Award.
7 December	President Gorbachev, in the course of a major address to the UN General Assembly, announces unilateral Soviet conventional force reductions. A major earthquake in Armenia devastates several cities and causes massive loss of life.
8 December	Alliance Foreign Ministers welcome Soviet reductions in conventional forces and publish a statement outlining the Alliance's proposals for forthcoming negotiations on conventional stability and further confidence and security building measures.

1989

7-11 January	149 countries participate in an international Conference on Chemical Weapons in Paris.
18 January	President Gorbachev provides further details of intended reductions in Soviet armed forces referred to in his address to the United Nations on 7 December 1988, announcing cuts of 14.2 percent in Soviet defence expenditure and 19.5 percent in the production of arms and military equipment.
19 January	Conclusion of the Vienna CSCE Follow-up Meeting and adoption of a Concluding Document including mandates for new negotiations on Conventional Armed Forces in Europe (CFE) and new negotiations on Confidence and Security Building Measures (CSBMs).
23-27 January	Future reductions in conventional forces and military budgets are announced by the German Democratic Republic, Poland, Hungary, Czechoslovakia, and Bulgaria. They are

welcomed by Alliance countries as contributions to the reduction of conventional force imbalances in Europe.

2 February	Final meeting of the Vienna negotiations on Mutual and Balanced Force Reductions.
11 February	The Central Committee of the Hungarian Communist Party endorses "gradual and steady" transition to a multi-party political system.
15 February	The Soviet Union completes the withdrawal of military forces from Afghanistan in accordance with the schedule announced by President Gorbachev.
6 March	Foreign Ministers of CSCE states meet in Vienna to mark the opening of new negotiations on Conventional Armed Forces in Europe (CFE) among the 23 members of NATO and the Warsaw Treaty Organisation and on Confidence and Security Building Measures among all 35 CSCE participating states.
26 March	The first multi-candidate elections to the new USSR Congress of People's Deputies result in major set-backs for official Party candidates in many constituencies.
4 April	The fortieth anniversary of the signing of the North Atlantic Treaty is marked by a special session of the North Atlantic Council and other ceremonies at NATO and in capitals.
5 April	Agreements signed in Warsaw by Government and opposition negotiators on measures leading to political reforms in Poland including free elections and registration of the banned trade union movement Solidarity.
18 Apil-23 May	CSCE Information Forum, London.
12 May	President Bush proposes "Open Skies" régime to increase confidence and transparency with respect to military activities. The proposal envisages reciprocal opening of airspace and acceptance of overflights of national territory by participating countries.
29-30 May	Summit Meeting of the North Atlantic Council in Brussels attended by Heads of State and Government. Announcement by President Bush of major new initiatives for conventional force reductions in Europe. Adoption of the Alliance's Comprehensive Concept of Arms Control and Disarmament and publication of a Summit Declaration.
30 May-23 June	First meeting of the CSCE Conference on the Human Dimension (CDH) in Paris.
31 May	During a visit to the Federal Republic of Germany President Bush outlines proposals for promoting free elec-

	tions and pluralism in Eastern Europe and dismantling the Berlin Wall.
3-4 June	Chinese leaders use armed forces in Peking to suppress unarmed student-led popular demonstrations in favour of democracy, causing large-scale loss of life and leading to major unrest in other cities, purges and infringements of basic rights.
4 and 18 June	Free elections for the Polish Senate and partial elections involving 35 percent of seats in the Sejm result in major electoral success for Solidarity.
8-9 June	Ministerial Meeting of the Defence Planning Committee. Defence Ministers consider implications for defence planning of Western proposals for reduction of conventional forces in Europe.
16 June	Imre Nagy, leader of the 1956 Hungarian revolution who was hanged in 1958, is reburied with full honours in Budapest.
19 June	Re-opening of Strategic Arms Reduction Talks (START) in Geneva.
2 July	Death of veteran Soviet Foreign Minister and former President Andrei Gromyko.
9 August	A statement is issued by NATO's Secretary General on behalf of the Allies concerning the situation of ethnic Turks in Bulgaria, calling upon the Bulgarian government to respond positively to appeals to meet its responsibilities in accordance with CSCE commitments.
24 August	Tadeusz Mazowiecki becomes Prime Minister of the first non-communist led government in Poland in 40 years. The Polish United Workers' (Communist) Party retains four ministries.
10 September	Hungary opens its Western border, enabling large numbers of East German refugees to leave the country for destinations in the West.
3 October	Following the exodus of 6 390 East German citizens from Western embassies in Prague on 1 October under arrangements made by the East German Government, some 20 000 East German emigrants congregate in the Prague and Warsaw embassies of the Federal Republic of Germany.
6-7 October	Mikhail Gorbachev, attending 40th Anniversary Parade in East Berlin, urges reforms in the GDR.
16 October	CSCE Meeting on Environmental Protection in Sofia.

18 October	Erich Honecker, General Secretary of the Socialist (Communist) Unity Party since 1971, is replaced by Egon Krenz as leader of the German Democratic Republic as East German citizens demonstrate for political reform and large numbers of refugees continue to leave the German Democratic Republic through Prague and Budapest.
23 October	The new constitution adopted by the Hungarian Parliament on 18 October brings into being the Republic of Hungary as a "free, democratic, independent legal state" and opens the way for multiparty elections in 1990.
7 November	Resignation of the East German Cabinet following rallies in many cities calling for free elections and the abolition of the Communist monopoly on power and calls from within the Party for major changes at the highest level. The move is followed the next day by the joint resignation of the ruling Politburo.
9-10 November	Opening of the Berlin Wall. In an atmosphere of political uncertainty and a crisis of authority in East Berlin, East and West Berliners tear down the wall and celebrate the beginning of the process of unification. Following widespread demonstrations and demand for political reform, the government of the German Democratic Republic announces the lifting of travel restrictions to the West and sets up new crossing points.
10 November	Removal of Todor Zhivkov, Bulgarian Communist Party leader since 1954, followed by further sweeping changes in the party leadership.
14 November	East German Parliament elects Hans Modrow as Prime Minister. Portugal and Spain sign the Treaty of Accession to the Western European Union.
17 November	Violent dispersal of Prague student demonstrations triggers popular movement against the government. Emergence of Civic Forum, led by Vaclav Havel.
20 November	Mass demonstrations in Leipzig voice popular call for German unification.
24 November	Resignation of the Czechoslovak Party leadership. Karel Urbanek becomes General Secretary and invites dialogue with Civic Forum.
3 December	Resignation of new East German Politburo and Central Committee amid revelations of Communist leadership's misrule and corruption.

4 December	NATO Summit Meeting in Brussels. US President George Bush briefs NATO leaders on his talks with Soviet President Gorbachev at the US-Soviet Summit Meeting in Malta on 2-3 December. The Summit Meeting of leaders of the Warsaw Treaty Organisation in Moscow publishes a joint statement denouncing the 1968 invasion of Czechoslovakia by Warsaw Pact forces and repudiates the Brezhnev Doctrine of limited sovereignty.
7 December	Resignation of President Gustav Husak and formation of coalition government in Czechoslovakia. NATO's Atlantic Award for 1989 is bestowed on Sir Michael Howard, President and co-founder of the International Institute for Strategic Studies (IISS).
11 December	Popular demonstrations in Bulgaria lead to the promise of free elections and renunciation of the leading role of the Communist Party.
14-15 December	Ministerial Meeting of the North Atlantic Council in Brussels. Foreign Ministers review accelerating political change in Central and Eastern Europe.
19 December	Soviet Foreign Minister Eduard Shevardnadze visits NATO Headquarters for talks with NATO Secretary General Manfred Woerner and Permanent Representatives of NATO countries, the first such visit by a Minister of a Central or Eastern European government.
20 December	Troops and police open fire on thousands of anti-government protesters in the Romanian town of Timisoara.
22 December	Fall of Ceausescu regime. Nicolai Ceausescu is arrested by the Romanian armed forces and executed on 25 December. The National Salvation Front headed by Ion Iliescu takes control and promises free elections.
29 December	The Polish Parliament abolishes the leading role of the Communist Party and restores the country's name as the Republic of Poland. Vaclav Havel is elected President of Czechoslovakia.

1990

15 January	Bulgarian government abolishes the Communist Party's 44-year monopoly on political power.
16 Jan.-5 Feb.	35-nation Seminar on Military Doctrines in Vienna in the framework of the CSCE.
6 February	In an unprecedented speech to the Plenary Session of the Central Committee of the Communist Party of the Soviet Union, Mikhail Gorbachev addresses major aspects of his

reform programme including the abandonment of the leading role of the Communist Party and the introduction of political pluralism.

12-14 February	Foreign Ministers of NATO and Warsaw Treaty Organisation countries, with observers from other CSCE states, meet in Ottawa at the opening of the "Open Skies" Conference.
13 February	On the margins of the "Open Skies" Conference in Ottawa, agreement is reached by the Foreign Ministers concerned to hold discussions on external aspects of the establishment of German unity in a "Two Plus Four" framework. NATO and Warsaw Treaty Organisation Foreign Ministers also agree on steps to enable a CFE agreement to be concluded in 1990.
3 March	Czechoslovak Foreign Minister Jiri Dienstbier visits NATO Headquarters for discussions with NATO Secretary General Manfred Woerner.
8 March	At a meeting attended by Chancellor Helmut Kohl, consultations take place in the North Atlantic Council on the position of the Government of the Federal Republic on developments in Germany and related security matters.
11 March	The Lithuanian Parliament votes to break away from the Soviet Union and regain its independence.
17 March	Warsaw Treaty Organisation Foreign Ministers meeting in Prague support the continuation of both NATO and the Warsaw Pact.
18 March	In their first free elections in 40 years the citizens of the German Democratic Republic give an overwhelming majority to the conservative "Alliance for Germany", marking a further key step in the process of the unification of Germany.
19 March-11 April	CSCE Conference on Economic Cooperation in Europe, Bonn.
21 March	Krzystof Skubiszewski, Foreign Minister of Poland, visits NATO Headquarters for discussions with Secretary General Manfred Woerner and Permanent Representatives of NATO countries.
26 March	The Czechoslovak Government orders border installations along its frontiers with Austria and the Federal Republic of Germany to be dismantled.
27 March	Formal entry of Portugal and Spain to the WEU on completion of the ratification process.

7 April	Elections in Hungary result in a decisive victory for the Hungarian Democratic Forum (centre-right party).
12 April	The coalition government of the German Democratic Republic pronounces itself in favour of unification with the Federal Republic of Germany on the basis of Article 23 of the Basic Law and the membership of the unified country in the North Atlantic Alliance.
3 May	President Bush announces the cancellation of modernisation programmes for nuclear artillery shells deployed in Europe and for a "follow-on" to the LANCE short-range nuclear missile. He calls for negotiations on US and Soviet short-range nuclear missiles to begin shortly after a CFE treaty is signed.
4 May	The Latvian Parliament declares the independence of the Baltic Republic.
8 May	The Estonian Parliament modifies the Republic's name and constitution and restores its pre-war flag and national anthem.
9-10 May	NATO Defence Ministers, meeting in the Nuclear Planning Group in Kananaskis, Canada, discuss the implications of political changes taking place in Europe for NATO's security policy.
20 May	Following elections in Romania, former Communist Government member Ion Iliescu is elected President despite opposition accusations of electoral irregularities. The National Salvation Front obtains a majority in Parliament.
22-23 May	NATO Defence Ministers, meeting in the Defence Planning Committee, assess the implications for NATO security policy of the changes taking place in Europe and initiate a review of NATO's military strategy. Hungary's new Premier, Josef Antall, announces his government's intention to withdraw from the Warsaw Treaty Organisation following negotiations.
30 May	Boris Yeltsin is elected President of the Russian Republic in the third round of elections.
30 May-2 June	US-Soviet Summit Meeting in Washington.
5 June	Foreign Ministers of the 35 countries participating in the second CSCE Conference on the Human Dimension (CHD2) in Copenhagen agree to accord observer status to Albania.
7-8 June	At the Ministerial Meeting of the North Atlantic Council at Turnberry in Scotland, Alliance Foreign Ministers publish a

	"Message from Turnberry" in which they express their determination to seize the opportunities resulting from the changes in Europe and extend to the Soviet Union and all other European countries the hand of friendship and co-operation.
8 June	Parliamentary elections in Czechoslovakia. Civic Forum and allied parties win a majority in the Federal Assembly.
10 and 17 June	Elections in Bulgaria result in a parliamentary majority for the Bulgarian Socialist Party.
18 June	NATO announces the award of 70 research fellowships for 1990/91 including 55 fellowships for research on democratic institutions awarded for the first time to citizens of both NATO and Central and Eastern European countries.
28 June	At the Copenhagen CSCE Conference on the Human Dimension, Eastern European countries (excluding Albania, which joined the CSCE process in June 1991) commit themselves to multiparty parliamentary democracy and to the rule of law.
29 June	Geza Jeszensky, Foreign Minister of Hungary, is received at NATO Headquarters by Secretary General Manfred Woerner.
2 July	Monetary union is established between the Federal Republic of Germany and the German Democratic Republic. Taro Nakayama, Foreign Minister of Japan, is received by Secretary General Manfred Woerner at NATO Headquarters.
6 July	NATO Heads of State and Government meeting in London publish the "London Declaration" on a Transformed North Atlantic Alliance. The Declaration outlines proposals for developing cooperation with the countries of Central and Eastern Europe across a wide spectrum of political and military activity, including the establishment of regular diplomatic liaison between those countries and NATO.
10 July	The Foreign Minister of the German Democratic Republic, Markus Meckel, visits NATO.
13-17 July	NATO Secretary General Manfred Woerner visits Moscow at the invitation of Foreign Minister Shevardnadze for talks with the Soviet leadership following publication of the London Declaration.
16 July	Chancellor Kohl and President Gorbachev agree on measures enabling Germany to regain full sovereignty and to exercise its right to remain a full member of the North Atlantic Alliance.

17 July	Conclusion of the "Two Plus Four" Conference in Paris on the unification of Germany.
18 July	Hungarian Prime Minister Josef Antall visits NATO Headquarters.
2 August	Iraqi troops invade Kuwait following a dispute between the two countries on exploitation of oil rights in the Gulf.
6 August	The UN Security Council agrees unanimously on wide-ranging sanctions against Iraq and demands Iraqi withdrawal from the occupied territory of Kuwait.
8 August	The UN Security Council declares the Iraqi announcement of its de facto annexation of Kuwait null and void.
10 August	Special Meeting of the North Atlantic Council at the level of Foreign Ministers for consultations and exchange of information on developments in the Gulf.
22 August	The legislature of the German Democratic Republic votes in favour of the unification of the GDR with the Federal Republic of Germany on 3 October 1990 and agrees to hold elections in the unified country on 2 December 1990.
4 September	The nine member countries of the Western European Union agree on guidelines for the coordination of their naval operations in the Gulf region in order to reinforce the international embargo against Iraq. A number of WEU and other countries send forces to the area.
5-8 September	NATO Secretary General Manfred Woerner visits the Czech and Slovak Federal Republic for discussions with the President, Prime Minister and President of the Parliament.
7 September	Consultations continue in the North Atlantic Council on political, military and economic developments in the Gulf in the framework of the harmonisation of allied policies and the commitment of the Allies to work for the application of United Nations resolutions in relation to the Gulf crisis.
10 September	The United States Secretary of State James Baker briefs a special meeting of the North Atlantic Council in Ministerial session on the outcome of the US-Soviet summit meeting on the Gulf crisis.
12 September	In a statement issued on the occasion of the signing of the "Two Plus Four" Treaty in Moscow, the Alliance welcomes this historic agreement which paves the way for the unification of Germany and its return to full sovereignty.
13-15 September	NATO Secretary General Manfred Woerner on his first visit to Poland addresses the Sejm on the historic opportunities

	for creating a durable order of peace and prosperity in Europe based on cooperation and friendship.
14 September	Initiation of Allied consultations in NATO's Special Consultative Group on future negotiations on short-range nuclear forces as called for in the London Declaration. In a statement condemning the forced entry by Iraqi soldiers into the residences of NATO embassies in Kuwait, the Alliance calls upon Iraq to free those seized and to refrain from further aggressive acts.
24 Sept.-19 Oct.	CSCE Meeting on the Mediterranean, Palma de Mallorca.
1-2 October	CSCE Conference of Foreign Ministers in New York passes resolution condemning Iraqi aggression against Kuwait.
3 October	On the day of German unification the North Atlantic Council marks the occasion by a special meeting and welcomes the united country as a full member of the Alliance.
15 October	Mikhail Gorbachev is awarded the 1990 Nobel Peace Prize.
23 October	Petre Roman, Prime Minister of Romania, is received at NATO Headquarters by Secretary General Manfred Woerner.
25-26 October	Visit to NATO by First Deputy Minister of Defence and Chief of the Soviet General Staff, General M.A. Moiseyev.
26 October	Dr. Lajos Fur, Defence Minister of the Republic of Hungary, visits NATO.
15 November	Luben Gotsev, Foreign Minister of Bulgaria, is received at NATO Headquarters by Secretary General Manfred Woerner.
17 November	CSCE negotiators adopt the "Vienna Document" on Confidence and Security Building Measures (CSBMs).
19 November	In the framework of the CSCE Summit Meeting in Paris, the 22 member states of NATO and the Warsaw Treaty Organisation sign a major Treaty on Conventional Armed Forces in Europe and publish a Joint Declaration on non-aggression.
21 November	CSCE Heads of State and Government publish the Charter of Paris for a New Europe and endorse the adoption of the Vienna Document on Confidence and Security Building Measures (CSBMs).
22-25 November	NATO Secretary General Manfred Woerner visits Hungary.
26-28 November	The North Atlantic Assembly meeting in London accords associate delegate status to parliamentarians from the

	Soviet Union, Bulgaria, Czechoslovakia, Hungary and Poland.
6-7 December	Ministerial meeting of the Defence Planning Committee and the Nuclear Planning Group in Brussels. Defence Ministers support UN Resolution 678 demanding that Iraqi forces withdraw from Kuwait by January 1991. They review progress in developing a new strategic concept for NATO and other steps being taken to adapt NATO forces to the new strategic environment in Europe.
9 December	Lech Walesa is elected President of Poland.
11 December	Albania's Communist Party announces the legalisation of political opposition parties after 45 years of one-party dictatorship.
13 December	Romanian Secretary of State for Defence, General Vasile Ionel visits NATO.
15 December	At a Summit Meeting in Rome EC leaders open Intergovernmental Conferences on Economic and Monetary Union and Political Union.
17-18 December	Ministerial meeting of the North Atlantic Council in Brussels. Foreign Ministers review progress made since the July Summit Meeting in fulfilling the objectives of the London Declaration and issue a statement on the Gulf Crisis.
20 December	Soviet Foreign Minister Eduard Shevardnadze resigns, warning of the risks of renewed dictatorship in the Soviet Union.

1991

2 January	NATO deploys aircraft of the ACE Mobile Force (AMF) to south-east Turkey in an operational role.
8 January	Soviet troops are deployed around the Lithuanian capital to enforce mandatory conscription.
9 January	At a Geneva meeting between the US and Iraqi Foreign ministers, Iraq maintains its refusal to withdraw its forces from Kuwait.
11 January	NATO issues a statement urging Soviet authorities to refrain from using force and intimidation in the Baltic Republics.
15 Jan.-8 Feb.	CSCE Experts' Meeting on Peaceful Settlement of Disputes in Valetta proposes establishment of Dispute Settlement Mechanism.
17 January	Coalition forces launch air attacks against Iraq at the beginning of the Gulf War, following Iraq's refusal to with-

	draw from Kuwait in accordance with UN Security Council Resolutions.
9 February	Eighty-five percent of those voting in a Lithuanian plebiscite favour moves towards independence.
18 February	WEU Secretary General Wim van Eekelen visits NATO for discussions with NATO Secretary General Manfred Woerner in the framework of ongoing consultations on the development of the European Security and Defence Identity and cooperation between NATO and the WEU.
19 February	An eleventh-hour Soviet peace plan for averting the Gulf War falls short of Allied demands for an unconditional withdrawal of Iraqi forces.
24 February	Coalition forces begin ground offensive into Kuwait.
25 February	Representatives of the six countries of the Warsaw Pact convene in Budapest to announce the dissolution of its military structure. The Warsaw Pact Committee of Defence Ministers, its Joint Command, and its Military, Scientific and Technical Council are disbanded.
27 February	Czechoslovak Foreign Minister Jiri Dienstbier visits NATO.
28 February	Coalition forces liberate Kuwait. US President George Bush suspends allied coalition combat operations. Iraq accepts unconditionally all 12 UN resolutions relating to the withdrawal of its forces from Kuwait.
3 March	In referendums held in Estonia and Latvia, votes favour independence by 77 percent and 73 percent, respectively.
4 March	The Soviet legislature ratifies the Treaty permitting German unification, formally ending the authority of the quadripartite arrangements concerning Germany introduced after World War II.
5 March	NATO's Allied Mobile Force is withdrawn from Turkey following the end of the Gulf War.
13-26 March	Completion of United States withdrawal of missiles from Europe in accordance with the INF Treaty.
21 March	Visit to NATO by the President of the Czech and Slovak Federal Republic, Vaclav Havel. In a historic speech, President Havel addresses the North Atlantic Council.
31 March	Formal dissolution of the military structures of the Warsaw Pact.
5 April	Inauguration in London of the European Bank for Reconstruction and Development (EBRD), established to assist Eastern European countries and the Soviet Union in developing democracy and a market economy.

23-24 April	Visit by the Chairman of NATO's Military Committee, General Vigleik Eide, to the Czech and Slovak Federal Republic.
25-26 April	Conference on The Future of European Security in Prague sponsored jointly by the Foreign Minister of the Czech and Slovak Federal Republic and the Secretary General of NATO.
29 April	NATO's annual Atlantic Award is presented posthumously to Senator Giovanni Malagodi of Italy.
30 April	Visit to NATO Headquarters by Bulgarian Prime Minister, Dimitar Popov and Colonel General Mutafchiev, Minister of Defence.
7 May	The Yugoslav Defence Minister declares that his country is in a state of civil war.
12 May	Elimination by the Soviet Union of remaining SS20 missiles in accordance with the INF Treaty.
21 May	The US House of Representatives calls for a reduction of US troop strength in Europe from 250 000 to 100 000 by 1995. The Supreme Soviet passes a bill liberalising foreign travel and emigration.
23 May	Visit to NATO by Poland's Defence Minister, Piotr Kolodziejczyk.
28-29 May	Ministerial Meetings of NATO's Defence Planning Committee and Nuclear Planning Group. Ministers agree inter alia on the basis of a new NATO force structure.
28 May-7 June	CSCE Cultural Heritage Symposium, Cracow.
1 June	US and Soviet officials report resolution of outstanding differences on the CFE Treaty.
6-7 June	NATO Foreign Ministers meeting in Copenhagen issue Statements on Partnership with the Countries of Central and Eastern Europe, NATO's Core Security Functions in the New Europe, and the Resolution of Problems Concerning the CFE Treaty.
12-14 June	NATO Secretary General Manfred Woerner pays an official visit to the Republic of Bulgaria.
19 June	Albania becomes 35th CSCE participating state.
19-20 June	Meeting of CSCE Council, Berlin. Foreign Ministers create a CSCE Emergency Mechanism allowing for meetings of Senior Officials to be called at short notice subject to agreement by 13 states, and endorse the Valetta Report on the Peaceful Settlement of Disputes.

20 June	German legislators vote to reinstate Berlin as the country's official capital.
25 June	Parliaments of Slovenia and Croatia proclaim independence.
28 June	Dissolution of COMECON.
1 July	The Warsaw Treaty Organisation is officially disbanded in accordance with a protocol calling for a "transition to all-European structures."
1-19 July	CSCE Experts' Meeting on National Minorities, Geneva.
3 July	Polish President Lech Walesa visits NATO.
4-5 July	NATO's Secretary General Manfred Woerner visits Romania.
30 July	Russian President Boris Yeltsin signs a treaty with Lithuania recognising its independence.
30-31 July	US and Soviet Presidents proclaim their two-day summit as opening a new era in bilateral relations and sign START Treaty reducing strategic nuclear weapons.
19 August	Soviet President Gorbachev is removed from office in a coup and replaced by an "emergency committee". Meeting in emergency session, the NATO Council warns the Soviet Union of "serious consequences" if it abandons reform. Western aid programmes are suspended. Russian President Boris Yeltsin calls for a general strike while loyalist tanks flying Russian flags position themselves near the Russian parliament building.
21 August	Ministerial meeting of the North Atlantic Council. Foreign Ministers review the political situation in the Soviet Union and publish a statement condemning the unconstitutional removal of President Gorbachev and calling for the restoration of democratic reform. President Gorbachev returns to Moscow as the 19 August coup collapses and its leaders are arrested. Western leaders praise President Yeltsin's role in resisting the coup and lift a freeze on aid to the Soviet Union. Romanian Foreign Minister Adrian Nastase visits NATO.
25 August	The Soviet Union announces a wholesale purge of the Military High Command. President Gorbachev proposes that the Communist Party be disbanded and resigns as its General Secretary.
26 August	President Gorbachev indicates that the demands of secession-minded republics for independence can no longer be resisted. EC countries agree to establish diplomatic ties with the three Baltic states.

28 August	President Gorbachev appoints Boris Pankin, former Ambassador to Czechoslovakia, as Foreign Minister, strips the KGB of its troops and orders an investigation of its activities.
29 August	Soviet legislators vote to suspend all activities of the Communist Party.
5 September	The Soviet Congress of Peoples Deputies, before disbanding, agrees to hand over key powers to the Republics.
10 Sept.-4 Oct.	Third CSCE Meeting of the Conference on the Human Dimension, in Moscow. Estonia, Latvia and Lithuania become participating CSCE States.
17 September	Estonia, Latvia and Lithuania are admitted to the UN.
27 September	US President Bush announces sweeping cuts in US nuclear weapons and calls upon the Soviet Union to do likewise. The US cuts include the destruction of all US ground-launched tactical nuclear missiles and the removal of nuclear cruise missiles from submarines and warships.
6 October	Meeting in Cracow, the Foreign Ministers of Poland, Hungary and Czechoslovakia state their wish for their countries to be included in NATO activities. President Gorbachev announces the abolition of Soviet short-range nuclear weapons and the removal of all tactical nuclear weapons from ships, submarines and land-based naval aircraft.
17 October	NATO Defence Ministers meeting in Taormina, Italy, announce reductions in the current NATO stockpile of sub-strategic nuclear weapons in Europe by approximately 80 percent.
21 October	Visit to NATO by Soviet Deputy Foreign Minister Deryabin.
24-25 October	Seminar on Civil/Military Coordination of Air Traffic Management at NATO with participation from NATO and Central and Eastern European countries.
28 October	Hungarian Prime Minister Josef Antall visits NATO.
30 October	The first Peace Conference on the Middle East opens in Madrid under the joint chairmanship of the United States and the Soviet Union.
4-15 November	CSCE Experts' Seminar on Democratic Institutions, Oslo.
7-8 November	Summit Meeting of the North Atlantic Council in Rome. Heads of State and Government publish the Alliance's new Strategic Concept and issue the Rome Declaration on Peace and Cooperation.

11 November	NATO Secretary General Manfred Woerner receives Polish Foreign Minister Krzystof Skubiszewski at NATO.
12 November	Estonian Foreign Minister Lennart Meri is received at NATO.
	Bulgarian Foreign Minister Stoyan Ganev visits NATO.
14 November	Bulgarian President Zhelyu Zhelev visits NATO.
25 November	Romanian Minister of National Defence Lt. General Nicolae Spiroiu is received at NATO.
1 December	In a referendum 90 percent of the voters in Ukraine opt for independence from the Soviet Union.
8 December	Representatives of the three former Soviet Republics of Russia, Belarus and Ukraine meet in Minsk and agree to set up a Commonwealth of Independent States to replace the Soviet Union.
9-10 December	At the Maastricht European Council, Heads of State and Government of the EC adopt treaties (subject to ratification) on Economic and Monetary Union and Political Union. WEU Member States also meeting in Maastricht invite members of the European Union to accede to the WEU or to become observers, and other European members of NATO to become associate members of the WEU.
12-13 December	Ministerial meeting of the Defence Planning Committee in Brussels. Defence Ministers review major changes in force structures called for in the Alliance's new Strategic Concept, including substantial reductions in troops and equipment.
13 December	First Deputy Prime Minister of Russia, Gennadij Burbulis, visits NATO for discussions with Secretary General Manfred Woerner on the situation in the Soviet Union following the foundation of the Commonwealth of Independent States by Russia, Ukraine and Belarus.
17 December	During talks in Moscow President Yeltsin and President Gorbachev agree that the transition to the Commonwealth of Independent States would take place at the end of December 1991.
19 December	Ministerial meeting of the North Atlantic Council in Brussels. Foreign Ministers condemn the violence in Yugoslavia and pursue initiatives taken at the Rome Summit Meeting in November, inter alia on NATO assistance in providing humanitarian aid to the Soviet Union.
20 December	Inaugural meeting of the North Atlantic Cooperation Council attended by Foreign Ministers and Representatives of 16 NATO countries and 9 Central and

	Eastern European countries. On the same day, developments in Moscow mark the effective end of the USSR.
21 December	Eleven of the constituent republics of the former Soviet Union meet in Alma Ata and sign agreements creating a new Commonwealth of Independent States.
25 December	President Gorbachev announces his resignation as Soviet President and signs a Decree relinquishing his function as Supreme Commander-in-Chief of Soviet Forces.

1992

1 January	Boutros Boutros-Ghali of Egypt becomes Secretary General of the United Nations on the retirement of Javier Perez de Cuellar of Peru.
7-8 January	NATO participates in arrangements for airlifting EC humanitarian assistance to Moscow and St Petersburg in aircraft provided by the Canadian and German governments.
8-10 January	Meeting of CSCE Senior Officials, Prague.
10 January	At the first meeting of an informal High Level Working Group established by the North Atlantic Cooperation Council to discuss ratification and implementation of the CFE Treaty, agreement is reached on a phased approach for bringing the CFE Treaty into force.
22-23 January	A 47-nation international coordinating conference in Washington on assistance to the former Soviet Union, sponsored by the United States, is attended by NATO's Secretary General Manfred Woerner and representatives of other international organisations.
28 January	In his State of the Union Address, US President Bush proposes major new arms control and disarmament initiatives.
30 January	The first Summit Meeting of the 15 nation UN Security Council is attended by Boris Yeltsin, President of the Russian Federation.
30-31 January	Meeting of CSCE Council of Foreign Ministers in Prague recognises the Russian Federation as the continuation of the legal personality of the former Soviet Union and admits 10 former Soviet Republics as CSCE participating states.
19 February	Prime Minister Gasanov of Azerbaijan visits NATO.
21 February	Manfred Woerner, Secretary General of NATO, visits Romania and opens a new Euro-Atlantic Centre in Bucharest.
22-23 February	Secretary General Manfred Woerner visits Ukraine.

24-25 February	Secretary General Manfred Woerner visits Russia.
26 February	The Canadian Government informs the Alliance of its decision to cancel plans to maintain 1 100 Canadian forces in Europe after 1994, but confirms its intention to fulfil other commitments to the Alliance and to its Integrated Military Structure. The North Atlantic Council, in a Statement on Yugoslavia, appeals to all parties to respect cease-fire arrangements in order to allow the deployment of a UN peacekeeping force.
5-6 March	Foreign Ministers of Denmark, Estonia, Finland, Germany, Latvia, Lithuania, Norway, Poland, Russia and Sweden, meeting in Copenhagen, announce the formation of the Council of Baltic Sea States.
10 March	Extraordinary Meeting of the North Atlantic Cooperation Council. Foreign Ministers and Representatives of the NACC countries publish a Work Plan for Dialogue, Partnership and Cooperation.
11 March	President of the Italian Republic Francesco Cossiga visits NATO.
11-12 March	Secretary General Manfred Woerner visits Poland and opens a Seminar on "Security in Central Europe".
13-16 March	NATO Secretary General Manfred Woerner visits the Baltic States at the invitation of the Governments of Latvia, Estonia and Lithuania.
24 March	Opening of Fourth CSCE Follow-Up Meeting in Helsinki. Croatia, Georgia and Slovenia become CSCE participating states. Signature of Open Skies Treaty permitting overflights of national territory on a reciprocal basis.
	Mission of experts sponsored by the Medical Working Group of the Washington Coordinating Conference on Assistance to the Commonwealth of Independent States visits 10 cities on board a NATO Boeing 707 to assess medical needs.
1 April	NATO Defence Ministers meet with Cooperation Partners and identify areas for further cooperation in defence-related matters.
8-10 April	NATO Economics Colloquium on External Economic Relations of the Central and Eastern European countries.
10 April	First Meeting of the NATO Military Committee in Cooperation Session with Chiefs of Defence and Chiefs of General Staff of Central and Eastern European States.

30 April	NATO's Naval On-Call Force for the Mediterranean is replaced by a Standing Naval Force Mediterranean (STANAVFORMED).
4 May	Visit to NATO by Japanese Minister of State for Defence, Sohei Miyashita.
7 May	Meeting of Russian Secretary of State Gennady Burbulis with Acting Secretary General of NATO Amedeo de Franchis at NATO Headquarters.
11 May	Visit of the Foreign Ministers of Estonia, Latvia and Lithuania to NATO Headquarters.
11-12 May	CEAC Seminar with Cooperation Partners at NATO Headquarters on civil/military coordination of air traffic management.
15 May	Agreements signed at the fifth Summit Meeting of the leaders of the Commonwealth of Independent States in Tashkent include the apportionment of rights and obligations between the eight former Soviet states concerned with respect to the CFE Treaty.
20-22 May	NATO Defence Conversion Seminar with Cooperation Partners.
21 May	First formal meeting of the North Atlantic Council with the Council of the Western European Union at NATO Headquarters.
26-27 May	Ministerial Meetings of NATO's Defence Planning Committee and Nuclear Planning Group. Defence Ministers discuss NATO support for CSCE peacekeeping activities.
4 June	NATO Foreign Ministers, meeting in Ministerial Session in Oslo, announce their readiness to support conditionally peacekeeping activities under the responsibility of the CSCE on a case-by-case basis. Foreign Ministers also issue statements on the crisis in the territory of the former Yugoslavia and on the crisis in Nagorno-Karabakh.
5 June	Foreign Ministers and Representatives of the countries participating in the NACC, meeting in Oslo, consult on regional conflicts and other major security issues. Georgia and Albania are welcomed as members of the NACC. Finland attends as observer. The Final Document issued at the conclusion of an Extraordinary Conference held in Oslo in conjunction with these meetings formally establishes the obligations under the CFE Treaty of the eight countries of the former Soviet Union with territory in the area of application of the Treaty.

11-12 June	Seminar with Cooperation Partners conducted by NATO's Verification Coordinating Committee on implementation of the CFE Treaty.
16 June	Agreement is reached by US President Bush and Russian President Yeltsin to cut nuclear warheads on strategic missiles significantly beyond the limits of the START Treaty.
19 June	Foreign and Defence Ministers of WEU member states meet at Petersburg, near Bonn, and issue a Declaration setting out guidelines for the Organisation's future development.
1-3 July	High Level Seminar on Defence Policy and Management at NATO Headquarters, attended by officials from 30 Allied and Cooperation Partner countries.
2 July	The United States notifies its Allies of the completion of the withdrawal from Europe of land-based nuclear artillery shells, LANCE missile warheads and nuclear depth bombs, in accordance with the initiative announced on 27 September 1991, as well as the removal of all tactical nuclear weapons from US surface ships and attack submarines.The Parliament of Kazakhstan approves the ratification of START.
8 July	Visit to NATO by Leonid Kravchuk, President of Ukraine.
10 July	At the conclusion of the Helsinki CSCE Follow-Up Conference at Summit Level, leaders of the 51 participating nations approve a Final Document ("The Challenges of Change") addressing, inter alia, support for CSCE peacekeeping activities by NATO and other international organisations. The Concluding Act of the Negotiations on Personnel Strength of Conventional Armed Forces in Europe (CFE 1A), is also signed. The North Atlantic Council in Ministerial Session in Helsinki agrees on a NATO maritime operation in the Adriatic in coordination and cooperation with the operation by the WEU, to monitor compliance with UN sanctions imposed on Serbia and Montenegro by Security Council Resolutions 713 and 757.
16 July	WEU member countries meet in Rome with representatives of Denmark, Greece, Iceland, Ireland, Norway and Turkey to discuss steps towards enlargement.
16-18 July	Official visit to Hungary by the Secretary General of NATO Manfred Woerner.

17 July	The CFE Treaty, signed on 19 November 1990, enters into force provisionally, allowing verification procedures to be implemented.
26-28 August	London Conference on Yugoslavia.
28 August	Signature of NATO-Spanish coordination agreement on air defence.
2 September	The North Atlantic Council agrees on measures to make available Alliance resources in support of UN, CSCE and EC efforts to bring about peace in the former Yugoslavia, including the provision of resources for the protection of humanitarian relief and support for UN monitoring of heavy weapons.
3 September	An Italian relief plane is shot down west of Sarajevo in Bosnia and Herzegovina.
8 September	Czechoslovak Foreign Minister Jozef Moravcik visits NATO.
12-13 September	UN begins monitoring of heavy weapons in Bosnia and Herzegovina. NATO Allies express readiness to support the UN in this endeavour.
22 September	The CSCE Forum for Security Cooperation (FSC), established at the Helsinki Summit in July 1992, is inaugurated in Vienna. UN General Assembly votes to exclude Serbia and Montenegro and rules that Belgrade must make an application to be admitted to the United Nations.
23 September	Visit to NATO by Lithuanian President, Vytautas Landsbergis.
29 September	The Swedish Foreign Minister, Margaretha af Ugglas, is received at NATO by Secretary General Manfred Woerner. Foreign Minister of Argentina, Guido di Tella, visits NATO for discussions with Secretary General Manfred Woerner.
1 October	US Senate ratifies START Treaty, cutting US and Russian nuclear forces by one-third.
2 October	NATO's new Allied Command Europe (ACE) Rapid Reaction Corps (ARRC) is inaugurated at Bielefeld, Germany, by SACEUR, General John Shalikashvili.
7 October	Visit to NATO by Poland's Prime Minister, Hanna Suchocka.
14 October	WEU Permanent Council meets at Ambassadorial level with eight Central and Eastern European countries. The North Atlantic Council authorises the use of a NATO airborne early warning and control force (AWACS) to monitor the UN-mandated "no-fly" zone in effect over Bosnia and Herzegovina.

20-21 October	NATO Ministers of Defence meeting in the Nuclear Planning Group (NPG) at Gleneagles, Scotland, focus on the implications of the Alliance's role in peacekeeping activities for NATO's collective defence planning. New political guidelines providing for reduced reliance on nuclear weapons are also adopted.
28 October	Finnish President Mauno Koivisto meets with NATO Secretary General Manfred Woerner in Brussels.
30 October	The Atlantic Club of Bulgaria becomes the first Partner country organisation to be associated with the Atlantic Treaty Association (ATA) as an observer.
1-5 November	Secretary General Manfred Woerner visits Belarus, Kazakhstan and Kyrgyzstan.
3 November	Governor Bill Clinton, the Democratic candidate, wins the US Presidential election.
6 November	NATO supplies UN Protection Force in Bosnia and Herzegovina with an operational headquarters, including a staff of some 100 personnel, equipment, supplies and initial financial support.
9 November	The CFE Treaty officially enters into force after ratification by all 29 signatory states.
16 November	SACEUR, General John Shalikashvili, meets with President Leonid Kravchuk during a visit to Ukraine.
20 November	NATO's Secretary General, Manfred Woerner, is invited for the first time to attend WEU Ministerial meeting in Rome. Greece is invited to become the tenth WEU member; Denmark and Ireland are granted WEU observer status; and Turkey, Norway and Iceland are granted WEU associate member status.
22 November	Enforcement operations in support of UN sanctions by NATO and WEU naval forces in the Adriatic begin as an extension of the maritime monitoring operations which began in July 1992.
25 November	Estonia's President, Lennart Meri, visits NATO Headquarters.
27 November	NATO Secretary General Manfred Woerner visits Russian troops stationed in former East Germany.
4 December	European NATO Defence Ministers decide to dissolve the IEPG and transfer its functions forthwith to the WEU.
11 December	Defence Ministers participating in NATO's Defence Planning Committee state that support for UN and CSCE peacekeeping should be included among the missions of NATO forces and headquarters.

14 December	The Alliance commemorates the 25th anniversary of NATO's Harmel Report.
15 December	UN Secretary General Boutros Boutros-Ghali requests access to NATO contingency plans for possible military operations in former Yugoslavia, including enforcement of the no-fly zone over Bosnia and Herzegovina, establishment of safe havens for civilians in Bosnia, and ways to prevent the spread of conflict to Kosovo and the former Yugoslav Republic of Macedonia*.
16 December	Albanian President Sali Berisha meets with Secretary General Manfred Woerner at NATO Headquarters.
17 December	At the Ministerial Session of the North Atlantic Council, Foreign Ministers announce their readiness to back further action by the UN in former Yugoslavia, and agree to strengthen Alliance coordination in peacekeeping and develop practical measures to enhance the Alliance's contribution in this area.
18 December	NACC Foreign Ministers and representatives agree to exchange experience and expertise on peacekeeping and related matters and issue the 1993 NACC Work Plan.

1993

1 January	The Czech Republic and the Republic of Slovakia become independent states.
3 January	Presidents Bush and Yeltsin sign the START II Treaty in Moscow, further reducing US and Russian strategic offensive arms by eliminating all their multiple warhead Intercontinental Ballistic Missiles (ICBMs) and reducing their strategic nuclear stockpiles by two-thirds.
13 January	The Chemical Weapons Convention (CWC), completely banning chemical weapons, opens for signature in Paris and is signed by 127 nations.
14 January	Allies agree on plans for enforcement of no-fly zone over Bosnia and Herzegovina, if requested to do so by the UN.
21 January	Signature of the agreement on conditions for employing the European Corps within the Alliance framework by NATO Supreme Allied Commander Europe and the Chiefs of Defence of France and Germany.
26-27 January	NATO's Verification Coordinating Committee holds a seminar with Cooperation Partner countries on Cooperation in the Implementation of the CFE Treaty.
27 January	WEU Secretary General Willem Van Eekelen meets with Secretary General Manfred Woerner at NATO

Headquarters for first time since WEU transferred its offices to Brussels on 18 January, to discuss practical cooperation between the two organisations.

1 February	Nursultan Nazarbayev, President of Kazakhstan, meets with the NATO Secretary General at NATO Headquarters.
4 February	Belarus ratifies START I Treaty.
17 February	President of Romania, Ion Iliescu, meets with Secretary General Manfred Woerner at NATO Headquarters.
23 February	The Prime Minister of Slovakia, Vladimir Meciar, pays an official visit to NATO Headquarters. NATO's CCMS, meeting for the first time in formal session with Cooperation Partners, discusses, inter alia, the problems of cross-border environmental pollution.
24 February	The NATO Secretary General issues a statement supporting the US decision to undertake air drops of humanitarian assistance in eastern Bosnia.
25 Feb.-4 March	NATO conducts crisis management procedural exercise ("NATO CMX 93").
26 February	Special Ministerial meeting of the North Atlantic Council at NATO Headquarters, with the participation of the new US Secretary of State, Warren Christopher.
1-3 March	On a visit to the US, NATO Secretary General Manfred Woerner meets with President Clinton, Secretary of State Christopher, Secretary of Defence Aspin, and key congressional leaders.
4 March	The President of Italy, Oscar Luigi Scalfaro, visits NATO Headquarters.
8 March	Greek Prime Minister Constantin Mitsotakis visits NATO Headquarters.
8-9 March	The Chairman of the NATO Military Committee, Field Marshall Sir Richard Vincent, pays an official visit to Albania.
9 March	The Prime Minister of Bulgaria, Lyuben Berov, visits NATO Headquarters.
	Czech Foreign Minister Josef Zieleniec visits NATO Headquarters.
	The Foreign Minister of Poland, Krzysztof Skubiszewski, visits NATO Headquarters.
10 March	The North Atlantic Council directs NATO Military Authorities to develop contingency options for possible implementation of a UN peace plan for Bosnia and Herzegovina.

15 March	North Korea ejects inspectors from the International Atomic Energy Agency (IAEA) and announces its intention to withdraw from the Nuclear Non-Proliferation Treaty (NPT) régime.
16 March	Italy conducts the first joint multinational CFE inspection led by a NATO member state with the participation of Cooperation Partners (Azerbaijan, Hungary and Poland) to verify a declared site in Romania.
18-20 March	NATO Secretary General Manfred Woerner makes an official visit to Albania.
26 March	Czech Defence Minister Antonin Baudys meets with the NATO Secretary General and the Chairman of the Military Committee at NATO Headquarters.
29 March	Meeting of NATO Defence Ministers with Cooperation Partners to review progress in cooperation on defence-related matters, as well as to exchange views on broader security issues.
2 April	The North Atlantic Council directs SACEUR to take preparatory steps to implement UN Resolution 816, authorising enforcement of the no-fly zone over Bosnia and Herzegovina.
3-4 April	The first US-Russian Summit between Presidents Clinton and Yeltsin takes place in Vancouver.
12 April	Beginning of the NATO operation to enforce the no-fly zone over Bosnia and Herzegovina, under the authority of UN Security Council Resolution 816 and decided by the North Atlantic Council on 8 April. Fighter and surveillance aircraft from several allied nations participate, as well as aircraft from NATO's Airborne Early Warning Force (NAEWF).
19 April	US search and rescue units join Russians in Siberia in the first US-Russian joint training exercise on Russian soil since the Second World War.
22 April	UN Secretary General Boutros Boutros-Ghali meets NATO Secretary General Manfred Woerner in Brussels, to discuss the situation in former Yugoslavia, NATO's role in peacekeeping and NATO-UN relations in general.
28 April	The Military Committee meets at Chief of Defence/Chief of General Staff level with Cooperation Partners at NATO Headquarters.
6 May	US Secretary of State Warren Christopher visits NATO Headquarters to discuss the Bosnia crisis.

17 May	Hungarian Foreign Minister, Dr. Geza Jeszensky, visits NATO Headquarters.
	Bosnian Serbs reject the Vance-Owen Peace Plan.
22 May	Joint Action Programme on Bosnia and Herzegovina announced by members of the UN Security Council (France, Russia, Spain, United Kingdom, United States) to stop the fighting, including provisions for "safe areas".
24 May	Eurogroup Defence Ministers transfer Eurogroup training and medical activities to NATO and Eurogroup publicity and communications activities to the WEU.
25-26 May	DPC/NPG Ministerial meeting at NATO Headquarters to discuss, inter alia, defence planning implications of support for UN and CSCE peacekeeping activities and defence aspects of the proliferation of weapons of mass destruction.
8 June	At the joint session of the North Atlantic Council and the Council of the Western European Union at NATO Headquarters, the two organisations approve a single command and control arrangement for the combined NATO/WEU naval operations in the Adriatic for the enforcement of the UN embargoes against Serbia and Montenegro.
10 June	At the Ministerial meeting of the North Atlantic Council in Athens, NATO Foreign Ministers offer to provide protective air power in case of attack against UNPROFOR in the performance of its overall mandate, if so requested by the UN.
11 June	NACC Foreign Ministers, meeting in Athens, announce a programme of cooperation in preparation for joint peacekeeping activities in support of the UN and CSCE and publish a report by the NACC Ad Hoc Group on Cooperation in Peacekeeping.
18 June	The UN Security Council approves deployment of 300 US troops to the former Yugoslav Republic of Macedonia* to join the 700 UN troops already there as a preventive measure to keep the Bosnian conflict from spreading.
23 June	Eduard Shevardnadze, the Chairman of Parliament and Head of State of Georgia pays an official visit to NATO Headquarters.
28-30 June	The Chairman of the NATO Military Committee, Field Marshall Sir Richard Vincent, visits the Czech Republic.
30 June-2 July	NACC High Level seminar on peacekeeping is held in Prague, to further the work of the NACC Ad Hoc Group on Cooperation in Peacekeeping.

30 June-2 July	The 1993 Economics Colloquium is held at NATO Headquarters on the theme "Economic Developments in Cooperation Partner Countries from a Sectoral Perspective".
22 July	Belarus formally accedes to the NPT as a non nuclear weapon state, in accordance with the 1992 Lisbon Protocol to START I.
2 August	At a special meeting on the situation in Bosnia and Herzegovina the North Atlantic Council announces immediate preparations for undertaking stronger measures, including air strikes against those responsible, if the strangulation of Sarajevo and other areas continues, including wide-scale interference with humanitarian assistance.
9 August	The North Atlantic Council approves the operational options for air strikes in Bosnia and Herzegovina, as called for by the Council on 2 August, to be implemented on the authorisation of the UN Secretary General.
	Albert II, King of the Belgians, accedes to the throne following the death of King Baudouin I on 31 July.
16-18 August	The Chairman of the Military Committee, Field Marshall Sir Richard Vincent, pays an official visit to Romania and Moldova.
31 August	Russia completes the withdrawal of its troops from Lithuania.
1 September	NATO Secretary General Manfred Woerner meets with UN Secretary-General Boutros Boutros-Ghali in Geneva to discuss prospects for a peaceful settlement in Bosnia and Herzegovina and NATO's role in support of the UN's peacekeeping mission in the former Yugoslavia, as well as the development of closer links between NATO and the UN.
18 September	Ukrainian Foreign Minister Anotoly Zlenko visits NATO Headquarters.
20 September	NACC representatives meeting at NATO Headquarters issue a statement calling for an end to fighting in Georgia and condemning the cease-fire violations of the Abkhazian forces.
21 September	The Chief of Defence of the Czech Republic, Major General Jiri Nekvasil, visits NATO Headquarters. Russian President Boris Yeltsin suspends parliament and calls for fresh elections on 11-12 December. Vice-President Alexander Rutskoi and the Parliamentary Chairman Ruslan Khasbulatov urge the armed forces to resist the

	suspension. They and other hardliners occupy the Russian White House.
22 September	Thorvald Stoltenberg and Lord Owen, Co-Chairmen of the International Conference on the Former Yugoslavia, visit NATO Headquarters to discuss the implementation of an eventual peace plan for Bosnia and Herzegovina with the Secretary General and the Chairman of the Military Committee.
29 September	Official visit of the President of Turkmenistan, Saparmurad Niyazov, to NATO Headquarters.
4 October	Troops loyal to Russian President Yeltsin pound the White House, headquarters of the Russian Parliament, with tanks and machine gun fire, ending the occupation of the building by parliamentarian hardliners opposing President Yeltsin's reform programme.
	The Security Council extends the mandate of UN peace-keepers in Croatia and Bosnia for six months. It authorises the peacekeepers in Croatia *"to take the necessary measures, including the use of force, to ensure its security and its freedom of movement"*.
6-7 October	NATO Secretary General Manfred Woerner, on a visit to the US, meets with President Bill Clinton in Washington, and with UN Secretary General Boutros Boutros-Ghali in New York.
18 October	The Prime Minister of the Republic of Estonia, Mart Laar, pays an official visit to NATO Headquarters.
20-21 October	NATO Defence Ministers meet in Travemünde, Germany, to discuss informally a range of subjects including the Partnership for Peace proposal and the CJTF concept and proliferation of weapons of mass destruction.
2-3 November	The Chairman of the NATO Military Committee, Field Marshal Sir Richard Vincent, pays an official visit to Bulgaria, meeting with President Zhelyu Zhelev.
4 November	The President of the Slovak Republic, Michael Kovac, pays an official visit to NATO Headquarters.
15-17 November	NATO's Verification and Coordinating Committee conducts a seminar at NATO Headquarters with NACC Partner Countries on cooperation in the verification and implementation of conventional arms control provisions, including the CFE Treaty.
30 November	NATO Secretary General Manfred Woerner addresses the CSCE Council of Foreign Ministers meeting in Rome.

2 December	At the Ministerial meeting of the North Atlantic Council, NATO Foreign Ministers discuss the concept of Partnership for Peace and related proposals, in preparation for the January 1994 Summit.
3 December	At the NACC Ministerial, NATO and NACC Foreign Ministers approve a second report by the NACC Ad Hoc Group on Cooperation in Peacekeeping, as well as the NACC Work Plan for 1994.
7 December	EUROGROUP Ministers announce that several sub-groups will either be incorporated into NATO or transferred to the WEU, and that the EUROGROUP itself will cease to exist as of 1 January 1994.
8-9 December	NATO Defence Ministers meeting in the DPC/NPG in Brussels discuss new defence tasks of the Alliance, including support for UN and CSCE peacekeeping, and the concept of Combined Joint Task Forces. Ministers express their strong support for the Partnership for Peace.
9 December	NATO Secretary General Manfred Woerner meets with Russian President Boris Yeltsin in Brussels.
12 December	First multiparty parliamentary elections in Russia since 1917. A new constitution giving increased power to the President is approved by 58.4 percent of votes cast.
14 December	Joint meeting of the North Atlantic Council and the Council of the WEU at ambassadorial level at WEU Headquarters in Brussels.

1994

10-11 January	At the Brussels Summit, Alliance Heads of State and Government launch Partnership for Peace (PfP), issuing an invitation to all NACC partner countries and CSCE states able and willing to participate. The PfP Framework Document is published. The concept of Combined Joint Task Forces is endorsed, as well as other measures to support the development of a European Security and Defence Identity. NATO Heads of State and Government reaffirm NATO's readiness to carry out air strikes to prevent the strangulation of Sarajevo and other UN-declared safe areas in Bosnia and Herzegovina.
14 January	The Presidents of US, Russia and Ukraine sign a trilateral agreement in Moscow detailing procedures for the transfer of Ukrainian nuclear warheads to Russia and associated compensation and security assurances. US President Clinton and Russian President Yeltsin sign an accord

	bringing to an end the targeting of long-range nuclear missiles at each other's countries with effect from 30 May 1994.
18 January	Elections for the Russian State Duma (Parliament) result in large gains for opponents of President Yeltsin.
20 January	The President of Bosnia and Herzegovina, Alija Izetbegovic, visits NATO Headquarters.
24-27 January	Second NATO/CCMS International Conference on the Role of the Military in Protecting the Ozone Layer. Participants pledge to meet the deadlines set by the Montreal Protocol on Substances that Deplete the Ozone Layer.
26 January	Romania's Foreign Minister, Teodor Melescanu, comes to NATO Headquarters to sign the Partnership for Peace Framework Document.
27 January	The President of Lithuania, Algirdas Brazauskas, pays an official visit to NATO Headquarters to sign the PfP Framework Document.
A programme of military cooperation between Russia and NATO, signed in Moscow, provides for exchanges of visits by senior commanders and military experts and for joint exercises and training.
1 February	Sergio Silvio Balanzino (Italy) succeeds Ambassador Amedeo de Franchis as Deputy Secretary General of NATO.
2 February	Polish Prime Minister Waldemar Pawlak signs the PfP Framework Document at NATO Headquarters.
3 February	Juri Luik, Estonian Minister of Foreign Affairs, signs the PfP Framework Document at NATO Headquarters.
The Ukrainian Parliament rescinds the conditions attached to its earlier ratification of START I on 18 November 1993, authorising the government to exchange instruments of ratification.
6 February	UN Secretary General Boutros Boutros-Ghali requests NATO to prepare for possible air strikes against artillery positions in and around Sarajevo, following a mortar attack on a crowded market place in the city with extensive loss of life.
8 February	Hungary's Minister of Foreign Affairs, Geza Jeszenszky, visits NATO Headquarters to sign the PfP Framework Document.
Anatoly Zlenko, Foreign Minister of Ukraine, signs the PfP Framework Document at NATO Headquarters.

9 February	The North Atlantic Council condemns the continuing siege of Sarajevo and announces that heavy weapons of any of the parties remaining in an area within 20 kilometres of the centre of the city after 20 February would be subject to NATO air strikes conducted in close coordination with the UN Secretary General, consistent with the NAC's decisions of 2 and 9 August 1993. The Prime Minister of Slovakia, Vladimir Meciar, signs the PfP Framework Document at NATO Headquarters.
14 February	Zhelyu Zhelev, President of Bulgaria, visits NATO Headquarters where he signs the PfP Framework Document.
	Latvian Prime Minister Vladis Birkavs signs the PfP Framework Document at NATO Headquarters.
	Kazakhstan formally accedes to the Non-Proliferation Treaty (NPT) as a non-nuclear weapon state, in accordance with the 1992 Lisbon Protocol to START I.
14-15 February	The Chairman of the NATO Military Committee, Field Marshall Sir Richard Vincent, pays an official visit to Poland, under the auspices of the NACC programme.
15 February	The UK and Russia agree to reprogramme their nuclear missiles so that, as of 30 May 1994, they are no longer targeted at one another.
21 February	Following expiry of the deadline of 9 February to withdraw heavy weapons from the Sarajevo exclusion zone, NATO's Secretary General announces that, because the objectives were being met, UN and NATO officials had recommended not to use air power at this stage.
23 February	The President of Albania, Sali Berisha, comes to NATO Headquarters to sign the PfP Framework Document.
28 February	Four warplanes violating the UN-mandated no-fly zone over Bosnia-Herzegovina are shot down by Alliance jets.
4 March	The first shipment of 60 nuclear warheads are transferred from the Ukraine to Russia, under the terms of the Tripartite Statement of 14 January 1993 between Ukraine, Russia and the US.
10 March	Vaclav Klaus, the Prime Minister of the Czech Republic, signs the PfP Framework Document at NATO Headquarters.
14-17 March	Field Marshall Sir Richard Vincent, Chairman of the Military Committee, pays an official visit to Estonia, Latvia and Lithuania to discuss NATO's Military Cooperation Programme and the security interests of each country.

16 March	The President of Moldova, Mircea Snegur, visits NATO Headquarters to sign the PfP Framework Document.
23 March	Alexander Chikvaidze, Foreign Minister of Georgia, signs the PfP Framework Document at NATO Headquarters.
30 March	The Prime Minister of Slovenia, Janez Drnovsek, visits NATO Headquarters to sign the PfP Framework Document.
10 April	Following a request from the UN Force Command, NATO aircraft provide close air support to UN personnel in Gorazde, a UN-designated safe area in Bosnia and Herzegovina, under the guidance of a UN forward air controller.
16 April	A British Sea Harrier jet is shot down while on a NATO close air support mission to protect UNPROFOR troops in Bosnia and Herzegovina.
22 April	In a response to a request of 18 April by the UN Secretary General, the North Atlantic Council takes further decisions regarding the use of air power to protect UN personnel throughout Bosnia and Herzegovina and UN-designated safe areas. The Council also authorises air strikes unless all Bosnian Serb heavy weapons are withdrawn by 27 April from an area within 20 kilometres of Gorazde. This deadline also applies to any of the other UN-designated safe areas if they are attacked by heavy weapons.
25 April	Poland's Defence Minister, Piotr Kolodziejczyk, visits NATO Headquarters to submit his country's PfP Presentation Document.
27 April	The NATO Council, reviewing the implementation of its decisions of 22 April concerning the situation in and around Gorazde and other safe areas in Bosnia and Herzegovina, determines that there is general compliance with the deadline. The NATO Military Committee meets in Cooperation Session at Chiefs of Defence/Chiefs of General Staff level at NATO Headquarters.
27-29 April	NACC seminar on Planning and Management of National Defence Programmes is held in Budapest, Hungary.
28 April	Opening ceremonies of the Partnership Coordination Cell, collocated with SHAPE at Mons, Belgium. Defence Minister Gheorghe Tinca submits Romania's PfP Presentation Document at NATO Headquarters.
4 May	The President of Azerbaijan, Gaidar Aliyev, signs the PfP Framework Document at NATO Headquarters.

9 May	The Foreign Minister of Sweden, Baroness Margaretha af Ugglas, and the Foreign Minister of Finland, Heikki Haavisto, visit NATO Headquarters to sign the PfP Framework Document.
	Meeting of the WEU Council of Ministers in Kirchberg, Luxembourg, with Foreign and Defence Ministers of Bulgaria, the Czech Republic, Estonia, Hungary, Latvia, Lithuania, Poland, Romania and Slovakia. A new status is agreed whereby these countries become Associate Partners of the WEU.
10 May	Finland and Sweden submit their PfP Presentation Documents to NATO.
	Turkmenistan's Deputy Prime Minister, Boris Shikmuradov, signs the PfP Framework Document at NATO Headquarters.
11-14 May	The Chairman of the NATO Military Committee, Field Marshall Sir Richard Vincent, visits Slovakia and Russia to meet with high ranking military and civilian government officials in both countries in the context of the NACC.
17 May	The Czech Republic submits its PfP Presentation Document to NATO.
24 May	At the DPC/NPG Ministerial meeting, NATO Defence Ministers review progress on the defence implications of PfP, the CJTF concept, counter-proliferation and peace-keeping efforts.
	Russian Defence Minister Pavel Grachev comes to NATO Headquarters to brief NATO Defence Ministers on Russia's new defence doctrine.
25 May	NATO Defence Ministers meet with Defence Ministers and Representatives of Cooperation Partner countries including, for the first time, those from Finland, Sweden and Slovenia, under the auspices of PfP, to discuss cooperation in defence-related matters, including peacekeeping.
	Slovakia and Ukraine submit their PfP Presentation Documents to NATO.
26-27 May	Inaugural Conference on a Pact on Stability in Europe, in Paris. European Foreign Ministers discuss a new initiative aimed at averting conflicts over borders and the rights of minorities, promoting good neighbourly relations in Central and Eastern Europe, and strengthening regional cooperation and democratic institutions.

27 May	The Foreign Minister of the Republic of Kazakhstan, Kanet Saudabaev, visits NATO Headquarters to sign the PfP Framework Document.
1 June	President Askar Akayev of Kyrgyzstan signs the PfP Framework Document at NATO Headquarters.
3 June	Deputy Secretary General Sergio Balanzino formally opens the offices for Partners in the Manfred Woerner Wing at NATO Headquarters.
6 June	Bulgaria and Hungary submit their PfP Presentation Documents to NATO.
9 June	NATO Foreign Ministers meeting in Istanbul review progress on the implementation of the Brussels Summit decisions, noting that 20 countries had already joined PfP. Ministers adopt an overall policy framework on the Alliance's approach to the proliferation of weapons of mass destruction.
10 June	Ministerial meeting of the NACC in Istanbul. Foreign Ministers issue a third Report on Peacekeeping by the Ad Hoc Group on Cooperation in Peacekeeping. Foreign Ministers from Finland, Sweden and Slovenia also attend. Lithuania submits its PfP Presentation Document.
22 June	Russian Foreign Minister Andrei Kozyrev visits NATO Headquarters to sign the PfP Framework Document and to hold discussions with the Council. A Summary of Conclusions of the discussions is issued.
26-28 June	General George Joulwan (SACEUR) visits Moscow for discussions on Russia's participation in PfP as well as a specific cooperation programme with Russia.
29 June	The Special Representative of the Secretary General of the UN, Yasushi Akashi, accompanied by Lt. Gen. Bertrand de Lapresle, Commander of the United Nations Protection Forces (UNPROFOR) in former Yugoslavia, and Lt. Gen. Sir Michael Rose, Commander of UNPROFOR in Bosnia and Herzegovina, visit NATO Headquarters to meet with the Deputy Secretary General, Sergio Balanzino.
29 June-1 July	The annual NATO Economics Colloquium takes place, focusing on privatisation in the defence industry.
5 July	Poland's PfP Individual Partnership Programme with NATO is formally accepted. Russia submits its PfP Presentation Document.
8 July	Estonia submits its PfP Presentation Document.

11 July	The North Atlantic Council issues a statement reiterating the willingness of the Alliance to participate in the implementation of a peace agreement in Bosnia and Herzegovina; and agreeing that steps envisaged in the plan issued by Foreign Ministers in Geneva on 5 July could result in the assumption of new tasks by the Alliance in former Yugoslavia at the request of the UN.
12 July	The German Federal Constitutional Court clarifies the constitutional basis for the deployment of German forces abroad, removing constitutional objections to German participation in UN, NATO or WEU peacekeeping missions.
13 July	The Foreign Minister of Uzbekistan, Saidmukhtar Saidkasimov, and Defence Minister Rustam Ahmedov visit NATO Headquarters to sign the PfP Framework Document.
18 July	Latvia submits its PfP Presentation Document.
20 July	Slovenia submits its PfP Presentation Document.
5 August	NATO aircraft attack a target within the Sarajevo Exclusion Zone at the request of UNPROFOR, after Bosnian Serbs seize weapons from a UN collection site near Sarajevo.
13 August	Death of NATO Secretary General Manfred Woerner in Brussels. Deputy Secretary General Sergio Balanzino assumes duties as Acting Secretary General.
18 August	Commemorative meeting of the NAC in honour of the late Secretary General Manfred Woerner.
22 August	Sweden's PfP Individual Partnership Programme with NATO is formally accepted.
31 August	The last Russian troops leave Estonia, completing their withdrawal from the three Baltic States.
1 September	Russian troops leave Berlin, completing their withdrawal from German territory.
2-10 September	The first joint US-Russian manoeuvres held on Russian territory focus on peacekeeping training exercises.
6 September	Moldova submits its PfP Presentation Document to NATO.
8 September	The US, UK and France withdraw remaining Allied troops from Berlin.
12-16 September	The first joint training exercise under PfP (Cooperative Bridge) is held near Poznan, Poland, with participation by soldiers from 13 NATO and Partner nations.
13 September	Lt. Gen. John Sheehan is appointed Supreme Allied Commander Atlantic (SACLANT).
14 September	Romania's PfP Individual Partnership Programme with NATO is formally accepted.

22 September	Following an attack on an UNPROFOR vehicle near Sarajevo, NATO aircraft carry out an air strike against a Bosnian Serb tank, at the request of UNPROFOR. Albania submits its PfP Presentation Document.
28 Sept.-7 Oct.	Maritime PfP exercise Cooperative Venture takes place in the Skagerrak area of the North Sea, with NATO and Cooperation Partner maritime forces conducting peacekeeping, humanitarian and search and rescue operations.
29 September	The North Atlantic Council, meeting at the level of Foreign Ministers in New York, invites Willy Claes, Belgian Minister of Foreign Affairs, to become Secretary General of NATO.
29-30 September	The Defence Ministers and representatives of the 16 Alliance nations meet in Seville, Spain, for informal discussions on a range of subjects of mutual interest and concern, including the situation in the former Yugoslavia; peacekeeping and the concept of Combined Joint Task Forces; defence cooperation with Central and Eastern Europe, including Partnership for Peace; and security in the Mediterranean.
5 October	The Minister of Foreign Affairs of Armenia, Vahan Papazian, signs the PfP Framework Document at NATO Headquarters.
5-7 October	Seminar on Peacekeeping and its Relationship to Crisis Management at NATO Headquarters in Brussels, with participation of 38 countries in addition to other international organisations.
10 Oct.-2 Dec.	CSCE Review Conference in Budapest.
12 October	Finland's PfP Individual Partnership Programme with NATO is formally accepted. German President Roman Herzog pays an official visit to NATO Headquarters.
17 October	Willy Claes, former Deputy Prime Minister and Minister of Foreign Affairs of Belgium, succeeds Manfred Woerner as Secretary General of NATO.
17 Oct.-8 Nov.	The Alliance's Rapid Reaction Corps (ARRC) holds exercises in Denmark.
21-28 October	The first PfP joint peacekeeping training exercise held on Allied territory "Cooperative Spirit" takes place in the Netherlands, with participation by 12 NATO and Partner countries.
28 October	NATO and the UN issue a joint statement on the use of NATO airpower in Bosnia and Herzegovina in support of relevant UN resolutions. NATO Secretary General Willy

	Claes addresses the 40th General Assembly of the Atlantic Treaty Association in The Hague.
4 November	Ion Iliescu, President of Romania, visits NATO Headquarters.
7 November	Special Joint Meeting of allied National Armament Directors to address equipment implications of peace-keeping operations.
11 November	NATO Secretary General Willy Claes issues a statement on the announcement of limitations to United States participation in Operation Sharp Guard.
14 November	Meeting of the WEU Council of Ministers with the participation of Foreign and Defence Ministers of the nine Associate Partner countries. Publication of the Noordwijk Declaration endorsing inter alia preliminary policy conclusions on the formulation of a Common European Defence Policy.
15 November	Hungarian Foreign Minister Laszlo Kovacs and Defence Minister Gyoergy Keleti visit NATO. Hungary's PfP Individual Partnership Programme with NATO is formally accepted.
21 November	NATO aircraft attack the Udbina airfield in Serb-held Croatia at the request of and in close coordination with UNPROFOR, in response to attacks launched from Udbina against targets in the Bihac area of Bosnia and Herzegovina.
23 November	Following attacks against NATO aircraft, NATO forces carry out an air strike on a surface-to-air missile site south of Otoka, in accordance with self-defence measures previously announced.
	Slovakia's PfP Individual Partnership Programme with NATO is formally accepted.
24 November	The North Atlantic Council issues a statement condemning recent attacks on the UN safe area of Bihac by Bosnian Serb and Krajinan Serb forces; and announcing measures being taken in support of United Nations negotiating efforts.
25 November	Czech Vice-Minister of Foreign Affairs Alexander Vondra and Vice-Minister of Defence Jiri Pospisil visit NATO. The Czech Republic's PfP Individual Partnership Programme with NATO is formally accepted.
	Bulgarian Deputy Foreign Minister Todor Tchourov visits NATO. Bulgaria's PfP Individual Partnership Programme with NATO is formally accepted.

30 November	Lithuanian Secretary of State for Foreign Affairs, Albinas Januska visits NATO. Lithuania's PfP Partnership Programme with NATO is formally accepted.
1 December	Ministerial Meeting of the North Atlantic Council in Brussels attended by Russian Foreign Minister Andrei Kozyrev.
5 December	Signature of the Nuclear Non-Proliferation Treaty (NPT) by President Kuchma of Ukraine, at the CSCE Summit Meeting in Budapest.
5-6 December	Summit Meeting of CSCE Heads of State and Government in Budapest, attended by NATO Secretary General Willy Claes.
	The CSCE is renamed the Organisation for Security and Cooperation in Europe (OSCE).
	The Budapest Document "Towards a Genuine Partnership in a New Era'" is published.

1995

1 January	Four months cease-fire in Bosnia begins.
	Austria, Finland and Sweden join the European Union.
	The World Trade Organisation (WTO) is established as the successor to GATT.
11 January	The Minister of Foreign Affairs of Belarus, Uladzmir Syanko, visits NATO and signs the Partnership for Peace Framework Document.
13 January	1993 UN Chemical Weapons Convention fails to be enacted: only 20 countries ratify the treaty. To be implemented 65 countries are needed.
18 January	The NATO Council agrees on a NATO standardisation programme to improve the coordination of allied policies and programmes for materiel, technical and operational standardisation.
23 January	The Albanian Vice-Minister of Foreign Affairs, Arjan Starova, and Vice Minister of Defence, Alfred Moisiu, visit NATO and declare acceptance of the Albanian Individual Partnership Programme.
24 January	The NATO Council agrees on the establishment of a new NATO Standardisation Organisation.
31 January	US announces a one-year extension of its unilateral moratorium on nuclear testing.
8 February	The Latvian Defence Minister, Janis Trapans, visits NATO and declares acceptance of the Latvian Individual Partnership Programme. NATO approves plans for direct

dialogue with Egypt, Israel, Mauritania, Morocco and Tunisia to combat the threat of Islamic fundamentalism.

9 February	Visit to NATO by Hungarian Prime Minister Gyula Horn.
10 February	The Austrian Minister of Foreign Affairs, Alois Mock, visits NATO to sign the PfP Framework Document.
14-21 February	Ukraine's Minister of Defence, Valery Shmarov, meets with the Chairman of NATO's Military Committee and signs a protocol on mutual cooperation between Ukraine and NATO.
16 February	The Vice-President of the Muslim-Croatian Federation approves an international plan for the suspension of economic sanctions against Serbia in exchange for recognition of Bosnia and Croatia under the condition of a completely closed Bosnian-Serbian border.
23 February	Belarus suspends its weapons destruction programme, violating the CFE Treaty.
24 February	NATO opens talks in Brussels with Morocco, Egypt, Mauritania, Tunisia and Israel to discuss security in North Africa.
27 February	The Defence Ministers of Estonia, Latvia and Lithuania sign an agreement on military cooperation covering international policy and logistics. Visit to NATO by US Vice-President Al Gore.
1 March	The US, France, Germany and Italy agree in the scope of allied armaments cooperation to develop a Medium Extended Air Defence System (MEADS). Estonia signs an individual military cooperation programme with NATO following their membership of PfP since 1994.
6 March	Croatia forms a military alliance with the Bosnian Muslim-Croat federation. UNPROFOR remains in Croatia.
8 March	Secretary General Willy Claes and US President Bill Clinton meet in Washington to discuss a possible pullout of UN peacekeeping forces from Croatia and Bosnia.
16 March	A Slovak-Hungarian agreement is reached over a treaty on minority rights.
18-20 March	A Pan-European Security Conference meeting in Paris, attended by 50 countries, adopts a stability pact to eliminate the dangers of crisis in Europe and agrees on a series of measures relating to borders and the rights of ethnic minorities.
30-31 March	Meeting of the OSCE Senior Council discusses a Common and Comprehensive Security Model for the 21st

century - a comprehensive, inclusive concept of security, designed to benefit all participating states.

11 April	The UN Security Council adopts Resolution 984, guaranteeing assistance for non-nuclear states that have signed the 1970 nuclear Non-Proliferation Treaty (NPT) if subjected to nuclear threat or attack.
26 April	The Deputy Prime Minister and Minister of Foreign Affairs of Malta, Professor Guido de Marco, signs the Partnership for Peace Framework Document (Malta subsequently withdraws from PfP).
7 May	Commemoration of 50th anniversary of the end of World War II.
11 May	The Non-Proliferation Treaty is extended indefinitely by consensus.
15 May	The Ministers of Foreign Affairs and Defence of the WEU gathered in Lisbon, where they discussed the future relationship between the WEU and NATO.
25 May	In response to a request from the UN, NATO aircraft attack a Bosnian Serb ammunition depot near Pale. This is followed by a second attack the next day.
27 May	At a meeting, the North Atlantic Council demands that the Bosnian Serbs stop their attacks on UN safe areas and comply with the UNPROFOR ultimatum to remove all heavy weapons from the Sarajevo exclusion zone or place them under UN control. It condemns the killing and detention of UN peacekeepers.
30-31 May	The NATO Foreign Ministers and the North Atlantic Cooperation Council meet in Noordwijk, the Netherlands. At a special meeting with Russian Foreign Minister Kozyrev, Russia formally accepts the Russian Individual Partnership Programme under PfP and the document on "Areas for Pursuance of a Broad, Enhanced NATO-Russia Dialogue and Cooperation."
	In a statement on the situation in former Yugoslavia, the North Atlantic Council condemns the escalation of violence by the parties and hostile acts against UN personnel.
1 June	President of Ukraine, Mr. Leonid Kuchma, visits NATO.
28-30 June	A NATO Economic Colloquium attended by participants from NATO and Partner countries discusses the status of economic reforms in Cooperation Partner countries.
2 July	Srebrenica receives heaviest shelling since being declared a UN safe area. The UN War Crime Tribunal for-

	mally indicts Mr. Karadzic and General Mladic with charges of genocide and crimes against humanity.
11 July	NATO aircrafts attack targets in the Srebrenica area of Bosnia and Herzegovina.
12 July	The North Atlantic Council strongly condemns Bosnian Serb attacks in the safe area of Srebrenica.
1 August	US House of Representatives votes to lift Bosnian arms embargo.
	NATO launches Operation Deliberate Force, attacking Serb positions with aircraft and artillery in response to the shelling of Sarajevo.
30 August	NATO aircraft strikes against Bosnian Serbs positions near Sarajevo.
1 September	NATO aircraft resume bombing of Bosnian Serb positions; Bosnian Serbs respond by shelling Sarajevo.
	NATO aircraft attack Bosnian Serb targets near Pale.
	NATO suspends Operation Deliberate Force after Bosnian Serbs agree to withdraw heavy weapons from the 20 km exclusion zone around Sarajevo.
	Agreement on the framework of constitutional arrangements for Bosnia and Herzegovina is signed in New York.
2 September	NATO military commanders are authorised by the NATO Council to resume air strikes on Bosnian Serb positions at any time to counter further aggression against UN-designated safe areas.
5 September	NATO aircraft resumed attacks on Bosnian-Serb military targets.
12 September	A framework for the Wassenaar Arrangement, the successor to COCOM, establishing export controls on certain conventional weapons and dual-use technologies is reached in The Hague.
14 September	Greece and the former Yugoslav Republic of Macedonia* sign an agreement to establish diplomatic relations and economic ties.
	The NAC meets in a special session with the Ministers of Foreign Affairs of Ukraine, Gennadi Udovenko, to discuss the strengthening of NATO-Ukraine relations.
	Bosnian Serb military and political leaders sign an agreement to withdraw their heavy weapons from the 20 km exclusion zone around Sarajevo.
20 September	Council meeting with Russia on the implementation of the CFE Treaty.

21 September	NATO ambassadors approve a Study on NATO Enlargement outlining the membership requirements for countries wanting to join the Alliance.
25 September	The Review Conference of the UN Conventional Weapons opens in Vienna.
26 September	NATO presents a draft proposal of a "Political Framework for NATO-Russia Relations" to Russian Ambassador Churkin.
28 September	NATO presents the conclusions of the Study on NATO Enlargement to NACC and PfP Cooperation partners.
2 October	Croats and Serbs strike deal over Eastern Slavonia to place it under Croatian administration after a transition period.
	Three Serb SAM sites are attacked by NATO aircrafts.
	The cease-fire in Bosnia comes into effect.
5-6 October	NATO Ministers of Defence meet in Williamsburg, USA.
12 October	Visit to NATO by President Sali Berisha of Albania.
13 October	UN Conference on Conventional Weapons ends without agreement on a global ban on anti-personnel landmines.
19 October	NATO Council meets with Russian representative to discuss Peace Implementation Planning in Bosnia.
21 October	Willy Claes resigns as NATO Secretary General.
27 October	A Memorandum of Understanding is signed between NATO and the WEU to enable direct and plain communication between both organisations.
	Visit to NATO by Special Representative of the UN Secretary-General and Special Envoy to NATO, Kofi Annan.
1 November	Bosnian peace talks start in Dayton, Ohio. An agreement is signed in Dayton on the reintegration of Eastern Slavonia into Croatia.
	The UN Security Council suspends sanctions on the former Yugoslavia.
8 November	US Secretary of Defence William Perry and Russian Defence Minister General Pavel Grachev visit NATO to discuss participation of Russian forces in IFOR.
13 November	The US Senate Foreign Relations Committee and the Armed Services Committee block the ratification of the Chemical Weapons Convention.
14 November	The Ministers of Foreign Affairs and Defence of the WEU nations meet in Madrid and affirm the objective of developing the WEU as a means to strengthen the European pillar in NATO.

15 November	The President of the former Yugoslav Republic of Macedonia*, Branko Crvenkovski, visits NATO. His country joins PfP.
22 November	Visits to NATO by President Martti Aktisaari of Finland, and OSCE Chairman Lazlo Kovacs.
27 November	Recipients from 14 Alliance countries receive medals for service in relation to former Yugoslavia.
28 November	The European Union and 12 Mediterranean neighbours sign an agreement in Barcelona on future political and economic cooperation.
1 December	Javier Solana Madariaga is appointed Secretary General of NATO.
5 December	The NAC meets at ministerial level. Foreign and Defence Ministers of all 16 nations affirm their commitment to continue the Alliance's efforts to bring peace to Bosnia and Herzegovina.
	NATO formally endorses the deployment of 60 000 troops in Bosnia. The German Parliament votes to contribute 4 000 troops.
	In Paris, the Presidents of Bosnia and Herzegovina, Croatia and Serbia sign the General Framework Accord for peace in Bosnia and Herzegovina.
	US troops arrive in Tuzla and UN hands over commands of military operations in Bosnia to NATO.
	NATO Commander, Admiral Leighton Smith, turns down requests by the Bosnian Serb Assembly leader, Momcilo Krajisnik, for delay of at least nine months in transferring Bosnian Serb areas of Sarajevo to Muslim control.
	France announces that it will resume its seat in the NATO Military Committee. The French Minister of Defence will also regularly attend the Defence Planning Committee and other meetings.
7-8 December	OSCE Ministerial Council in Budapest gives guidelines for Security Model and confirms its role in Bosnia and Herzegovina.
14 December	President Slobodan Milosevic of Serbia, President Alya Izetbegovic of Bosnia and Herzegovina and President Franjo Tudjman of Croatia sign the Bosnian Peace Agreement in Paris.
15 December	The UN Security Council adopts Resolution 1031 on the establishment of a Multinational Military Implementation Force.

16 December	Beginning of the deployment of the NATO-led Implementation Force (IFOR) in Bosnia.
19 December	Twenty-Eight countries sign the Wassenaar Arrangement on armament and technology export controls.
20 December	UN peacekeeping forces (UNPROFOR) hand over command of military operations in Bosnia to the NATO-led Implementation Force (IFOR).

1996

3 January	US Defence Secretary William Perry flies to Sarajevo to discuss peacekeeping with NATO military officers and Bosnian leaders.
4 January	Negotiations open in Vienna under OSCE auspices on confidence building and arms control measures in Bosnia. The parties to the Peace Agreement sign agreements on measures to enhance mutual confidence, reduce the risk of conflict, restrict military power and improve political cooperation.
5 January	Russian parliament votes in favour the deployment of Russian forces to Bosnia to join the NATO-led peacekeeping mission. Special arrangements apply to the command and control of Russian forces in IFOR.
11 January	Prince El-Hassan Bin Talal of Jordan meets with Secretary General Solana in the context of NATO's Mediterranean Dialogue.
13 January	Beginning of deployment of Russian troops supporting IFOR in Bosnia.
15 January	The UN Security Council authorises a 5 000 men strong force backed by NATO air power for Eastern Slavonia.
17 January	Visits to NATO by President Aleksander Kwasniewski of Poland and by Hans Koschnik, EU Administrator for Mostar.
19 January	Richard Goldstone, Prosecutor of UN War Crimes Tribunal, visits NATO.
23 January	General George Joulwan (SACEUR) visits Russia for discussions with the Russian Defence Minister and Chief of Staff.
24 January	Tiit Vähi, Prime Minister of Estonia, visits NATO.
26 January	The Russian Federation joins the Council of Europe.
	The American Senate ratifies the START II Treaty, which will reduce the levels of both American and Russian strategic nuclear missiles.

29 January	The Secretary General of the OSCE begins a two-day visit to former Yugoslavia to pave the way for OSCE's supervision of postwar free elections.
12 February	The NATO Secretary General visits Mostar.
	Bosnian authorities give their approval for the release of two Bosnian Serb officers to the International War Crimes Tribunal.
26 February	Visit to NATO by Austrian Vice-Chancellor Wolfgang Schüssel.
	Austria signs its Individual Partnership Programme (IPP) with NATO.
8 March	Permanent Representatives on the North Atlantic Council visit Sarajevo.
13 March	Russia signs IFOR Participation and Financial Agreements.
15 March	US Secretary of State Warren Christopher visits SHAPE to meet with Supreme Allied Commander Europe, General George Joulwan, to discuss efforts to obtain compliance with the Dayton Peace Agreement on Bosnia and the subject of NATO enlargement.
20-21 March	NATO Secretary General Solana pays an official visit to Moscow to discuss NATO and Russia relations. He meets with Russian President Yeltsin, the Speaker of the Duma, Seleznev Gennady and other senior officials.
20 March	A Memorandum of Understanding on Civil Emergency Cooperation between NATO and Russia is signed in Moscow.
23 March	The Foreign Ministers of the contact group on the former Yugoslavia meet in Moscow.
25 March	President Jelev of Bulgaria visits NATO.
26 March	The Prime Minister of Belarus, Mikhail Chygir, the President of Latvia, Guntis Ulmanis, and the President of Estonia, Lennart Meri visit NATO.
23 April	Visits to NATO by Georgian President Eduard Shevardnadze and President of Armenia, Levon Ter Petrossian.
24 April	The Minister of Foreign Affairs and Deputy Prime Minister of Malta, Professor Guido de Marco, visits NATO.
26 April	HM King Juan Carlos of Spain visits NATO.
29 April	The NAC states that IFOR has brought a secure environment to Bosnia and Herzegovina during its first four months of mission.

2 May	NATO Secretary General Javier Solana and WEU Secretary-General José Cutileiro sign a security agreement. The Agreement sets out procedures for protecting and safeguarding classified information and material provided by either organisation.
7 May	The Ministers of Foreign Affairs and Defence of the WEU nations meet in Birmingham.
8 May	Carl Bildt, High Representative responsible for coordinating civilian aspects of the peace agreement for the former Yugoslavia, visits NATO.
9 May	SHAPE and the International Criminal Tribunal for the former Yugoslavia conclude a Memorandum of Understanding which codifies practical arrangements for the detention and transfer of persons indicted for war crimes.
15-31 May	First CFE Treaty Review Meeting is held in Vienna. Negotiations achieve a solution to the "Flank Agreement" and agreement on further negotiations relating to the Treaty.
16 May	NATO Secretary General Solana visits Banja Luka and Belgrade along with General George Joulwan, SACEUR.
19-21 May	Representatives from NATO and Cooperation Partner countries meet near Bonn to review worldwide efforts to destroy and dismantle chemical, nuclear and conventional weapons.*
21 May	Visit to NATO by Prime Minister Janez Drnovsek of Slovenia.
3 June	Meeting of NATO Foreign Ministers in Berlin. Ministers agree to build up the European Security and Defence Identity within NATO as part of the internal adaptation of the Alliance.
12 June	The former Yugoslav Republic of Macedonia* signs the individual Partnership for Peace Programme.
13 June	The NAC meets in Defence Minister session.
14-15 June	NATO Secretary General Solana visits Zagreb and Sarajevo.
18 June	Following the termination of the UN arms embargo on the former Yugoslavia, Operation Sharp Guard is suspended.
26-28 June	NATO Economics Colloquium on Economic Developments and Reforms in Cooperation Partner countries.
1 July	Establishment of a new NATO Consultation, Command and Control (C3) Agency.

3 July	Boris Yeltsin is re-elected President of the Russian Federation.
17 July	Admiral Leighton Smith is honoured with the NATO medal for his role as Commander of the Implementation Force and Commander in Chief Southern Region.
19 July	The North Atlantic Council endorses an overall NATO Standardisation Programme involving 50 harmonised standardisation objectives.
13 August	NATO Secretary General Solana and US Secretary of State Warren Christopher meet in Brussels to discuss the Bosnian election, enlargement of the Alliance and relations with Russia.
27 August	An agreement signed on ending the conflict in Chechnya which began at the end of 1995 is brokered by Russian special envoy Alexander Lebed.
14 September	IFOR troops provide security for elections held in Bosnia and Herzegovina to be monitored by the OSCE.
16 September	Visit to NATO of Hungarian President Arpad Göncz.
20 September	Meeting of Secretary General Solana with Russian Foreign Minister Primakov in Vienna.
24 September	China, France, Russia, United Kingdom and United States sign a Comprehensive Test Ban Treaty.
25-26 September	Informal meeting of NATO Defence Ministers in Bergen, Norway to discuss the peacekeeping operation in Bosnia.
2 October	The WEU Council decides to end the Danube Embargo Enforcement Operation against the Federal Republic of Yugoslavia.
7 October	Secretary of the Security Council of the Russian Federation, General Alexander Lebed, visits NATO Headquarters.
16 October	President Algirdas Brazauskas of Lithuania visits NATO.
17 October	Visit to NATO by President Michal Kovac of Slovakia.
19 October	Russian President Boris Yeltsin replaces his recently-appointed Secretary of the Security Council Alexander Lebed by the Speaker of the Duma Ivan Rybkin.
29 October	Malta announces its intention to withdraw from the Partnership for Peace Programme.
5 November	Bill Clinton is re-elected President of the United States.
13 November	President of Uzbekistan Islam Karimov visits NATO.
14 November	The Spanish Parliament endorses Spanish participation in NATO's new military structure.
27 November	Prime Minister Paavo Lipponen of Finland visits NATO.

2-3 December	OSCE summit in Lisbon on European Security issues adopts a Declaration on a Common and Comprehensive Security Model for Europe for the 21st Century.
9 December	German Chancellor Kohl and French President Jacques Chirac sign an agreement on mutual security and defence.
10 December	Ministerial meeting of the North Atlantic Council at NATO Headquarters in Brussels confirms NATO readiness to organise and lead a Stabilisation Force (SFOR) in Bosnia and Herzegovina, subject to a UN Security Council mandate. Ministers also announce further steps to be taken in the internal and external transformation of the Alliance in preparation for the July 1997 Madrid Summit. NATO issues a statement on the stationing of nuclear forces.
11 December	Switzerland signs the Partnership for Peace Framework Document, during a meeting with the North Atlantic Council.
17 December	Kofi Annan becomes Secretary General of the United Nations.
18 December	H.M. The Sultan of Brunei visits NATO.
20 December	NATO's Implementation Force (IFOR) in Bosnia is replaced by SFOR (Stabilisation Force).

1997

16-17 January	NATO Secretary General Javier Solana visits Austria and meets Federal Chancellor Franz Vranitzky and other political leaders.
17 January	Richard C. Holbrooke receives the first Manfred Woerner Medal for his contribution to peace in the former Yugoslavia.
19-21 January	First round of talks between Secretary General Javier Solana and Russian Foreign Minister Yevgeni Primakov on a NATO-Russia Document in Moscow.
21 January	Negotiations on a revision of the 1990 CFE treaty start in Vienna.
22 January	Prime Minister Thorbjörn Jagland of Norway visits NATO.
28 January	NATO Secretary General Javier Solana visits Paris to meet French President Jacques Chirac.
29 January	Visits to NATO by Bulgarian President Petar Stoyanov and Romanian President Emil Constantinescu.
30 January	NATO Secretary General Javier Solana addresses the Parliamentary Assembly of the Council of Europe.

4 February	In his State of the Union address American President Bill Clinton vows to pursue NATO's enlargement by 1999 and to establish a "stable partnership" with Russia.
5-6 February	Secretary General Javier Solana meets Turkish President Suleyman Demirel and Prime Minister Necmettin Erbakan in Ankara to discuss the expansion of the Alliance and the broader issue of Turkey's place in Europe.
10-14 February	NATO Secretary General Javier Solana visits Moldova, Georgia, Armenia and Azerbaijan to meet Heads of State and government and other leading politicians.
12 February	Former guerrilla leader Aslam Maskhadov is sworn in as new Chechen President.
18 February	Newly-appointed US Secretary of State, Madeleine Albright attends her first NATO Foreign Ministers Meeting in Brussels and proposes the creation of a permanent Russia-NATO brigade.
19 February	EU High Representative in Bosnia Carl Bildt visits NATO.
20 February	NATO allies propose major changes to the CFE Treaty, which limits conventional forces in Europe. NATO now accepts the principle of limits on the arsenals of individual countries as opposed to regions. The Alliance also accepts Russia's wish on having territorial rather than national limits on troops deployment, which effectively prevents NATO from massing troops in one particular area near Russia's borders.
21 February	Visit to NATO by Polish Prime Minister Wlodzimierz Cimoczewicz.
23 February	NATO Secretary General Javier Solana meets Russian Foreign Minister Yevgeni Primakov for a second round of talks on a NATO-Russia document in Moscow.
7 March	US Defence Secretary William Cohen makes his first visit to NATO headquarters in Brussels.
9-10 March	Secretary General Javier Solana meets Russian Foreign Minister Yevgeni Primakov in Moscow for the third round of negotiations on a document to lay out the basis for NATO-Russia relations.
10-15 March	Secretary General Javier Solana visits PfP members in Central Asia: Kazakhstan, the Kyrghyz Republic, Uzbekistan and Turkmenistan.
11 March	WEU conference in Athens to discuss security problems in the light of NATO and EU enlargement.
16 March	EU Foreign Ministers meet in Apeldoorn, the Netherlands, to discuss EU enlargement among other issues.

20-21 March	US President Bill Clinton and his Russian counterpart Boris Yeltsin meet in Helsinki to talk about future NATO-Russian relations. The parties do not issue a joint statement on NATO plans to expand eastwards, but sign a general statement about European security.
21 March	Official visit to NATO by HM Albert II, King of the Belgians.
24-25 March	NATO Secretary General Javier Solana and General George A. Joulwan (SACEUR) visit the former Yugoslav Republic of Macedonia* and the Republic of Bosnia and Herzegovina.
2 April	Baltic Defence Ministers meet in Vilnius, Lithuania, to discuss the formation of a joint peacekeeping battalion (BALTBAT) and a joint naval squadron (BALTRON).
9-11 April	NATO Secretary General Javier Solana meets US Secretary of State Madeleine Albright on NATO-Russian relations and visits Canada.
15 April	NATO Secretary General Javier Solana meets Russian Foreign Minister Yevgeni Primakov in Moscow for a fourth round of talks on a NATO-Russia document.
	The first of 6 000 Italian-led multinational security landing force arrive at Tirana's airport. Operation Alba aims at the protection of humanitarian aid to Albania.
	WEU members agree that non-members Turkey and Norway would have the option of playing a full role in any WEU operations launched with NATO equipment.
17 April	Poland announces it will reduce its number of troops from 220 000 to 180 000 over the next seven years to meet NATO standards.
24 April	US Senate approves the Chemical Weapons Convention, a global treaty banning chemical weapons. (The Convention comes into force on 29 April).
6 May	NATO Secretary General Javier Solana has a fifth round of talks with Russian Foreign Minister Primakov in Luxembourg on a NATO-Russia document.
7 May	NATO Secretary General Javier Solana visits Ukraine to meet President Leonid Kuchma and inaugurates a NATO Information and Documentation Centre in Kyiv.
12-13 May	Foreign and Defence Ministers from 28 European countries meet in Paris, under the auspices of the WEU, to discuss security issues.
13-14 May	NATO Secretary General Javier Solana and Russian Foreign Minister Yevgeni Primakov meet in Moscow for a sixth round of negotiations on a NATO-Russia document

14 May	NATO Secretary General Javier Solana and Russian Foreign Minister Yevgeni Primakov reach agreement on the "Founding Act on Mutual Relations, Cooperation and Security between NATO and the Russian Federation".
22 May	Russian President Boris Yeltsin replaces Minister of Defence Igor Rodionov by Viktor Samsonov.
27 May	NATO-Russia Summit Meeting in Paris. Signature of the Founding Act on Mutual Relations, Cooperation and Security between NATO and the Russian Federation.
29 May	On the margins of the meeting of NATO Foreign Ministers in Sintra, Portugal, NATO Secretary General Solana and Ukrainian Foreign Minister Udovenko initial a "Charter for a Distinctive Partnership Between NATO and Ukraine".
30 May	Concluding meeting of the North Atlantic Cooperation Council (NACC) and inaugural meeting of the Euro-Atlantic Partnership Council (EAPC) in Sintra, Portugal. NATO and Cooperation Partner Foreign Ministers approve the EAPC Basic Document.
2 June	Signature of Treaty of Friendship and Cooperation between Romania and Ukraine.
12-13 June	NATO's Defence Ministers meet in Brussels for their annual spring meetings.
16-17 June	European Council summit in Amsterdam agrees on a new EU treaty, but makes no significant move towards taking charge of their joint defence. The WEU remains an independent body sub-contracted to carry out humanitarian, peace-keeping and crisis management missions for the Union.
16-27 June	PfP naval exercise "Baltic Operations 1997" (BALTOPS) takes place in Poland and Germany to conduct maritime search and rescue operations, coastal surveillance and customs enforcement. Participants are the United States, Denmark, Estonia, Finland, Germany, Latvia, Lithuania, the Netherlands, Norway, Poland, Russia, Sweden and the United Kingdom.
20-22 June	Russia joins the "G7" Summit (hereafter "G 8").
25-27 June	NATO Economics Colloquium on Economic Developments in Cooperation Partner countries.
26 June	The Conference on Disarmament (CD) in Geneva agrees to break its deadlock and to open global negotiations for the gradual elimination of land mines. The 61 participating countries appoint Ambassador John Campbell of Australia

	as special coordinator. Separate negotiations on a global land mine ban, initiated by Canada, continue in Brussels.
8 July	Madrid Summit Meeting of the North Atlantic Council. NATO Heads of State and Government agree to invite the Czech Republic, Hungary and Poland to begin accession talks with NATO with a view to becoming members of the Alliance, after completion of the ratification process, in April 1999. They reaffirm that NATO remains open to new members under Article 10 of the North Atlantic Treaty and agree to review the process at their next meeting in 1999.
	Formal signature of the Charter on a Distinctive Partnership between NATO and Ukraine.
	NATO Heads of State and Government issue a special declaration on Bosnia and Herzegovina reaffirming their commitment to the full implementation of the Peace Agreement and to the establishment of Bosnia and Herzegovina as a single, democratic and multiethnic state.
9 July	Meeting of the Heads of State and Government of NATO and Cooperation Partners under the aegis of the Euro-Atlantic Cooperation Council (EAPC). The meeting focuses on how the EAPC can most effectively be used to contribute to security and stability.
11 July	US Army General Wesley Clark replaces General G. Joulwan to become the new Supreme Allied Commander Europe (SACEUR).
16 July	Coordination of assistance for flooding in Poland takes place through NATO's Disaster Relief Policy at the request of the Polish government.
18 July	First meeting of the NATO-Russia Permanent Joint Council (PJC) at Ambassadorial level in Brussels agrees on organisational and procedural arrangements.
22 July	The WEU issues a Declaration on the Role of the Western European Union and its Relations with the European Union and the Atlantic Alliance.
10 September	Representatives from Hungary begin accession talks with NATO.
15 September	Operation Kozatskiy Step 97 under Partnership for Peace begins in Ukraine, involving NATO, Polish and Ukrainian troops. The exercise is designed to simulate an ethnic conflict.
16 September	Representatives from Poland begin accession talks with NATO.
22 September	Swedish Prime Minister Göran Persson visits NATO.

23 September	Representatives from the Czech Republic begin accession talks with NATO.
24 September	Latvian Prime Minister Guntars Krasts visits NATO.
26 September	NATO and Russian Foreign Ministers meet for the first time as the NATO-Russia Permanent Joint Council. A Work Plan is approved, providing for consultations on confidence building measures in arms-control, joint peacekeeping in Bosnia and the stationing of Russian military representatives at NATO.
30 September	NATO Ministers of Defence held two days of informal meetings in Maastricht, the Netherlands. The planned opening up of NATO to new members, the continuation of NATO's mandate in Bosnia and the adaptation of Alliance's command structure are discussed.
1 October	Russia's Defence Minister, Igor Sergeyev, meeting with NATO Defence Ministers, agrees that Russia will send a military liaison officer to the Alliance's Brussels Headquarters in the near future.
	At the request of the High Representative in Bosnia, SFOR takes action against Serbian Radio and TV transmitters, following violations and misuse.
2-8 October	General Assembly of the Atlantic Treaty Association in Sofia, hosted by the Atlantic Club of Bulgaria.
8 October	High Representative in Bosnia Carlos Westendorp and Ambassador Robert H. Frowick visit NATO.
9 October	Ukraine and Hungary become the first non-NATO countries to open diplomatic missions to the Alliance.
13 October	43rd Annual Session of North Atlantic Assembly takes place in Bucharest.
24 October	Following the 23 October visit to NATO of the Russian Chief of General Staff, General Kvashnin, participants in the third meeting of the NATO-Russia Permanent Joint Council at Ambassadorial level issue a statement welcoming the appointment of Lieutenant-General Zavarzin as Russia's military representative to NATO.
16 November	Hungarians voted overwhelmingly (85 percent) to join NATO in a national referendum.
18 November	Foreign and Defence Ministers of the WEU met in Erfurt, Germany and agreed on harmonising the EU and WEU presidencies.
25 November	Russian military representative to NATO, Lieutenant-General Viktor Zavarzin, held his first official meeting with NATO Military Committee Chairman, Klaus Naumann.

27 November	Visit to NATO by Polish Prime Minister Jerzy Buzek.
2-3 December	First meeting of the NATO-Russia Permanent Joint Council at Defence Ministers level. Military chiefs of staff from 44 countries also meet in the framework of the Euro-Atlantic Partnership Council. Defence Ministers of 15 NATO member countries meet within the Nuclear Planning Group and Defence Planning Committee. The 16 members of the Alliance meet shortly afterwards in the North Atlantic Council.
4 December	Meeting of NATO-Russia PJC at Chiefs of Staff level.
16 December	NATO and Ukraine sign a Memorandum of Understanding on Civil Emergency Planning and Disaster Preparedness.
16-17 December	NATO Foreign Ministers sign Protocols of Accession for the Czech Republic, Hungary and Poland in the presence of their respective Foreign Ministers.
18-19 December	OSCE General Assembly meeting concludes with an agreement on guidelines to work out a European Security Charter.

1998

14 January	Euro-Atlantic Partnership Council (EAPC) publishes its Action Plan for 1998-2000. Visit to NATO by UN High Commissioner for Refugees, Sadako Ogata.
26 January	Visit to NATO by President Petra Lucinschi of Moldova.
4 February	Visit to NATO by the Prime Minister of the former Yugoslav Republic of Macedonia*, Branko Crevenkovski.
11 February	Inauguration of the NATO Documentation Centre for European Security Issues at the Institute of Scientific Information for Social Sciences (INION) in Moscow.
12-18 February	Annual NATO Crisis Management Exercise involving active participation of NATO Partner Countries for the first time.
20 February	NATO announces readiness to organise and lead a multi-national force in Bosnia and Herzegovina after the expiry of SFOR's mandate in June 1998, subject to UN Security Council mandate.
23 February	Visit to NATO by President Saparmurat Niyazov of Turkmenistan.
25 February	The Secretary General of NATO welcomes the agreement between the UN Secretary General and Iraq on a diplomatic solution to the Iraq crisis. He underlines the importance of providing immediate unconditional and unre-

stricted access to UNSCOM weapons inspectors in accordance with UN Security Council resolutions.

The NATO-Russia Permanent Joint Council discusses NATO-Russia cooperation in SFOR with a view to its continuation in the framework of the multinational force in Bosnia following the end of SFOR's current mandate in June 1998.

4 March	The North Atlantic Council welcomes UN Security Council Resolution 1154 relating to Iraq and gives its strong support to UN insistence on full compliance by Iraq.
5 March	The North Atlantic Council issues a statement expressing its concern over recent violent incidents in Kosovo and calls on all sides to take immediate steps to reduce tensions.
	The Council issues a statement supporting the efforts of the OSCE Mission to Croatia relating to the resettlement of refugees and displaced persons and reminds Croatia of its obligations under the Bosnian Peace Agreement.
11 March	Ambassadors and representatives of EAPC countries discuss the serious developments in Kosovo and enumerate the conditions needed for peaceful settlement.
7 April	Official inauguration of the Manfred Woerner Building adjacent to the NATO Headquarters in Brussels, housing Partner countries' diplomatic missions to NATO.
20 April	Permanent Representatives on the North Atlantic Council visit Bosnia and Herzegovina, accompanied by Secretary General Javier Solana and Chairman of the Military Committee General Naumann.
23 April	Visit to NATO by President Valdas Adamkus of Lithuania.
27-28 April	EAPC seminar in Bratislava on Democratic Control of Defence Expenditures.
28 April	Visit to NATO by Mr. Josef Tosovsky, Prime Minister of the Czech Republic.
20 May	The North Atlantic Council condemns India's decision to conduct nuclear tests.
28 May	At the NATO-Russia Permanent Joint Council Meeting in Luxembourg, NATO and Russia condemn nuclear tests conducted by India and Pakistan.
	At the meeting a Memorandum of Understanding on Scientific and Technological Cooperation between NATO and the Ministry of Science and Technology of the Russian Federation, is signed.

	At the meeting of the North Atlantic Council, NATO Foreign Ministers issue a statement expressing concern over the situation in Kosovo and outline measures being taken to contain the crisis and to seek a peaceful resolution.
29 May	Establishment of the Euro-Atlantic Disaster Response Coordination Centre (EADRCC) at NATO under the aegis of the EAPC.
30 May	The NATO Secretary General condemns further nuclear tests by Pakistan and calls on India and Pakistan to halt nuclear and missile testing, adhere to the NPT and CTBT and begin a dialogue to reduce tensions.
12 June	The NATO-Russia Permanent Joint Council (Defence Ministers) agrees to continue NATO-Russia cooperation in SFOR and condemns Belgrade's use of force in Kosovo as well as attacks by Kosovar extremists.
15 June	NATO air exercise "Determined Falcon" takes place in Albania and the former Yugoslav Republic of Macedonia* in agreement with the respective governments.
18 June	At a meeting of the NATO-Russia Permanent Joint Council, NATO and Russia reaffirm their determination to contribute to international efforts to find a peaceful solution to the crisis in Kosovo.
17-19 June	NATO Economics Colloquium on Economic Developments and Reforms in Cooperation Partner Countries takes place in Ljubljana, Slovenia.
2-3 July	NATO Information Seminar takes place in Sarajevo, aimed at encouraging the development of democratic practices in Bosnia and Herzegovina.
10 July	Visit to NATO by Bulgarian President Petar Stoyanov.
24 July	Visit to NATO by Hungarian Prime Minister Viktor Orban.
12 August	NATO Secretary General Javier Solana expresses deep concern over the continuing violence in Kosovo, indicating that the North Atlantic Council had reviewed military planning for options to bring an end to the violence and create conditions for negotiations.
14 September	NATO Secretary General Javier Solana calls on all sides to show restraint and establish conditions for a return to a peaceful and stable environment throughout Albania.
18 September	M. Hubert Védrine, Minister of Foreign Affairs of France, becomes President of the North Atlantic Council[3].

---

3   An honorary position held in rotation by a Foreign Minister of one of the Member countries.

24 September	The North Atlantic Council approves the issuing of an activation warning (ACTWARN) for both a limited air option and a phased air campaign in Kosovo.
24-25 September	Informal meeting of NATO Defence Ministers in Vilamoura, Portugal.
30 September	At a meeting of the Permanent Joint Council, NATO and Russia discuss continuation of NATO-Russia cooperation in SFOR and reiterate concern about the humanitarian situation in Kosovo.
5 October	Visit to NATO by President Milan Kucan of Slovenia.
7 October	Visits to NATO by the Prime Minister of the Czech Republic, Milos Zeman and by the Prime Minister of Bulgaria, Ivan Kostov.
9 October	NATO and Russia express full support for diplomatic efforts aimed at securing a political solution to the crisis in Kosovo and stress the need for immediate full and irreversible compliance with UN Security Council Resolutions 1160 and 1199.
13 October	In the absence of compliance by the Federal Republic of Yugoslavia with UNSCR 1199, the North Atlantic Council reviews the situation in Kosovo and issues activation orders (ACTORDs) for both limited air strikes and a phased air campaign in Yugoslavia after approximately 96 hours.
13-15 October	Under the aegis of the NATO Air Defence Committee, a first joint exercise is held at Kayseri airbase in Turkey, involving the strategic loading of a NATO mobile air defence radar by a Russian Illuyshin 76 heavy transport aircraft. The exercise is in preparation for potential cooperation in combined peace support operations.
15 October	Visits to NATO by the President of Latvia, Guntis Ulmanis and by the Prime Minister of Poland Jerzy Buzek.
	NATO Secretary General Javier Solana visits Belgrade, accompanied by the Chairman of the Military Committee General Naumann and Supreme Allied Commander Europe (SACEUR) General Clark, to insist upon full and immediate compliance by President Milosevic with UNSCR 1199 relating to Kosovo. Agreement is signed on air verification force over Kosovo.
16 October	The North Atlantic Council announces its decision to maintain its readiness to launch air operations against Yugoslavia and extends the period before execution of air strikes to 27 October.

20 October	Supreme Allied Commander Europe (SACEUR) General Clark meets Serbian leadership in Belgrade over the Kosovo crisis.
21 October	Carlos Westendorp, the High Representative responsible for coordinating the civilian organisations and agencies in Bosnia and Herzegovina, visits NATO for discussions with the Secretary General and to address the North Atlantic Council.
	At a meeting of the NATO-Russia Permanent Joint Council, Ambassadors discuss the situation in Bosnia and Herzegovina and in Kosovo. NATO and Russia support the aims of securing a political solution to the crisis in Kosovo based on strict compliance with UNSCR 1160 and 1199.
20 October	Visit to NATO by Radu Vasile, Prime Minister of Romania.
22 October	Visit to NATO by the Prime Minister of the former Yugoslav Republic of Macedonia* Branko Crvenkovski.
24-25 October	The Chairman of the NATO Military Committee General Naumann and General Clark return to Belgrade to meet the Serbian leadership over the Kosovo crisis.
27 October	NATO Secretary General Javier Solana issues a statement noting improvement of the security and humanitarian situation in Kosovo following the decisions taken by the North Atlantic Council on 13 October; reaffirming the need for full compliance with UNSCR 1199 and 1203; announcing the maintenance of NATO's ACTORD for limited air operations subject to decision and assessments by the Council and maintenance of the ACTORD for a phased air campaign; and calling for equal compliance with UNSC Resolutions by the Kosovar Albanians.
4 November	Visit to NATO by President Lennart Meri of Estonia.
5 November	Visit to NATO by Mikulas Dzurinda, Prime Minister of Slovakia.
11 November	Meeting of the NATO-Ukraine Commission. Members welcome information on the State Programme of Ukraine on Cooperation with NATO recently approved by President Kuchma and discuss other matters including the stationing of two NATO liaison officers in Kyiv to facilitate Ukraine's participation in PfP.
16 November	NATO Secretary General attends WEU ministerial meeting in Rome, Italy.
18-20 November	NATO Secretary General meets UN Secretary General Kofi Annan and senior US administration officials and US Senators in New York and Washington.

19 November	First meeting of the NATO-Russia Joint Science and Technological Cooperation Committee in Moscow, Russia. The North Atlantic Council expresses concern about the deteriorating situation in Kosovo, insisting that all parties must comply fully with relevant United Nations Security Council resolutions.
25 November	The President of Romania, Dr. Emil Constantinescu, visits NATO Headquarters.
26 November	NATO Secretary General and Supreme Allied Commander Europe visit the former Yugoslav Republic of Macedonia* to discuss the situation in Kosovo with President Kiro Gligorov and senior government officials.
26-27 November	Ukraine's State Inter-Agency Commission visits NATO to present Ukraine's programme of cooperation with NATO (1999-2001).
27 November	Visit to NATO of the Prime Minister of Slovakia, Mikulas Dzurinda.
30 November	NATO-Russia Permanent Joint Council discusses NATO-Russia cooperation in SFOR in Bosnia and Herzegovina and ways to cooperate in support of the international verification mission in Kosovo.
2 December	NATO Secretary General Javier Solana issues a statement on the detention by SFOR troops of indicted war criminal, General Radislav Krstic. The former Yugoslav Republic of Macedonia* agrees to allow a NATO force to be stationed on its territory, to evacuate international personnel involved in the OSCE verification mission in neighbouring Kosovo, if called upon to do so.
3 December	Visit to NATO by the Prime Minister of Albania, Pandeli Majko.
7 December	Visit to NATO by the Prime Minister of the former Yugoslav Republic of Macedonia*, Ljubco Georgievski.
8 December	The North Atlantic Council meets at foreign minister level, with the participation of the three invitee countries - the Czech Republic, Hungary and Poland. Ministers discuss preparations for the Washington Summit in April 1999, review the situation in Bosnia and Herzegovina and the future of SFOR, and consult on the situation in Kosovo. They also review progress made on the internal adaptation of NATO and on updating the Alliance's Strategic Concept. A separate statement is issued on behalf of the 19 Governments on the adaptation of the CFE Treaty.

The Euro-Atlantic Partnership Council meets at foreign minister level. Ministers discuss future security challenges and NATO-Partner cooperation in the context of EAPC and PfP, focusing on the situations in Bosnia and Herzegovina and in Kosovo. They review progress on the implementation of the EAPC Basic Document and the enhancement of the Partnership for Peace, and endorse an updated EAPC Action Plan for 1998-2000.

Foreign Minister of Austria, Wolfgang Schüssel, in his capacity as President of the Council of the European Union, meets with the NATO Secretary General for an informal exchange of views on issues of common concern, including the situations in Kosovo and Bosnia and Herzegovina.

9 December	The NATO-Russian Permanent Joint Council meets at foreign minister level. Ministers review implementation of the 1998 PJC Work Programme, welcoming progress made on developing a strong, stable partnership and emphasising the usefulness of the PJC in promoting consultation, coordination, and joint action.
	The NATO-Ukraine Commission meets at foreign minister level. Ministers review the implementation of the NATO-Ukraine Charter and agree on the work programme for 1999. A Memorandum of Understanding is signed concerning the appointment of two NATO Liaison Officers in Kyiv. NATO Ministers welcome the announcement of Ukraine's "State Programme of Cooperation with NATO to the Year 2001".
10 December	The Secretary General of NATO visits Bosnia and Herzegovina accompanied by General Wesley K. Clark (SACEUR).
17 December	The North Atlantic Council meets at defence minister level, with the participation of the three invitee countries - the Czech Republic, Hungary and Poland. Ministers review progress on the implementation of the decisions of the Madrid Summit in the defence field, discuss NATO's defence capabilities and preparations for the Washington Summit. They also take stock of the situation in Bosnia and Herzegovina and in Kosovo.
	Ministerial meeting of the Defence Planning Committee and the Nuclear Planning Group. Ministers approve the 1998 Ministerial Guidance providing political guidance to

NATO's Military Authorities for the period up to 2006 and beyond.

NATO Secretary General issues a statement calling for President Saddam Hussein to comply fully with all Iraq's obligations and to resume cooperation with the United Nations Special Commission on disarmament (UNSCOM).

18 December   The Euro-Atlantic Partnership Council meets at defence minister level to discuss future security challenges and NATO-Partner cooperation in the context of EAPC and PfP from the defence perspective. Ministers also exchange views on the situation in Bosnia and Herzegovina and stress the need for an early negotiated settlement to the crisis in Kosovo. NATO ministers welcome the willingness of Partners to contribute to the NATO-led Kosovo air verification mission.

The NATO-Ukraine Commission meets at defence minister level to review the implementation of activities related to defence and military cooperation between NATO and Ukraine.

1999

1 January   The NATO Science Programme is revised and restructured so as to direct support towards collaboration between scientists from NATO and Partner countries.

A European single currency, the Euro, is adopted by 11 member states of the European Union.

7 January   The NATO Secretary General visits the former Yugoslav Republic of Macedonia* to meet the Minister of Foreign Affairs, Aleksander Dimitrov, and the Minister of Defence, Nikola Kljusev. The Secretary General also visits the Kosovo Verification Coordination Cell (KVCC) in Kumanovo and the NATO Extraction Force.

9 January   NATO Secretary General issues a statement on the action by French SFOR troops resulting in the shooting of indicted war criminal Dragan Gagovic in the course of his resisting arrest.

17 January   NATO Secretary General, on behalf of the North Atlantic Council, condemns the massacre of Kosovar Albanians by Serb forces in Racak and calls on the Yugoslav authorities to cooperate fully with the ICTY in accordance with UN resolutions and to bring those responsible to justice.

18 January   NATO Generals Wesley Clark, Supreme Allied Commander Europe, and Klaus Naumann, Chairman of

	the Military Committee, go to Belgrade to impress upon the Yugoslav President Slobodan Milosevic the gravity of the situation in Kosovo.
20 January	The NATO-Russian Permanent Joint Council reviews the deteriorating situation in Kosovo and reaffirms their full support for the OSCE verification mission. NATO and Russia call on all parties to end the violence and open the path for a negotiated settlement.
28 January	NATO Secretary General issues a statement in support of the Contact Group's proposals to mediate the conclusion of an interim political settlement in Kosovo within a specified timeframe. NATO decides to increase its military preparedness to ensure the demands of the international community are met.
	United Nations Secretary General, Kofi Annan, visits NATO and addresses the North Atlantic Council. Discussions focus on the situations in Bosnia and Herzegovina and in Kosovo.
	The six-nation Contact Group on the former Yugoslavia call on the government of the Federal Republic of Yugoslavia and representatives of the Kosovar Albanians to begin negotiations at Rambouillet, France.
30 January	The North Atlantic Council authorises air strikes on the territory of the Federal Republic of Yugoslavia and delegates authority for implementing this decision to the Secretary General of NATO in case of non-compliance with the demands of the international community. The Council announces that appropriate measures will also be taken if the Kosovar Albanian side fails to comply.
	United Kingdom Foreign Secretary Robin Cook flies to Belgrade and issues warnings to President Milosevic to stop the killings or face NATO air strikes against Serbian positions responsible for conducting repression in Kosovo.
3 February	Joint NATO-WEU crisis management seminar on building the European Security and Defence Identity (ESDI) is held at NATO HQ.
7 February	Kosovo Peace talks begin between Serb and Kosovo Albanian representatives in Rambouillet, France.
9 February	The Hungarian parliament votes overwhelmingly in favour of NATO membership.
10-12 February	NATO's Political Committee visits Ukraine for discussions with senior officials in the context of the implementation of the NATO-Ukraine Charter.

12 February	As the deadline approaches for the conclusion of the Rambouillet negotiations on Kosovo, the North Atlantic Council reiterates its earlier demands and emphasises that NATO's forces are ready to take whatever measures are necessary to avert a humanitarian catastrophe and achieve a political settlement.
17 February	NATO-Russia Permanent Joint Council discusses the situation in Bosnia and Herzegovina and in Kosovo, stressing the importance of peace talks at Rambouillet and urging the parties to work responsibly and intensively to achieve an interim political agreement.
	Both houses of the Polish parliament vote overwhelmingly in favour of NATO membership.
18 -19 February	NATO Secretary General and General Wesley Clark, Supreme Allied Commander Europe, visit the former Yugoslav Republic of Macedonia* as well as Bosnia and Herzegovina.
23 February	Secretary General, Javier Solana, issues a statement appealing to the parties involved in the Kosovo Peace Talks to accept the Contact Group Peace Plan in its entirety.
24-26 February	NATO ambassadors and representatives of Mediterranean Dialogue Countries meet jointly for the first time at a conference in Valencia to discuss the way ahead in conjunction with NATO's Mediterranean Dialogue.
1 March	The North Atlantic Council approves activation requests for the headquarters of the new NATO military command structure.
3 March	US and European Union Special Envoys for Kosovo, Ambassador Christopher Hill and Wolfgang Petritsch, brief the North Atlantic Council.
5 March	The NATO Secretary General welcomes the announcement of the Independent Arbitrator, Mr Robert Owen, on the future neutral status of Brcko and calls on all sides to honour the decision, guaranteeing freedom of movement for all citizens of Bosnia and Herzegovina through the Brcko district.
	The NATO Secretary General expresses his support for the decision of the High Representative, Carlos Westendorp, in accordance with the powers vested in him by the General Framework Agreement for Peace in Bosnia and Herzegovina, to remove Nikola Poplasen from the Office of President of Republika Srpska.

12 March	The Czech, Hungarian and Polish Foreign Ministers deposit their instruments of accession to the Washington Treaty at the Truman Library, Independence, Missouri in accordance with Article 14 of the North Atlantic Treaty. With this act, the Czech Republic, Hungary and Poland officially become members of the Alliance.
15 March	The negotiations on an Interim Peace Agreement for Kosovo resume in Paris.
16 March	A flag-raising ceremony at NATO Headquarters and a special meeting of the North Atlantic Council mark the accession of the Czech Republic, Hungary and Poland.
17 March	At the meeting of the NATO-Russian Permanent Joint Council, Ambassadors continue consultations on the crisis in Kosovo, underscoring the importance of the negotiations in Paris.
19 March	Paris negotiations on an Interim Peace Agreement for Kosovo are suspended as the Federal Republic of Yugoslavia (FRY) announces its decision not to sign the Interim Peace Agreement.
22 March	Following the suspension of the Paris negotiations on 19 March and in response to Belgrade's intransigence, the North Atlantic Council authorises NATO Secretary General to decide, subject to further consultations, on a broader range of air operations to end the repression in Kosovo.
	At a meeting of the NATO-Ukraine Commission, Ambassadors discuss the deteriorating security situation in Kosovo, urging the Federal Republic of Yugoslavia to accept the Interim Agreement signed by the Kosovar Albanian delegation. NATO allies express their appreciation for Ukraine's offer to contribute to the Kosovo air verification mission and to a possible NATO-led peace implementation force.
23 March	NATO Secretary General Javier Solana directs General Wesley Clark (SACEUR) to initiate air operations in the Federal Republic of Yugoslavia, aimed at halting the violence and bringing to an end the humanitarian crisis in Kosovo, preventing the spread of instability in the region and securing a political settlement.
24 March	NATO Secretary General, Javier Solana, announces NATO's intention to pursue military action against the Federal Republic of Yugoslavia following the breakdown of political negotiations to end the Kosovo crisis. He emphasises that the objectives of NATO actions are to prevent

further human suffering and violence and the spread of instability in the region and are directed against the repressive policies of the Serb leadership. NATO air operations commence against military targets.

27 March	NATO Secretary General directs SACEUR to initiate a broader range of air operations in the Federal Republic of Yugoslavia, intensifying action against Yugoslav forces.
3 April	The North Atlantic Council authorises the Commander of the Allied Command Europe (ACE) Rapid Reaction Corps (ARCC), General Sir Michael Jackson, to coordinate Allied humanitarian efforts in the former Yugoslav Republic of Macedonia*, making use of all NATO forces in the area.
4 April	The North Atlantic Council holds a meeting at NATO HQ with EU member states, the OSCE Chairman-in-office, the UN High Commissioner for Refugees, the Council of Europe and the Western European Union to coordinate efforts to address the grave humanitarian crisis caused by the actions of Serb forces in Kosovo.
5-7 April	Deputy NATO Secretary General, Ambassador Sergio Balanzino, visits Romania, Bulgaria, the former Yugoslav Republic of Macedonia* and Albania to meet with the authorities of these countries. He also visits NATO troops in the former Yugoslav Republic of Macedonia* and views at first hand the refugee situation in the area.
6 April	NATO Secretary General Javier Solana issues a statement rejecting as insufficient the cease-fire proposed by the Federal Republic of Yugoslavia, emphasising that the international community's demands must be met before a cease-fire can be considered.
9 April	Foreign Minister Aleksander Dimitrov and Defence Minister Nikola Kljusev of the former Yugoslav Republic of Macedonia* meet with the North Atlantic Council at NATO HQ. The Allies reiterate their appreciation of the vital role the country is playing in addressing the refugee crisis and the severe consequences for the country itself.
12 April	Extraordinary Ministerial Meeting of the North Atlantic Council. NATO foreign ministers issue a formal statement on the situation in and around Kosovo, reaffirm the solidarity of the Alliance in acting on behalf of the international community to end the conflict, and enumerate the five conditions which must be fulfilled by the Yugoslav leadership (end of military action and repression; withdrawal of all Serb forces; acceptance of an international military pres-

ence; return of refugees; willingness to enter negotiations towards a political settlement based on the Rambouillet Accords).

14 April	Visit to NATO by the UN High Commissioner for Refugees, Sadako Ogata.
21 April	Bulgarian Prime Minister Ivan Kostov visits NATO Headquarters.
23 April	Opening of the NATO Liaison Office in Kyiv.
23-25 April	Washington Summit Meeting of the North Atlantic Council. Alliance leaders commemorate the 50th anniversary of the Alliance and reiterate their determination to end the repressive policies of the Yugoslav regime in Kosovo and to continue with the air campaign until the five conditions of the international community are met.

Work is launched or completed on a series of initiatives to prepare NATO for the challenges of the 21st century. NATO leaders issue the Washington Declaration and announce approval of an updated Strategic Concept as well as initiatives designed to improve defence capabilities; address risks posed by weapons of mass destruction; further the process of developing the European Security and Defence Identity within the Alliance; strengthen the operational dimension of PfP as well as EAPC consultation and cooperation; pursue NATO's Mediterranean Dialogue; and assist countries aspiring to NATO membership through a Membership Action Plan.

A meeting is held with representatives of the countries neighbouring the Federal Republic of Yugoslavia to discuss the impact of the continuing crisis in and around Kosovo. Alliance leaders propose measures to enhance regional security and promote regional cooperation in South Eastern Europe.

Heads of State and Government of the 19 member states of the Alliance and Ukraine meet for the first time at Summit level to review the implementation of the Charter on a Distinctive Partnership; the situation in Kosovo; challenges facing Euro-Atlantic security; the adaptation of the Alliance; and Ukraine's contribution to stability in Europe.

Meeting of the Euro-Atlantic Partnership Council at Summit Level, Washington DC. EAPC leaders endorse a report by the Political Military Steering Committee on Partnership for Peace ("Towards a Partnership for the 21st

	Century - The Enhanced and More Operational Partnership").
28 April	The North Atlantic Council extends till the end of 1999 the mission of the team of experts from NATO and Partner countries training the Albanian military in the clearance of unexploded munitions.
3 May	Russian Balkan envoy, Victor Chernomyrdin arrives in Washington after visiting Rome, Bonn, and Belgrade, to meet with President Clinton and UN Secretary General Kofi Annan in the context of initiatives to find a diplomatic solution to the crisis in Kosovo.
4 May	President Clinton visits NATO Headquarters for discussions on the Kosovo crisis.
10 May	European Defence and Foreign Ministers agree to work for a common defence capability to tackle crises such as the conflict in the Balkans.
14 May	UN High Commissioner for Human Rights Mary Robinson condemns ethnic cleansing in Kosovo.
18 May	Visit to NATO by Dr. Ibrahim Rugova, Leader of the Democratic League of Kosovo.
20 May	Visit to NATO by Italian Prime Minister, Massimo D'Alema. He issues a statement proposing a halt to the bombing in Yugoslavia for three days pending an accord by NATO nations and Russia on a draft UN Security Council resolution.
25 May	Visit to NATO by the President of the Government of the Kingdom of Spain, José María Aznar. Visit to NATO by the Prime Minister of Albania, Pandeli Majko.
1 June	NATO-EAPC Research Fellowships Programme 1999-2001 announces award winners. Visit to NATO by the Prime Minister of Slovenia, Janez Drnovsek.
4 June	NATO Secretary General, Javier Solana, is appointed to the new post of EU High Representative for Common Foreign and Security Policy.
10 June	NATO Secretary General Javier Solana issues a statement on the suspension of air operations after President Milosevic agrees to withdraw his troops from Kosovo following 78 days and nights of air strikes. The UN Security Council authorises the deployment of an international force (KFOR) to Kosovo, with NATO at its core, under the terms of the Military Technical Agreement signed by

	Lt. General Sir Michael Jackson, Commander of KFOR and Yugoslav representatives.
11 June	Russian troops enter Pristina in advance of KFOR troops.
18 June	At an Extraordinary Meeting of Foreign and Defence Ministers of the North Atlantic Council held at NATO, a further statement is issued on "The Situation In and Around Kosovo".
20 June	The NATO Secretary General announces that all Yugoslav military and police forces have departed Kosovo in compliance with the Military Technical Agreement.
23 June	NATO Secretary General, Javier Solana, visits Kosovo. Visit to NATO by the President of Armenia, Robert Kocharian.
29 June	The first Partnership for Peace (PfP) Training Centre opens in Ankara, Turkey.
12 July	Former Bosnian Serb Deputy Prime Minister, Radislav Brdjanin appears before the UN war crimes tribunal.
13 July	Visit to NATO by Bernard Kouchner, Special UN Representative for Kosovo. Visit to NATO by the President of Slovakia, Rudolf Schuster.
23 July	Statement issued by the NATO-Russia Permanent Joint Council on the security situation in Kosovo, affirming commitment to full implementation of the provisions and goals of United Nations Security Council Resolution 1244.
30 July	A Stability Pact for South East Europe is agreed by the European Union Council of Ministers in Köln, Germany.
2 August	Statement issued by the Secretary General of NATO, Javier Solana, on SFOR's action against indicted war criminal, Radomir Kovac.
4 August	The Secretary General of NATO, Javier Solana, announces that Lord George Robertson, Minister of Defence of the United Kingdom, will become the next Secretary General of NATO.
19 August	The United States and Russia affirm that a 1972 treaty banning missile defence systems is the cornerstone of strategic stability between the two nations.
6 September	NATO Secretary General, Javier Solana, visits Kosovo.
8 September	Visit to NATO by the High Representative Wolfgang Petritsch, responsible for coordinating the work of civilian organisations in Bosnia and Herzegovina.

9 September	NATO-Ukraine Commission welcomes KFOR's accomplishments and endorses Ukraine's future participation in the international security presence in Kosovo.
9-11 September	Inauguration of the new site of the NATO Defense College in Rome in the presence of Permanent Representatives on the North Atlantic Council.
10 September	Appointment of General Dr. Klaus Reinhardt, German Army, to succeed Lt. General Sir Michael Jackson as Commander of KFOR.
10-11 September	Leaders of more than 20 Black Sea and Baltic states gather in Yalta, Ukraine to discuss issues of European integration.
13 September	Troops from Germany, Poland, Denmark, Romania, and Lithuania participate in military exercises held in central Lithuania.
15 September	The NATO-Russia Permanent Joint Council discusses the situation in and around Kosovo and NATO-Russia cooperation in the international security presence in Kosovo.
21 September	Secretary General of NATO, Javier Solana, welcomes the statement by KFOR that the Kosovo Liberation Army has complied with its commitment to demilitarise.
21-22 September	Informal meeting of NATO Defence Ministers in Toronto.
23 September	The European Union welcomes the completion of the disarmament of the Kosovo Liberation Army and the formation of a multi-ethnic Kosovo Protection Corps.
24 September	Russian warplanes begin a bombing campaign in areas around the rebel province of Grozny in an escalation of the conflict in Chechnya.
6 October	Visit to NATO by the President of the Federal Republic of Germany, Johannes Rau.
11 October	NATO and Ukraine sign an agreement to provide civilian training for retired Ukrainian army officers.
13 October	NATO issues a statement on research, development and acquisition programmes relating to non-lethal weapons.
14 October	Lord Robertson takes up his appointment as NATO Secretary General, succeeding Javier Solana, whose term ended on 6 October.
15 October	President of Montenegro, Milo Djukanovic, meets with NATO Secretary General Lord Robertson, to discuss the situation in Montenegro and the Balkan region. The Secretary General emphasises the need for all leaders in the Balkan region to work for stability and democratisation.

	Fifth NATO-Japan Security Conference at NATO Headquarters.

| 19 October | NATO Secretary General and Permanent Representatives on the North Atlantic Council visit Bosnia and Herzegovina, Kosovo and the former Yugoslav Republic of Macedonia*. |

Visit to NATO by the Prime Minister of Hungary, Viktor Orban.

21 October   NATO Secretary General Lord Robertson announces reductions in SFOR.

26 October   Visit to NATO by the President of Latvia, Vaira Vike-Freiberga.

27 October   At a meeting of the Permanent Joint Council at Ambassadorial level NATO and Russia discuss the situation in and around Kosovo and NATO-Russia cooperation in the international security presence in Kosovo.

3 November   NATO announces the appointment of General Joseph W. Ralston, U.S. Air Force, to succeed General Wesley K. Clark as Supreme Allied Commander, Europe (SACEUR).

4 November   The Council of Europe holds an emergency debate to discuss the Russian offensive in Chechnya.

17 November   The NATO-Russia Permanent Joint Council at Ambassadorial level stresses commitment to the full implementation of UN Security Council Resolution 1244 and reiterates the determination of NATO and Russia to cooperate closely in ensuring the protection of Kosovo's minorities and the establishment of a multiethnic, democratic society.

18-19 November   OSCE Summit in Istanbul, Turkey. 54 nations sign a new Charter for European Security and an updated Conventional Forces in Europe (CFE) arms control treaty.

29 November   Meeting of NATO-Ukraine Commission in Ambassadorial session.

Visit to NATO by the High Representative Wolfgang Petritsch, responsible for coordinating activities of civilian organisations and agencies in Bosnia and Herzegovina.

1 December   The Minister of Foreign Affairs of Ireland, David Andrews visits NATO and signs the PfP framework document. Ireland becomes the 25th member of the PfP programme.

3 December   Meeting of the NATO-Ukraine Commission in Defence Ministers Session.

Meeting of the Euro-Atlantic Partnership Council in Defence Ministers Session.

6 December	Statement by the Secretary General of NATO, Lord Robertson, on the OSCE Report on Kosovo, confirming that a pre-planned systematic campaign of persecution had been carried out by the Serb security forces against the ethnic Albanian population.
8 December	The United Nations, the OSCE and the Council of Europe issue a joint declaration urging Russia to respect human rights in Chechnya.
10 December	Turkey becomes an official candidate for accession to the European Union.
13 December	Statement by Lord Robertson, Secretary General of NATO welcoming the results of the Helsinki European Council on strengthening the European role in security and defence.
15-16 December	NATO Foreign Ministers meeting in Brussels discuss the outcome of the EU Council in Helsinki, NATO-led military operations in Bosnia and Herzegovina and in Kosovo, relations with Russia and the situation in Chechnya.
16 December	Approval by the Euro-Atlantic Partnership Council (EAPC) of its Action Plan for 2000-2002.
31 December	Boris Yeltsin announces his resignation as President of Russia and hands over the acting presidency to Prime Minister Vladimir Putin, pending elections in 2000.

2000

19 January	Visit to NATO by the Prosecutor of the International Criminal Tribunal for the former Yugoslavia (ICTY), Carla Del Ponte. The NATO-Russia Permanent Joint Council reiterates the determination of NATO and Russia to cooperate closely in ensuring the protection of Kosovo's minorities.
25 January	Statement by Secretary General of NATO, Lord Robertson on the detention of Mitar Vasiljevic, indicted for war crimes in Bosnia and Herzegovina.
14 February	Statement by NATO Secretary General Lord Robertson on attacks against KFOR troops in Kosovska Mitrovica.
15 February	Visit to NATO by the Prime Minister of Croatia, Ivica Racan.
16 February	Publication of joint statement on the occasion of the visit of NATO Secretary General Lord Robertson to Moscow, affirming the intention of NATO and Russia to intensify dialogue and cooperation.
1 March	Publication of statement following the first meeting of the NATO-Ukraine Commission in Kyiv.

5 March	Statement by NATO Secretary General, Lord Robertson, concerning the detention of Dragoljub Prcac indicted for war crimes in Bosnia and Herzegovina.
8 March	Statement by NATO Secretary General, Lord Robertson, following North Atlantic Council Meeting, condemning further violence in Mitrovica.
14 March	Algeria becomes a participant in NATO's Mediterranean Dialogue.
15 March	NATO-Russia Permanent Joint Council reaffirms NATO and Russia's determination to intensify mutual dialogue and cooperation.
21 March	NATO Secretary General Lord Robertson publishes his personal report to the North Atlantic Council on the anniversary of the Alliance's military intervention in the Kosovo conflict ("Kosovo One Year On: Achievement and Challenge").
22 March	Maart Laar, Prime Minister of Estonia, visits NATO.
26 March	Vladimir Putin is elected President of the Russian Federation.
28 March	Representatives from the six countries of the Contact Group for the former Yugoslavia meet to examine ways to advance the peace progress in Kosovo.
28 March	Lord Robertson congratulates Vladimir Putin on his election as President of Russia and underlines NATO readiness to strengthen cooperation with Russia.
31 March	International donors commit 2.4 million euros to the Stability Pact for the Balkans.
3 April	NATO Secretary General Lord Robertson issues a statement on the arrest of Momcilo Krajisnik, aide to former Serb leader Radovan Karadjic.
12 April	Supreme Allied Commander Europe, General Wesley Clark receives NATO medals for his role in the former Yugoslavia and Kosovo from NATO Secretary General Lord Robertson.
13 April	NATO Secretary General Lord Robertson visits the International War Crimes Tribunal for the former Yugoslavia (ICTY) in The Hague.
14 April	The State Duma (lower house of the Russian parliament) ratifies the Russian-American strategic arms reduction treaty (START II).
19 April	The Federation Council (upper house) of the Russian Parliament ratifies the START II Treaty.

2 May	US General Joseph Ralston succeeds General Wesley Clark as Supreme Allied Commander Europe (SACEUR).
4 May	Visit to NATO by Ambassador Wolfgang Petritsch, High Representative responsible for coordinating the civilian organisations and agencies in Bosnia and Herzegovina.
5 May	Visit to NATO of the President of the Republic of Italy, Carlo Azeglio Ciampi.
9 May	Croatian Prime Minister Ivica Racan visits NATO.
22 May	Visit to NATO by the Prime Minister of Ukraine, Viktor Yuschenko.
24 May	Ministerial meeting of the North Atlantic Council in Florence. NATO Foreign Ministers discuss progress in SFOR and KFOR and other developments in the former Yugoslavia, implementation of the Defence Capabilities Initiative (DCI), and future dialogue with the European Union, as well as other areas of Alliance policy.
	Ministerial meeting in Florence of the NATO-Russia Permanent Joint Council (PJC) reviews progress in NATO-Russia cooperation and the situation in the former Yugoslavia, and approves a PJC Work Programme for the remainder of 2000.
25 May	Meeting in Florence at the level of Foreign Ministers, the Euro-Atlantic Partnership Council (EAPC) discusses a range of security issues including the South East Europe Initiative and developments in Kosovo and in Bosnia and Herzegovina.
	Croatia becomes the 46th member of the EAPC and joins the Partnership for Peace (PfP).
	Ministerial meeting in Florence of the NATO-Ukraine Commission discusses progress of the NATO-Ukraine partnership, the situation in Kosovo and other regional issues.
	Dr. Alexander Yuschenko of the Kharkov State Polytechnic University of Ukraine is awarded the Manfred Woerner Fellowship for the year 2000.
7 June	NATO condemns recent attacks against border guards of the former Yugoslav Republic of Macedonia*.
8 June	NATO Defence Ministers, meeting in the ministerial session of the North Atlantic Council in Brussels, issue statements on NATO's Defence Capabilities Initiative and on the situation in the Balkans.

	At a meeting of the Defence Planning Committee and the Nuclear Planning Group, NATO Defence Ministers adopt a new set of NATO Force Goals covering the period to 2006. Meeting in Defence Ministers' session, the NATO-Ukraine Commission discusses NATO-Ukrainian cooperation in KFOR, Ukraine's participation in PfP, Ukraine's plans for restructuring its armed forces, and other aspects of the partnership.
9 June	Meeting in Defence Ministers' session, the Euro-Atlantic Partnership Council (EAPC) welcomes the development of the first full set of Partnership goals and receives a Summary Report on the Partnership for Peace Planning and Review Process (PARP).
	Meeting at ministerial level, the NATO-Russia Permanent Joint Council (PJC) welcomes steps to strengthen consultation and cooperation, discusses the situation in the former Yugoslavia and examines defence-military priorities for the NATO-Russia dialogue.
13 June	NATO announces the award of 54 NATO-EAPC Research Fellowships to citizens of EAPC member nations.
19-20 June	At the meeting of the Council of the European Union in Feira, Portugal, proposals are adopted for establishing four ad hoc working groups to address NATO-EU cooperation.
25 June	NATO Secretary General Lord Robertson issues a statement on the detention by SFOR of Dusko Sikirica, indicted by the International War Crimes Tribunal for the former Yugoslavia (ICTY).
27 June	Visit to NATO by the President of Kazakhstan, Nursultan Nazarbayev.
28 June	Appointment of US Lt. General Kernan to succeed Admiral Gehman as Supreme Allied Commander Atlantic (SACLANT) from September 2000.
17 July	Croatian President Stipe Mesic visits NATO.
17-19 July	North Atlantic Council fact-finding mission to the Balkans.
24 July	General Valery Manilov, First Deputy Chief of the General Staff of Russia's Armed Forces, briefs the NATO-Russia Permanent Joint Council on Russia's military doctrine and on the Russian perspective on the Alliance's Strategic Concept.
24-29 July	Seminar in the framework of NATO's security cooperation programme with Bosnia and Herzegovina hosted by the

	Norwegian Defence International Centre in Sessvollmoen, Norway.
27 July	NATO Secretary General Lord Robertson issues a statement welcoming the Airlie House Declaration by prominent Kosovar Albanian and Serbs as an important step towards reconciliation between all of Kosovo's ethnic groups.
10 August	Appointment of Lt. General Thorstein Skiaker, Norwegian Army, as Commander of KFOR from Spring 2001.
22 August	NATO offers condolences to Russia on the loss of the crew of the "Kursk" submarine.
1 September	NATO Secretary General Lord Robertson issues a statement on the US decision to continue testing and development of a limited National Missile Defence system, emphasising the importance of continuing consultation with allies.
8 September	US General Michael L. Dodson replaces US General Ronald E. Adams as Commander of SFOR.
13 September	Slovenian Prime Minister Andrei Bajuk visits NATO. Carl Bildt, UN Special Envoy for the Balkans, briefs the North Atlantic Council at NATO Headquarters.
18 September	George Papandreou, Minister of Foreign Affairs of Greece, becomes Président d'Honneur of the North Atlantic Council succeeding Joschka Fischer, Minister of Foreign Affairs of Germany.
19 September	First meeting of the North Atlantic Council and the interim Political and Security Committee of the European Union takes stock of progress in EU-NATO ad hoc working groups set up to define arrangements for EU access to NATO collective assets and permanent consultation mechanisms between NATO and the EU.
20-29 September	A Disaster Relief Exercise - "Transcarpathia 2000" - simulating major flooding, is conducted in Western Ukraine in the framework of Partnership for Peace and the NATO-Ukraine Work Plan. Three hundred and fifty personnel from disaster response elements of 11 EAPC countries participate.
27 September	Prime Minister Kjubco Georgievski of the former Yugoslav Republic of Macedonia* visits NATO for discussions with Secretary General Lord Robertson.
4-6 October	NATO's Political Committee visits Ukraine.
5 October	Visit to NATO by UN Secretary General, Kofi Annan, to discuss security challenges in the Balkans and NATO's contribution to UN peace-keeping operations.

6 October	Following contested elections of 24 September, protests in Belgrade and the occupation of the federal parliament, Vojislav Kostunica, leader of the democratic opposition of Serbia, is internationally recognised as the new president of Yugoslavia, forcing former president Slobodan Milosevic from office.
10 October	At an informal meeting of NATO Defence Ministers in Birmingham in the United Kingdom, NATO Secretary General Lord Robertson welcomes the democratic transition taking place in the Federal Republic of Yugoslavia and offers a hand of friendship to its people.
13 October	Statement by Secretary General of NATO Lord Robertson on the SFOR operation to arrest Janko Janjic under indictment for war crimes.
13-14 October	Seminar on Political/Military Tools for Conflict Prevention within the Euro-Atlantic Partnership Council (EAPC)/ Partnership for Peace Programme (PfP) in Ljubljana, Slovenia.
16 October	General Carlo Calsigiosu of Italy replaces General Juan Ortuño of Spain as Commander of KFOR.
18 October	Meeting at NATO of the NATO-Ukraine working group on scientific and environmental cooperation.
	Carla Del Ponte, prosecutor of the International War Crimes Tribunal for the former Yugoslavia (ICTY) in The Hague, addresses the Euro-Atlantic Partnership Council (EAPC) at NATO.
30 October	Statement by Lord Robertson on the successful holding of local elections in Kosovo on 28 October.
	The OSCE declares Ibrahim Rugova, leader of the Democratic League of Kosovo, winner of municipal elections.
31 Oct.-3 Nov.	General Assembly of the Atlantic Treaty Association in Budapest.
1-10 November	Exercise Cooperative Determination takes place in Lucerne, Switzerland. Nine NATO and 11 Partner countries, as well as international organisations, including the International Committee of the Red Cross and the UN High Commission for Refugees, take part in the exercise to train participants in procedures for peace-support operations.
2-3 November	Representatives of the Verkhovna Rada (Ukrainian parliament) and of the NATO Parliamentary Assembly meet at

	NATO headquarters in Brussels to discuss NATO-Ukraine cooperation.
9 November	North Atlantic Council meeting with the interim Political and Security Committee of the European Union.
	Visit to NATO by George Soros for discussions with NATO Secretary General Lord Robertson on possible cooperation in strengthening democratic society in South Eastern Europe and central Asia.
10 November	Yugoslavia is admitted to the Organisation for Security and Cooperation in Europe (OSCE) as the 55th participating State.
11 November	General elections in Bosnia and Herzegovina result in significant gains for nationalist parties in all three ethnic groups.
13 November	The Council of Ministers of the Western European Union (WEU), meeting in Marseilles, takes decisions relating to the transfer of the WEU's operational functions to the European Union and arrangements for the WEU's residual functions and structures.
15-17 November	The NATO Military Committee visits Bosnia and Herzegovina and Kosovo.
16 November	The Verkhovna Rada (parliament) of Ukraine ratifies the Comprehensive Test Ban Treaty.
20 November	Bulgarian Prime Minister Ivan Kostov visits NATO.
21 November	At a Capabilities Commitment Conference in Brussels, Defence Ministers of European Union and Partner countries pledge substantial forces to provide the military capabilities to meet the EU Headline Goal agreed upon at Helsinki in December 1999, to enable the EU to deploy, by 2003, military forces of up to 60 000 troops for crisis management operations.
22 November	Visit to NATO by the Chancellor of the Federal Republic of Germany, Gerhard Schröder.
24 November	Visit to NATO by Mikulas Dzurinda, Prime Minister of Slovakia.
28 November	Visit to NATO by Vaira Vike-Freiberga, President of Latvia.
	Visit to NATO by Aleksander Kwasniewski, President of Poland.
29 November	Statement by NATO Secretary General Lord Robertson on upsurge of violence in southern Serbia, near the boundary with Kosovo.
5 December	Meeting at the level of Defence Ministers, the NATO-Russia Permanent Joint Council emphasises its commit-

ment to a strong and stable NATO-Russia partnership aimed at enhancing Euro-Atlantic stability and security. The Council also discusses the situation in the former Yugoslavia, progress in cooperation between NATO and Russian military officers at SHAPE, cooperation between NATO and Russian forces in SFOR and KFOR, possibilities for expanding future cooperation, and the opening of a NATO Military Liaison Office in Moscow.

6 December   NATO Secretary General Lord Robertson announces that talks on Confidence Building Measures between Greece and Turkey have led to an agreement between the two countries to notify each other in advance of national exercises.

7 December   Summit Meeting of the European Union in Nice. EU leaders adopt further measures to strengthen the European policy on security and defence and establish arrangements for consultation and cooperation between NATO and the EU.

Boris Trajkovski, President of the former Yugoslav Republic of Macedonia* visits NATO.

14 December   NATO Defence Ministers meeting in Brussels review national defence plans for 2001-2005 and adopt a 5-year force plan addressing the requirements of the future security environment. New Ministerial Guidance is also approved, providing the framework for NATO and national defence planning in the period up to 2008.

George W. Bush is nominated President-Elect of the United States following the decision of the US Supreme Court in favour of the Republican presidential candidate.

Ministerial meeting of the NATO-Ukraine Commission in Brussels. Foreign Ministers welcome positive progress in different fields of NATO-Ukraine cooperation and endorse an ambitious Work Plan for 2001. Foreign Ministers review the status of cooperation in the Balkans, Partnership for Peace, parliamentary contacts, civil emergency planning, defence reform and measures against proliferation of weapons of mass destruction. Ministers express appreciation for the decision to close the Chernobyl nuclear power plant.

15 December   Ministerial meeting of the EAPC. Foreign Ministers review the situation in the former Yugoslavia and examine other aspects of cooperation including the EAPC's future role

and contribution to regional cooperation initiatives. The EAPC Action Plan for 2000 to 2002 is published.

Ministerial meeting of the North Atlantic Council. Foreign Ministers review progress across the spectrum of Alliance activities, including NATO's dialogue with the European Union and the process of establishing arrangements for NATO/EU cooperation in the context of ESDI.

NATO issues a report on Options for Confidence and Security Building Measures (CSBMs), Verification, Non-proliferation, Arms Control and Disarmament.

Ministerial meeting of the NATO-Russia Permanent Joint Council. Foreign Ministers examine the situation in the former Yugoslavia, welcoming the peaceful democratic changes in the Federal Republic of Yugoslavia. Ministers also review progress in NATO-Russia cooperation in relation to discussions on strategy and doctrine, arms control, proliferation, military infrastructure, nuclear weapons, retraining of military personnel and search and rescue at sea.

Foreign Ministers exchange letters on the establishment of a NATO Information Office in Moscow to improve public understanding of evolving NATO-Russia relations.

2001

10 January   Visit to NATO by the Foreign Minister of the Federal Republic of Yugoslavia, Goran Svilanovic.

Statement by the Secretary General on the use of Depleted Uranium Munitions in the Balkans.

12 January   Establishment of a NATO Ad Hoc Committee on Depleted Uranium to act as a clearing house for information sharing and coordination on this issue.

18 January   Command authority for the NATO-led forces in Kosovo (KFOR) is transferred from Supreme Allied Headquarters Europe (SHAPE) to Allied Force Southern Europe (AFSOUTH), based in Naples.

24 January   Visit to NATO by the Romanian Prime Minister, Adrian Nastase.

Launch of an international Architectural Design Competition for the new NATO Headquarters.

At a meeting of the NATO-Russia Permanent Joint Council, Ambassadors agree on steps to implement the PJC Work Programme for 2001.

25 January	A humanitarian assistance project is undertaken by NATO and Partner countries, under the direction of NATO's Maintenance and Supply Agency (NAMSA), to assist Albania in destroying stockpiled anti-personnel mines.
30 January	Visit to NATO by the former Special Representative of the Secretary General of the United Nations in Kosovo, Bernard Kouchner.
31 January	Visit to NATO by Rolandas Paksas, Prime Minister of the Republic of Lithuania.
5 February	First meeting of the North Atlantic Council and the EU Political and Security Committee at Ambassadorial level, under new permanent NATO-EU consultation arrangements. Discussions centre on NATO-EU relations and the contribution of both organisations to the management of the crisis in the Western Balkans.
6 February	Visit to NATO of Ruud Lubbers, newly appointed UN High Commissioner for Refugees.
14-16 February	Annual Seminar on implementation aspects of the Treaty on Conventional Armed Forces in Europe (CFE) hosted by the NATO Verification Coordinating Committee, with the participation of representatives from the 30 States Parties to the Treaty.
15 February	Nebojsa Covic, Serbian Deputy Prime Minister and Yugoslav Foreign Minister Svilanovic, brief the North Atlantic Council on the initiative to seek a peaceful resolution to the conflicts in southern Serbia.
15-21 February	NATO conducts an annual Crisis Management Exercise (CMX 2001) involving, for the first time, the participation of 14 Partnership for Peace countries.
16 February	The Secretary General of NATO issues a statement condemning the attack on a bus near Podujevo, Kosovo, in which Serb civilians were killed or injured.
18 February	Statement by the Secretary General condemning the escalation of violence in southern Serbia.
18-22 February	Forces from NATO's Standing Naval Force Atlantic conduct a humanitarian assistance exercise in the Caribbean, testing capabilities for providing humanitarian aid following tropical storms and hurricanes.
20 February	Inauguration of the new NATO Information Office in Moscow by NATO Secretary General, Lord Robertson.
23 February	The Secretary General of NATO issues a statement, welcoming the creation of a new government in Bosnia and Herzegovina, formed from moderate parties.

26 February	NATO and Ukraine sign an agreement on the Practical Implementation of the NATO-Ukraine Programme concerning retraining of discharged or to be discharged military personnel in Ukraine for the year 2001.
27 February	Meeting of the North Atlantic Council in Foreign Ministers' Session, attended by the new US Secretary of State, Colin Powell.
	Representatives of the UN, the EU, the OSCE, the UNHCR and NATO meet at NATO Headquarters, Brussels to discuss growing tensions in the Presevo Valley, focusing on ways of coordinating their efforts to help reduce the number of armed incidents and to prevent a spill-over of violence in the region.
	The North Atlantic Council reiterates concern over the situation in southern Serbia and condemns continuing acts of violence.
	In the context of the Partnership for Peace, NATO issues details of planning being undertaken by the NATO Maintenance and Supply Agency (NAMSA) to provide assistance and training to the government of Moldova for the destruction of anti-personnel land mines and other munitions.
28 February	Visit to NATO by the Special Representative of the Secretary General of the United Nations in Kosovo, Hans Haekkerup.
	The NATO-Russia Permanent Joint Council discusses developments in the Federal Republic of Yugoslavia and NATO-Russia cooperation in Kosovo (KFOR).
	Secretary General Lord Robertson announces NATO's readiness to implement a phased and conditional reduction of the ground safety zone on the border of Kosovo and appoints a personal representative to the region to assist in developing a peaceful solution to the conflict.
2 March	The Secretary General of NATO issues a statement condemning violent incidents in the border area of the former Yugoslav Republic of Macedonia*.
4 March	Following agreement between NATO and the Yugoslav government, Yugoslav troops entered the Ground Safety Zone, the five-kilometre strip of southern Serbia bordering Kosovo, for the first time since their withdrawal from Kosovo in June 1999.
5 March	Visit to NATO by the President of Bulgaria, Petar Stoyanov.

8 March	The North Atlantic Council announces measures relating to southern Serbia and the former Yugoslav Republic of Macedonia*, including a phased reduction of the Ground Safety Zone.
9 March	Visit to NATO by the Foreign Minister of the former Yugoslav Republic of Macedonia*, Srgjan Kerim.
13 March	NATO welcomes publication of the United Nations Environment Programme (UNEP) report on possible health hazards associated with the use of Depleted Uranium munitions in Kosovo.
19 March	Visit to NATO by the High Representative for Bosnia and Herzegovina, Wolfgang Petritsch.
20-29 March	At a NATO-sponsored Advanced Study Institute in Budapest, experts analyse scientific and technical issues related to the implementation of the Protocol of the Biological and Toxin Weapons Convention (BTWC).
21 March	The North Atlantic Council approves further measures to enhance stability in the southern Balkans and to demonstrate its support for the government in Skopje, including the appointment of Ambassador Hans-Joerg Eiff as NATO's senior civilian representative to Skopje.
	Meeting of the Euro-Atlantic Partnership Council (EAPC). Ambassadors express support for the government of the former Yugoslav Republic of Macedonia*, condemn extremist violence, and welcome measures to enhance border security.
	Visit to NATO by Jakob Kellenberger, President of the International Committee of the Red Cross.
26 March	NATO Secretary General Lord Robertson and European Union High Representative Javier Solana visit Skopje to reaffirm support for the government of the former Yugoslav Republic of Macedonia* and to urge restraint in responding to the present conflict.
28 March	Meeting of the NATO-Russia Permanent Joint Council. Ambassadors discuss the situation in the Balkans and NATO-Russia cooperation in KFOR and welcome international efforts to prevent the escalation of ethnic tensions in the region.
29 March	Statement by NATO Secretary General on mortar explosions near Krivenik in Kosovo, in which civilians have been killed or injured.

ILLUSTRATIONS

NATO's Civil and Military Structure

Principal NATO Committees

Principal Institutions of Partnership Cooperation and Dialogue

The NATO International Staff

Divisions of the International Staff

NATO's Military Structure

The Military Structure - Allied Command Europe

The Military Structure - Allied Command Atlantic

The International Military Staff

NATO's Civil and Military Structure

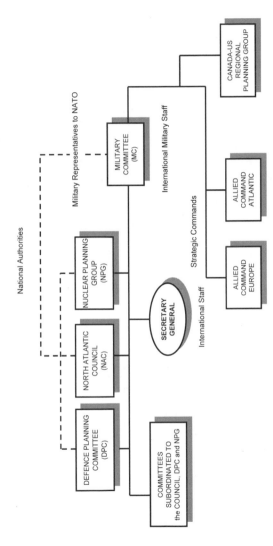

National Authorities

Military Representatives to NATO

DEFENCE PLANNING COMMITTEE (DPC)

NORTH ATLANTIC COUNCIL (NAC)

NUCLEAR PLANNING GROUP (NPG)

MILITARY COMMITTEE (MC)

SECRETARY GENERAL

COMMITTEES SUBORDINATED TO the COUNCIL, DPC and NPG

International Staff

International Military Staff

Strategic Commands

ALLIED COMMAND EUROPE

ALLIED COMMAND ATLANTIC

CANADA-US REGIONAL PLANNING GROUP

Principal NATO Committees

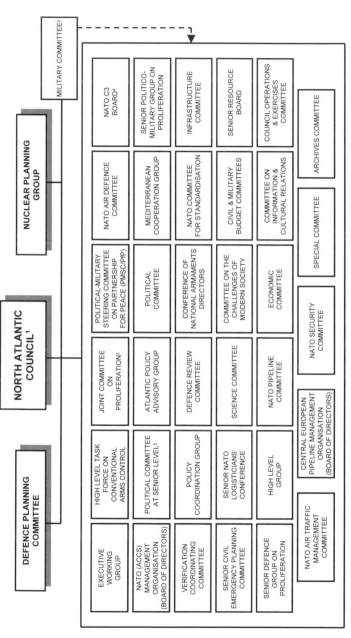

DEFENCE PLANNING COMMITTEE

NORTH ATLANTIC COUNCIL[1]

NUCLEAR PLANNING GROUP

MILITARY COMMITTEE[2]

EXECUTIVE WORKING GROUP

HIGH LEVEL TASK FORCE ON CONVENTIONAL ARMS CONTROL

JOINT COMMITTEE ON PROLIFERATION[3]

POLITICAL-MILITARY STEERING COMMITTEE ON PARTNERSHIP FOR PEACE (PMSC/PfP)

NATO AIR DEFENCE COMMITTEE

NATO C3 BOARD[4]

NATO (ACCS) MANAGEMENT ORGANISATION (BOARD OF DIRECTORS)

POLITICAL COMMITTEE AT SENIOR LEVEL[5]

ATLANTIC POLICY ADVISORY GROUP

POLITICAL COMMITTEE

MEDITERRANEAN COOPERATION GROUP

SENIOR POLITICO-MILITARY GROUP ON PROLIFERATION

VERIFICATION COORDINATING COMMITTEE

POLICY COORDINATION GROUP

DEFENCE REVIEW COMMITTEE

CONFERENCE OF NATIONAL ARMAMENTS DIRECTORS

NATO COMMITTEE FOR STANDARDISATION

INFRASTRUCTURE COMMITTEE

SENIOR CIVIL EMERGENCY PLANNING COMMITTEE

SENIOR NATO LOGISTICIANS' CONFERENCE

SCIENCE COMMITTEE

COMMITTEE ON THE CHALLENGES OF MODERN SOCIETY

CIVIL & MILITARY BUDGET COMMITTEES

SENIOR RESOURCE BOARD

SENIOR DEFENCE GROUP ON PROLIFERATION

HIGH LEVEL GROUP

NATO PIPELINE COMMITTEE

ECONOMIC COMMITTEE

COMMITTEE ON INFORMATION & CULTURAL RELATIONS

COUNCIL OPERATIONS & EXERCISES COMMITTEE

NATO AIR TRAFFIC MANAGEMENT COMMITTEE

CENTRAL EUROPEAN PIPELINE MANAGEMENT ORGANISATION (BOARD OF DIRECTORS)

NATO SECURITY COMMITTEE

SPECIAL COMMITTEE

ARCHIVES COMMITTEE

(1) Most of the above committees report to the Council. Some are responsible to the Defence Planning Committee or Nuclear Planning Group. Certain committees are joint civil and military bodies which report both to the Council, Defence Planning Committee or Nuclear Planning Group and to the Military Committee.

(2) The Military Committee is subordinate to the North Atlantic Council and Defence Planning Committee but has a special status as the senior military authority in NATO. The role of the Military Committee is described in Chapter 11.

(3) Senior Politico-Military Group on Proliferation plus Senior Defence Group on Proliferation.

(4) NATO C3 (Consultation, Command and Control) Board

(5) Reinforced with experts as required.

Principal Institutions of Partnership Cooperation and Dialogue

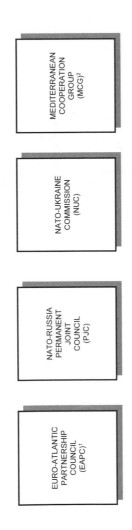

EURO-ATLANTIC PARTNERSHIP COUNCIL (EAPC)[1]

NATO-RUSSIA PERMANENT JOINT COUNCIL (PJC)

NATO-UKRAINE COMMISSION (NUC)

MEDITERRANEAN COOPERATION GROUP (MCG)[2]

(1) Many NATO Committees regularly meet in EAPC or Partnership for Peace format (see Principal NATO Committees).

(2) In addition to meetings among Allies, the Mediterranean Cooperation Group also meets with representatives of countries participating in the Alliance's Mediterranean Dialogue.

The NATO International Staff

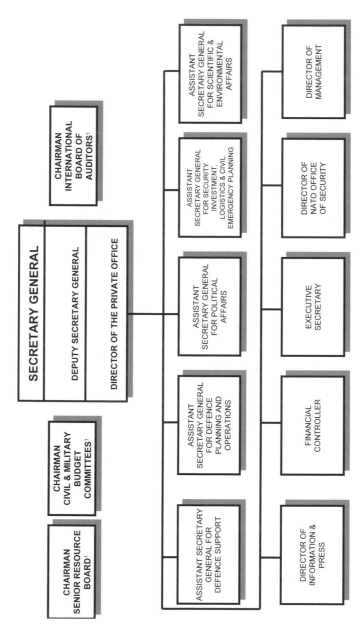

CHAIRMAN SENIOR RESOURCE BOARD[1]

CHAIRMAN CIVIL & MILITARY BUDGET COMMITTEES[1]

SECRETARY GENERAL

DEPUTY SECRETARY GENERAL

DIRECTOR OF THE PRIVATE OFFICE

CHAIRMAN INTERNATIONAL BOARD OF AUDITORS[1]

ASSISTANT SECRETARY GENERAL FOR DEFENCE SUPPORT

ASSISTANT SECRETARY GENERAL FOR DEFENCE PLANNING AND OPERATIONS

ASSISTANT SECRETARY GENERAL FOR POLITICAL AFFAIRS

ASSISTANT SECRETARY GENERAL FOR SECURITY INVESTMENT, LOGISTICS & CIVIL EMERGENCY PLANNING

ASSISTANT SECRETARY GENERAL FOR SCIENTIFIC & ENVIRONMENTAL AFFAIRS

DIRECTOR OF INFORMATION & PRESS

FINANCIAL CONTROLLER

EXECUTIVE SECRETARY

DIRECTOR OF NATO OFFICE OF SECURITY

DIRECTOR OF MANAGEMENT

(1) These positions are not filled by members of the International Staff but by national chairmen appointed by the Council.

Divisions of the International Staff

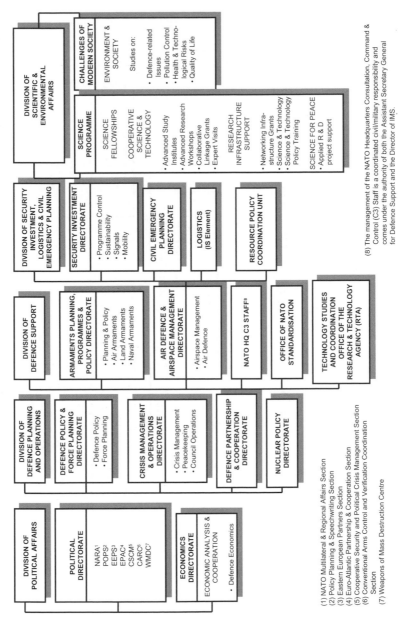

DIVISION OF SCIENTIFIC & ENVIRONMENTAL AFFAIRS

CHALLENGES OF MODERN SOCIETY

ENVIRONMENT & SOCIETY

Studies on:
- Defence-related Issues
- Pollution Control
- Health & Technological Risks
- Quality of Life

SCIENCE PROGRAMME

SCIENCE FELLOWSHIPS

COOPERATIVE SCIENCE & TECHNOLOGY
- Advanced Study Institutes
- Advanced Research Workshops
- Collaborative Linkage Grants
- Expert Visits

RESEARCH INFRASTRUCTURE SUPPORT
- Networking Infra-structure Grants
- Science & Technology Policy Training

SCIENCE FOR PEACE
- Applied R & D project support

DIVISION OF SECURITY INVESTMENT, LOGISTICS & CIVIL EMERGENCY PLANNING

SECURITY INVESTMENT DIRECTORATE
- Programme Control
- Sustainability
- Signals
- Mobility

CIVIL EMERGENCY PLANNING DIRECTORATE

LOGISTICS (IS Element)

RESOURCE POLICY COORDINATION UNIT

DIVISION OF DEFENCE SUPPORT

ARMAMENTS PLANNING, PROGRAMMES & POLICY DIRECTORATE
- Planning & Policy
- Air Armaments
- Land Armaments
- Naval Armaments

AIR DEFENCE & AIRSPACE MANAGEMENT DIRECTORATE
- Airspace Management
- Air Defence

NATO HQ C3 STAFF[8]

OFFICE OF NATO STANDARDISATION

TECHNOLOGY STUDIES AND COORDINATION OFFICE OF THE RESEARCH & TECHNOLOGY AGENCY (RTA)

DIVISION OF DEFENCE PLANNING AND OPERATIONS

DEFENCE POLICY & FORCE PLANNING DIRECTORATE
- Defence Policy
- Force Planning

CRISIS MANAGEMENT & OPERATIONS DIRECTORATE
- Crisis Management
- Peacekeeping
- Council Operations

DEFENCE PARTNERSHIP & COOPERATION DIRECTORATE

NUCLEAR POLICY DIRECTORATE

DIVISION OF POLITICAL AFFAIRS

POLITICAL DIRECTORATE

NARA[1]
POPS[2]
EEPS[3]
EPAC[4]
CSCM[5]
CARC[6]
WMDC[7]

ECONOMICS DIRECTORATE

ECONOMIC ANALYSIS & COOPERATION
- Defence Economics

(1) NATO Multilateral & Regional Affairs Section
(2) Policy Planning & Speechwriting Section
(3) Eastern European Partners Section
(4) Euro-Atlantic Partnership & Cooperation Section
(5) Cooperative Security and Political Crisis Management Section
(6) Conventional Arms Control and Verification Coordination Section
(7) Weapons of Mass Destruction Centre

(8) The management of the NATO Headquarters Consultation, Command & Control (C3) Staff is a coordinated civil/military responsibility and comes under the authority of both the Assistant Secretary General for Defence Support and the Director of IMS.

521

NATO's Military Structure

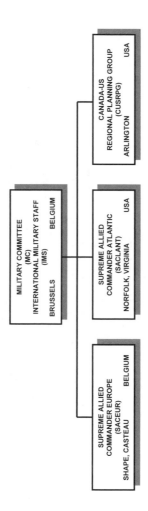

MILITARY COMMITTEE (MC)
INTERNATIONAL MILITARY STAFF (IMS)
BRUSSELS   BELGIUM

SUPREME ALLIED COMMANDER EUROPE (SACEUR)
SHAPE, CASTEAU   BELGIUM

SUPREME ALLIED COMMANDER ATLANTIC (SACLANT)
NORFOLK, VIRGINIA   USA

CANADA-US REGIONAL PLANNING GROUP (CUSRPG)
ARLINGTON   USA

The Military Structure
ALLIED COMMAND EUROPE

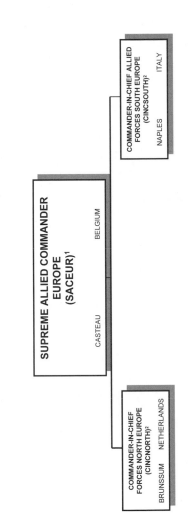

SUPREME ALLIED COMMANDER EUROPE (SACEUR)[1]

CASTEAU   BELGIUM

COMMANDER-IN-CHIEF FORCES NORTH EUROPE (CINCNORTH)[2]

BRUNSSUM   NETHERLANDS

COMMANDER-IN-CHIEF ALLIED FORCES SOUTH EUROPE (CINCSOUTH)[2]

NAPLES   ITALY

(1) Strategic Commander
(2) Regional Commander

The Military Structure

ALLIED COMMAND ATLANTIC

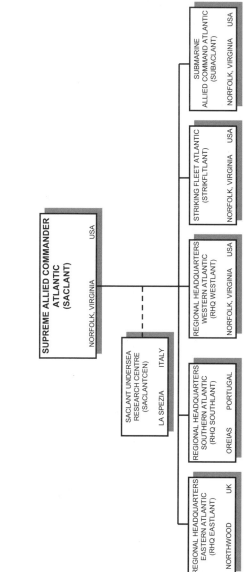

SUPREME ALLIED COMMANDER ATLANTIC (SACLANT)
NORFOLK, VIRGINIA — USA

SACLANT UNDERSEA RESEARCH CENTRE (SACLANTCEN)
LA SPEZIA — ITALY

REGIONAL HEADQUARTERS EASTERN ATLANTIC (RHQ EASTLANT)
NORTHWOOD — UK

REGIONAL HEADQUARTERS SOUTHERN ATLANTIC (RHQ SOUTHLANT)
OEIRAS — PORTUGAL

REGIONAL HEADQUARTERS WESTERN ATLANTIC (RHQ WESTLANT)
NORFOLK, VIRGINIA — USA

STRIKING FLEET ATLANTIC (STRIKFLTLANT)
NORFOLK, VIRGINIA — USA

SUBMARINE ALLIED COMMAND ATLANTIC (SUBACLANT)
NORFOLK, VIRGINIA — USA

The International Military Staff

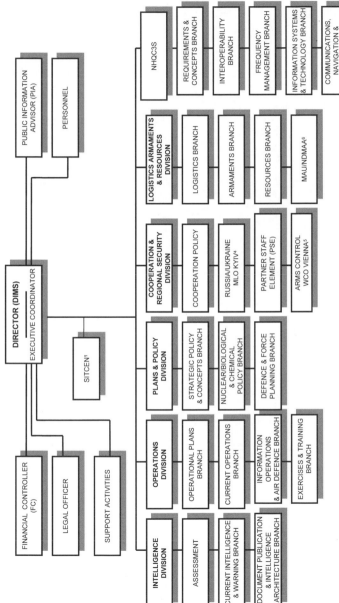

(1) The Situation Centre (SITCEN) reports to the Assistant Secretary General for Defence Planning & Operations but is directed on a day-to-day basis by the Director of the International Military Staff.
(2) The Information Systems and Technology Branch serves both the International Staff and International Military Staff.
(3) The NATO Headquarters Consultation, Command and Control (C3) Staff is managed jointly by the Director (IMS) and the Assistant Secretary General for Defence Support.
(4) MLO: Military Liaison Office.
(5) WCO: Western Consultation Office.
(6) Management Advisory Unit/NATO Defence Manpower Advisory Authority.

THE NORTH ATLANTIC TREATY
Washington DC, 4 April 1949

The Parties to this Treaty reaffirm their faith in the purposes and principles of the Charter of the United Nations and their desire to live in peace with all peoples and all governments.

They are determined to safeguard the freedom, common heritage and civilisation of their peoples, founded on the principles of democracy, individual liberty and the rule of law.

They seek to promote stability and well-being in the North Atlantic area.

They are resolved to unite their efforts for collective defence and for the preservation of peace and security.

They therefore agree to this North Atlantic Treaty:

ARTICLE 1

The Parties undertake, as set forth in the Charter of the United Nations, to settle any international dispute in which they may be involved by peaceful means in such a manner that international peace and security and justice are not endangered, and to refrain in their international relations from the threat or use of force in any manner inconsistent with the purposes of the United Nations.

ARTICLE 2

The Parties will contribute toward the further development of peaceful and friendly international relations by strengthening their free institutions, by bringing about a better understanding of the principles upon which these institutions are founded, and by promoting conditions of stability and well-being. They will seek to eliminate conflict in their international economic policies and will encourage economic collaboration between any or all of them.

ARTICLE 3

In order more effectively to achieve the objectives of this Treaty, the Parties, separately and jointly, by means of continuous and effective self-help and mutual aid, will maintain and develop their individual and collective capacity to resist armed attack.

ARTICLE 4

The Parties will consult together whenever, in the opinion of any of them, the territorial integrity, political independence or security of any of the Parties is threatened.

ARTICLE 5

The Parties agree that an armed attack against one or more of them in Europe or North America shall be considered an attack against them all, and consequently they agree that, if such an armed attack occurs, each of them, in exercise of the right of individual or collective self-defence recognised by Article 51 of the Charter of the United Nations, will assist the Party or Parties so attacked by taking forthwith, individually, and in concert with the other Parties, such action as it deems necessary, including the use of armed force, to restore and maintain the security of the North Atlantic area.

Any such armed attack and all measures taken as a result thereof shall immediately be reported to the Security Council. Such measures shall be terminated when the Security Council has taken the measures necessary to restore and maintain international peace and security.

ARTICLE 6[1]

For the purpose of Article 5, an armed attack on one or more of the Parties is deemed to include an armed attack:

- on the territory of any of the Parties in Europe or North America, on the Algerian Departments of France[2], on the territory of Turkey or on the islands under the jurisdiction of any of the Parties in the North Atlantic area north of the Tropic of Cancer;

- on the forces, vessels, or aircraft of any of the Parties, when in or over these territories or any area in Europe in which occupation forces of any of the Parties were stationed on the date when the Treaty entered into force or the Mediterranean Sea or the North Atlantic area north of the Tropic of Cancer.

ARTICLE 7

The Treaty does not affect, and shall not be interpreted as affecting, in any way the rights and obligations under the Charter of the Parties which are members of the United Nations, or the primary responsibility of the Security Council for the maintenance of international peace and security.

---

[1]   As amended by Article 2 of the Protocol to the North Atlantic Treaty on the accession of Greece and Turkey.

[2]   On 16 January 1963 the Council noted that insofar as the former Algerian Departments of France were concerned the relevant clauses of this Treaty had become inapplicable as from 3 July 1962.

ARTICLE 8

Each Party declares that none of the international engagements now in force between it and any other of the Parties or any third State is in conflict with the provisions of this Treaty, and undertakes not to enter into any international engagement in conflict with this Treaty.

ARTICLE 9

The Parties hereby establish a Council, on which each of them shall be represented to consider matters concerning the implementation of this Treaty. The Council shall be so organised as to be able to meet promptly at any time. The Council shall set up such subsidiary bodies as may be necessary; in particular it shall establish immediately a defence committee which shall recommend measures for the implementation of Articles 3 and 5.

ARTICLE 10

The Parties may, by unanimous agreement, invite any other European State in a position to further the principles of this Treaty and to contribute to the security of the North Atlantic area to accede to this Treaty. Any State so invited may become a party to the Treaty by depositing its instrument of accession with the Government of the United States of America. The Government of the United States of America will inform each of the Parties of the deposit of each such instrument of accession.

ARTICLE 11

This Treaty shall be ratified and its provisions carried out by the Parties in accordance with their respective constitutional processes. The instruments of ratification shall be deposited as soon as possible with the Government of the United States of America, which will notify all the other signatories of each deposit. The Treaty shall enter into force between the States which have ratified it as soon as the ratification of the majority of the signatories, including the ratifications of Belgium, Canada, France, Luxembourg, the Netherlands, the United Kingdom and the United States, have been deposited and shall come into effect with respect to other States on the date of the deposit of their ratifications.[3]

ARTICLE 12

After the Treaty has been in force for ten years, or at any time thereafter, the Parties shall, if any of them so requests, consult together for the purpose of reviewing the Treaty, having regard for the factors then affecting peace and

---

[3] The Treaty came into force on 24 August 1949, after the deposition of the ratifications of all signatory states.

security in the North Atlantic area including the development of universal as well as regional arrangements under the Charter of the United Nations for the maintenance of international peace and security.

ARTICLE 13

After the Treaty has been in force for twenty years, any Party may cease to be a Party one year after its notice of denunciation has been given to the Government of the United States of America, which will inform the Governments of the other Parties of the deposit of each notice of denunciation.

ARTICLE 14

This Treaty, of which the English and French texts are equally authentic, shall be deposited in the archives of the Government of the United States of America. Duly certified copies will be transmitted by that government to the governments of the other signatories.

NOTES

NOTES

NOTES

NOTES

NOTES

NOTES